100 *Best*
Romantic
Resorts
of the World

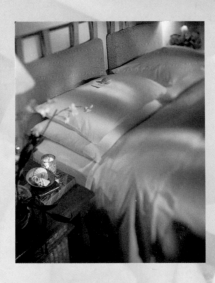

Fourth Edition

KATHARINE D. DYSON

The
Globe
Pequot
Press

GUILFORD, CONNECTICUT

Interior design by Nancy Freeborn/Freeborn Design

ISSN 1540-6822
ISBN 0-7627-2331-9

Printed in Korea
Fourth Edition/First Printing

> The prices and rates listed in this guidebook were confirmed at press time but under no circumstances are they guaranteed. We recommend that you call establishments before traveling to obtain current information.

To my husband, John, for his never-ending
support and patience

Author's Thanks

Because the quality of a resort can change dramatically in a short time, I have ensured that each place comes with a first-person, recent recommendation, preferably (and in most cases) mine. However, because of the time constraints involved in researching and writing such a book, it would have been physically impossible for me to personally revisit each of the one hundred resorts within the allotted time frame and still get the material to the publisher on deadline. Thus I am indebted to many fellow travel writers and others who have generously helped me put together an accurate, up-to-date account of these one hundred most romantic resorts around the globe.

My deepest appreciation to the following people who helped me update this fourth edition: Anamary Pelayo, for her profiles of Amangani and Snake River Lodge & Spa in Wyoming; Lynn and Scott Prowitt-Smith, who shared their impressions of their honeymoon resort, Maroma, Mexico, with me; Risa Weinreb, for her contributions in Hawaii and Tahiti. Christopher Pinckney, for Hyatt Regency Aruba and Sandals St. Lucia, where, he and his wife, Cathy, report, their honeymoon was a perfect "ten"; Georgina Kassalty, for Hyatt Regency Grand Cayman; and Merrie Murray, for Four Seasons Maui. Thanks also to Frank "Poncho" Shiell, for help in Ixtapa/Zihuatanejo; Richard Kahn, of Kahn Travel Communications; Marcella Martinez, of Marcella Martinez Associates; Norman Pieters, of Kavell's African Dream Vacations; Karen Hoffman, for her Africa expertise; Kristin Wherry, of PPR; Rosann Valentini, of Relais & Chateaux; Karen Preston, of Leading Hotels of the World; and Sara Southworth. Also thanks to Jan Cronan at Globe Pequot Press for her patience and hard work.

CONTENTS

INTRODUCTION

In preparing the material for the fourth edition of 100 Best Romantic Resorts of the World I have noticed a couple of new trends: an increasing number of smaller, boutique-style resorts and the growth of in-house spa facilities.

Since the last edition, I have continued to travel widely, discovering many wonderful resorts to tell you about, places that extend a heartwarming welcome without overpowering you by being intrusive. When I check into a hotel, I am not looking to find a "new best friend." I don't need someone knocking on my door every ten minutes to replace towels or do a turndown when I've just stepped into the shower. With the really cool resorts, your needs are taken care of, your bed is made, and the dirty glasses replaced but you haven't a clue when it happened.

Really comfortable beds, linens, and pillows are so important. No matter how great the room looks, if the bed is lumpy, the linens coarse or worn, or the pillow a Flintstone throwback, your beauty rest may be hard to come by. Frette linens are nice, but there are others that work just as well; a good hotelier knows what they are. Down duvets, white goose down pillows, and quality options for those who are allergic to down are important, too.

Another of my pet peeves (now that I'm on a roll) is a pretentious staff. A satisfying resort experience has nothing to do with glitz or pretension. And little things count. I like good lights on either side of the bed, a full-length mirror, plenty of light in the bathroom, hooks on the back of the bathroom door, and hangers that don't require Houdini to get them off the rod.

Above all, a smile goes a long way.

Each of the "100 Best Romantic Resorts of the World" has unique, special qualities—some may even be a bit quirky. In my travels and research, I came across some marvelous places that perhaps didn't quite fit the definition of a full-service resort. Nonetheless, because they are especially romantic and may be just what you're looking for, I've included them in the book.

Each of the 100 Best is characterized by the following:

1. Has a romantic setting

2. Rates best in category/region for overall quality

3. Caters primarily to vacationers seeking recreation, entertainment, and escape from the "real world"

4. Is easy to reach

5. Is in a safe location

6. Provides excellent, friendly service

7. Has one or more restaurants on or within walking distance of the property

8 Is spiffy clean and superbly maintained

9. Appeals to couples in love

10. Offers good value

Romantic setting. This is highly subjective. What will it be? A cabin in the woods, a castle on a hilltop, an over-the-water bungalow, a thatched beachfront cottage? I invite you to browse through these profiles and decide for yourself.

Best in category. It might have made my job easier had I simply selected the most expensive and exclusive places in each region. Expense doesn't necessarily add up to value, though, and since many honeymooners are just starting out, I've included a number of reasonably priced resorts as well as the pricier hotels to give you a range of choices—all which represent the best in their price category for ambience and quality.

Recreation, entertainment, and escape. These resorts are more than just a place to spend the night. Most have pools and/or beaches for swimming, tennis courts, and fitness facilities. Recreation covers a wide spectrum—it might be skiing, hiking, horseback riding, sailboarding, or croquet—and entertainment could be anything from soft piano music to disco. The bottom line is that these resorts cater to travelers who are on vacation, rather than on a business trip. The 100 Best exist for fun and romance.

Easy to reach. The majority of the resorts in this book are within reasonable traveling distance of North America. This is particularly important for honeymooners. After all the excitement of the wedding festivities, you could very well be exhausted. It would help if your trip to your destination is a quick and easy one. I have, however, included some properties in exotic faraway places for those who feel adventurous and have the time.

Safe location. You want to feel safe and secure. Going to an iffy area with a history of turbulence is not a good idea if you want to relax and simply enjoy each other. The 100 Best are located in what are considered (at press time) safe, stable areas. If you have any questions, you can check the U.S. Travel Advisories available on the Internet. Remember that no matter where you go, you should always take necessary precautions, such as putting your money in traveler's checks, stowing cash in two or three different places, and bringing along an ATM card, often the best way to get additional cash abroad. Carry all the "must have" items with you on the plane (don't check them with your luggage) and put your valuable items in the hotel safe. Better yet, leave expensive jewelry at home, and you won't have to worry about it.

Excellent, friendly service. When you order room service at 3:00 A.M., you'd like to get your order before the sun rises. When your waiter greets you at the table, it would be nice to see a smile. All these things help to enhance your resort experience.

Choice of restaurants. It's good to have two or more places to eat, ranging from gourmet/formal to casual. A range of prices, ambience, and kinds of cuisine is also important. The most important element, however, is good food, whether the resort has one restaurant or several, or is located in an area where there are several good restaurants.

Clean and superbly maintained. There's nothing like a leaky faucet dripping in the middle of the night or a dust ball behind a chair to turn the romance level down a notch or two. The 100 Best get high ratings in the cleanliness and maintenance departments.

Appeals to couples in love. Now here's where it gets tricky. I discovered some great resorts that met all my other criteria except this one. Perhaps the kids took over the pool most of the day. Or the resort was just too exclusive, geared to the hopelessly well-off and out of reach to all but 2 percent of our readers (who probably already know where they are jetting off to and don't need anyone to tell them where to go). Resorts like these didn't make it.

Good value. Very important. I tried to eliminate any place that was unreasonable or doing the "big rip-off." If prices are steep to begin with and you know it, you can budget for it. If rates at first sound reasonable and then the cash register starts ringing up every time you go waterskiing, play an hour of tennis, or walk into the nightclub, your good deal starts to drift into the sunset. Whenever possible, I have listed romance packages and other plans that give you the biggest bang for your buck. And remember: Even if a package is not listed in the book, ask the resort if it offers any special plans, such as ones for tennis, scuba diving, or golf. Many do; they just may not promote them.

One of the best bets for some budget-minded travelers is the all-inclusive resort, where one price pays for everything, including drinks, meals, and sports activities. No surprises here at checkout time.

HELPFUL TIPS FOR USING THIS BOOK

Each resort profile in this guide begins with a complete description of the resort, including its special features, ambience, decor, cuisine, and activities offered. Following the description is a section of at-a-glance information about the resort—types of accommodations, rates, sports and facilities available, and so on. Most of this information is self-explanatory, but the following clarification of a few items should help you utilize this book to the fullest as you plan your romantic holiday.

Rates: Each resort has its own unique way of putting together its rate schedule. Although I have tried to give you the rates in as consistent a manner as possible, you will see several variations on such details as seasons— some offer seasonal rates, some do not. In some cases package rates are quoted. I have given you my best shot in describing these rates so that you can understand what is and is not offered.

Following are terms used throughout the book in reference to rates.

Rack Rates: Published rates—usually the top retail price without any discounts

MAP: Modified American Plan; includes accommodations, breakfast, and dinner

AP: American Plan; includes accommodations, breakfast, lunch, and dinner

EP: European Plan; includes no meals

Package Rates: Promotional packages geared in some cases to specific-interest groups such as honeymooners. Most include a number of extra features, such as champagne and room upgrade.

All-Inclusive: Usually this means that the rate includes accommodations, all meals, sports, and other activities. A truly all-inclusive rate will include all beverages, including name-brand liquors; some even include the wedding ceremony. Occasionally resorts advertise an all-inclusive rate but still require you to pay for your beverages. Read the fine print and make sure you know what you're buying.

Room Upgrade: This means getting a better room than you paid for. It is dependent on whether one is available and is usually not guaranteed. If you are on your honeymoon, tell the resort manager. Upgrades are often given to newlyweds.

Seasonal Rates: Prices are geared to the time of year and can vary widely from hotel to hotel. The high season is the most expensive and is the time when the resort is the busiest. In the Caribbean this means the colder months; in Europe it's usually spring, summer, and fall; in New England it is often fall foliage season; and in Bermuda, it's summer. Christmastime is also considered high season by many places. Low-season rates are the least expensive and are available when the resort is not in such great demand. Some resorts do not use season designations but instead give you a schedule of periods during the year with corresponding rates. Some offer just one year-round rate.

("Shoulder" season rates are those between high and low.)

Deposit: Deposit and refund policies vary greatly with each hotel. Some require only a guarantee with a credit card. Typically you get your money back if you cancel within a particular period. Check with the hotel and be sure you understand their policy

Exchange Rates: You'll find that some of the rates in this book are in U.S. dollars, others in local currency. Often when a hotel has a U.S. representative, you'll find rates quoted in U.S. dollars. Some hotels, however, quote only in their local money. For these we have provided an approximate rate in U.S. dollars. To convert to U.S. dollars, look up the exchange rate in the daily paper (usually in the business section) or on the Internet.

Arrival/Departure: Transfers mentioned under this item refer to the resort's arrangements for getting you from and to the airport—by bus, boat, van, private car, or otherwise.

Weddings: If you want to get married at your honeymoon destination, make sure you inquire well ahead of time as to residency requirements, documents required, etc. Your travel agent, resort, and/or country tourism office representative in the United States can help you with this. Many resorts offer the services of an in-house wedding planner.

A Note About Electricity: Dual-voltage appliances such as hair dryers often have a special switch that allows you to convert to either 110 or 220 volts. You will also, however, need a special plug for your appliances when traveling to many places out of the country. Hardware stores generally sell these plugs in sets.

TIPS FOR THOSE PLANNING A HONEYMOON

Attention to the following details can make the difference between having an OK honeymoon and a great one.

1. Book a late flight the morning after the wedding, when possible.

2. Know what your budget is and work within these limits. If money is tight, look into an all-inclusive resort, where you know ahead of time what you'll spend. Many resorts sound reasonably priced until you add up all the extra charges. Checkout time can be a mind-blower.

3. Book the best room you can afford. Complaints from returning honeymooners tend to focus on the quality of their accommodations.

4. Ask about bed size. In some parts of the world, double beds may be smaller than what you'd expect. In Europe you'll find a lot of twin-bedded rooms, so if you're Europe-bound, you might want to ask for a "matrimonial bed."

5. Both the bride and the groom should take part in deciding where to go and how much to spend.

6. Unless you want to keep your honeymoon a secret, let the hotel know ahead of time that you are newly married (your travel agent can do this for you). Honeymooners often enjoy special perks, such as champagne and breakfast in bed.

7. It is often helpful to be in the travel agent's office while your room is being booked so that you can answer any special questions the hotel might have.

8. If being directly on the beach overlooking the water is very important to you, make sure the hotel and the room you book are just that. Sometimes properties advertised as "beachfront hotels" are in reality not right on the beach, but close by. Rooms may also have a view of the garden instead of the water.

9. Ask about the best way to get from the airport to your resort. Are you being met? Do you need to look for someone in particular? How much is a taxi or van service?

10. If you are renting a car, find out ahead of time about insurance requirements. Check with your credit card company to see if you are covered by collision damage waiver.

11. Check what travel documentation you will need and get everything in order. Carry two forms of photo identification in two separate places. If you lose one you'll still be able to get on the plane with the other. Remember, a valid photo ID is required to board. No ID, no flight.

12. On international travel it is good to fax hotels a few days before your arrival date to reconfirm your arrangements. This is particularly important when the booking was made well in advance. This is one vacation you want to make sure runs like clockwork. Your travel agent should do this for you, but be sure to request that it be done.

13. I highly recommend purchasing trip cancellation insurance. If you have to cancel for any reason (heaven forbid), you'll get your deposit back. Ask your travel agent about this.

14. If you are traveling to a place such as Africa or the South Pacific, check with your doctor or local health authority to find out if you need any special inoculations or medicines to take either prior to or during your trip. In some areas you must show proof that you are up to date on certain disease-preventing immunizations (e.g., yellow fever and malaria) in order to enter the country.

15. If you are not leaving for your vacation destination until a day or two after your wedding, you may want to stay at a relaxing, romantic inn on your first night. Most couples find they are quite exhausted after the festivities and need some time to unwind.

16. Book your airline seats at the same time you make plane reservations. This is also the time to order special meals if you have any dietary restrictions.

HONEYMOON COUNTDOWN

Don't wait until the last minute to plan your honeymoon. Good groundwork can really pay off when it comes to lining up the perfect romantic holiday. Here are some guidelines.

- Five months before your wedding: Select a travel agent, read up on destinations, and nail down your budget. Be sure to include spending money in your calculations.

- Four months: Decide where you're going and book your reservations with your travel agent.

- Three months: Get your travel documents together. Allow up to six weeks to process the paperwork for a new passport. Applications are available at the main branch of your local post office and at U.S. government passport agencies.

- Two months: Get your confirmation numbers for hotel, airlines, rental cars, and so forth

- One month to one week: Purchase film for your camera. Check to make sure your camera batteries are working. Get out the converter plugs for your hair dryer, and so on, or purchase them from a hardware store. Confirm your reservations and get your traveler's checks.

This book offers a wide range of resorts to choose from. You and your partner should look through it individually and select a few establishments that appeal to each of your tastes. Then compare notes and narrow down the list to the ones that sound wonderful to both of you. The next step is to contact your travel agent for brochures and more information.

TIPS FOR PACKING

1. Plan ahead. The layered look is in. Temperatures in many areas can soar one day, plunge the next.

2. Limit your color choices to basics. Gray, white, black, and beige work. Add color with silk scarves, belts, and jewelry.

3. Take costume jewelry. Take nothing you couldn't bear losing unless you wear it all the time.

4. Bring no more than three pairs of shoes unless you want to squeeze in a pair of sandals.

5. Pack mix-and-match outfits—shirts, slacks, etc.— that can be worn two or more times in different combinations.

6. Wear your bulkiest (and most comfortable) things on the plane.

7. Think silk, tencel, and anything else that is thin and will not wrinkle easily.

8. Pack or wear a basic all-purpose jacket. Black works great.

9. Don't carry large bottles of anything. Use small bottles, containers, and plastic bags. Film cartridge canisters are handy for things like pills and pins.

10. Put together a mini-medicine kit (just in case), and carry it in a small sandwich-size baggie.

11. Before you pack, lay out on your bed everything you want to take. Put aside all those things that you absolutely can't live without. Pack them. Put everything else back in the closet.

12. Take a midsize wheely bag and a small carry-on. Bring nothing you cannot easily move yourself and preferably carry on the plane. Movability is flexibility. And remember that cars in Europe are smaller than most of those in the United States.

13. Check out special travel collections featuring clothes and other items available by catalogue and on the Net from companies such as Travel Smith and L.L. Bean Travel.

My hope is that your holiday will be far more romantic than you ever dreamed; that you'll have the opportunity to get off the beaten track and create memories that will last a lifetime as you discover what is unique and special about a place, its people, and its traditions.

If you have any suggestions for how this guide could be improved, please feel free to e-mail your comments to editorial@globe-pequot.com, or send them to The Globe Pequot Press, Reader Response, P.O. Box 480, Guilford, Connecticut 06437.

For more information check the author's Web site, www.honeymoonsaway.com.

UNITED STATES

THE BOULDERS
Arizona

As you approach the resort, you see just ahead some huge, reddish boulders. At first you don't see the resort itself—it blends so well into its environment. Individual casitas are molded into the terrain; colors blend perfectly. Here and there you catch a view of the golf courses with their green tees and greens looking very much like neat toupees sitting on the red-tan desert ground. This is the Boulders, one of the country's most romantic resorts.

You know you are in the desert. The air is hot yet dry. The days are sunny and warm, the nights cool. The sky goes on forever. Giant fingers of the saguaros, several times as tall as you are and much older, stick up out of the desert scrub, silhouetted against the brilliant sunset skies and morning sunrises.

Granite boulders, their edges rounded and smoothed by millions of years of wear, sit one atop another in a bit of a hodgepodge, just as they have lain for centuries, like silent sentries watching over the desert. Tucked in the crevices and cracks and rooted in the land are the flowers and plants of this rich desert environment.

The 160 casitas, made of earth-tone adobe, were hand-molded and rubbed to follow the contours of the rocks, and, like the ancient boulders themselves.

Each individual casita has a sitting area and fireplace, a balcony or patio, a minibar, a large tiled bath with a vanity, and comfortable leather chairs, ottomans, and sofas upholstered in flame stitch and earthy fabrics reflecting the rich colors and patterns of the desert. Stone floors,

hand-hewn beamed ceilings, area rugs, baskets, clay pots, and regional art objects and paintings add to the Southwestern ambience. Lights are perfectly placed for reading or for romance. And many of the Indian weavings and paintings hanging on the walls are for sale—just ask.

Life at the Boulders revolves around the main lodge, the pool, and the two superb golf courses. A trail nearby leads up a steep, rocky hill; at the top you get sweeping views of the beautiful Sonoran Desert with its armies of erect saguaro cactus and low-growing bushes and flowers.

In the main lounge a lofty ceiling has been installed using the latilla and viga method of construction: Spokes of wood radiate from a center "pole" much like a giant umbrella. Adobe walls are brightened by original artwork, such as an 1890s chief's blanket and antique tapestries.

Every evening as the sun goes down and things get cooler, the giant fireplace inside the lodge and the one just outside the entrance are lit, sending the sweet spicy odor of shaggy juniper into the air. The aroma lingers the next day, buoyed by additional fires in the restaurants and casitas.

The five restaurants at the Boulders place a strong emphasis on healthful eating. You can enjoy food such as mesquite-grilled meats and fish, roast range chicken, anchiote-basted veal chop with sun-dried tomato orzo, grilled salmon and quesadilla with Anaheim chiles. The chef seeks out local farmers who produce organically grown fruits and vegetables, finds sources for fresh meat and special seafood items like "diver scallops," and harvests such things as cactus fruits right from the desert.

You really don't have to leave the grounds to find both a variety of restaurants and a change in moods. Through its large windows the Latilla restaurant affords marvelous views of the Sonoran landscape and a softy lit waterfall. The Palo Verde restaurant, with its colorful exhibition kitchen, features Southwestern cuisine.

The informal Boulders Club, located in the golf course clubhouse, is a popular choice for lunch and dinner, and you can eat in the main dining room. You also can stay "home" and enjoy a private breakfast or dinner on your balcony or patio or get cozy in front of your fireplace while the wood fire blazes away.

The Boulders' two excellent golf courses have been carefully integrated into the landscape. One ancient cactus sits smack in the center of a rather formidable sandtrap. These are true desert courses: No plants are growing here that are not indigenous to the area, and local grasses are

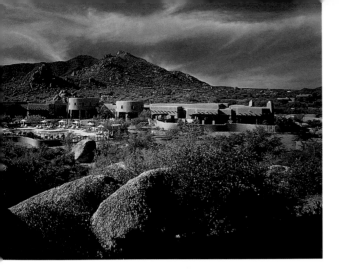

used that require much less water than the type normally associated with golf courses. Named by *Golf Magazine* as a Gold Medal Golf Resort 1999–2000, The Boulders treats its players to stunning vistas from elevated tees—on one hole you actually tee off from the top of a boulder.

In addition to the two golf courses, the Boulders Club, a private country club reserved exclusively for resort guests and club members, includes a tennis center with seven Plexi-cushioned courts, and one classic clay court, a pro shop, and another pool. Clinics and private lessons are offered daily.

The Boulders is home to the new Golden Door Spa, a 33,000-square-foot facility. A sibling to the original Golden Door in Escondido, California, this luxury spa blends eastern and western influences in its architectural design, healing methods, treatments, and philosophies. Here you'll find a labyrinth for reflection, fitness center, movement studio, and classroom for wellness lectures.

For the ultimate romantic indulgence, book the spa's couples' suite with views of the desert garden. Share a relaxing Golden Door aromatherapy or reflexology massage and, to enhance the treatment, enjoy your own private pool.

You can explore the area on horseback or hike on the Apache Trail, which passes by lakes, volcanic rock formations, and awesome buttes. You can take a sunset jeep tour or a moonlight horseback ride. Or tackle the desert trails on foot or bike; ask for a special hike and gourmet picnic lunch designed just for the two of you. There is also rock climbing and night-vision hikes using infrared goggles. You can spend hours in the colorful market area, El Pedregal, which contains more than forty boutiques, restaurants, and art galleries, plus an amphitheater.

Just as any great resort cannot stand on its physical beauty and facilities alone, the Boulders goes to the top of the class for its personal people skills. You are greeted warmly on your arrival, and if you come back for more visits (and you will), you are remembered and catered to.

The Boulders

Location: Nestled in the high Sonoran Desert northeast of Phoenix and Scottsdale, Arizona, on 1,300 acres

Romantic Highlights: Vast beauty of the desert setting; fireplaces in your private casita; hikes on the magnificent grounds; balloon rides over the desert

Address/Phone: P.O. Box 2090, 34631 North Tom Darlington Drive, Carefree, AZ 85377; (480) 488–9009; fax: (480) 488–4118

Web Site: www.wyndham.com

U.S. Reservations: (800) 553–1717

Owner/Manager: Fred Kleisner, CEO and president of Wyndham International, Mark Vinciquerra, vice-president and general manager

Arrival/Departure: Pickup at either the Scottsdale or the Phoenix Airport can be arranged.

Distance from Scottsdale Airport: 13 miles (30 minutes); 33 miles from Phoenix Sky Harbor Airport

Distance from Phoenix: 16 miles

Accommodations: 160 adobe-style guest casitas; 50 one-, two-, and three-bedroom Pueblo Villas

Most Romantic Room/Suite: If you like water views, try one of the casitas near the end, overlooking the pond

Amenities: Air-conditioning, ceiling fans, wood-burning fireplace, minibar, large dressing area, TV, toiletries, padded hangers, umbrella, room service, telephone, robes

Electricity: 110 volts

Sports and Facilities: 2 championship 18-hole golf courses; tennis park, featuring 8 tennis courts (1 classic clay) and pro shop; fitness center with aerobic studio, weight room, heated outdoor lap pool, hiking program; desert jeep tours, hot air ballooning, horseback riding; Golden Door Spa

Dress Code: Casually smart

Weddings: Can be arranged

Rates/Packages: $205–$625 per room for casitas; $245–$750 for a one-bedroom/den pueblo villa. Golden Door Romance, $1,550–$2,858, including 2 nights' casita accommodations, breakfasts, dinners, gift, and hot air balloon ride or en suite couples' massage

Payment/Credit Cards: Most major

Deposit: Two-night deposit or half the package rate to be applied to first and last night's stay. Cancel 3 weeks in advance of arrival date for full refund.

Government Taxes: 10.67 percent tax on accommodations; 7.4 percent tax on food and beverage charges

Service Charges: $27 per night in lieu of cash gratuities for all resort personnel, excluding food and beverage, and daily entrance to the Golden Door Spa.

THE AHWAHNEE
California

Sounds of birds, the rustle of grasses and trees, glimpses of a coyote, badger, or even a bear along with awesome views of rock cliffs, red-woods, rivers, and lakes await those who visit the Ahwahnee and Yosemite National Park. The main

attraction here is nature, which provides the perfect get-away destination for those who love the outdoors.

The Ahwahnee is nestled in the heart of Yosemite Valley, an ideal location as just getting in and out of the center of the park can take an hour or more. Yosemite is huge. There are rustic cottages nearby, operated by the Yosemite Concession Service Corporation, as is the Ahwahnee. But if you are looking for any kind of luxury and a candlelit dinner at the end of a day of exploring the more than 350 miles of marked trails, climbing a mountain, or taking a horseback ride through the hills, then the Ahwahnee is the place to be.

When Lady Astor, England's first female member of Parliament, came to Yosemite in the early 1920s she thumbed her nose at her unheated room and bathroom, which was down the hall. She checked out and returned to the gentler comforts of the city. This prompted Stephen T. Mather, director of the National Park Service, to order that a new luxury hotel be built to attract more people to his beloved park.

Since the seven-story granite-and-timber structure and cottages were built, the Ahwahnee has welcomed such important guests as Queen Elizabeth II, President John F. Kennedy, Judy Garland, Winston Churchill, Ronald Reagan, and First Lady Laura Bush.

From the beginning the theme of the furnishings and decor was derived from Native American culture. The public rooms are massive with soaring ceilings that replicate the park's towering pines and giant sequoias. Large windows as well as the long outdoor terrace are oriented toward Glacier Point and Sentinel Dome. Pull out your binoculars and look carefully; you may be able to spot someone climbing the sheer rock faces.

Although it was used as a Navy hospital for three years during World War II, it has primarily served as a gracious place to stay in the woods. Over the years it has been refurbished and redecorated, but some things have stayed the same. The original big oak tables, wrought-iron chandeliers in the Great Lounge, the beautiful Native American carpets hanging on the walls, and the intricate rubber mosaic tiles in the entrance lobby are still here.

Accommodations are located in the main lodge and in the cottages that are strung along paths leading from the hotel. Beautifully decorated in Native American prints and rusts, browns, black, greens, and blues, the rooms have all necessary amenities, including cable television and mini-fridges.

For privacy the cottages are great and come with stone patios furnished with a wrought-iron table and chairs. You won't see much beyond the trees that surround the cottages, and the decor is a bit more rustic; still you have basically the same amenities as the rooms in the main lodge along with a small dressing room, separate vanity area, and a sitting area. Most cottages are furnished with king-size beds with wood headboards edged by a twig border. A few cottages are furnished with double beds.

Inside the lodge, the Great Lounge is huge (77 feet long, 55 feet wide, and 24 feet high) and the fireplace is

The Ahwahnee

Location: Inside Yosemite National Park

Romantic Highlights: Spectacular vistas of forests, waterfalls, and mountains; miles of trails to explore on foot and horseback; private cottages in the woods

Address/Phone: Yosemite National Park, Yosemite, CA 95389; (209) 372–1407; fax (209) 372–1463

Web Site: www.yosemitepark.com

U.S. Reservations: (559) 252–4848; fax (559) 456–0542

Owner/Manager: Larry Ross, general manager

Arrival/Departure: Car rentals available at San Francisco and Oakland Airports

Distance from San Francisco Airport: 214 miles (4 to 5 hours); Fresno Airport, 105 miles (2½ hours)

Distance from Yosemite: Right in the park

Accommodations: 127 rooms and cottages

Most Romantic Room/Suite: Mary Tresidder Room (605), a mini-suite with balcony and huge bath; The Duke's Suite (602), a spacious suite with a king-size bed, library, fireplace; cottages for those who want rustic privacy

Amenities: Hair dryer, mini-refrigerator, TV, coffeemaker (cottages), toiletries, robes, ice service, concierge service, valet parking, turndown service, complimentary morning coffee, *USA Today* delivered to your door

Electricity: 110 volts

Sports and Facilities: Pool, walking, hiking, fishing, horseback riding, mountain climbing, Alpine and cross-country skiing, ice skating, art classes, river rafting; golf at Wawona outside the valley

Dress Code: Jackets required in main dining room, dinner only

Weddings: Can be arranged

Rates/Packages: $366.00 per couple per night for rooms; $713.00–$1,813.00 for suites. Romance Package (January 30–March 5) $1,162.49 for 3 nights including accommodations, in-room candlelight dinner, one breakfast in bed, picnic lunch, champagne, rose, and gifts (available Sunday through Thursday)

Payment/Credit Cards: Most major

Deposit: By credit card

Government Taxes: 10 percent

Service Charges: Not included

large enough to roast a cow. The dining room is equally impressive, especially at night when the chandeliers and candles set a romantic mood. For casual dining and drinks you can order such items as turkey quesadillas, salads, and sandwiches in the bar.

You will probably run out of time before you run out of things to do in Yosemite. In addition to the obvious—hiking, biking, riding, climbing—have the hotel pack a lunch basket or stop at the convenience store for some wine, bread, and cheese. Then drive up to Tuolumne Meadows, stopping at Tenaya Lake for a picnic by the shore. The lake is surrounded by tall pines and the north side is blessed by a lovely sand beach. The lake is sparkling clean and swimmable if you like your water briskly cool.

Keep in mind that the drive up to Tuolumne is about 50 miles and takes about one and one-half hours. You can visit the giant sequoias on the way or head to Mariposa for a guided tour of the massive trees with trunks so large that you could drive a truck through the middle.

For an overview of the valley, sign on for a two-hour valley floor tour, a 26-mile journey in an open-air tram. (If you are driving a convertible, you can use a map and do it yourself.) If you like to paint, join one of the art classes that are offered every day April through November.

If you want a break head to the Ahwahnee pool for a soothing swim and soak up the dramatic views from your lounge chair.

AUBERGE DU SOLEIL
California

Location, location, location is yours to savor at this luxury resort in the heart of Napa Valley wine country. Snuggled in an olive grove in the eastern foothills, Auberge du Soleil overlooks a tapestry of vineyards, stone wineries, and the rugged ridge of the Mayacamas Mountains. A Relais & Châteaux property, it's the perfect hideaway for couples wanting to sample the best of the wine country lifestyle—tasting rooms and fine restaurants, smart boutiques and antiques stores, hot air ballooning and bicycling.

Auberge cossets guests in tranquil beauty from the moment they enter the lobby with its oversize floral display placed on a massive wood and stone table. The grounds are spectacular, with gardens and courtyards cached in nooks and crannies accented by pergolas, fountains, and gigantic pots overflowing with ivy geraniums.

A four-acre olive grove provides a unique venue for appreciating alfresco works in the inn's sculpture garden. The collection of sixty works by well-known local and national artists are fun and unique. A shapely pair of stone legs sprawl under a tree; cheerful metal flowers "grow" in the gardens; a dancer turns on her toe in the wind; giant nails are hammered in the ground; colorful rings frolic on the hillside.

Accommodations are tucked into two-story cottages staggered up the hillside. Stuccoed in warm earth tones, each cottage has a patio or terrace. Inside, the decor is class, not flash, embellished with cool Mexican tile floors and rawhide chairs. Color schemes percolate in vibrant hues of hot pink and yellow. Two new cottages are a whopping 1,800 square feet and come with nonstop views and every imaginable amenity.

Everything encourages you to relax, from the two chaise lounges poised on the terrace with the comfortable padded cushions, chairs for two, and sofas with huge overstuffed pillows. Music is piped from a CD/stereo player, logs are laid in your fireplace, and candles and amber bath salts wait by the side of the tub (some units have Jacuzzis for two). The king-size bed is primped with a medley of colorful pillows; live orchids and flowers are everywhere. Original artwork, such as large canvasses and three-dimensional pieces, reflects the sunny warmth of the Napa Valley.

If perfection lies in details, Auberge has it all figured out. Light switches are marked for location, including one to spotlight the art . . . even the extra roll of toilet paper comes "gift wrapped" with a bow. Both drawer and closet spaces are ample, and the wet bar includes a refrigerator stocked with drinks and snacks.

In fine weather (almost a certainty here in Northern California), you'll enjoy basking by the lovely swimming pool, heated to a comfy 85 degrees year-round. Broad wooden decks provide plenty of space for sunning, while a flotilla of market umbrellas seems to mirror the contours of distant mountain peaks. You can play tennis or work out in the well-equipped gym.

The new Spa du Soleil, tucked into an olive garden near the entrance, occupies a 7,000-square foot stucco building where windows open to superb views of the valley. The centerpiece of the spa, a courtyard punctuated by fountains and hundred-year-old olive trees, reflects a French-country spirit.

Six treatment rooms with French doors are arranged

around the courtyard and there is a private guest patio, with an outdoor shower and tub, and a Tranquility Room with a fireplace. Massage, facial, exfoliation, masque and wrap, foot therapy, and hair and scalp treatments make use of things from the outdoors: The Valley (mud and minerals), The Grove (olive oil), The Garden (herbs and flowers), and The Vineyard (grapes).

You will certainly want to explore several of Napa's more than 220 vineyards. Ask Auberge to prepare a picnic basket for your day in the valley, and pick up a special wine along the way.

For wining and dining there's the Auberge du Soleil Restaurant, with meals served either indoors in a country-French dining room or outdoors on a trellis-covered wooden deck with awesome views of the valley. No need to worry about a chilly evening while savoring the sunset—overhead heaters keep you cozy. Service is friendly, not intrusive. Advice on wine and cuisine choices is delivered by the maître d' and highly knowledgeable waiters.

New executive chef Richard Reddington comes from California's Jardiniere where he was chef de cuisine. He continues to enhance Auberge's reputation as an elite dining venue with his fusion of French-Mediterranean-California cuisine. Dishes such as Sonoma rabbit with Swiss chard, soft polenta and lardons, and wild striped bass with French lentils, shallot confit, and wild mushroom broth showcase his skills in the kitchen. Paired with Auberge's expansive selection of rare and fine wines, meals here are indeed a memorable experience. To complement the Spa du Soleil, new menu item are being created incorporating freshly harvested ingredients indigenous to the Napa Valley.

Time your reservation so that you catch the last glow of the sun going down, flaming behind the mountains. By dessert, the stars will be twinkling out *good night*.

Auberge du Soleil

Location: Thirty-three–acre olive grove in the Rutherford foothills

Romantic Highlights: Knockout views of Napa Valley's most illustrious vineyards (each room has a private deck and fireplace); half-mile nature trail studded with more than sixty sculptures

Address/Phone: P.O. Drawer B, 180 Rutherford Hill Road, Rutherford, CA 94573; (707) 963–1211; fax (707) 963–8764

E-mail: reserve@aubergedusoleil.com

Web Site: www.aubergedusoleil.com

U.S. Reservations: (800) 348–5406; Relais & Châteaux, (800) RELAIS–8

Owner/Manager: Philippa Perry, general manager

Arrival/Departure: Car rentals available at airports; limousine service available from San Francisco at $175 each way

Distance from San Francisco Airport: 65 miles north (1½ hours)

Distance from Rutherford: 5 minutes

Accommodations: 50 rooms, one-, two-, and three-room suites, each with valley views and fireplaces

Most Romantic Room/Suite: The 2 private cottages are the most spectacular, with a bedroom, living room, den and huge patio with stainless Jacuzzi outdoor tub.

Amenities: Air-conditioning, fireplace, refrigerator stocked with drinks and snacks, TV, VCR, coffeemaker, toiletries, skylights in bath, double sinks, some rooms with Jacuzzis, hair dryer, valet, 24-hour room service, down comforter, bathrobes, slippers, twice-daily maid service, full-service beauty salon, voice mail, and business center

Electricity: 110 volts

Sports and Facilities: Swimming pool and large sundeck; whirlpool, massage, and steam rooms; gym/Spa du Soleil; tennis court (instruction available); golf, horseback riding, bicycling, hot air ballooning, and jogging nearby

Dress Code: Casually smart

Weddings: Can be arranged

Rates/Packages: $400–$600 per couple per night for rooms; $800–$950 for suites; $2,500 for private cottages

Payment/Credit Cards: Most major

Deposit: Prepayment is required at time of booking to secure your reservation. Your reservation will be confirmed in writing upon receipt of full payment. Reservations must be canceled 14 days prior to scheduled arrival date to receive a refund.

Government Taxes: 10.5 percent

Service Charges: Not included

CHATEAU DU SUREAU
California

This red-roofed palace with its stone tower, balustrades, gardens, and wrought-iron balconies beckons to all the Romeos and Juliets in the world. There may be plenty to explore in nearby Yosemite, but Chateau du Sureau, a member of the Relais & Château group, seduces you to linger. Discover unusual treasures—one-of-a-kind pieces of furniture, accessories, and artwork, all carefully collected by Erna Kubin-Clanin, Chateau du Sureau's owner, whose inspiration and superb taste is revealed throughout the property, which consists of the Erna's Elderberry House Restaurant, the Chateau, and the exquisite new two-bedroom Villa Sureau.

Imagine hand-painted ceilings and alcoves, a 1780s tapestry, Oriental carpets, period prints, urns, china, beamed ceilings, tall arched windows, period light fixtures, a 1,000-year-old floor obtained from a chateau in Paris, gardens, and the herringbone pattern brick fireplace in the Grand Salon.

Growing up in Vienna, Austria, castles and romance were woven into Erna's dreams from an early age. In 1962 Erna came to New York, found her way to Yosemite, and was responsible for turning the rather lackluster Redwood Inn into one of the finest restaurants around.

When it came time for her to renew the lease, the government clamped down on the use of parkland, sending Erna hunting for a new challenge. She found it: nine wooded hillside acres full of pines, black oak, manzanita, and elderberry bushes reminding her of her native land. First she built her restaurant, Elderberry House, named for the elderberries she found on the property.

Over the door she placed a sign quoting Oscar Wilde: I HAVE THE SIMPLEST OF TASTES: I WANT ONLY THE BEST. That's what she demanded and that's what her customers got. The restaurant's reputation for superb cuisine and meticulous service brought diners from San Francisco and beyond, people like Robert DeNiro and Kevin Bacon. One day Craig Claibourne stopped in. His glowing article in the *New York Times* that followed brought "foodies" from everywhere to

Erna's restaurant. Reservations were hard to get. Erna's success with the restaurant served as a springboard for the fulfillment of Erna's second dream: to build a place where people could stay overnight in complete comfort.

With her new husband, Rene, Erna built the ten-room Chateau du Sureau and, most recently, the two-bedroom Villa Sureau. She has used her creative talents and boundless energy to fill the rooms with authentic antiques and other unique pieces gathered from around the world.

Each room is different and named after Provençal herbs and flowers: elderberry, thyme, rosehip, sweet geranium, mint, lavender, chamomile, rosemary, and saffron. The Saffron Room is decorated in bold golds and yellows and boasts a handsome 1834 Napoleonic ebony armoire and bed inlaid with ivory; the Lavender Room features delicate lavender-and-white fabrics and wall coverings and the Elderberry Room has a canopy bed with blue-and-white flowered drapes. Baths are trimmed in hand-painted French tile and beds are dressed with down duvets and Italian linens. There are massive four-poster beds, sleigh beds, canopies with flowing side draperies, fireplaces, and oversize tubs. Fresh flowers are everywhere.

An ornate gazebo overlooks a pond, a nice place to sip a cup of tea or a cocktail; nearby, a giant chess game is tucked into its own garden setting.

Four full-time gardeners keep flowers and shrubs looking their best and supply fresh blooms for arrangements and herbs and vegetables for the kitchen. Staff is always on hand to see that your every wish is granted. Chambermaids dressed in crisp black uniforms with ruffled white aprons deliver room service orders, make the beds, resupply fluffy fresh towels, and keep everything spotless.

Chef Robert Riescher presides over the award-winning kitchen creating a California-French cuisine with fresh fruits, vegetables, and meats. A six-course prix-fixe dinner in the red-toned candlelit dining room costs $85.00; Sunday Brunch $32.50. The menu changes each

Chateau du Sureau

Location: Poised in the foothills of the Sierras on nine wooded acres south of Yosemite National Park

Romantic Highlights: Balconies and fireplaces, canopy beds, intimate dining in Erna's Elderberry House Restaurant

Address/Phone: 48688 Victoria Lane, Oakhurst, CA 93644; (559) 683–6800; fax (559) 683–0800

E-mail: chateau@chateausureau.com

Web Site: www.chateausureau.com

U.S. Reservations: (559) 683–6800; Relais & Châteaux, (800) RELAIS-8

Owner/Manager: Erna Kubin-Clanin; Lucy Royse, director

Arrival/Departure: Car rentals available at San Francisco, Oakland, and Fresno/Yosemite airports

Distance from San Francisco Airport: 210 miles (3 hours); Fresno airport, 35 miles (45 minutes)

Distance from Yosemite: 17 miles

Accommodations: 10 rooms and suites plus the two-bedroom Villa Sureau

Most Romantic Room/Suite: It's a tough call. The Lavender Room's balcony overlooks the pool; the Rosehip Room features Empire-period furniture and a tub-for-two with a view out a large window; Mint has a wonderful wide canopy; Elderberry, a corner room, is decorated in blue and yellow and has a high, vaulted ceiling. If you really want to splurge, take the Villa Sureau. All rooms are no-smoking.

Amenities: Hair dryer, CD/VCR stereo system, toiletries, robes, TV on request

Electricity: 110 volts

Sports and Facilities: Pool, chess, walking, hiking, bocce ball; Yosemite about 17 miles away

Dress Code: Jackets requested in main dining room

Weddings: Can be arranged for guests staying in the Chateau. In addition to the gazebo and gardens, there is a mini-chapel in the Chateau with just 3 pews.

Rates/Packages: $350–$550 per room per couple, including full European breakfast and complimentary bar in the Grand Salon; $2,800 for Villa Sureau with a private butler

Payment/Credit Cards: Most major

Deposit: 50 percent at time of booking; cancel 14 days prior to arrival for refund less 10 percent service fee

Government Taxes: 9 percent

Service Charges: 12 percent

night and might include grilled foie gras with apples, braised turnips and elderberry grappa emulsion, vegetable couscous, brochette of rib eye and shiitake mushrooms with boudin noir mashed potatoes and celery root and black trumpet sauce—topped off by semolina flummery, a white and dark chocolate pâté plum sorbet. The wine list offer more than 700 choices; be sure to stop at the wine cellar bar for a drink.

The newest addition to Erna's kingdom, Villa Sureau, goes over the top in elegance and amenities and is furnished with turn-of-the-century pieces from France: original art, stained-glass windows, massive carved wood doors, fireplaces, highly polished marble-topped tables, full-length gold-gilt mirrors, Oriental carpets, crystal chandeliers, a king-size bed swathed from floor to ceiling with filmy turquoise-and-gold organdy, hand-painted trompe l'oeil detailing, a grand piano, library of leather-bound books, and an opulent black-marble bath with columns— Nero would love it. There is a private gate, a garden with a fountain, and another beautiful bedroom. And let's not forget the butler and the outdoor Roman spa.

At Chateau du Sureau, fairy tales do come true.

FOUR SEASONS BILTMORE
California

Celebrating its seventy-fifth anniversary in 2002, the Four Seasons Biltmore reigns as the red-tile–roofed queen of Santa Barbara. You can't beat the vintage 1920s style or the California dream setting, with the deep-blue Pacific glimmering just across the way.

The resort glows with the burnished patina of a classic. It opened in 1927 as part of the original Biltmore chain; the property became a Four Seasons resort in 1987. Over the years the clientele has included everyone from Douglas Fairbanks to Michael Douglas and President Ronald Reagan. (The Reagan ranch is located in the nearby Santa Ynez foothills.)

Set on nineteen acres, the Spanish-Mediterranean resort is composed of a main building plus separate wings and cottages. Public areas resemble the castle of a Spanish grandee, with high, coffered ceilings; thick, red-tile floors; and hand-painted tiles adorning the corridors and stairways. Red-tile or flagstone walkways ramble past bright green lawns and impeccable flower borders. Giant blue gum trees, broad Monterey cypress, and spreading camphor trees shade the grounds.

Accommodations all differ in layout and view; there are also separate cottages poised along the back ridge of the property in a lush garden setting. Furnishings reflect classic good taste and have recently been updated using rich colors and fabrics. You can slide open the white plantation shutters for an airy country cottage feel. Extremely well laid out, the white-marble bathrooms are replete with such nice touches as Chinese ceramic containers to hold cotton balls. Some rooms have fireplaces, balconies, or private patios.

The executive chef, Martin Frost, who had garnered top notices while at the Four Seasons Nevis in the Caribbean, presides over the Biltmore's three superb restaurants. Dining in The Patio is like eating in a country garden—there's even a glass roof with retractable panels to open or close to fit the weather's moods. The nightly buffet earns raves, and Sunday brunch is a Santa Barbara tradition, with huge platters of fresh seafood, a stir-fry table, omelet and Belgian waffle stations, and lots more.

Afternoon tea is served in the Sala Lounge, an elegant drawing room beautified with a high, open-beamed ceiling and a fireplace. La Marina is known for romantic dining, with flowers, candlelight, and arched windows framing the seaward view. In addition to a la carte selections, Chef Frost presents a four-course tasting menu, where choices might include squab with scallion polenta and mission figs, followed by roast tenderloin of veal. Heading to a polo match or into Santa Barbara wine country? The hotel can customize a picnic basket for you.

Guests enjoy preferred tee-time privileges at Sandpiper Golf Course, one of the top-rated public golf layouts in the country, and the newly opened Rancho San Marcos. For tennis players there are three lighted courts. On the property you'll also find an eighteen-hole putting green, croquet, and shuffleboard; the concierge can make arrangements for sportfishing, horseback riding, and sailing.

The recently refurbished workout room comes with an ocean view—along with treadmill, bikes, free weights, and stair machines—and lolling by the Olympic-size swimming pool on the edge of the Pacific makes life luxuriously wonderful. But the biggest treats of all may just be the guest privileges at the Art Deco–era Coral Casino, a private club that has been the center of Santa Barbara social life for over half a century.

Four Seasons Biltmore

Location: Across the street from Butterfly Beach, in the exclusive Montecito enclave

Romantic Highlights: Beachfront setting, Roaring Twenties panache (the hotel opened in 1927), glamorous public areas

Address/Phone: 1260 Channel Drive, Santa Barbara, CA 93108; (805) 969–2261; fax (805) 565–8323

Web Site: www.fourseasons.com

U.S. Reservations: (800) 332–3442

Owner/Manager: Managed by the Four Seasons Hotels & Resorts

Arrival/Departure: Transfers can be arranged; car rentals available at airport

Distance from Santa Barbara Airport: 12 miles

Distance from downtown Santa Barbara: 2 miles (5 minutes)

Accommodations: 213 rooms, suites, and cottages, many with balconies or private patios and fireplaces

Most Romantic Room/Suite: Cottage suites; Odell Cottage suite is top of the heap.

Amenities: Ceiling fan, hair dryer, 3 phones, VCR, TV, in-room safe, air-conditioning, minibar, bathrobes, AM/FM clock radio, toiletries; in-room spa treatments available, 24-hour room service, twice-daily maid service, shoeshine

Electricity: 110 volts

Sports and Facilities: 3 tennis courts, 2 swimming pools, bicycles; golf and whale-watching expeditions nearby (February to mid-April). A new Fitness Center with several personal treatment rooms offers a variety of services.

Dress Code: Casually elegant

Weddings: Can be arranged; popular sites include outdoor courtyards and the ocean view ballroom

Rates/Packages: $395–$450 per couple per night for a room, $1,000 and up for a suite. Romance package (3 days, 2 nights) $950–$1,150 per couple; includes welcome bottle of champagne, dinner for two at La Marina restaurant.

Payment/Credit Cards: Most major

Deposit: Deposits are required within 14 days of making reservation. Cancellations are accepted with a full refund up to 72 hours prior to the expected arrival date.

Government Taxes: 10 percent

Service Charges: Not included

THE INN AT SPANISH BAY
California

You pass through the staffed gate of Pebble Beach's highly privileged enclave that juts into the Pacific, drive along the narrow winding roads, and turn into the landscaped entrance of the Inn at Spanish Bay, one of the famed Pebble Beach Resorts. It has all the things you require in a top-rate hotel: beautiful flowers and grounds, bellmen, multiple restaurants, elevators, a pool, a golf course, a tennis complex, a health club, walkways along the beach, and miles of sea to ponder.

Golfing couples will be in heaven. Laid along the sea and winding among the snaggly shrubs, trees, and grass is the often windy Links at Spanish Bay. The area's newest golf course, designed by Robert Trent Jones Jr., Tom Watson, and Frank "Sandy" Tatum, is reminiscent of Scotland's wild and gritty dune classics. Pebble Beach, a course on every golfer's wish list, is just down the way. As a guest at Spanish Bay, you have a good shot of getting tee times at Pebble Beach Resorts' other two courses on the Peninsula.

The Inn at Spanish Bay

Location: In the Del Monte Forest on the south coast of the Monterey Peninsula

Romantic Highlights: Fireplaces; views of the sun setting over the sea

Address/Phone: 2700 17-Mile Drive, Pebble Beach, CA 93953; (831) 647–7500; fax (831) 644–7955

U.S. Reservations: (800) 654–9300

Owner/Manager: David Oliver, general manager

Arrival/Departure: Car rentals available at San Francisco International, Monterey, San Jose, and Oakland airports

Distance from San Francisco Airport: 130 miles (2–3 hours); Monterey Airport, 7 miles (15 minutes)

Distance from Carmel-By-The-Sea: 3 miles

Accommodations: 270 rooms and suites

Most Romantic Room/Suite: Ocean-view suites

Amenities: Hair dryer, clock radio, telephone, TV, iron, toiletries, wall safe, double vanities, minibar, CD player, fireplace

Electricity: 110 volts

Sports and Facilities: Golf, 8 Plexi-paved tennis courts (2 lighted), health club, pool, sauna, steam room, walking, hiking, biking, horseback riding, spa

Dress Code: Resort casual

Weddings: Can be arranged

Rates/Packages: $425–$575 per room, per night; $795–$2,395 for suites; golf $210–$350 per person

Payment/Credit Cards: Most major

Deposit: By credit card

Government Taxes: 10.5 percent

Service Charges: $20 per room per day

Tennis players will appreciate the eight-court complex, and fitness buffs will be more than happy with the full-service health club.

At Spanish Bay red-tile–roofed groups of interconnected low-rise buildings huddle close to the shoreline, inviting walks along the sea to catch the early morning mists or the glowing sunsets. The 17-mile drive is a popular route for bikers; Carmel-by-the-Sea, Clint Eastwood's trendy domain, is just fifteen minutes away.

This low-key resort is high on service and luxury. Airy rooms decorated in soft tones of creams and sand echo the grassy dunes just outside. Comfortable chairs flank the corner fireplace—just flick a switch and the fire comes to life. A bar is stocked with every imaginable snack and beverage; the spacious Italian-marble baths are roomy enough for two. Rooms are so comfortable, they're hard to leave. They come with overstuffed pillows, sofas, and chairs; downy comforters; and large balconies.

When it comes time to eat, you have several choices. Roys is always popular; Peppoli serves authentic Tuscan-style dishes; the Clubhouse Bar and Grill is perfect for lunch or dinner after golf; and for a change of pace, there are the facilities and restaurants of the Lodge at Pebble Beach.

Be sure to catch the plaintive sounds of the lone bagpiper as he walks the course at sunset. It's just one of the traditions at Spanish Bay you'll long remember.

LA VALENCIA
California

Since it was built in 1926, La Valencia, the legendary "Pink Lady of La Jolla," has been a San Diego tradition attracting the rich and notable such as Groucho Marx, Lillian Gish, and Mary Pickford. More recent famous guests have included Pearl Jam, Madonna, Rush Limbaugh, and Ellen DeGeneres.

Reigning over La Jolla Cove, this elegant pink palace is planted in the heart of the trendy seaside town of La Jolla, within walking distance of many great little boutiques and restaurants. Since my last visit, fifteen new villa suites have been added that just about knock your socks off. These new accommodations, which came with a $10 million price tag, have been tucked into the terraced hillside without jogging the overall ambience one little bit. In fact, I had a hard time trying to remember just what it had looked like before the change.

Villas, which range from 400 to 1,200 square feet, come with separate sitting room, patio or balcony, dining area, and huge bath. Most have fireplaces and are designed so that from your king-size bed you can look through the living room out to the patio, gardens, and sea. Room features include hand-painted Mexican tiles; a Lyceum digital audio system; bathroom with steam shower; down duvets; Italian marble floors, sinks, and bath; Jacuzzi tub; and a private butler service. The television in the living room rises by remote control out of a handsome wood cabinet—very cool. The shower has two oversized rain showerheads that give you the feeling you are standing under Victoria Falls. (Even if you don't need a shower, take one. So sensual.)

Most of the 117 guestrooms have terraces or patios with views of the sea and gardens. Each room is different, each with its own charm. I especially like the rooms with French doors opening onto balconies where flowers tumble down terraces below and the sea glistens beyond. All rooms have windows that open, allowing you to enjoy the fresh sea air and fragrant tropical flowers.

La Valencia has a decidedly Mediterranean flavor with elegant appointments such as Oriental carpets, grand potted plants, antique furniture and accessories, Spanish mosaics, and hand-painted murals and ceilings. The hand-painted coffered ceiling in the elegant La Sala lounge is magnificent. What better place to sip a cocktail while listening to piano music and gazing out to sea.

Dining options include French cuisine in the Sky Room Restaurant on the tenth floor where there are but twelve tables offering 180-degree views of the Pacific; the more casual Whaling Bar & Grill; the Mediterranean Room overlooking the Pacific; or alfresco dining at the Tropical Patio, poolside cafe, or Ocean View Terrace. A variety of picnic baskets can be prepared for a special day excursion with that someone special.

On the ocean side there is a park and a coastal walk leads to a small cove, a popular hangout for seals. With an average year-round temperature of 70 degrees, you can almost be guaranteed springlike weather whenever you come.

La Valencia

Location: Terraced up a flower-filled hillside overlooking the Pacific in the seaside community of La Jolla

Romantic Highlights: French doors opening onto balconies looking out to the sea; tiered gardens, a riot of color; fireplaces; private butler service

Address/Phone: 1132 Prospect Street, La Jolla, CA 92037; (888) 320–2600, (858) 454–0771; fax (858) 456–1664

E-mail: info@lavalencia.com

Web Site: www.lavalencia.com

U.S. Reservations: (800) 451–0772

Owner/Manager: Michael J. Ullman, managing director

Arrival/Departure: Private limousine service can be arranged from the San Diego Airport. If you drive, there is valet service at the door.

Distance from San Diego Airport: 12 miles

Distance from San Diego: 12 miles

Accommodations: 117 rooms, suites, and villas

Most Romantic Room/Suite: Ultraprivate La Valencia suite

Amenities: Air-conditioning, fans, cable TV and VCR, custom toiletries, terry robes, hair dryer, complimentary shoeshine, morning newspaper, 24-hour room service, valet parking, in-room safe, iron/ironing board, minibar

Electricity: 110 volts

Sports and Facilities: Pool, Jacuzzi, fitness center, sauna; golf and tennis can be arranged

Dress Code: Casually elegant

Weddings: Can be arranged

Rates/Packages: Per night from $250–$1,200, rooms; $650–$3,500, suites and villas

Payment/Credit Cards: Most major

Deposit: Credit card

Government Taxes: Included

Service Charges: Included

MEADOWOOD NAPA VALLEY
California

You'll be treated like Napa Valley landed gentry while staying at this luxury resort located in the area's most prestigious country club. Meadowood Napa Valley is a picture-perfect property tucked into a 250-acre valley off the Silverado Trail. A member of the Relais & Châteaux group, this elegant hideaway is surrounded by vineyards and trees.

You'll feel as though you've stepped back in time when you enter the turn-of-the-century farmhouse-style lobby, with its huge fireplace, bowls of apples ready for the taking, and glass-fronted cabinets filled with books and knickknacks. It almost feels as though you're in New England. Meadowood's casual, clubby atmosphere reflects hominess and coziness, not glitz; it's conducive to doing nothing—yet it offers all the facilities of a full-service luxury resort.

Over the years the property served as a Christmas tree farm and rice paddy, before being groomed into one of the area's preeminent country clubs in the 1960s. The resort itself opened in 1984, and today guests rub shoulders with the "who's who" of Napa Valley, especially during the many top social events that are held here, including the annual Napa Valley Wine Auction in June.

Guests dwell in gray clapboard cottages, which look part Martha's Vineyard, part California wine country, with gables, white trim, cathedral ceilings, and stone fireplaces. There is more than a little romance in these gracious abodes nestled into the woods of tall California oaks and conifers. What a place to go and hide out—with the scent of pine permeating the airy rooms, a fine Chardonnay resting in an ice bucket next to two flutes, plush down comforters, and piles of fat pillows stacked on the king-size bed; and in the cooler months, a cozy fire crackling in your fireplace. With room service available, who needs to go anywhere?

One of the best features of the cottages are the wrap-around porches, each with an oh-so-private sitting area furnished with chairs and tables. In your room you'll find rattan furniture, a writing desk and minibar, and tasteful decor. Bathrooms are spacious and come with all the modern comforts. Some cottages have kitchenettes.

Meadowood offers a tantalizing array of choices for the sports-minded. In addition to miles of hiking and walking trails, where it would not be unusual for a deer or two to cross your path, you can swim in two pools and play croquet on the primped and clipped croquet lawns, which are trimmed as meticulously as a golf green and have wickets just the thickness of a nickel wider than the ball.

You can shake out your golf game on the resort's nifty and narrow nine-hole course, play tennis, explore the area by bike, or be pampered with a variety of soothing treatments at the health spa. The aerobics room provides a setting for classes ranging from a thirty-minute abs-intensive workout to yoga, and the air-conditioned exercise room features Cybex equipment, bikes, stair machines, and more. The masseur will even do treatments in your room—one of life's great happinesses.

Want to check out Napa Valley and the grapes? You can get an overview of more than one hundred vineyards from a lofty perch in a hot air balloon, or you can hop in a car and explore the area. Pick up a loaf of sourdough bread (a specialty in the region), a bottle of wine, and some good cheese and have a picnic on the way. Meadowood can help you with directions and suggestions for visiting not only the vineyards but also the scores of art galleries and boutiques in the vicinity.

The Restaurant at Meadowood offers the most extensive wine list in the valley, with more than 600 selections. Practically every vineyard in the valley is represented, and bottles are all fairly priced. Overlooking gnarled oaks and the golf course, the dining room makes an especially pretty picture at night, with floral displays, table lamps, and spotlighted watercolors. The menu tempts you with country-style rack of lamb with rice, beans, fennel, tomatoes, wilted arugula, olives, and garlic sauce or chilled Dungeness crab with three caviars, mango, and avocado, and lemon-cilantro vinaigrette. Desserts are hard to resist, but the flourless chocolate cake is rich enough to satisfy the most audacious of chocoholics. All this, of course, is accompanied by a fine wine—would you expect anything less here!

Breakfast, lunch, and dinner are served in the casual Meadowood Grill, and snacks and a limited lunch menu are available during the summer months at the Poolside Terrace. The food and other services are delivered by a caring, attentive staff in a friendly, unobtrusive manner.

Meadowood is a peaceful and unspoiled sanctuary in the midst of one of the nation's most interesting areas. Little more than an hour's drive from San Francisco, it is an exceptional retreat that has great charm and style. With its woodsy privacy it can help you put the outside world on hold.

Meadowood Napa Valley

Location: In the heart of the Napa Valley wine region, just outside the charming town of St. Helena

Romantic Highlights: Wood-burning fireplaces; private cottages hidden up a long, winding lane; great spa facilities (a well-kept secret)

Address/Phone: 900 Meadowood Lane, St. Helena, CA 94574; (707) 963–3646; fax (707) 963–3532

U.S. Reservations: (800) 458–8080; Relais & Chateâux, (800) RELAIS–8

Owner/Manager: Kenneth B. Humes, managing director; H. William Harlan, managing partner

Arrival/Departure: Limousine service available from airport

Distance from San Francisco Airport: 70 miles; Santa Rosa Airport, 20 miles; Oakland Airport, 60 miles

Distance from Downtown San Francisco: 70 miles

Accommodations: 85 rooms are scattered throughout the property. All rooms have a private entrance and porch; some are located in the woods overlooking the pool, others by the tennis courts and golf course fairways, and 13 are located in the Croquet Lodge. All have king-size beds; most have fireplaces.

Most Romantic Room/Suite: The Hillside Terrace cottages, set deep in the woods, with huge porches, stone hearths, and plenty of privacy

Amenities: Air-conditioning, TV, minibar, toaster, coffeemaker, hair dryer, terry robes, toiletries, duvets, fireplaces in most rooms, fresh fruit basket, newspaper, room service

Electricity: 110 volts

Sports and Facilities: 7 championship tennis courts, 2 regulation croquet lawns, 2 pools (one is a heated, 25-yard pool and is open year-round), 9-hole golf course, bicycling, hiking trails; full-service health spa with sauna, Jacuzzi, classes, quality equipment, and massage treatments

Dress Code: Informal; casually elegant attire requested for dinner at the Restaurant; white clothing and flat-soled shoes are required on the croquet lawns.

Weddings: May be arranged by calling (707) 963–3646; e-mail: catering@meadowood.com

Rates/Packages: $395–$2,915 per couple per night

Payment/Credit Cards: Most major

Deposit: Guarantee with 2-night deposit (use a credit card); cancel 14 days prior to arrival for refund

Government Taxes: 10.5 percent

Service Charges: Not included

POST RANCH INN
California

They sometimes have problems with deer grazing on the roofs. That challenge reflects the uniqueness of Post Ranch Inn, a magnificent resort located in one of the most majestic spots on earth—Big Sur. Opened in 1992, Post Ranch was the first new hotel in nearly twenty years to debut along this untamed, almost mythological coastline, which over the decades has attracted avant-garde writers and actors such as Henry Miller, Jack Kerouac, and Orson Welles. Big Sur was one of America's last frontiers, a place where roads did not arrive until the 1930s, electricity until the 1950s.

To win the approval of development-abhorring locals and legislators, the resort had to meet stringent environmental standards. In part, the property was planned by Bill Post III, whose great-grandfather had homesteaded the land (he paid $4.00 an acre for 160 acres) some 130 years previously. The resultant enclave manages to feel both rustic and futuristic—*Star Wars* meets the Old West.

Planked with redwood, the accommodations seem more like private houses than hotel rooms. Although rooms vary in layout and view, all offer the same amenities and square footage and make extensive use of gold-gray rajah slate, quarried by hand in India, for the floors. Railings and doors in Cor-Ten steel weather to the same brown-red tone of the neighboring oaks and madrone trees. Furnishings are comfortable, with features such as curvilinear sofas or window seats. Color schemes of blue, green, and earth tones soothe the spirit. Bathrooms are embellished with slate and granite; many have tubs next to windows positioned so that no one can see you but you can enjoy a 100-mile view. Bath towels are thick, the down comforters plump.

Tree Houses live up to their name, built on stilts so as not to disturb the adjoining redwoods. Walls are angled to maximize views and privacy. Personal favorites are the Ocean Houses, which hunker into the ridgeline—the terrain rising from the back to form the sod-covered roofs,

the aforementioned salad bar for perambulating deer. Out front, views of the Pacific surge to the horizon. The fireplace is arranged so that you can view it from both the living room and the bathroom.

Because Michael Freed and Myles Williams, Post Ranch's creators, wanted to spotlight the splendor of nature rather than the playthings of man, distractions are kept to a minimum. Rooms have no TVs (though they do come with pretty nifty stereo/CD systems), and there are no tennis courts or golf courses. What you have are miles of big-country hiking trails through redwood forests into the valleys snaking hillward behind Highway 1. Some guided hikes are offered, including nature treks and off-property hikes; herb garden talks are also available. The lap pool awaits, a warm 80 degrees year-round. A fitness room offers a step machine, free weights, and exercise machines; yoga classes are held poolside in the morning. Dramatic seascapes can be enjoyed at Pfeiffer and Andrew Molera Beaches, both less than 5 miles to the north.

Rates include an elaborate continental breakfast, served in your room or in the restaurant. Choices generally include fresh fruits, home-baked breads, granola, and quiche. Floor-to-ceiling glass windows (each of which took nine people to carry into position during construction) of the Sierra Mar restaurant afford cliff-hanging views of the water. So as not to compete with the vistas, decor is simple, with slate floors and a big fireplace.

Superintended by executive chef Craig von Forester, the Californian menu dallies with flavors from around the world. Entrees might feature a grilled venison chop with fermented black beans or John Dory (a fish that is like sole) with lemongrass, papaya, chili, and roasted peanuts. Prices run $73 per person for the four-course, prix-fixe dinner. The wine list is phenomenal, encompassing 2,000 different wines.

Not much is known about the Ohlone Indians, the original inhabitants of the Northern California coast. From their celebrations only a line from a song remains, "dancing on the brink of the world." From your cliffside perch at Post Ranch Inn, you'll probably experience a similar feeling of joy.

Post Ranch Inn

Location: On ninety-eight acres amid
Big Sur

Romantic Highlights: Endless views
villas' ridge-top perches; a large, night
tub on the edge of a cliff; guided natu
tarot reader and astrologer; stargazing through a 10-inch Meade electronic tracking telescope

Address/Phone: P.O. Box 219, Highway 1, Big Sur, CA 93920; (831) 667–2200; fax (831) 667–2824

U.S. Reservations: (800) 527–2200

Owner/Manager: Michael Freed and Myles Williams, general partners; Dan Priano, general manager

Arrival/Departure: Easily accessible by car

Distance from Monterey Airport: 35 miles south; 90 miles south of San Jose Airport; 150 miles south of San Francisco International Airport

Distance from Carmel: Approximately 30 miles south; 150 miles south of San Francisco

Accommodations: 30 villas, each with ocean or mountain views, in four styles: 5 Ocean Houses recessed into ridge with sod roofs, 7 Tree Houses on stilts, 10 Coast Houses, 2 Mountain Houses, and 6 guest accommodations in three-level Butterfly House

Most Romantic Room/Suite: Top-of-the-line Ocean Houses hang on the brink of the cliff and feature private, slate-floored terraces. These often book up way in advance.

Amenities: Wood-burning fireplace, bathtub/Jacuzzi, satellite stereo/CD music system, in-room massage table, coffeemaker, minibar, toiletries, terry-cloth robes, hair dryer

Electricity: 110 volts

Sports and Facilities: A "basking pool" (a giant hot tub); fitness center and spa; hiking and walking trails

Dress Code: Casually elegant

Weddings: Can be arranged

Rates/Packages: $485–$935 per couple per night

Payment/Credit Cards: Most major

Deposit: Reservations require guarantee or deposit in advance. Cancellations must be made 14 days in advance.

Government Taxes: 10 to 15 percent

Service Charges: Not included

RANCHO VALENCIA
California

Rancho Valencia, a Relais & Châteaux all-suite property, sits atop a forty-acre plateau in the rolling hills of Rancho Santa Fe. The fifty-five pink-and-white adobe bungalows, red-tile roofs, mountains of bougainvillea, and red clay pots brimming over with hot pink flowers create a virtual garden of Eden. Walkways wind through the grounds, which are liberally planted with vibrantly blooming flowers and shrubs: Impatiens, agapanthus, hibiscus, geraniums, palms, and wildflowers burst in great exuberance in the gardens and on the hillsides. Trumpet flower vines in red, orange, and pink surround the tennis courts and cover trellises and casita walls, and fragrant honeysuckle wafts through the air.

Built in 1989, Rancho Valencia has welcomed guests such as Bill Gates, President Clinton, Michael Jordan, Regis Philbin, and Rene Russo. These elite guests might occupy the Hacienda, a luxurious three-suite adobe brick home built in the 1940s, but perchance if the Hacienda is taken, they should be quite happy, thank you, in the suites which are spacious and private.

It's a tough call as to which suite style to recommend. The 1,200-square-foot Rancho Santa Fe suite comes with a separate bedroom and sitting room; the Del Mar suite gobbles up 850 square-feet of open space with a low, tile-topped divider that contains a desk, built-in bureau, and bar, defining the sleeping area and sitting area. The new Grove suites are spacious and offer private patios with outdoor Jacuzzis, huge steam showers with large rainhead sprays, and large whirlpool tubs.

All configurations reflect a combination of California chic and traditional hacienda with whitewashed, beamed cathedral ceilings, earth-toned stucco walls, French doors, and a mix of white carpets and red-tile floors. Suites feature walk-in closets, separate vanities, wet bar, gas fireplaces, patios or balconies, wonderful red clay and glazed pots planted with live orchids and tropical plants. There are wicker baskets, plantation shutters, and a color palette that reflects nature. Bathrooms are so large that you don't fog up the mirror after a hot, steamy shower.

Furnishings combine Southwestern antiques and antique reproductions. King-size beds are dressed in creamy white and, if high-quality linens are important to you, you'll love the Italian duvet cover and sheets that are dreamy high-thread-count Fili D'Oro Egyptian cotton. Pillows are fine goose down. (Synthetic-filled pillows are available for those who have allergy problems.)

Each suite has a CD player and a collection of CDs. (In my room I had *Romancing the Guitar* by Ron Freshman, *Dream Melodies*, and selections by Mozart and Tchaikovsky.)

The pool is surrounded by gardens, palms, and plenty of chaise lounges. There is a fitness center, croquet lawn, and a golf course nearby. Once the John Gardener Tennis Center, Rancho Valencia has an impressive array of tennis facilities with eighteen tennis courts, eight pros, and a program of clinics and private lessons available to guests. It's no wonder that Rancho Valencia has been consistently rated as one of the Top Ten Tennis Resorts in the country by *Tennis Magazine*.

When you get up in the morning, you'll find glasses of fresh-squeezed orange juice, the daily newspaper and a flower just outside your door on a tiled ledge. Although you might be tempted to linger on your patio sipping your juice and reading the paper, you'll be rewarded with a sumptuous breakfast in the Sunrise Room where cobalt blue, white, and yellow tiles cover

the walls. Eat inside or just outside where the French doors open onto flower-filled patios overlooking lines of lemon trees and the tennis courts.

Breakfast might be Belgian waffles surrounded by fresh raspberries, blackberries, blueberries, and currants or Valencia Eggs Benedict. For those wishing lighter fare, there are always choices from the alternative spa menu such as Rancho Frittata made with egg whites and oat bran waffles served with berries and fresh fruit.

The Main Dining Room is casually elegant with white-linen–topped tables, crystal, and superb vistas of the countryside. Other places to eat and drink include the light and airy Terrace Room and the open-air Fountain Courtyard where a kiva fire casts a romantic glow in the evening and large mazeta pots filled with clouds of bougainvillea fill the space with color.

California-Mediterranean cuisine features the freshest of local produce. Chef Steven Summer uses fresh herbs grown on the property, and guests enjoy fresh oranges, grapefruit, limes, lemons, and tangerines from Rancho Valencia's orchards.

Lunch choices include items such as Spicy Sautéed Crabcake on a bed of shiitake mushrooms or mesculin salad with champagne vinaigrette and pear tomatoes. Dinner may start with chilled white asparagus salad with Chino's baby greens or lobster bisque with Armagnac. Entrees are equally tempting: pan-roasted veal chop with Valencia garden herb gnocchi or sautéed duck breast served with roasted tricolor potatoes and a black-cherry balsamic bigarade sauce and mushrooms and a Madeira demi-cream sauce. Then if you have room for dessert, you can try the flourless chocolate soufflé served with roasted espresso sauce and vanilla bean cheesecake. And of course you have a choice of some excellent wines from California and France as well as from all over the world.

Rancho Valencia

Location: 30 miles north of San Diego

Romantic Highlights: Flower-studded hilltop setting; private courtyards; fireplaces; luxuriously dressed king-size beds

Address/Phone: P.O Box 9126, Rancho Santa Fe, CA 92067-4126; (800) 548–3664, (858) 756–1123; fax (858) 756–0165

E-mail: reservations@ranchovalencia.com

Web Site: www.ranchovalencia.com

U.S. Reservations: (800) 548–3664

Owner/Manager: Michael J. Ullman, general manager

Arrival/Departure: Most arrive by car; pickup can be arranged.

Distance from San Diego Airport: 30 minutes

Distance from San Diego: 30 minutes

Accommodations: 49 suites

Most Romantic Room/Suite: The Grove suites, with private patios and Jacuzzis, fireplaces, and large baths; Room #100, a Rancho Santa Fe suite that is close to the pool and the dining rooms; and the Del Mar open-plan suites

Amenities: Walk-in closets, separate vanities, gas fireplace, 2 cable TVs and a VCR, CD player, terry robes, turndown service, wet bar and mini-fridge, coffee/tea maker, clock radio, safe, full-length mirror, hair dryer, 24-hour room service, fine toiletries, valet parking. The Grove suites feature Jacuzzi tubs on patios, whirlpool tubs, and steam showers with rainheads.

Electricity: 110

Sports and Facilities: Pool, 18 Deco-Turf tennis courts, croquet lawn, boutique, pro shop, biking, hiking, fitness center; golf and hot air ballooning nearby

Dress Code: Resort casual

Weddings: Can be arranged

Rates/Packages: Daily rates per suite range from $450 to $875. A two-night "Romantic Getaway" including accommodations, champagne, dinner for two, breakfasts on your patio or in the dining room, 1 aromatherapy massage or European Facial per person, use of tennis courts and fitness center, all taxes, and restaurant and spa gratuities is $1,425 to $1,705 per couple. Tennis packages are also available.

Payment/Credit Cards: Most major

Deposit: By credit card

Government Taxes: Included in package

Service Charges: Not included

SONNENALP RESORT
Colorado

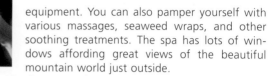

You don't have to go all the way to Austria to find the archetypal European ski and mountain resort. Just grab your skis and head to Vail, where the Fässler family has created a resort that fairly sings with charms of the Old World. The Sonnenalp Resort is actually three separate inns within easy walking distance of one another. Each has its own restaurants and personality.

The Austria Haus Club & Hotel, located next to Vail's covered bridge, is the smallest and coziest. It has a bar, a Jacuzzi, a sauna, on-site ski storage, and an intimate lobby with a large fireplace. Many of the thirty-seven rooms, with their antique brick and barn-board walls and washed pine furniture, overlook picturesque Gore Creek.

The Sonnenalp Resort of Vail, winner of *Snow Country Magazine*'s National Design Award for ski area lodges and hotels, as well as several other awards, consists of the elegant Ludwig's Restaurant, the more casual Bully Ranch Restaurant, and the King's Club Lounge, with its piano bar and library.

The light, airy, 5,000-square-foot spa features a 1,200-square-foot indoor/outdoor pool, indoor and outdoor Jacuzzis, a sauna, steam rooms, and an exercise room with the latest in exercise and weight-lifting equipment. You can also pamper yourself with various massages, seaweed wraps, and other soothing treatments. The spa has lots of windows affording great views of the beautiful mountain world just outside.

The largest and most luxurious of the three inns, Sonnenalp Resort of Vail has eighty-eight suites decorated with handcrafted woodwork, original artwork of Native American scenes, gas fireplaces, cozy sitting areas, European fixtures, and warm, natural wood furniture. Bathrooms have heated marble floors, double sinks, and large tubs just right for soaking out kinks acquired on the ski slopes.

With its white exterior trimmed with wooden balconies and stone arches and a roofline that swoops over towers and gables, Sonnenalp Resort of Vail is reminiscent of a lovely palace chalet. Covered with snow, it's a picture postcard. Send this one to your friends, and they won't believe it's not somewhere in the Alps.

At the Swiss Hotel & Spa, just half a block away from Sonnenalp Resort of Vail, you'll find a European treatment spa offering aromatherapy and massage and body treatments as well as facials, manicures, and other pampering services. The spa also has an indoor Jacuzzi, an outdoor heated pool, a cold plunge pool, a fitness room, Finnish saunas, Turkish steam rooms, and a juice bar as well as a full bar serving beverages and light meals.

The fifty-seven rooms and two suites at the Swiss Hotel & Spa feature pine armoires and beds, Alpine decor, and views of the creek or the village. Be sure to try the fondue and raclette, specialties at the Swiss Chalet Restaurant.

The Cosmetique Boutique and the Sonnenalp Resort Shop, located in the Swiss Hotel & Spa, feature a tempting array of items, including jewelry, accessories, perfumes, and unique gifts. Those staying at the Austria Haus Club & Hotel and the Swiss Hotel & Spa have access to the Swiss Spa; those staying at the Sonnenalp Resort of Vail can use both the Sonnenalp Spa and the Swiss Spa.

During the summer months Sonnenalp is a wonderful base for those who love hiking, biking, swimming, horseback riding, tennis, and exploring this lovely mountain area. The Sonnenalp Golf Club features an eighteen-hole, links-style course.

If you've got Europe on your mind but want to leave your passports at home, Sonnenalp Resort is highly recommended.

Sonnenalp Resort

Location: Three separate houses set in the center of Vail

Romantic Highlights: Sitting by a blazing fire in your suite while the snow falls softly outside; sleeping under fluffy down duvets; moonlight sleigh ride; European ambience

Address/Phone: 20 Vail Road, Vail, CO 81657; (970) 476–5656; fax (970) 476–1639

E-mail: info@sonnenalp.com

Web Site: www.sonnenalp.com

U.S. Reservations: (800) 654–8312; fax (970) 476–5449

Owner/Manager: Johannes Fässler, owner/general manager

Arrival/Departure: Colorado Mountain Express shuttle service available at $62 one-way from Denver International Airport and $42 one-way from Eagle.

Distance from Denver International Airport: 2 hours. Eagle County Airport is only a 45-minute drive.

Distance from Denver: 100 miles west

Accommodations: Sonnenalp Resort of Vail, 2 rooms, 88 suites; Swiss Hotel & Spa, 57 rooms, 2 suites; Austria Haus Club & Hotel, 19 rooms and 6 suites

Most Romantic Room/Suite: Suites in Sonnenalp Resort of Vail; spacious Bald Mountain Suite overlooks creek and comes with a separate bedroom. Lodgepole Suite also roomy and luxurious, with view of Vail Village or Gore Creek. Creekside Room in Austria Haus Club & Hotel has view of mountain and creek and is cozy and less expensive.

Amenities: Hair dryer, bathrobes, iron and ironing board, toiletries, telephone, high-speed Internet access in rooms, TV, VCR, down duvet, minibar, air-conditioning (Sonnenalp Resort of Vail only). Suites have fireplace, minibar, double vanity, soaking tub, balcony, separate living room, and loft.

Electricity: 110 volts

Sports and Facilities: Vail Mountain has 4,000 skiable acres serviced by 25 lifts; in addition to Alpine and cross-country skiing, you can go snowboarding, snowshoeing, bobsledding, paragliding, dogsledding, snowmobiling, and ice skating. There is also an 18-hole golf course with pro shop, pool, and clubhouse; outdoor Jacuzzi, indoor and outdoor heated pools; 2 European spas; 4 tennis courts.

Dress Code: Casual; for Ludwig's, neat casual attire

Weddings: Can be arranged

Rates/Packages: Romance in the Rockies, $149–$219 per person, double occupancy, including suite accommodations, flowers, champagne, chocolate-covered strawberries, breakfast, and dinner (rates higher in winter season).

Payment/Credit Cards: Most major

Deposit: 1 night's lodging due within 10 days of booking

Government Taxes: 8.4 percent

Service Charges: Not included

DISNEY'S GRAND FLORIDIAN RESORT & SPA
Florida

If you thought Walt Disney World was just for kids, think again. This area, with all its various attractions, is one of the top honeymoon destinations in the world. And within this complex of fun and games, the Grand Floridian Resort & Spa is just about the most romantic place you can stay. Special Concierge honeymoon rooms overlook the lagoon with a veiw of Cinderella's Castle in the Magic Kingdom or of the palm-studded pool. This Victorian-style hotel rests like an oasis right in the heart of all the action just beyond its entrance.

Designed in the grand manner of the Victorian era and reminiscent of the setting for *The Great Gatsby*, the Grand Floridian, with its sprawling white facade accented by gabled roofs, intricate latticework, and ornate balustrades, is set amid gardens and lawns planted with canary palms, magnolias, hibiscus, and other lush tropical flora. This grand hotel boasts wide verandas with wicker rockers, more than 120 miles of decorative scrollwork, white towers, and a red-shingle roof.

A curious touch in the lofty, five-story atrium lobby is an open-cage elevator that whisks guests up and down. Look up and admire the lobby's ceiling, with its three illuminated stained-glass domes, ornate chandeliers, and metal scrolls.

Rooms, which are located in a 225,000-square-foot main building and in five lodge buildings, carry out the early 1920s mood, though the colors used are softer and lighter. Applied with flair are printed wall coverings coordinated with fabrics, light woods, marble-topped sinks (but with old fashioned–looking fittings), and Victorian woodwork. Most rooms have two queen-size beds; some have kings. Suites include a parlor plus one or more bedrooms.

The mood may hark back to the turn of the century and the days of John D. Rockefeller and Thomas Edison, but the amenities are pure twenty-first century modern, with monorail service and air-conditioning—the monorail stops right beside the Grand Lobby. The resort has five restaurants, four lounges, two snack bars, five shops, a 9,000-square-foot spa and health club, a marina, and children's facilities. One of the two pools overlooks the Seven Seas Lagoon and has a waterfall that drops from a 27-foot-high stone mountain. A water slide carries you on a thrilling ride through the mountain, past trees, and under a waterbridge.

The opportunities for fun and romance are seemingly unlimited. At the spa you can unwind with a soothing massage, a native Floridian floral bath, or a hydrating paraffin body wrap. Or rent a boat from the marina and explore the lagoon. At Epcot you can visit the cultures and entertainment worlds of many countries as well as thrill at the sharks and tropical fish at The Living Seas. You can ride the spine-tingling Thunder Mountain at the Magic Kingdom; whiz down the 120-foot-high Summit Plummet from the top of Mt. Gushmore at the sixty-six-acre Blizzard Beach water park; thrill to an alien encounter in Tomorrowland; go on "safari" at the new Disney Animal Kingdom Park; and dodge (imaginary) flying objects at the 3-D exhibit, "Honey, I Shrunk the Audience." Later, back in the resort, you can dine by candlelight in the privacy of your room and enjoy a moonlit walk on the white-sand beach.

You can go nightclub hopping at Pleasure Island (yes, that man's eyes in the portrait at the Adventurers Club really do follow you), where you will most likely laugh at the comedians at the Comedy Warehouse, and dance up a storm at the Mannequins Dance Palace. See how films

Disney's Grand Floridian Resort & Spa

Location: On 40 acres in the heart of Walt Disney World Resort on the west side of Seven Seas Lagoon

Romantic Highlights: Walt Disney World at your doorstep; luxurious spa; champagne cruise; couples' massages

Address/Phone: P.O. Box 10,000, Lake Buena Vista, FL 32830-1000; (407) 824–3000; fax (407) 824–2968

U.S. Reservations: (407) W–DISNEY

Owner/Manager: Georgina Sussan, general manager

Arrival/Departure: Transfers can be arranged at an additional cost for the Disney Fairy Tale Honeymoon Package.

Distance from Orlando International Airport: 26 miles

Distance from Orlando: 25 miles southwest

Accommodations: 867 rooms and suites

Most Romantic Room/Suite: Honeymoon rooms have all the amenities included in the Concierge rooms, with a few differences. Some are octagonal; some have balconies; some Jacuzzis. Lodge suites, located in a separate building, enjoy such special amenities as afternoon tea, complimentary continental breakfast, and hors d'oeuvres and wine.

Amenities: Air-conditioning, ceiling fans, hair dryer, telephone, minibar, in-room safe, bathrobes, turndown service, room service, iron and ironing board (on request), and toiletries. Main building Concierge rooms also include special shampoos and lotions, slippers, VCR, continental breakfast, tea, hors d'oeuvres, and late-night dessert and cordials.

Electricity: 110 volts

Sports and Facilities: A 275,000-gallon swimming pool and a second pool overlooking the Seven Seas Lagoon with a waterfall and slide; beach, marina, water sports; health club, exercise room, saunas, massage room. Also in the Disney complex are 5 championship golf courses, tennis courts, jogging paths, horseback riding, ponds, and pools.

Dress Code: Casual; dressier at Victoria & Albert's

Weddings: The glass-enclosed Fairy Tale Wedding Pavilion, on an island in the Seven Seas Lagoon, offers a magical site for the ceremony. You can also arrange for a wedding and Cinderella reception at the Grand Floridian or a Sunset Beach wedding. Call (407) 828–3400 for details.

Rates/Packages: The three-night Disney Fairy Tale Honeymoon Package, priced from $2,670 per couple, includes accommodations, unlimited admission to Disney World attractions; breakfast, lunch, and dinner daily; fireworks cruise; 50-minute spa treatment; admission to Cirque du Soleil; private golf and tennis lessons; and use of health club.

Payment/Credit Cards: Most major

Deposit: Two-night deposit at time of booking to cover first and last nights' accommodations

Government Taxes: 11 percent sales tax on rooms; 6 percent on food

Service Charges: Some gratuities included in honeymoon packages

are made and special effects created at Disney's MGM Studios and shop at the many, many stores.

Restaurants at the Grand Floridian range from the formal fare served in Victoria & Albert's to the hamburgers and hot dogs of Gasparilla Grill and Games. At V&A's the menu changes daily, and what you get depends on what is available in the local market that day. Selections include fresh seafood and meat. A nice touch is the red rose you are given at the end of your meal.

For a market-fresh blend of Florida and Mediterranean cooking, try Citricos, and for Southern specialties head for the Grand Floridian Cafe. The 1900 Park Fare serves a Disney-character breakfast and dinner buffet; Narcoosee's features a variety of seafood. All serve baked goods prepared in the hotel bakery.

At the close of the evening, the night sky lights up at Epcot with a spectacular display of fireworks during IllumiNations, a laser and water spectacular—it's guaranteed you'll see stars!

LITTLE PALM ISLAND
Florida

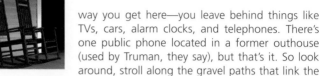

It used to be a rustic fishing retreat for America's presidents and high-profile stars. It still attracts people like Mario Andretti, Robert Wagner, Jill St. John, and Ivana Trump, but Little Palm Island is no longer rustic. The South Seas–style thatched bungalows, which stand on stilts amid the more than 250 coconut palm trees, tropical foliage, and gardens of this idyllic island Shangri-la, just 3 miles offshore in the Lower Florida Keys, come with air-conditioning, whirlpool baths, king-size beds, and fully stocked minibars. Little Palm Island, which opened as a public resort in 1988, succeeds in combining the best of both worlds.

Once your boat pulls into the pier—and that's the only way you get here—you leave behind things like TVs, cars, alarm clocks, and telephones. There's one public phone located in a former outhouse (used by Truman, they say), but that's it. So look around, stroll along the gravel paths that link the cottages to the pool area and beach, find a hammock, settle in, and relax. Since young children are not allowed here, you'll have the pool and the beach all to yourself.

You share the island, maintained as a nature preserve, with a variety of species of birds and animals, including herons, parrots, manatees, Key deer, and loggerhead turtles, which lay their eggs each year on the beach. A recently completed $2 million landscape program includes a Zen garden.

The sugar-white sand beach runs in a thin strip around the five-acre island and broadens out at one end, where you'll find a vast tidal flat, home to a fascinating number of birds and other creatures, which are best seen in the early morning or evening. During the day, from your lounge on the beach you need only plant your pink flag in the sand to summon a member of the ever-watchful staff, who will be quick to take your drink or snack order.

Sunsets are special here. Look carefully and you can see the green flash just as the sun drops below the horizon. Walk completely around the island in the early evening and watch the colors brighten and mellow.

Your suite has a soaring pitched ceiling of thatch and bamboo, a ceiling fan, a king-size bed draped with a filmy white net canopy, a sitting area furnished in traditional British colonial style, wraparound sundecks, a dressing area, and a bathroom decorated with Mexican tile.

Although each bathroom comes with a whirlpool tub, the most popular way to freshen up is to use your outdoor shower, which is enclosed by bamboo walls and is totally private. On Little Palm's list of ways to conserve natural resources is the suggestion to "shower with a friend."

Louvered wood walls (with screens) open to let the sea breezes in—you rarely need to turn on your air-conditioning; some never do.

Of course you'll have to make major decisions, like whether to go snorkeling or try out one of the canoes, whether to loll at the lagoonlike pool or head to the spa for a massage. Since the water off the beach is usually too shallow to swim in, you'll need the pool for your lap work. Nearby are superb dive sites for scuba enthusiasts. Just 3 miles away, Looe Key, a long reef protected by the National Park Service, stretches for miles and is home to myriad multicolored fish and other sea creatures.

There is a small library with a good selection of books to borrow, and nearby are hammocks strung in the trees. At Little Palm, hammocks are in. And if you really can't stand all this serenity and good living, you can sneak down to the Quarter Deck, which is located on the dock, and rent a TV/VCR.

You can dine indoors in the main restaurant or outside on the terrace. You can also dine at the casual, literally on-the-beach restaurant, where your dining chairs and table sit on wood "island" platforms set right on the sand. And the food prepared by executive chef Adam Votaw is as good as it looks—using mostly fresh local ingredients.

Especially tasty are the fresh dolphin, grouper, tuna, grilled salmon, rack of lamb, and homemade soups and pastas. Fresh herbs and seasonings are just right, sauces splendid, desserts impossible to resist. On Sundays it's brunch time. Everything can be accompanied by a bottle of red or white from Little Palm's impressive wine cellar.

Physically, Little Palm Island is fifteen minutes from shore; psychologically, it's another world, where cares wash away and romance blooms.

Little Palm Island

Location: Off the tip of Little Torch Key, 120 miles southwest of Miami and 28 miles east of Key West

Romantic Highlights: Your own thatched cottage—it's like being in the South Pacific, only you don't have to knock yourself out getting there.

Address/Phone: 28500 Overseas Highway, Little Torch Key, FL 33042; (305) 872–2524; fax (305) 872–4843

E-mail: getlost@littlepalmisland.com

Web Site: www.littlepalmisland.com

U.S. Reservations: (800) 3–GET–LOST; Relais & Châteaux, (800) RELAIS–8

Owner/Manager: John Leinhardt, general manager

Arrival/Departure: Transfer and van service to the Little Torch Key Shore Station (mile marker 28.5) is available from both Key West and Marathon Airports. Little Palm's shuttle service will meet you and take you to their shore station, where you will board a boat for the 3-mile, 15-minute ride to the island. Limousine service can also be arranged from Miami International.

Distance from Miami International Airport: 120 miles; Key West International Airport, 28 miles

Distance from Key West: 28 miles

Accommodations: 30 one-bedroom suites located in 15 thatched-cottage bungalows; 2 Island Grand suites

Most Romantic Room/Suite: Although all rooms have a view of the sea, the Island Grand suites are the most coveted.

Amenities: Air-conditioning, minibar, wet bar, coffee bar, whirlpool bath, outdoor shower, ceiling fans, bathrobes. (TVs, telephones, and alarm clocks are "banned" from the island. There is one public phone, located in the former out-house, and it takes credit cards only.)

Electricity: 110 volts

Sports and Facilities: Pool, beach, full-service spa, exercise room; sailing, kayaking, canoeing, fishing, snorkeling; pontoon boats and Sun-Kat motorized lounge chairs can be rented; deep-sea fishing, scuba diving, guided nature tours can be arranged.

Dress Code: Casually elegant

Weddings: Can be arranged

Rates/Packages: $595–$1,895 per suite per night; dinner plans available at additional cost

Payment/Credit Cards: Most major

Deposit: First and last nights' lodging at time of booking, refundable if canceled no later than 30 days prior to arrival date; $50 service charge applies. Deposit will be forfeited if canceled 30 days or less prior to arrival date.

Government Taxes: 11.5 percent

Service Charges: 10 percent

FOUR SEASONS RESORT MAUI AT WAILEA
Hawaii

Everything about the Four Seasons Resort Maui at Wailea since the resort opened in 1990 is as it should be—geared for the pleasure of its guests. Most would agree that chilled towels, ice water, and Evian mist brought to your poolside cabana throughout the day are not necessities. But boy are they appreciated! The Four Seasons' propensity for pampering and attention to detail has helped it earn the distinction of ranking consistently among the top hotels in the world.

The young, energetic staff look more like winners from central casting for a new California surfing movie than their real-life roles as dispensers of goodwill, frosty drinks, and fluffy towels. Four Seasons in Maui has managed to put together a great package, combining exquisite facilities with superb personnel.

A study of elegance and style, the property has the look and feel of a plantation home settled in perfect harmony with its seaside surroundings. The lofty, open design integrates the vibrant blues of the Pacific with pastel-colored walls, floor-to-ceiling wooden shutters, ceiling fans, and plump-cushioned rattan couches. Gen-

tle trade winds keep a profusion of white orchids in constant motion. Scattered throughout the lobby and other (un)common areas are pieces of art and period furniture.

Measuring a generous 600 square feet, the guest rooms are both elegant and comfortable and are decorated in a decidedly tropical mode. The in-room safe is simple to use; the light in the closet, a welcome touch; and sitting on your bedside table is a reading light.

Catering to the diversity of its many guests, the Four Seasons maintains the delicate balance between too much activity and not enough, and successfully separates activities geared for children and adults. With two pools, water sports galore, a health club/spa, a jogging trail, aerobics, and more, there is no lack of things to do. Sea kayaks and water scooters are available nearby.

A special surprise (priced at $215) awaits the unsuspecting: A trail of flower petals is laid from your bedroom door to a drawn bubble bath. Candles, CD music, roses, and champagne set the mood. At the heart of the resort, royal palms define the borders of a large swim-

ming pool, which boasts an adjacent computer-controlled fountain; it's programmed to react to the whims of the trade winds so its spray keeps within defined boundaries. Two Jacuzzis spill into the pool; one is for adults only. Hundreds of flowers follow a sweeping stairway from the upper lobby to the pool area and beyond. Beneath the stairway two tropical birds greet visitors as they pass. A manicured lawn between the pool and Wailea Beach provides an additional lounging area, and even the sand is water-cooled, making it easygoing on bare feet when the sun is hot.

Nearby, a waterfall cools guests as they swim in the smaller, second pool, effectively hidden by tropical plants. The resort also has two tennis courts; cold, wet towels are provided.

Dining options abound and range from casual to elegant haute cuisine. Wolfgang Puck's new Spago restaurant is a treat for even the most assiduous gourmet. The offerings are varied and exceptional, with the Pacific Rim menu featuring fresh island fish and local ingredients. All are presented with pride in a pleasing, open setting with wonderful ocean views.

Soft breezes and a breathtaking view also factor in at the Pacific Grill, where guests can enjoy a sumptuous buffet breakfast, lunch, or dinner. For more casual dining there is Ferraro's at Seaside for informal fare served during the day. At night try authentic Italian cuisine and watch the sunset while enjoying seductive Italian music.

A car isn't necessary, as other dining options, shops, and golf are just a short walk away along Wailea's 2-mile ocean pathway. A complimentary shuttle is also available within the Wailea Resort. However, if you want to go off on your own and go exploring, you will probably want to rent a car for a couple of days. There is a lot to see and do on Maui. You can get up early in the morning, be driven up to the top of the volcano, and then ride back down the mountain on a bike, and you can visit some of the small nearby villages and browse in the shops. Or you can stay just where you are on your lounge and wait for someone to come by and refresh you with a light mist of cool Evian water.

Four Seasons Resort Maui at Wailea

Location: On 15 waterfront acres between the slopes of the Haleakala Crater and the Pacific shore in Wailea, along Maui's southwestern coast

Romantic Highlights: Breathtaking views of the rugged volcanic coast and moonlit surf; huge marble bath; the ultimate romantic dinner for two on a grassy knoll, high above the sea; limo picnic lunch with champagne; outdoor massages along the ocean

Address/Phone: 3900 Wailea Alanui, Wailea, Maui, HI 96753; (800) 334–6284 or (808) 874–8000; fax (808) 874–2222

Web Site: www.fourseasons.com

U.S. Reservations: (800) 332–3442 or (800) 334–6284

Owner/Manager: Shimizu Development, owner; Radha Arora, general manager

Arrival/Departure: Airport limousine transfers; Budget rental cars; motor-coach minibus and van service can be arranged.

Distance from Kahului Airport: 17 miles

Distance from Kihei: 4 miles

Accommodations: 380 spacious rooms and suites, all with one or more lanais (porches); 85 percent have ocean views

Most Romantic Room/Suite: Ocean-view or executive suite

Amenities: Air-conditioning, ceiling fans, hair dryer, bathrobes, room safe, double vanity as well as separate vanity, built-in refrigerator bar, separate soaking tub, TV, cosmetic mirror, toiletries, complimentary morning coffee

Electricity: 110 volts

Sports and Facilities: 2 pools, 2 whirlpools, beach, use of 3 golf courses at Wailea Golf Club, tennis at the 14-court Wailea Tennis Center (including 3 grass courts), complimentary use of 2 on-site tennis courts lighted for night play, health club with exercise machines and steam room; full-service spa; running paths, snorkeling, scuba diving, sailing instruction, aerobics, aqua exercise, power walking

Dress Code: Casually elegant

Weddings: Packages range from $3,800 for the Ku'uipo Wedding, with ceremony, leis, solo musician, and a bottle of champagne, to $14,000 for the more elaborate Lokelani Wedding.

Rates/Packages: $400 per couple per night for a room with a garden view; $625–$925 for an executive suite; $735–$2,400 for a room or suite on the Club floor; $735–$2,750 for a one-bedroom suite.

Payment/Credit Cards: Most major

Deposit: 1-night deposit plus tax

Government Taxes: 11.416 percent

Service Charges: Not included

HALEKULANI

Hawaii

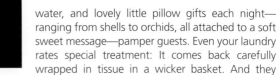

Originally a private oceanfront estate, the quietly posh Halekulani, on the middle of Waikiki Beach, has been welcoming guests since 1917. Over the years ownership has changed and buildings have been built and demolished and built again. What remains of the original hotel is a 1930s building (now called the "main building") that has been incorporated into the overall design, consisting of five interconnected structures. Throughout the resort you'll find lots of marble, Italian terrazzo, and fine woods in creating this Hawaiian oasis.

From your languorous lanai you'll see the exquisite oval pool and, beyond that, the beach and sea. Halekulani, which means "house befitting heaven," has everything you'll require to make it your own personal paradise.

Wraparound lanais with nonstop views of the sunsets, the sea, and Diamond Head are only the beginning. Decorated in soft whites and neutrals enlivened by the color of orchids and flowers so perfect you'll wonder if they're real, rooms are furnished with rattan and upholstered furniture, glass-top tables, king-size beds, louvered-window walls, and plush carpets. Everything is quietly elegant. You'll not find any Hawaiian clichés lurking in the decorating schemes of these rooms.

Baths have marble vanities, ceramic tiles with outrigger motifs, and mirrored doors opening into a closet. Open the louvered doors on the other (bedroom) side of the closet and you can watch the surfers ride the waves while you relax in your tub. You'll also have a desk, plenty of drawers, extra shelves in the closet, padded hangers, an in-room safe, a minibar, and a TV that slides into a wall cabinet. The Halekulani gets my vote for the best designed room I've ever seen: not necessarily the largest or the poshest, but a space perfectly crafted for its size in visual beauty and ease of use. Even the toiletries, which are in small, sleek containers, fit into your hand or cosmetic bag just right.

Your room comes with all the amenities you'd expect, such as hair dryers and state-of-the-art phones, but there is more. A phone in the enclosed toilet area, spa-type bottled water, and lovely little pillow gifts each night—ranging from shells to orchids, all attached to a soft sweet message—pamper guests. Even your laundry rates special treatment: It comes back carefully wrapped in tissue in a wicker basket. And they really go over the top with honeymooners and deliver champagne to help celebrate the happy occasion.

Your opportunities for dining are no less impressive. Orchids, an oceanside indoor/outdoor restaurant open for all meals, specializes in international seafood cuisine along with Hawaiian items created by chef Jean-Pierre Maharibatcha. Living up to its name, this three-tiered restaurant has live orchids placed throughout it.

House Without A Key, another indoor/outdoor restaurant, serves breakfast, lunch, and sunset cocktails with Hawaiian entertainment and dancing under the stars each night. Arrive in time to watch the sun go down—it's one of the best seats in town for this nightly spectacle.

French-style meals are served at La Mer, an elegant indoor restaurant in the main building, with great ocean views and high accolades from those who rate. You'll find several Hawaiian-produced products on the menu, such as yellowfin tuna, Kula tomatoes, and Big Island lobster. Plates appear at your elbow like a series of gifts. Even the names of your dishes, like fine wines, need to be rolled across the tongue: Tartares of Hamachi, Ahi, and Salmon with Three Caviars and Three Coulis, and Baked Moano Fillets with Opakapaka Mousse and Lobster Medallions.

Tea is served every afternoon in the living room in the main building, and cocktails hold center stage in Lewers Lounge each evening.

I took a tour of "the back of the house," those places tourists don't normally see. Very impressive. I saw the yogurt and ice-cream machines at work, chocolates being dipped, and exotic flowers being artfully arranged. In the bakery the wonderful aromas of freshly baked rolls and breads and the miniature muffins reminded me it was getting time for yet another meal.

Halekulani offers a full range of water sports as well as a fitness room and sight-seeing programs. And I loved the pool. A simple, elegant large oval, it has no diving boards, slides, or waterfalls—just a huge orchid "painted" in mosaic glass tiles on the bottom. It really takes your breath away and only gets more beautiful as night falls.

Even when the hotel is full, there is never a need for you to do the early-morning scramble to stake out your territory on a favorite chaise with your towel. There are more than enough chairs, tables, and lounges.

You may never want to leave the grounds, but if you do there's a whole other world out there filled with fun and excitement. If you want action like an outrigger canoe ride, party time every Sunday at Duke's just down the beach, or shopping at the countless upscale stores, you'll find that almost everything is within a five- to ten-minute walk. Discos, nightclubs, streetcars—all close by. Catch the latest exhibit at the Contemporary Museum; picnic in the park and lie back on a blanket while the Hawaiian Royal Band plays the "Kamehameha Waltz." Try some rainbow-flavored shaved ice from the Waiola Store; shop for wild-looking veggies in Chinatown; pick up a yummy *malasada* (fluffy Portuguese doughnut) at Leonard's Bakery; and eat some great Thai food at Singha. Cap off the evening in the Hard Rock Cafe.

If you really feel adventurous, hop on a bus and go to Hanauma Bay for some snorkeling, hike up to the top of Diamond Head for a fabulous view of Honolulu, or explore Waimea Falls Park on the North Shore, where you can sit on a rock overlooking the beach and watch the sailboarders.

At sunset on Halekulani's terrace of the House Without A Key, sip a cool Chardonnay or Mai Tai as Kanoe Miller, elegantly dressed in a long brown velvet skirt and white Victorian-style blouse, dances gracefully under an aged Kiawe tree to lilting Hawaiian music played by the trio just behind her. With a backdrop of palms and the sea and the sun sinking slowly, turning the sky a rich pink, you'll find it hard to believe you are but a few yards from Waikiki Beach. Here, it would seem, you can have it all.

Staying at Halekulani may not be at the low end of the budget scale, but for your vacation of a lifetime, it's worth going the extra mile.

Halekulani

Location: On 5 oceanfront acres on Waikiki Beach, Oahu

Romantic Highlights: At twilight sounds of Hawaiian music floating up to your balcony overlooking the sea; candlelight dinner on your own private lanai

Address/Phone: 2199 Kalia Road, Honolulu, HI 96815-1988; (808) 923–2311; fax (808) 926–8004

Web Site: www.halekulani.com

U.S. Reservations: (800) 367–2343

Owner/Manager: Fred Honda, general manager

Arrival/Departure: Taxis available at airport; one-way is approximately $25; limousine service is $80

Distance from Honolulu Airport: 10 miles (25 minutes)

Distance from Honolulu: You're in the center of the Waikiki action; downtown Honolulu is 4 miles (15 minutes) away.

Accommodations: 456 rooms and suites, located in 5 low-density buildings ranging in height from 2 to 17 stories; 90 percent have ocean views.

Most Romantic Room/Suite: Corner ocean-view suites have a separate bedroom, bathroom, powder room, living room, wet bar, and dining area. Club ocean-view suites come with two lanais, bedroom/sitting area, bathroom, wet bar, and cozy bay window.

Amenities: Air-conditioning, hair dryer, remote color cable TV, mini-refrigerator, 3 telephones, in-room safe, separate glassed-in shower with thermostatic control, bathrobes, chocolates, fruit bowl

Electricity: 110 volts

Sports and Facilities: Large 46-by-82-foot pool; new day spa; beach center where you can arrange outrigger canoes, surfing, snorkeling, deep-sea fishing, sailboarding, and golf and tennis lessons; fitness room with scheduled workouts and classes as well as massages

Dress Code: Evening, resort attire in restaurants; LaMer, long-sleeved collared shirt or jacket for gentlemen

Weddings: The Halekulani does a lot of weddings, each one personalized.

Rates/Packages: Rates per couple $325–$520 per night; $750–$4,500 for suites. Romance Package, 4 nights from $1,920 for room; from $3,200 for suites including round-trip limousine service, champagne, strawberries, and exotic flowers; daily breakfast, chef's special dinner in Orchids, and Halekulani champagne flutes

Payment/Credit Cards: Most major

Deposit: Guarantee with credit card

Government Taxes: 4.16 percent state tax; 7.25 percent occupancy tax (total 11.41 percent)

Service Charges: Not included

HOTEL HANA MAUI
Hawaii

Geography has played a key role in making Hotel Hana Maui one of the most romantic resorts in Hawaii. Located on the eastern end of Maui, Hana is isolated from the more developed touristy areas by deep valleys and ravines dividing this part of the island from areas around Kahana and Kaanapali. In order to reach Hana, you embark on a breathtaking 50-mile journey along the Hana Highway, called one of the most beautiful roads in the world.

Around many of the 617 bends of the road, which twists and wiggles along the rugged coastline, waterfalls bubble and gush, falling into deep pools of clear mountain water—bring your bathing suit and take a dip in these clean, cool mountain "Jacuzzis." Jungle vegetation, lush and dense, cloaks the hills in a rich, dark green blanket damp with moisture and glistening in the sun, which filters through during the fickle mood shifts in the weather.

Finally, after crossing about fifty-four bridges along the Hana Highway (from Kahului), you come to the small town of Hana. There's not much here except for a couple of small stores, a bank, a post office, a gas station, and a restaurant. And Hotel Hana Maui. Sitting prettily on the very end of the island, below the rainy slopes of Haleakala, this hideaway resort is located on sixty-six acres of rolling, landscaped grounds.

This land was once devoted to the production of sugarcane and later to raising cattle. In the early fifties Hotel Hana Ranch was created by Paul Fagan, the owner of the 14,000-acre Puu O Hoku cattle ranch, specifically to accommodate Fagan's wealthy friends. There are still several thousand head of cattle on the property, but the hub of activity for most who find their way here is the hotel itself.

Once you check in and stroll around the gardens and lawns, richly planted with heliconias, exotic palms, and a

wide variety of flowering shrubs, and walk to the top of the hill overlooking the coast, where waves crash against jagged black rocks, the spell of Hana will soon captivate. Whether you stay in one of the bay cottages or in the traditionally styled Sea Ranch cottages, you'll appreciate the appointments and details that make this place so special. Live orchids growing out of ceramic containers and baskets, original Hawaiian arts and crafts, teak furniture, and beautiful tiled baths designed so that you don't need a curtain or door lend an air of low-key elegance.

Bleached hardwood floors, stone countertops, and carpets of lahaula, along with rich, muted natural colors of soft browns and greens, appeal to those who love things that are warm and welcoming, not overdone. Bathrobes are yakuta-style, towels are thick and thirsty.

Your view from your trellised patio or deck could be a fragrant garden or the sea. The one-story cottage suites are quite different from the Sea Ranch accommodations. Cottage suites are nestled into the gardens, and the views from the patios are of flowers and palms and towering trees. You'll find it hard to resist scooping up the petals from the plumeria trees, which drop their fragrant blossoms along the walkways.

The Sea Ranch cottages have spacious, private decks, and some come with Jacuzzis that overlook the sea. Louvered-window walls allow the sea breezes to cool the rooms, which are comfortable, quiet, and secluded.

Hana has a number of recreational facilities on the grounds or nearby. A 1932 Packard sedan takes you on a five-minute ride to a silver-black sand volcanic beach right down the road, a beach James Michener called the most perfect crescent beach in the Pacific. The beach is public but never crowded, and the hotel has its own changing and refreshment house.

Early risers may want to join the morning walk. You can also go horseback riding along the sea or follow the trails up the lower slopes of Haleakala volcano. An excursion to Ulaino brings you to lovely waterfalls and a stream you can swim in as well as an idyllic pond called the Blue Pond.

You can also go bicycle riding; play tennis, croquet, and sand volleyball; or practice your golf on the three-hole pitch and putt, where tees are marked by coconuts. Take a nature hike into the forest, or head to the Wellness Center, located near the pool at the top of a grassy hill above the sea, where you'll find the latest in fitness equipment. Aquacise and yoga classes are offered daily. A variety of

treatments are available including a romantic en suite couples' massage.

The dining room, with its beautiful garden view and dramatic 35-foot open-beamed ceiling, overlooks the gardens and features a range of Hawaiian specialties along with Polynesian, American, and Oriental cuisine. The chef uses lots of local produce, such as herbs, vegetables, taro, coconut, mango, and bananas. The Paniolo Bar, on the covered lanai overlooking the bay, is the place to go for those who want to relax after dinner. The more casual Hana Ranch Restaurant is open daily for breakfast and lunch and on Friday and Saturday for dinner.

The marvelous Hana Coast Gallery features the finest in genuine Hawaiian art and master crafts, including paintings, pottery, sculpture, wooden bowls, and rare antique floral prints.

You'll find the staff extremely friendly and helpful. Most live in the village and walk to work. Some have been employed at the hotel since its opening in 1946!

The Hotel Hana Maui casts its spell with exquisite subtlety. Serene and lovely, it's a resort romantics must discover at some point in their lifetime. A honeymoon is a good place to start.

Hotel Hana Maui

Location: Eastern end of the island, in Maui's back pocket

Romantic Highlights: Quiet, secluded area recalling Old Hawaii; private Jacuzzis on bungalow decks overlooking Pacific

Address/Phone: P.O. Box 9, Hana, Maui, HI 96713-9989; (808) 248–8211; fax (808) 248–7202

U.S. Reservations: (800) 321–4262

Owner/Manager: Douglas Chang, general manager

Arrival/Departure: By car from Kahului Airport: a 55-mile drive along the scenic (and winding) Hana Highway. If you're going to rent a car, make arrangements in advance, and rent the car in Kahului. You'll pay more if you rent in Hana, and only Dollar has an office there. By air: a 15-minute flight to Hana from Kahului Airport by Pacific Wings. You can also fly from Honolulu to Hana via Pacific Wings (60 minutes) or take a private charter or private helicopter. The hotel's open jitney picks up guests at all flights coming into Hana Airport and transports them to the property, a 10-minute ride.

Distance from Kahului Airport: 55 miles

Distance from Hana: In town; 50 miles from Kahului

Accommodations: 78 rooms and suites, including garden lanais and Sea Ranch cottages on the ground sloping to the seacoast on the Pacific side

Most Romantic Room/Suite: Ranch cottages with private Jacuzzis

Amenities: Coffee bar with coffeemaker, grinder, and selection of Kona coffee beans; hair dryer, toiletries; ceiling fans and refrigerator with ice maker; minibar with complimentary snacks and refreshments

Electricity: 110 volts

Sports and Facilities: Beach, tennis court, pool, 3-hole pitch-and-putt course, hiking, horseback riding, snorkeling, croquet, volleyball

Dress Code: Casual by day; dressier during evening

Weddings: The wide veranda of the Plantation House and the beautiful lawn and gardens are popular sites.

Rates/Packages: $275–$795 per couple, per day, including tennis, bicycles, snorkeling, and beach equipment; $95 per person, per day for breakfast, lunch, and dinner; $75 for breakfast and dinner. Honeymooners get 10 percent off rack rates as well as dinner 1 evening, champagne, and a massage for two with minimum four-night stay.

Payment/Credit Cards: Most major

Deposit: 1 night, guaranteed with credit card

Government Taxes: 10.17 percent

Service Charges: 15 percent

KONA VILLAGE RESORT
Hawaii

Native grass shacks were never like the luxurious *hales* that loll along the crystal-blue bay at Kona Village Resort, a hideaway strung around peaceful lagoons and blessed by a natural black-and-white speckled beach. The setting is something of a miracle—a small oasis of coco palms and beach that was left untouched by a fiery lava flow in 1801. Today Kona Village remains a lush, eighty-two-acre paradise of emerald lawns and mirror-still ponds. It's a quiet retreat for simple pleasures: watching a coconut drift in with the tide or stopping to watch the nightly "water ballet" by the resident manta rays, which softly swirl near shore.

Located at the site of an ancient Hawaiian fishing community, the resort resembles an old Hawaiian village. Its paths are edged by fragrant pikake and plumeria blossoms, and bungalows are thatched with coconut fronds and planted on stilts beside the ocean and lagoons or on lava fields. The resort is, in fact, the largest group of thatched buildings in the state of Hawaii. Local materials, such as coral, stone, and koa and ohia woods, are used extensively.

Inside, however, twenty-first century accoutrements include king-size beds in most accommodations, a refrigerator stocked with juices and soft drinks, modern bathrooms, and dressing rooms. The designs of the *hales* reflect nine different Polynesian cultures. The Hawaiian accommodations, for example, have steeply pitched thatched roofs, while the Maori feature boldly patterned fronts and carved figures on the rooflines. Interiors are paneled with wood, and ceilings are lined with lauhala matting. Furnishings might include rattan chairs and tropical-print spreads. The *hales* are also notable for what they don't have—in-room telephones, radios, or television. Instead of air-conditioners, ceiling fans enhance nature's cooling trade winds. A coconut placed in front of your *hale*'s door alerts the staff to leave you alone.

Every mealtime is special, from the macadamia-nut pancakes with coconut syrup at breakfast to duck breast with taro leaves and mango coulis at dinner. Friday and Monday nights the resort hosts a traditional luau, one of the most authentic in the islands—many Big Island residents drop by to enjoy the feast. Kailua pig is roasted in the imu (underground oven), accompanied by other delicacies, such as lau lau (pork and fish in taro leaves) and lomi salmon.

Afterward a Polynesian revue showcases Pacific Island dances, including the Samoan fire dance and hip-quivering Tahitian tamure. Another favorite is the paniolo steak cookout, with ukulele music to accompany the kiawe-grilled steaks.

A bevy of water sports activities are available for guests, including outrigger canoeing and glass-bottom boat excursions. In addition to the crescent-shaped swimming beach, the property offers two freshwater pools and a whirlpool. The resort has three lighted outdoor Plexi-

Kona Village Resort

Location: On eighty-two acres amid palms, gardens, and historic fishponds along a natural black-and-white beach on Kahuwai Bay, the Big Island

Romantic Highlights: Luxury *hales* (cottages), each designed in a different Polynesian style, such as Tahitian, Fijian, and Samoan; privacy protected when you place coconut at door; private massage for two in garden setting; private Jacuzzis

Address/Phone: P.O. Box 1299, Kailua-Kona, HI 96745; (808) 325–5555; fax (808) 325–5124

E-mail: kvr@aloha.net

Web Site: www.konavillage.com; www.konavillage honeymoon.com

U.S. Reservations: (800) 367–5290 or (800) 423–5450 (in Hawaii)

Owner/Manager: Fred Duerr, general manager

Arrival/Departure: Transfers included in honeymoon package

Distance from Keahole-Kona Airport: 6 miles

Distance from Kailua-Kona: 15 miles

Accommodations: 125 thatched *hales* (cottages) in 9 architectural styles

Most Romantic Room/Suite: The luxurious Lava Tahitians are set out on the lava rock along the ocean, away from other *hales*. The Sand Marquesans are also very luxurious and are located on the water, with lots of greenery to provide privacy.

Amenities: Ceiling fans, hair dryer, toiletries, king-size bed, dressing room, refrigerator stocked with juices and soft drinks, coffeemaker

Electricity: 110 volts

Sports and Facilities: Sunfish sailboats, outrigger canoes, snorkeling, new Oceanside spa, 3 lighted tennis courts all available on premises; nearby activities include 5 18-hole championship golf courses, horseback riding, fishing

Dress Code: Tropically casual

Weddings: Can be arranged

Rates/Packages: $495–$870 per couple per night, including breakfast, lunch, and dinner daily. Prices also cover most resort activities, including tennis, kayaking, Sunfish sailing, historical and petroglyph tours, airport transfers in the Big Island, and more. The Honeymoon Hideaway package costs $1,440– $2,560 per couple for 3 nights; $3,365–$5,975 for 7 nights. It includes all meals, accommodations, and a line-art reproduction of your honeymoon *hale*.

Payment/Credit Cards: Most major

Deposit: 2 nights' deposit; guarantee with credit card

Government Taxes: 11.42 percent

Service Charges: Not included

paved tennis courts; you can take advantage of the complimentary adult clinic or sign on for the round-robin series for practice and fun.

At the new Oceanside Massage Hale, a variety of massages from lomi lomi to Thai and cranial-sacral therapy soothe weary travelers.

The grounds also include many Hawaiian archaeological sites, including fishponds, house sites, and shelter caves. You can learn more about Hawaiian culture on several different excursions, including historical walks, tidepool explorations, and petroglyph tours highlighting the powerful depictions of turtles, fish, dogs, and humans.

About half of the guests at Kona Village have stayed at the resort previously. You'll probably want to add your names to the roster of returnees soon.

THE MANELE BAY HOTEL
Hawaii

A dozen years ago the island of Lanai was about a twenty-five–minute flight from—and about fifty years behind—Honolulu. With 98 percent of the land owned by Castle & Cooke, Lanai was called the Pineapple Island, a laid-back world with one funky hotel and a one-room airport.

All that changed in the early 1990s with the debut of two elegant new sister resorts, among the most luxurious in Hawaii. In the short time they have been open, the hotels have wowed rich and famous guests such as Kevin Costner and Billy Crystal and hosted major sporting events such as the Merrill Lynch Senior Shoot-Out on the PGA tour.

Playful spinner dolphins often visit Hulopoe Bay, Lanai's best beach and the setting for the Manele Bay Hotel, which opened in May 1991. Architecturally, the resort combines both Hawaiian and Mediterranean detailing, with arcaded loggias and sloping roofs. White walls and a sea-green tile roof harmonize with plush lawns and ochre pathways. To maintain an intimate feeling, individual wings surround garden courtyards, each with a different theme, such as Hawaiian, Japanese, or bromeliad.

In the lobby, murals by John Wullbrandt depict the legend of Kaululaau, said to have chased evil spirits from the island. Honoring Lanai's pineapple-plantation heritage, bronze chandeliers incorporate leaves and fruit in their design; vintage Hawaiian prints line the corridors.

As you stroll through the lush grounds, you'll encounter staff members diligently pursuing perfection—perhaps a wizened gardener raking imaginary leaves from an immaculate lawn, or a housekeeper polishing a bronze urn until it's mirror bright.

Rooms are very large and decorated in chinoiserie chic, with bamboo-framed chairs, porcelains poised on the armoire, and a four-poster bed. Spacious bathrooms sparkle with marble floors and counters and a separate glass stall shower. In addition to the usual shampoos and soaps, the lavish toiletries basket also includes hair spray, a miniloofah, and prethreaded needles. The lanai (terrace) is designed to be enjoyed and is furnished with a plump-cushioned chaise lounge and two comfy armchairs. About half of the rooms have ocean views.

A diamond-bright crescent, Hulopoe is one of the loveliest beaches in the islands. When conditions are calm, there's good snorkeling along the rocks at the left (as you face the ocean).

Through the hotel, guests can arrange various excursions, including a snorkel cruise aboard the *Trilogy* trimaran. They can also sign on for an ocean rafting trip along Lanai's coast, which is lined by 1,000-foot cliffs and secret coves.

For dining-with-a-view, you can't top the outside terrace of the Ihilani, with sound effects courtesy of the rustling palm fronds and wash of surf. Accented by crystal chandeliers and murals, the Ihilani formal dining room re-creates the splendor of the Hawaiian monarchy and serves a French Mediterranean cuisine.

The Lodge at Koele, Manele Bay's sister property, is also extremely Hawaiian—but in a way mainlanders rarely imagine Hawaii to be. The upland setting—a cool 1,700-foot elevation where hills often wear clouds like misty halos—resembles a scene more from *The Sound of Music* than *South Pacific*. Styled after a turn-of-the-century plantation estate, the resort features 35-foot beamed ceilings, twin natural stone fireplaces in the Great Hall, and spacious verandas arranged with phalanxes of wicker armchairs.

Although Koele feels as though it has purred along in

Grand Hotel perfection for at least a century or two, it only opened in April 1990. Connoisseurs can happily browse among rarities, ranging from a Burmese elephant howdah in the foyer to the eighth-century Persian painting in the music room. At the same time, the ambience is friendly, thanks to interior designer Joszi Meskan's sprightly touches, such as monkeys cavorting among the 8-foot-tall chandeliers.

Coddling remains the byword here, from the butter-soft suede armchairs in the library to the real down pillows on your bed. Rooms encourage relaxing, with a lavishly cushioned window seat, two wicker armchairs, and a four-poster bed crowned with pineapples. Bathrooms feature exotic blue-marble countertops paired with Italian tile floors and hand-painted cups from Portugal. Look carefully at the walls—they're painstakingly hand-painted, not papered.

Lanai is golfers' heaven, with two spectacular eighteen-hole layouts. Designed by Jack Nicklaus, the championship Challenge at Manele opened in December 1993 to immediate acclaim. Every hole on the course offers an unobstructed ocean vista. Upland, the Experience at Koele, designed by Greg Norman and Ted Robinson, boasts panoramic views and several dramatic elevation drops from tees to greens. The newly renovated Spa at Manele is reminiscent of an old-style plantation home with bamboo, stone, wood, and water features.

It all adds up to the perfect choice for couples who love outdoor adventures by day and sumptuous accommodations at night.

The Manele Bay Hotel

Location: Southeastern coast of Lanai

Romantic Highlights: White-sand Hulopoe Beach; serene courtyard gardens; two hotels for the price of one—stay at Mahele Bay and enjoy facilities at the upcountry Lodge at Koele.

Address/Phone: P.O. Box 630310, Lanai City, HI 96763; (808) 565–7700; fax (808) 565–2483

Email: reservations@lanai-resorts.com

Web Site: www.islandoflanai.com

U.S. Reservations: (800) 321–4666 or (808) 565–3800

Owner/Manager: Mark Vinsko, hotel manager

Arrival/Departure: Shuttle service between both hotels, golf courses, and Lanai airport is provided.

Distance from Lanai Airport: 12 miles (20 minutes)

Distance from Koele: 11 miles (20 minutes)

Accommodations: 250 rooms and suites

Most Romantic Room/Suite: If you want to splurge, ask for one of the suites that includes butler service (e.g., the midpriced Mauka Mini Suite); deluxe oceanfront rooms are also very romantic.

Amenities: Air-conditioning, ceiling fans, hair dryer, minibar, toiletries, TV, radio, clock; coffee/tea service; room service. Some suites have butler service.

Electricity: 110 volts

Sports and Facilities: 36 holes of championship golf, 6 tennis courts, sporting clays, archery range, croquet, lawn bowling, swimming pool, snorkeling, sea kayaking, scuba-diving. The hotel can arrange scuba diving and snorkel sails.

Dress Code: Casually elegant

Weddings: Can be arranged

Rates/Packages: $350–$695 per couple per night for a room; $725–$3,000 for a suite. Honeymoon & Romance Package: from $1,996 for 4 nights; accommodations, limousine airport transfers, aromatic bath salts and oils, champagne and chocolates, nightly turndown, couples' massage, 4-wheel-drive vehicle for 1 day with picinc lunch, breakfast in bed, and 1 dinner for two.

Payment/Credit Cards: Most major

Deposit: Two-night deposit required within 14 days of the reservation request. Deposits will be refunded in full when cancellations are received at least 14 days prior to arrival.

Government Taxes: 11.41 percent

Service Charges: Not included

MAUNA LANI BAY HOTEL & BUNGALOWS
Hawaii

Its name means "mountain reaching heaven," a perfect visual for honeymooners, who will feel as though they've come close to finding paradise at the Mauna Lani Bay Resort. Located on the sunny, dry (only 7 inches of rain annually) Kohala Coast, this six-story hotel presents a bold, contemporary design. Shaped like an arrowhead thrust seaward toward Makaiwa Bay, Mauna Lani Bay is a true-blue haven fringed by pearl-white beaches. The lobby reflects a spare elegance, with koi ponds and banks of orchids, torch ginger, and birds of paradise flanking the atrium. Jet-weary travelers are immediately soothed by the whoosh of waterfalls, view of the sapphire-blue Pacific, and friendly ministrations of the concierge, who checks you in.

The resort is built around fifteen acres of ancient fishponds, once *kapu* (forbidden) to all but Hawaiian royalty. They're stocked with mullet, awa, and lemon butterflies, whose brilliant colors swirl like an aquatic kaleidoscope. Paths encourage peaceful wanderings.

Decorated in serene tones of white and sand, each of the accommodations measures more than 550 square feet and has a private lanai. Ceiling fans, polished teak furnishings, and live orchids complement the tropical oasis decor. Top-of-the-line accommodations are the five bungalows—private houses, really, encompassing more than 4,000 square feet. Each has a private swimming pool and whirlpool spa and is served by a butler who can handle everything from unpacking your bags to grilling mahimahi on the barbecue. Steven Spielberg and Roseanne are among the celebrities who have roosted amid the sumptuous decor, accented by koa wood, marble, and crystal.

The signature restaurant is the celebrated Canoe House, which has won accolades in magazines such as *Bon Appétit*. Poised on the brink of the ocean, it offers diners ringside views of the polychromatic Kohala Coast sunsets. The Pacific Rim menu highlights choices such as wok-fried *lilikoi* (passion fruit), shrimp, and lemongrass-crusted *ono* (a fish). The Honu Bar is open for late-night music and dancing. In all, Mauna Lani has five restaurants.

Carved from a sixteenth-century lava flow, the two championship golf courses (home to the 1999–2000 Senior Skins golf tournament) present dramatic juxtapositions between stark black lava rock, smooth emerald turf, and an ever-changing sea. Meanwhile *Tennis Magazine* has included the ten Plexi-pave tennis courts on its list of top U.S. resort facilities. The roster of activities also includes aerobics classes, hula and lei-making lessons, beach picnics, and more. In July 2001, Mauna Lani debuted its indoor/outdoor spa. Options range from private yoga classes at water's edge to lomi lomi hula, an ancient Hawaiian-style massage choreographed to Hawaiian music.

For relaxing and sunning Mauna Lani's two beaches are regarded as some of the finest on the Big Island. Try to snare one of the private cabanas, and lie back on the two-person lounge chairs shaded by a cabriolet roof. One of Hawaii's best scuba-diving locales, the waters off the Kohala Coast are stippled with lava tubes, archways, caves, canyons, and coral heads. Favorite sites include Turtles Reef, a cleaning station for Hawaiian green sea turtles. Dive packages are available.

According to Hawaiians, Mauna Lani Bay is set on sacred ground. Perhaps that explains the tremendous feeling of mana (spiritual power) that the resort exerts over all those who visit.

Mauna Lani Bay Hotel & Bungalows

Location: On 29 oceanfront acres at Kalahuipua'a, on the Big Island's Kohala Coast

Romantic Highlights: 2 white-sand beaches; 15 acres of ancient, spring-fed Hawaiian fishponds plus pools teeming with tropical fish; award-winning oceanfront restaurant

Address/Phone: 68–1400 Mauna Lani Drive, Kohala Coast, HI 96743; (808) 885–6622, fax (808) 885–1484

E-mail: maunalani@maunalani.com

Web Site: www.maunalani.com

U.S. Reservations: (800) 367–2323; (808) 885–6622 (in Hawaii); (800) 992–7987 (in Hawaii)

Owner/Manager: Tokyu Corporation, owner; Kurt Matsumoto, vice president hotel operations

Arrival/Departure: Taxis available at airport; transfers can be arranged

Distance from Keahole-Kona Airport: 23 miles north

Distance from Kona: 34 miles north

Accommodations: 350 rooms; 5 bungalows with private swimming pools and 24-hour butler service; 23 ocean villas. More than 92 percent of the accommodations have ocean views.

Most Romantic Room/Suite: Bungalows with pools, ocean villas

Amenities: Oversize TV (with cable) and on-command movies, VCR, honor bar, electronic safe, clock radio, umbrella, refrigerator, makeup mirror, toiletries, his and hers marble basins, robes and slippers, hair dryer, concierge service, 24-hour room service

Electricity: 110 volts

Sports and Facilities: 36 holes of golf, 10 tennis courts, heated swimming pool, full-service spa, fitness center with outdoor lap pool, sailing, snorkeling, sailboarding, boogie boarding, and surfing. Scuba diving and deep-sea fishing can be arranged.

Dress Code: Casually elegant

Weddings: Can be arranged

Rates/Packages: $375–$725 per couple per night for a room; $1,100 for a suite; $550 for a one-bedroom villa; $4,400–$4,900 per night for a bungalow. Romantic Interludes (3 nights): $1,950 per couple for oceanfront accommodations. Additional nights, $455. Includes a bottle of champagne and chocolate-dipped strawberries, lei greeting, rose petal turndown, candlelight dinner, daily breakfast in bed, picnic basket, and gifts. Couples can also custom-design their own romance package.

Payment/Credit Cards: Most major

Deposit: Two-night deposit to guarantee reservation

Government Taxes: 11.16 percent

Service Charges: None

THE WHITE BARN INN
Maine

The White Barn Inn, a cozy enclave consisting of cottages, an 1850s homestead, and two 170-year-old barns, has been carefully crafted by owner Laurence Bongiorno, to meet the expectations of guests who come to Kennebunkport looking for privacy, luxury, and over-the-top dining. They are not disappointed.

Bongiorno has raised the bar when it comes to setting standards for country inns. Hand-painted furniture, CD stereo systems, steam showers, fireplaces, a heated infinity granite-and-stone pool, and an award-winning restaurant where the cuisine and service live up to the highly romantic ambience, all score points in the above and beyond column.

There are contrasts here and they all seem to work. Rustic beams and formally attired waiters; primitive farm implements and white linen table cloths; elaborate international cuisine and simply grilled local fish; 40-foot ceilings and intimate cottages; primitive antiques and contemporary art.

In the main house, once the Boothbay boarding house, there are twelve rooms featuring whimsically painted beds and original art. The four garden rooms have queen-size sleigh beds, fireplaces, and whirlpool baths. The seven junior suites are furnished with four-poster king-size beds and come with sitting areas, fireplaces, and spacious marble baths with whirlpool.

May's Cottage, one of the most romantic places to stay, is located by the pool and has a king-size bed, double-sided fireplace, living room, whirlpool bath, and steam shower. The new loft suite features a private deck, cathedral ceilings, and a private entrance as well as a king-size bed, oversized marble bath, steam shower, and whirlpool bath.

All rooms and suites are decorated with a mix of traditional furnishings and contemporary accents with coordinated fabrics and wallcoverings that are stylish and handsome, not cutesy Americana. Furniture is mostly nineteenth-century polished traditional pieces such as carved mahogany four-poster beds and Chippendale chairs. Mantels frame wood-burning fireplaces. Suites were recently renovated.

Bedspreads are creamy white matelasse; towels are thick and luxurious. On your bedside table, you'll find a bottle of water and you may decide to delve into one of the current novels left for you to read.

Breakfast—including fresh-squeezed juices, eggs, cheeses, cereals, and breads—is served in the main house dining room each morning; tea is served in the parlor in the afternoon during the cooler months around a roaring fire. Port is offered as a fitting nightcap, perhaps after a brisk walk around town.

The White Barn Inn restaurant is adjacent to the cottages. As you walk into the lofty candlelit room, you'll see at once the huge window wall framing a changing tableau each season: in the spring, brilliant displays of flowers and greenery; at Christmas, close to twenty trees all silvery with balls, bows, and white lights dusted with snow. A pianist plays soft dinner music and service is attentive, not intrusive. If ever you were looking for a place to pop the question, this is it.

Table-to-floor white linen cloths topped by fanciful silver sculptures (of New England wildlife creatures such as lobsters and pheasants crafted by French artist Gerard Bouvier from silver spoons, forks, knives, and other flatware) along with elegant brocade upholstered chairs are juxtaposed against the rustic barn-

siding backdrop of highly varnished wide board floors, soaring ceilings, and displays of oldtime farm equipment and antique signs. A bar with a highly polished brass top is tucked into a corner.

And if the setting isn't enough to ooh and ahh you, the highly acclaimed and artfully presented cuisine prepared by executive chef, Jonathan Cartwright, will tip the scales (and probably yours). Paying homage to Maine produce and seafood, Chef Cartwright combines regional fish, seafood, game, and poultry with unusual ingredients such as truffles, wild mushrooms, and quail eggs. The prix-fixe menu at $79 changes weekly and features items such as steamed lobster on fettucine with a cognac butter sauce, chargrilled native salmon, roasted lamb rack, and Grand Marnier custard. Meals start with an *amuse-bouche* from the chef, perhaps a bit of chicken liver mousse with truffles.

Small dinner parties of fifteen or less can enjoy private dining in the Wine Room, which is decorated with a mural of Tuscany by local artist Judith Harden and an Italian chiaro marble floor. More than 7,000 bottles of fine wine are stored here.

During the summer, a light bistro menu is offered poolside from 12:30 to 2:00 P.M. It consists of baguette sandwiches, salads, and brick oven pizza. And of course frosty drinks.

The White Barn Inn celebrates all seasons. In the summer lawns, flowers, and shrubs invite you to linger; in the winter the courtyard is alive with tiny white lights that glow against the snow and purple light of night creating a beautiful fairyland. Spring is light and lacy with new flowering shrubs and trees; fall is bold and colorful.

There's not much nightlife in Kennebunkport, but then, who needs it?

The White Barn Inn

Location: In historic Kennebunkport

Romantic Highlights: Elegant candlelight dining in a rustic barn; wood-burning fireplaces; whirlpool baths for two; poolside cottage

Address/Phone: P.O. Box 560C, Beach Street, Kennebunkport, ME 04046; (207) 967–2321; fax (207) 967–1100

E-mail: innkeeper@whitebarninn.com

Web Site: www.whitebarninn.com

U.S. Reservations: Contact the hotel directly.

Owner/Manager: Laurence Bongiorno, proprietor; Roderick Anderson, hotel manager

Arrival/Departure: Rental cars available at Portland (35 minutes driving time) or Logan International Airports (Boston, 1½ hours driving time)

Distance from Portland Airport: 25 miles

Distance from Logan International Airport: 80 miles

Distance from Downtown Kennebunkport: In town

Accommodations: 25 rooms and suites

Most Romantic Room/Suite: May's Cottage, with a double-sided fireplace, living room, whirlpool bath, and steam shower. Loft Suite features a private deck, cathedral ceilings, private entrance, king-size bed, oversize marble bath, steam shower, and whirlpool bath.

Amenities: Air-conditioning, TV, hair dryer, terry robes, CD stereo system, toiletries, telephone, complimentary tea and port, turndown service. Some have fireplaces, whirlpool tubs, steam showers, and decks.

Electricity: 110 volts

Sports and Facilities: Heated "brimming" pool, canoeing, tennis, and biking. Horseback riding, whale watching, and picnics can be arranged.

Dress Code: Informal; jackets required at dinner

Weddings: Can be arranged

Rates/Packages: $285–$675, including breakfast; packages available

Payment/Credit Cards: Most major

Deposit: Required (depends on length of stay); cancel 30 days prior to arrival during summer (high season) for full refund; 14 days in low season.

Government Taxes: 7 percent

Service Charges: None

CHATHAM BARS INN
Massachusetts

When you walk into this weathered, gray-shingled Cape Cod landmark, which sits on a bluff above the Atlantic Ocean and Pleasant Bay, it is easy to imagine what life was like at the beginning of the last century. A spacious porch filled with comfy wicker furniture, a huge lounge with overstuffed chairs, vases of fresh flowers, marble-topped tables, comfortable sofas, blue-and-white striped beach cabanas, and a wood panelled library set the tone.

The inn has been welcoming guests since 1914 when it opened as a hunting lodge. At that time you could sit on the porch and sip a frosty glass of lemonade while watching the world go by on land and sea. You still can.

Accommodations are spread throughout the property. You can stay in the main inn itself, in one of the cottages or houses on the water, or in one of the spacious new master suites featuring hand-painted furniture, fireplaces, upholstered window seats, and sliding doors that open onto decks. The intent of the designers who orchestrated

a recent $35 million restoration was to create accommodations that felt more like a classic Cape Cod home than a hotel room. Comfort was key. Some rooms are themed, for example, fishing, sailing, horseback riding, hunting lodge, and English country cottage.

Fabrics are keyed to the room style, some light and cheerful chintz, perhaps flowers or plaids; others feature natural hickory furniture and rich colors and textures. Fireplaces are bordered by decorative ceramic tile and there are many interesting appointments throughout the rooms: ship models, wood carvings, baskets, and books.

The Main Dining Room, where expansive, panoramic windows offer superb views of the water, is the venue for a grand dining experience. Executive chef Hidemasa Yamamoto blends classic French cuisine with a Pan-Asian influence such as in poelle of Chatham lobster with mango, avocado, beets, and a cilantro-ginger sauce. More casual fare is available at the nautically appointed Tavern

and one of the best seats in the summertime is at the oceanfront Beach House Grill where you can eat breakfast, lunch, and dinner. The grill is also the scene of clambakes, barbecues, and festive beach parties.

The inn has a private beach, large pool on the edge of the beach, and tennis courts. Spa treatments, including Swedish, sports, deep-tissue, and aromatherapy massages and sea-salt scrubs, are offered at the Health & Wellness Centre. You can work out on Stairmasters and other state-of-the-art equipment in the fitness center.

The daily calendar of activities is impressive. There are fitness walks, harbor tours, clam and lobster bakes, pool Scrabble, croquet lessons, tennis clinics, and nature walks as well as bike tours, gardening walks, and water aerobics.

It's an easy walk into town where you can spend several hours browsing through Chatham's boutiques, gift shops, and art galleries. Although summer is the busiest time, when you can unwind on the beach perhaps under one of the canvas cabanas that dot the seafront, other seasons hold special delights. In the spring, the gardens that are located along pathways and throughout the property come alive, in fall the sea air is crisp and fresh, a wonderful time to play golf and tennis and take long walks. Winter, you can sip a mug of mulled wine in front of a blazing fireplace either in the privacy of your room or in the lounge.

The nine-hole Chatham Seaside Links course is just out the back door. It's good for a quick warm-up to get you ready for some of the better courses. The hilly layout (which is not owned by the inn) has potential, but in its present state is not for serious golfers. (The artificial turf on some of the tee boxes presented a real challenge when it came to putting in your tees.) Still there are some superb courses within a half-hour drive, including Ocean Edge, the two Captains Golf Courses in Brewster, and the New Seabury course in Mashpee, all highly rated.

Chatham Bars Inn

Location: Hugging the elbow of Cape Cod within walking distance of Chatham on 25 acres facing the Atlantic Ocean.

Romantic Highlights: Walks along the salty sea; fireplace in your suite; dinner by the sea

Address/Phone: 297 Shore Road, Chatham, MA 02633; (508) 945–0096 or (800) 527–4884; fax (508) 945–6785

E-mail: welcome@chathambarsinn.com

Web Site: www.chathambarsinn.com

U.S. Reservations: (800) 527–4884

Owner/Manager: Christopher Diego, managing director

Arrival/Departure: Guests arrive by car or taxi. Rental cars are available at Providence and Boston airports.

Distance from Logan International Airport: 90 miles (closest airport, Hyannis, 25 miles)

Distance from Boston: 90 miles

Accommodations: 205 rooms, including 41 suites, 28 cottages, and 11 master suites

Most Romantic Room/Suite: Master suites with balconies, wet bars, fireplaces; #110 rose-covered cottage, very private and overlooking the golf course

Amenities: Air-conditioning, hair dryer, toiletries, safe, TV, clock radio, telephone, dataport, iron, some fireplaces, fans, balcony or patio, nightly turndown service

Electricity: 110 volts

Sports and Facilities: Beach, outdoor heated pool, 3 clay tennis courts, croquet; Health & Wellness Centre; putting green, beach volleyball, summer launch service to Outer Bar Beach, bikes, adjacent 9-hole golf course.

Dress Code: Resort casual except for dinner in the Main Dining Room, which is dressier and where gentlemen are expected to wear jackets and ties

Weddings: Can be arranged; sites include the Main Dining Room and The Beach House

Rates/Packages: From $310 per room (summer season); from $250 (late spring and early fall); from $190 (early spring and late fall); and from $150 (value season, Jan. 1 to end of March; end of November to end of December). Master Suites range from $460 to $1,600 depending on the season.

Payment/Credit Cards: Most major

Deposit: A one-night deposit at time of reservation is required.

Government Taxes: 9.7 percent

Service Charges: Not included

THE WAUWINET
Massachusetts

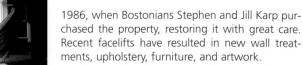

Situated 30 miles out to sea south of Cape Cod, Nantucket is a 50-square-mile island, town, and county of incredible natural beauty as well as a National Historic Landmark. Beach roads are lined with rugosa roses, beach plum, and blackberry bushes; cranberry bogs spread out over several acres; hundreds of deer roam the island; and ring-necked pheasant, piping plovers, terns, osprey, ducks, and geese make Nantucket a popular venue for bird-watchers.

Because of its proximity to the Gulf Stream, Nantucket is 10 percent cooler than the mainland in the summer and 10 percent warmer in the winter, making possible year-round golf, biking, and hiking as well as a plethora of water sports.

The weathered clapboard houses and tucked-away gardens brimming over with hollyhocks, black-eyed Susans, blue-and-purple hydrangeas, and cascades of roses tumbling over white picket fences are all part of Nantucket's inescapable charm. At the heart of it all is one of the oldest inns on the island, the Wauwinet. Located just about as far away as you can get from the noise and complexities of everyday life, the Wauwinet stands firmly planted on its grassy carpet, a bastion of peace and tranquility.

Its traditions reach back to the mid-1800s, when the inn was a restaurant, known as Wauwinet House, that served shore dinners to guests arriving by boat. In 1876 it became an inn and soon emerged as not only a Nantucket social center but a hot spot for Northeasterners to head for their vacation. It went through a period of decline until 1986, when Bostonians Stephen and Jill Karp purchased the property, restoring it with great care. Recent facelifts have resulted in new wall treatments, upholstery, furniture, and artwork.

On one side of the inn, a buff-colored ribbon of sand stretches for miles along the Atlantic providing a wonderful walking venue. In front of the inn, another beach runs along Nantucket Bay, reached by sandy paths and boardwalks from the Wauwinet's lawns. Both sides have private beaches for guests. Next door is a wildlife sanctuary.

Wicker chaises and white lawn chairs with superthick cushions entice you to settle back and relax while gazing out at the magnificent, endless ocean views, gentle grass-topped dunes, and wispy gardens of wildflowers and roses.

Rooms are individually decorated, many with an eclectic mix of English-style period pieces and pine country antiques. Chintz and stenciling add to the warmth of the decor, headboards are custom wood or upholstered. Around the rooms you'll find special touches such as baskets, hatboxes, books, and woodcarvings.

You have all the amenities you could wish for to ensure that you will be sublimely comfortable—extra things like Egyptian cotton bathrobes; armoires with soft, scented hangers; eyelet-trimmed linens; bottled water beside your bed; and fresh flowers. Windows are large, letting in lots of fresh air and light; ceilings are high.

Wauwinet's Topper's continues to garner rave reviews for its award-winning cuisine and wines. You can dine alfresco on the umbrella-shaded Bayview Terrace or eat inside in two indoor dining rooms. The executive chef, Chris Freeman, uses local produce, such as bushberries and cranberries, as well as fresh fish and seafood to prepare his American cuisine with a light touch. Lobster and fish caught from just offshore are prepared and served in a variety of flavorful dishes. Food is enhanced by fresh herbs from the Wauwinet's own herb gardens. A tasting menu featuring a delicious lobster course is served with appropriate wines. I found the staff very well trained. They knew how to serve and how to handle special guest requests and were well versed in what dishes and wines were being offered. And they were pleasant, not pretentious.

The inn's jitney is available to take you into Nantucket Town, always an interesting excursion. (You can also bicycle in.) Once one of the largest whaling centers in the world, Nantucket has a fascinating museum that details the history of the whaling industry. The town's streets are lined by more than 800 homes built between 1740 and

1840, many owned by whaling captains. You can spend hours browsing through the countless small shops, cozy restaurants, and art galleries. And take time to check out the harbor, where there are many lovely yachts riding at anchor or tied to the wharfs.

For a more intimate outing, ask the staff to prepare a gourmet basket lunch and take the *Topper, Too* launch to a secluded beach for a lazy afternoon of sunning and swimming.

Activities and sports at the Wauwinet are centered on Nantucket's natural assets. You can swim; go out in the inn's many boats and sailing craft; hike and jog through the trails that wind through the area; or play tennis or croquet. Golf can be arranged nearby.

Fishing is fabulous both from the beach and in the waters that surround the island, and biking is not only a favorite sport but a mode of transportation, especially during the summer when tourism swells the population from 10,000 to about 50,000. Paved bike paths link major areas of the island making it easy to get around even when the roads are teeming with traffic. The Wauwinet's fleet of bikes is available to guests.

But the Wauwinet is more than just a romantic place to stay. Its special hands-on programs give guests a chance to discover what the island and its people are all about. I can heartily recommend the lobster outing or shellfishing with Captain Rob McMullen, a native of Nantucket who truly "knows the ropes." Quite likely your catch of the day will be incorporated into the evening's meal by Chef Freeman.

Jeep safaris take you to Great Point or Coatue and through nature preserve lands. Your guide is an expert in wildlife and the history of the island. Other pleasures include cruising aboard the Wauwinet's two boats, whale-watching cruises, deep-sea fishing, surf fishing, sailing, yachting, golf, and biking.

During the crisper months, which some feel are the very best, after a walk through the dunes you can head to the cozy library, sit before the fire, and sip sherry or port.

Once you've stayed there, when you define the word *bliss*, you'll naturally think Wauwinet.

The Wauwinet

Location: On the northeastern end of the island of Nantucket

Romantic Features: Walks on windswept beaches; bike rides; picnics in a secluded cove; watching sunsets from the lawn chairs

Address/Phone: P.O. Box 2580, 120 Wauwinet Road, Nantucket, MA 02584; (508) 228–0145; fax (508) 228–6712

E-Mail: email@wauwinet.com

Web Site: www.wauwinet.com

U.S. Reservations: (800) 426–8718

Owner/Manager: Stephen and Jill Karp, owners; Russ and Debbie Cleveland, innkeepers

Arrival/Departure: Nantucket is accessible by ferry from Hyannis via 3 services: The Steamship Authority (508–477–8600 or 508–495–3278), Hy-Line Cruises (508–778–2600), and Freedom Cruise Line (508–432–8999). Air services are provided to the small Nantucket airport from Boston and other major gateways.

Distance from Nantucket Airport: 9 miles

Distance from Nantucket Town: 9 miles

Accommodations: 30 rooms; 25 located in the inn, 5 in private guest cottages

Most Romantic Room/Suite: Guest cottages are more private; deluxe rooms have king-size beds. French doors from corner room #101 open onto a generous covered porch with wonderful water views and lead directly to the lawn and beaches. Room #302 has huge views of the bay, and the cottage suite, Idlewild, has a fireplace, living room, and separate bedroom.

Amenities: Air-conditioning, ceiling fans, hair dryer, TV, VCR, cotton bathrobes, irons and ironing boards, telephone, evening turndown service

Electricity: 110 volts

Sports and Facilities: 2 Har-Tru clay tennis courts; jogging, hiking, and walking trails; swimming at 2 private beaches, sailing; jeep safaris, croquet, mountain bikes, fishing; golf (spring and fall)

Dress Code: Casually smart; jackets with or without ties or dress sweaters and slacks are requested for gentlemen dining at Topper's after 6:00 P.M.

Weddings: Can be arranged

Rates/Packages: Rates per couple, per night include room, breakfast, cheese, port and wine, tennis, use of bikes, boating, natural history excursions, jitney service into town: $200–$770 (spring/fall), $400–$900 (summer); Cottages: $580–$1,250 (spring/fall), $830–$1,650 (summer).

Payment/Credit Cards: Most major

Deposit: Prepayment required

Government Taxes: 9.75 percent room tax

Service Charges: Not included

Closed: November–late April

INN OF THE ANASAZI
New Mexico

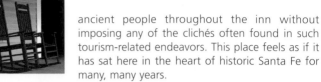

It's only been open since 1991, but its spirit stretches back over 700 years ago to a time when the creative Anasazi Indians lived in cliffs in the Southwest. The Indians, who were artistic and in tune with their surroundings, left a heritage of beautiful geometric designs that were found in everyday items such as pottery and weavings.

When the Inn of the Anasazi was built, the creators successfully captured the essence of the culture of this ancient people throughout the inn without imposing any of the clichés often found in such tourism-related endeavors. This place feels as if it has sat here in the heart of historic Santa Fe for many, many years.

Its romantic appeal is in both the low-key, classy way the inn has been designed and the warmth of the people who run it. Each room has its own private kiva fireplace, king-size bed (most rooms) with a fluffy duvet, fine, 100

percent cotton sheets, down pillows, and colors that carry you out to the desert.

Lie back on your bed and look up at the ceiling, which is made of authentic *vigas* and *latillas,* a traditional wooden beam and pole construction. Really interesting and indicative of the kind of thought that went into the inn's design.

The decor is pure Southwestern: massive hand-hewn furniture, Indian blankets, mellow brown leather chairs, stone-top tables; terra-cotta pots filled with cactus, original artwork and crafts by Native American artists, and antique Indian rugs. Baskets woven in Anasazi-style patterns, unpainted sandstone and adobe walls (hand-plastered), wide plank floors, a palette of desert earth tones, and handmade tile baths all add to a mood that is soft and seductive.

The ninety-two-seat restaurant serves a lot of fresh, organically grown food purchased from local farmers. The menu, which changes twice a year, is contemporary Southwestern fare and might include grilled corn tortilla soup with ginger pork; peanut-and-coconut–grilled prawns with watermelon salsa; Anasazi flat-bread with fire-roasted sweet peppers; and fresh herb-and-lime marinated rack of lamb.

Santa Fe has a lot going for it, and you're just steps away from it all. Right outside Anasazi's bold timbered entrance, you can stroll to the market stands of the Pueblo Indians who sell turquoise and silver jewelry and belts, and you can visit the many art galleries that feature wonderful, handcrafted pots, baskets, and paintings. The inn can arrange for you to visit the ancient Anasazi ruins of Chaco Canyon and see some of the northern pueblos that are in the area. You can also go hiking, whitewater rafting, and fishing. In the winter months you can head to the ski slopes not too far away.

Steeped in the earthy world of the Southwest, the Inn of the Anasazi will enchant those romantics who love the culture and spirit of the West. This place is really well done.

Inn of the Anasazi

Location: In the center of Santa Fe

Romantic Highlights: Seductive desert colors; private kiva fireplace; four-poster bed

Address/Phone: 113 Washington Avenue, Santa Fe, NM 87501; (505) 988–3030; fax (505) 988–3277

E-Mail: reservations@innoftheanasazi.com

Web Site: www.innoftheanasazi.com

U.S. Reservations: (800) 688–8100

Owner/Manager: Jeff Mahan, general manager

Arrival/Departure: By rail: Amtrak leaves passengers at Lamy, 17 miles from Santa Fe. Shuttle service is available into town by calling (505) 982–8829. By air: Shuttle service to downtown Santa Fe available at Albuquerque International Airport. Mesa Airlines operates a daily schedule of flights between Albuquerque and Santa Fe Municipal Airport. Transportation can be arranged to hotel. Taxis also available.

Distance from Albuquerque International Airport: 60 miles

Distance from Santa Fe: In the center of town

Accommodations: 59 rooms. Traditional rooms are fairly small; Superior rooms are larger, and Deluxe rooms, the largest, have small sitting areas. 53 rooms have king-size beds; 6 have 2 twins.

Most Romantic Room/Suite: Deluxe or superior rooms

Amenities: Hair dryer, air-conditioning; toiletries with organic bath oils, shampoo and soaps; minibar, bathrobe, TV, VCR, stereo, coffeemaker, safe, two-line telephone, 100 percent cotton sheets, duvet, down pillows, stationary bike for use in room on request; room service 6:00 A.M. to 11:00 P.M.

Electricity: 110 volts

Sports and Facilities: Massage therapist; white-water rafting and horseback riding can be arranged

Dress Code: Southwestern casual

Weddings: Can be arranged

Rates/Packages: Per couple per night rates (2002): $199–$399 (low season, January 6–February 28; December 2–19); $249–$439 (high season, March 1–June 27); $289–$459 (peak season, June 28–November 20; December 20–January 4, 2003). Romance packages available. $10 parking fee.

Payment/Credit Cards: Most major

Deposit: One-night deposit; cancel 72 hours prior to arrival for full refund

Government Taxes: 11.437 percent

Service Charges: Not included

MIRBEAU INN & SPA
New York

Mirbeau Inn & Spa easily recalls a French country chateau with its deep ochre stuccoed walls and blue trim and shutters, high pitched tile-like roofs, arched windows, and massive 300-year-old timbers that have been designed into the buildings. The inn's lodge along with the spa facility and four villa-cottages are arranged around a Monet-like water garden and pond in a twelve-acre setting studded with tall spruce trees. (Mirbeau loosely defined means "reflected beauty.")

A perfect base for exploring spectacular gorges, vineyards, and glacier lakes, Mirbeau's location in Skaneateles, one of the nation's loveliest little towns, is a big asset. Nestled around the northern end of the pristine 16-mile-long lake of the same name, Skaneateles, with less than 3,000 people, reigns as the prima donna of the Finger Lakes region. Its streets are lined with pristine vintage homes dating from the eighteenth and nineteenth centuries including several from the Victorian period. The lake's waters, which are known to be extremely pure, often change dramatically from swirls of deep cobalt to brilliant turquoise.

Mirbeau is a small inn with big services. When you arrive you are appointed a personal valet who escorts you to your room and helps you with whatever you might need, golf tee times, wine tasting information, or dinner reservations.

Guest rooms are spacious, superbly designed and appointed. Each is different. Fabrics were designed for Mirbeau in France; linens, including Frette, come from Italy; and duvets are filled with Canadian down. Furnishings include custom-made armoires and other furniture handcrafted by a cabinetmaker from Italy and antiques with fine inlays. Many rooms have beamed ceilings and are painted in deep red or gold. Each room has a fireplace and those on the first floor have a patio with wrought-iron tables and chairs. The large baths come with deep, French soaking tubs on feet, walk-in showers, and double vanities. The sound system is Bose with a CD player; music is chosen just for you.

Walls of the public rooms are faux-painted by hand in deep ochre; one has a border of grape vines tastefully rendered along the top of the room. Tile floors are accented by oriental carpets; lighting is subtle. The art and colors of Provence enhance the mood.

Even the fencing that defines the property is special, made of interwoven willow branches and arched iron trellises with climbing roses and wisteria to create romantic entries to the cottages.

Mirbeau's 10,000 square-foot full-service spa has ten treatment rooms, most with fireplaces and personal sound systems. A new concept for the region, the spa offers a wide variety of classic European body and facial treatments, classes, and on-site peaceful places that invite lingering, such as the "spruce cathedral," a grove of tall trees and wildflowers that is conducive to meditation.

Try a massage, wrap, seaweed bath, or facial, and while you wait for your treatment (or after it), relax in the elegant resting area modeled after a Roman bath with a subterranean foot-massage pool, soft lighting, columns, lovely wall frescos, teak chaises with soft comfortable cushions, and radiantly heated floors.

Two treatments are designed just for couples, both in front of a glowing fireplace. The Art of Living (80 minutes, $185) invites you to stretch out with a warm herbal soak in an oversized French tub for two as massage therapists perform their magic. It Takes Two (50 minutes, $160), a couples' massage, takes place in Mirbeau's signature couples' treatment room.

Other spa facilities include an aerobic workout and weight room, a motion studio, men's and women's locker rooms, herbal-infused steam, saunas, and a nail salon. Classes in aerobics, body sculpting, yoga, and meditation along with additional programs designed to treat body and mind are offered. Runners and walkers will find sidewalks just outside the property that lead to town and the lakeside parks, a ten-minute walk at the most.

The dining room, which leads out to a terrace, overlooks the pond with its arched bridge, water iris, and many other flowers and shrubs. Although this is one of the pricier dining venues in the area, most who have eaten here feel the cuisine is worth it: A four-course dinner is $49.

Executive Chef Edward Moro, whose credits include the Hotel Hershey and the Little Nell Hotel in Aspen, has created "Mirbeau Estate Cuisine," which can be defined as fresh, light American with French country accents. Moro's choices include butter-roasted Maine lobster tail with melted leeks and carrot-ginger sauce, Fallow Hollow Farm venison with apple conserve, rosemary fingerling potatoes, and sour cherry sauce and wild berry soufflé. Lunch and breakfast choices are equally tempting, the lemon soufflé pancakes with glazed blackberries and toasted almonds and the caramelized onion and white bean soup with Gruyère toast and mushroom salad, for example. Moro draws on herbs from Mirbeau's own gardens and local produce from the region's many farms.

In spite of its small size of less than 3,000 residents, no matter what time of year you come to Skaneateles, you will always find something going on. In the summer there are sight-seeing and dinner cruises on Skaneateles Lake on the *Judge Ben Wiles,* a two-decker replica of a lake steamer; free band concerts in a lakeside park Friday nights; the Musical Festival showcasing a feast of music under the stars; the Antique & Classic Boat Show; and polo matches on Sundays. Fall brings wine tastings in the Finger Lakes vineyards; and winter showcases a bevy of Dickens characters who stroll village streets during the holidays, and there is ice fishing, cross-country skiing, and ice skating.

Shoppers any time of year can enjoy browsing through the antiques shops, boutiques, bakeries, food shops, and speciality stores that open onto brick sidewalks lined with period lighting.

If you decide to go exploring, the Finger Lakes area has a lot to offer. There are more than seventy vineyards within an hour's drive, fifty public golf courses, several great parks with waterfalls and deep gorges, shopping galore, and museums such as Corning Glass Museum, the Erie Canal Museum, and Ste. Maria of the Iroquois, a fascinating indoor-outdoor exhibit featuring costumed period personalities who relive the interaction of Native Americans and French soldiers during an early period of the area's history.

The sun may not shine quite as much here as in most other places and winters can be rugged with lots of snow, but most folks don't seem to notice. For when the sun does come out, sparkling on the lake, burnishing the fall leaves, or glistening on the snow, there is no place prettier on earth.

Mirbeau Inn & Spa

Location: Tucked into a hillside within walking distance of Skaneateles, a pampered and prosperous town in the Finger Lakes region of middle New York State; vineyards and spectacular gorges of the Finger Lakes within easy driving distance

Romantic Highlights: Roman bath-style spa; flower-rimmed water garden; dinner on the terrace alongside the pond; side-by-side massages by the fireplace

Address/Phone: 851 West Genesee Street, Skaneateles, NY 13152; (877) MIRBEAU, (315) 685–5006; fax (315) 685–5150

E-mail: reservations@mirbeau.com

Web Site: www.mirbeau.com

U.S. Reservations: (877) MIRBEAU

Owner/Manager: Jack Burkam, general manager

Arrival/Departure: Most drive here or fly into Syracuse and rent a car.

Distance from Hancock International Airport, Syracuse: 20 miles (35–40 minutes)

Distance from Syracuse: 20 miles

Accommodations: 34 rooms

Most Romantic Room/Suite: Room #522 with a long, scenic view of the pond, bridge, and inn

Amenities: Air-conditioning, oversize bath, soaking tub, double sinks, Bose radio/CD player, TV, fireplace, hair dryer

Electricity: 110 volts

Sports and Facilities: 10,000-square-foot spa, aerobic workout and weight room, motion studio, library, sauna, nail salon

Dress Code: Resort casual

Weddings: Can be arranged

Rates/Packages: From $175 including use of spa facilities

Payment/Credit Cards: Most major

Deposit: 1 night required at time of booking via credit card

Government Taxes: 12 percent

Service Charges: Not included

THE WAWBEEK ON UPPER SARANAC LAKE

New York

Imagine loons gliding on the water, log cabins with private decks, pines so tall they hide in the early morning mist, miles of trails, and balsam-scented fresh air, and you get the picture. God's country. Who wouldn't find romance at the Waw-beek, a turn-of-the-century Adirondack Great Camp. Sprawled on more than forty wooded acres on Upper Saranac Lake, this is the great outdoors at its best—but with such comforts as heated cabins, warm blankets, and a superb restaurant.

The Wawbeek (Wawbeek is the Native American word for "big rock") is just one of a handful of Great Camps located in Adirondack State Park, the nation's largest state park. Constructed in the style we now call "Adirondack," these camps were built with dark wood exteriors, often logs, porches with railings made of thick branches, and large central great rooms with stone fireplaces.

The Wawbeek, my choice for a place that combines a rustic ambience with private cabins and candlelight dining, is managed by co-owners Nancy and Norman Howard, refugees from the corporate world in Connecticut, who preside over this glassy islet-studded lake.

The Wawbeek has its own fleet of canoes, paddleboats, and Sunfish promising days of water-oriented fun. Land-based amusements include two tennis courts, croquet, and a game house where you can challenge your mate to Ping-Pong, pool, darts, or a board game. Some evenings there may even be a campfire with a storyteller or guitar player.

Of the Wawbeek's twenty-nine rooms, six are located in Mountain House, a two-story building and one of the original houses built on the property. Some rooms open onto porches where you can look out to the shimmering lake and islands. There are eight rooms and suites with decks and firelaces in the new Lake House Lodge, which has a lofty two-story great room with a massive stone fireplace. Hannah's Lounge on the second floor is exclusively for Lake House Lodge guests.

Five rustic, traditional, log-cabin–style cottages come with sitting rooms, efficiency kitchens, pull-out sofas (for emergency snoring relief), and a spacious deck with glimpses of the water. Each cabin comes with a small kitchen; some have sitting rooms, fireplaces, screened porches or decks, and eating areas. Some are tucked into the hillside and are very private. Most have queen- or king-size comfortable beds with good quality linens, blankets, and quilts. All have updated fresh decor in pine

green, tan, and brown and are squeaky clean. Books and knitted afghans lend a homey touch.

Other rooms are in the Carriage House, including a spacious corner suite with a private entrance, king-size bed, and deck.

Bathrooms are modern, with a tub and shower combo and the new Lake House rooms have waterjet tubs. Wawbeek's rooms do not have telephones, TVs, or air-conditioning; however, if this creates any sense of panic, these contrivances can be arranged.

Nature trails fan out from the main reception area, leading to the lakefront and dock, to the restaurant, and to a secluded spot at water's edge where you can settle back in one of the Adirondack chairs, read, or simply savor the moment. The Adirondack Park's many hiking trails are right at your doorstep. You might follow the Bloomingdale Bog Trail, only 1.8 miles, or bike along the 7-mile Deer Pond Loop across the way or the 18-mile Paul Smith Loop up the road. Then cool off with a swim. The lake is clean and refreshing.

Nearby there are plenty of places to explore. The Adirondack Museum in Blue Mountain Lake is crammed with a day's worth or more of things to see, such as antique boats, trains, historical exhibits, survival tools, art exhibits, and more. There are miles of canoe routes and mountains to climb.

Spring, fall, and winter are lovely here, too. In the fall brilliant red, orange, and yellow leaves drift down, carpeting

the trails, and the air is brisk—perfect for long hikes. In the winter pristine snow blankets the ground in great drifts, catching the sunlight and making it sparkle. There are 100 miles of snowmobiling trails, endless cross-country ski trails, and snowshoeing and Alpine skiing down Big Tupper and Whiteface Mountains. There is ice skating on the lake and dinner and cocktails in the Wawbeek restaurant in front of a blazing fire. Early in February everyone in town turns out for Saranac Lake's Winter Carnival, renowned for its ice castle, and later for the annual Woodchuck Shuffle snowshoe event.

And Spring. Budding flowers poke up through the melting snow; energy levels turn up a notch or two. Things are waking up. It's a great time for brisk hikes, golf, and other outdoor pursuits—perhaps the Ice Breaker 5-mile canoe race on Saranac River.

All year long in the town of nearby Saranac Lake, there are stores to poke through, concerts, performances at the Pendragon Theatre, and sports events galore from canoe races to ski-jumping contests.

Once back at the Wawbeek, you can look forward to a really fine meal. The Wawbeek restaurant, which sits high on a rocky promontory overlooking the lake, delivers both romantic ambience and exceptional cuisine. Executive Chef Eric Rottner spins his magic, creating dishes such as Maple Chicken Dijon, Veal Wawbeek sautéed and topped with raisin chutney, and Duck Island Sauté (medallions of venison with forest mushrooms, roasted garlic, and fresh tarragon in a bourbon *demi-glace*). For dessert try Fried Ice Cream or Diane's Apple Torte. Chef Rottner prides himself on using as many fresh ingredients as he can find, including herbs and berries from the grounds, locally grown vegetables, fresh trout, and regional meats.

It is very quiet here at the Wawbeek—indeed so quiet that the scampering of a squirrel or two across your roof or the hoot of an owl in the night can put you into a momentary state of panic. "Just who is that?" No one. Go back to sleep. Listen to the rustle of the pines. You're in a good place where even the thought of locking your door may seem a bit silly. And when you must finally leave, listen carefully for the sounds of a pileated woodpecker tapping out "good-bye."

The Wawbeek on Upper Saranac Lake

Location: Adirondack Great Camp on 1,400 feet of shoreline in Tupper Lake.

Romantic Highlights: Canoeing on a pine-fringed glassy lake; hikes in the forest; dining on the porches overlooking the water; your own private cabin

Address/Phone: Panther Mountain Road, Tupper Lake, NY 12986; (800) 953–2656; (518) 359–2656; fax (518) 359–2475

E-mail: wawbeek@capital.net

Web Site: www.wawbeek.com

U.S. Reservations: (800) 953–2656

Owner/Manager: Nancy and Norman Howard

Arrival/Departure: Rental cars available at Adirondack Airport just 9 miles from Saranac Lake and Albany Airport

Distance from Albany Airport: 150 miles (2½ hours)

Distance from Tupper Lake: 10 minutes to village; 15 miles to Saranac Lake

Accommodations: 29 rooms in several buildings, including rustic cottages

Most Romantic Room/Suite: Partridgeberry, a secluded cabin with a fireplace, vaulted ceiling, and screened porch; Tamarack, a cottage close to the boat dock with a good view of the water from the corner deck; Mountain House Rooms 5 and 6; Carriage House Number 1

Amenities: Ceiling fans, coffee and tea making facilities, toiletries, grill, kitchen, laundry facilities. Some have fireplaces, fold-out queen-size sofas, daily housekeeping services.

Electricity: 110 volts

Sports and Facilities: Canoes, paddleboats, Sunfish, sloop; 2 tennis courts; swimming, walking, hiking, biking, skiing, snowshoeing, cross-country skiing, Alpine skiing, ice fishing; golf and horseback riding nearby

Dress Code: Informal

Weddings: Can be arranged

Rates/Packages: $155–$310 per couple, per night (summer); $135–$290 (fall and holidays); $170–$250 (winter/spring), including full breakfast and use of boats, bikes, and snowshoes. Weekly rates start at $625; three-day rates (winter/spring only) from $90 per night.

Payment/Credit Cards: Most major

Deposit: 50 percent deposit required to hold booking. Balance due on arrival. Cancel 30 days or more before arrival date for refund less 10 percent (60 days if booking more than one sleeping room).

Government Taxes: 7 percent

Service Charges: 10 percent recommended

THE EQUINOX
Vermont

The allure of Vermont's Green Mountains beckons to those who love the outdoors. From your base at the Equinox, a charming country inn resort that holds center stage in the small village of Manchester, you can hike; go horseback riding in the surrounding hills; play golf on a picturesque, par 71, 6,423-yard championship course; swim, fish, and ski. You can even learn off-road driving or falconry.

Close to the ski areas of Bromley and Stratton Mountains, the stately Equinox has a long history of welcoming guests. It started life in the 1700s as the Marsh Tavern (now one of the hotel's restaurants), and by the mid-1800s the hotel had put Manchester Village on the map as one of America's finest year-round destinations. In 1972 the resort was added to the National Register of Historic Places, and in 1991 the Equinox underwent an ambitious renovation program, including the restoration of all public areas and guest rooms as well as the golf course.

Anyone driving through the center of Manchester Vil-

lage could not possibly miss it. The Equinox, which faces the village green, is simply the most impressive structure in town. It boasts an imposing, white-pillared facade with a long porch set up with green rocking chairs and two wings that create an interior garden courtyard. Just across the street from the front entrance are a number of classy clothing and gift shops—fun to browse through, but bring lots of cash if you intend to buy. Also located here are a number of 200-year-old buildings, including the Congregational Church and Bennington County Courthouse.

You'll find the rooms at the Equinox very comfortable. Furnished in a traditional style in muted New England colors, some of these rooms include king-size beds, washed-pine armoires, desks, wing chairs, rich drapes and bedspreads, and marble-tiled baths.

Next door is the newest Equinox addition, the Charles Orvis Inn. Dating back to 1833, this house was originally used to accommodate guests during the winter months, when the main hotel was closed. Today it has been totally rebuilt and houses nine one- and two-bedroom deluxe suites, each with its own working fireplace, living room, dining room, full kitchen, and super appointments. Check in here and you'll have your own private en-suite Jacuzzi and the use of an intimate bar and billiard room.

If you're into golf, perhaps one of the best parts of staying here is that you can easily walk from the hotel to the first tee of one of the loveliest golf courses in New England. The Gleneagles course, originally designed by the legendary Walter Travis, has been improved and updated by the well-known golf course designer Rees Jones. The course's ups and downs will very likely do the same to your score card. It's hilly, challenging, and breathtaking in its beauty. As you hit your ball from the tee on the eighth hole, your ball will soar into the sky against a backdrop of dense green mountains and deep blue skies. Straight ahead is the white spire of a quintessential New England church, nestled at the base of a mountain. On the fifth hole you'll have to wait for those ahead of you to ring a bell before hitting over the blind hill. This is one course you can play again and again without getting bored—there are new challenges around every bend.

The Equinox has a great fitness spa, located at the back of the hotel's courtyard, as well as three Har-Tru tennis courts for year-round play, a 75-foot heated swimming pool outdoors, and a 47-foot heated indoor pool. You can rent bikes and cycle out to the many trails in the area and play

croquet. Hikers have a good selection of wooded mountain trails to explore. On the drawing board is a new spa facility as well as 3,400 square feet of additional meeting space.

Canoeing trips on the Battenkill River can be arranged, and if you ever wanted to try your hand at fly-fishing or shooting, the Equinox offers lessons on its own Equinox Pond or the Battenkill River. You can also attend the Orvis Fly-Fishing School, the oldest of its kind in the country, and the Orvis Shooting School, located right in Manchester Village.

You can eat breakfast, lunch, and dinner at the Marsh Tavern, a darkish, cozy place that dates back to 1769. You can also enjoy cocktails on the tavern's terrace during July and August. For a more elegant dining experience, head to the grand Colonnade, which features fine continental cuisine and wines and is open for dinner June to October on Wednesday through Sunday evenings and November to May on weekend evenings.

Some nights there is entertainment in the Marsh Tavern, and during the summer months a number of local performing art centers offer an assortment of concerts and theater productions. Come here if you love New England and all it offers. Your accommodations at the Equinox will be supremely comfortable; your choice of activities plentiful if you love exploring the countryside and participating in traditional sports.

Think of any name-brand clothing or sporting goods company and you'll find it in the outlet stores that line the roads leading into town. The stores are housed in attractive New England–style buildings of weathered wood and clapboard, in harmony with the surrounding countryside. If you have some wedding money you want to spend, you can easily fill the backseat of your car with bags full of bargains from Anne Klein, Liz Claiborne, Ralph Lauren, London Fog, Armani, Escada, and Donna Karan, to name a few.

The Equinox

Location: In the center of Manchester Village, in southern Vermont's Green Mountains

Romantic Highlights: Sleigh rides; late evening nightcaps in the cozy Marsh Tavern; en suite Jacuzzis and fireplaces

Address/Phone: Historic Route 7A, Manchester Village, VT 05254; (802) 362–4700; fax (802) 362–1595

E-mail: reservations@equinoxresort.com

Web Site: www.equinoxresort.com

U.S. Reservations: (800) 362–4747

Owner/Manager: A member of the Rockresorts collection; Gary S. Thulander, general manager

Arrival/Departure: Transfers via private car can be arranged at $85 per car, one-way, plus 15 percent gratuity.

Distance from Albany Airport: 64 miles (about 1½ hours)

Distance from Manchester Village: In the heart of town

Accommodations: 183 rooms and suites, including suites in the Charles Orvis Inn, next door.

Most Romantic Room/Suite: Try one of the new one-bedroom suites in the Charles Orvis Inn. Main building suites are also good.

Amenities: Toiletries, air-conditioning, telephone, clock radio, ironing facilities, cable TV, in-room movies, bathrobes, fireplaces (some), Jacuzzis (some); room service

Electricity: 110 volts

Sports and Facilities: Tennis (3 Har-Tru courts), swimming (indoor and outdoor pools), fishing, golf, fitness spa, downhill skiing nearby, snowmobiling, cross-country skiing, biking, ice skating, snowshoeing, hiking, horseback riding, canoeing, off-road driving school, falconry school

Dress Code: Casual in Marsh Tavern; jackets required in the Colonnade

Weddings: Can be arranged

Rates/Packages: $199–$899 per couple per night; add $75 per person for breakfast and dinner or $95 for breakfast, lunch, and dinner. Honeymoon Package: $468.75 per person, includes 3 nights in deluxe accommodations, flowers, champagne, use of fitness spa and mountain bikes. Fireside Package: $545 per person, includes 2 nights in a one-bedroom town house suite with fireplace, bottle of wine, breakfast and dinner daily, and use of the fitness spa.

Payment/Credit Cards: Most major

Deposit: One-night deposit required to confirm reservation and will be applied to last night of visit. Refunds will be issued only if cancellation is received 30 days before your scheduled arrival date. Cancellations are subject to a $35 processing fee.

Government Taxes: Vermont rooms and meals tax

Service Charges: $2.50 per room per night housekeeping gratuity

WOODSTOCK INN & RESORT

Vermont

If you are dreaming of a honeymoon in New England—with warm fires crackling and snow falling on the mountains, or brilliant fall foliage shading a village green lined by pristine clapboard houses, or perhaps lazy summer days strolling on woodland trails—your fantasies will turn into reality when you arrive in Woodstock, Vermont. At the heart of this beautiful little town of only about 2,500 people lies the stately Woodstock Inn & Resort, a lovely inn built by Laurance S. Rockefeller in 1969 on the site of the original inn and tavern, which dated back to 1793.

It's a resort you can enjoy all by itself. The impressive facilities include a putting green located in the courtyard of the inn; the Woodstock Country Club, with its superb golf course, Woodstock Health & Fitness Center, and Ski Touring Center; the nearby Suicide Six ski area; and many planned activities. But just outside your door is the delightful village of Woodstock, with all its eighteenth- and nineteenth-century homes, interesting shops, covered bridges, and historic places like the Billings Farm & Museum, an active historical museum and working dairy farm depicting what farm life was like in the nineteenth century, and the Marsh-Billings-Rockefeller National Historical Park.

Furnished in Colonial style, with soft reds, greens, and blues, the rooms—fifty recently renovated—are bright and cheery, many opening onto a central courtyard, where the putting green is located. Many have fireplaces—just ask and the staff will lay the logs for you. Beds are covered with handmade quilts and hand-loomed coverlets; bookshelves are filled with hardbacks and paperbacks; and built-in cupboards and bureaus give you plenty of storage space. You also have white louvered blinds that you can close when you wish privacy, as well as modern tile and marble baths.

The lobby area is most inviting, especially on a cold day when the massive, 10-foot fireplace is blazing away. Exceptional original artwork in various styles ranging from primitive to contemporary is located throughout the inn along with antique fixtures, lamps, and furniture.

You can dine in the main dining room at tables elegantly appointed with fine linen and gas lamps or enjoy a more casual meal in the Eagle Cafe. Particularly appealing is Richardson's Tavern, where you can settle into a comfortable sofa in front of the fireplace and sip a cognac before heading to your room. The cozy bar area is a popular gathering place.

Just a five-minute walk down South Street from the inn is the Woodstock Country Club. Here you'll find the 6,001-yard, eighteen-hole, Robert Trent Jones–designed golf course. It's narrow and lined with more than eighty bunkers and has some nasty water hazards guaranteed to give wild hitters more than a few nightmares—the Kedron Brook comes into play on all but six of the eighteen holes. (You might want to leave your driver in the car.) It's also one of the most interesting little courses you'll find in New England.

The 40,000-square-foot recently refurbished Woodstock Health & Fitness Center, located about 1 mile farther south from the Woodstock Country Club, has two indoor tennis courts, two squash courts, two racquetball courts, a 30-by-60-foot lap pool, a whirlpool, a gym, and a croquet court. Tennis buffs can enjoy ten outside tennis courts. Spa treatments include massages, facials, manicures, and pedicures.

In the winter the golf operations turn into the Woodstock Ski Touring Center. Ski trails lace the golf course and beyond, and equipment for sale or rent occupies the space where in the summer you find golf bags, balls, and accessories.

The personal, user-friendly Suicide Six ski area, which opened in 1937, has twenty-two trails in addition to the Face, which is served by two chairlifts and a beginner area with a J-bar. Although the more advanced skiers may prefer to head to nearby Killington, Suicide Six is still a good choice for skiers of all levels who want a pleasant, challenging ski experience. Here you'll find a ski school, ski

shop, cafeteria, and lounge-restaurant in the Base Lodge.

Other activities at your fingertips include hiking, biking, horseback riding, fishing, and cultural performances (Dartmouth College's Hopkins Center for the Performing Arts is just a half-hour's drive away). The inn serves morning coffee and afternoon tea and cookies in the Wicker Lounge, a greenhouselike lounge.

Your best bet, if you want to play golf or ski, is to look into a package that includes these activities. Otherwise you will be charged for the use of many of the sports facilities. For example, greens fees are $36.00–$65.00 per person; tennis is $10.00–$20.00 per person, per hour, and inn guests pay $8.00 per person for the use of the racquetball or squash courts. The use of the pool, sauna, steam room, whirlpool, exercise room, and croquet court is complimentary for Woodstock Inn guests.

The Woodstock Inn & Resort is a comfortable, friendly hotel boasting a staff that is eager to see to it you have everything you need. It has just enough spit and polish to make it a top-rated property, yet is not pretentious or stuffy. It's a place you'll want to come back to on your first anniversary.

Woodstock Inn & Resort

Location: Centrally located in Vermont near the New Hampshire border

Romantic Highlights: En suite fireplaces; village setting

Address/Phone: Fourteen the Green, Woodstock, VT 05091-1298; (802) 457–1100; fax (802) 457–6699

E-mail: email@woodstockinn.com

Web Site: www.woodstockinn.com (reservation requests accepted on-line)

U.S. Reservations: (800) 448–7900

Owner/Manager: Chet Williamson, president and general manager; Tom List, inn manager

Arrival/Departure: Daily air service available from New York, Hartford, and Boston to Lebanon, New Hampshire; taxi and car rentals available at Lebanon Airport

Distance from Lebanon Airport: 15 miles; 138 miles from Albany; 148 miles from Boston

Distance from Woodstock: In the heart of town

Accommodations: 144 rooms and suites, 23 with fireplaces

Most Romantic Room/Suite: The fireplace rooms or Suites 304 and 349

Amenities: Toiletries, air-conditioning, telephone, clock radio, ironing facilities, cable TV, VCR, bathrobes, fireplace (some), concierge services, room service, valet parking

Electricity: 110 volts

Sports and Facilities: Putting green, outdoor pool, 12 tennis courts (2 indoor, 6 clay, 4 all-weather), 18-hole golf course, 2 squash courts, 2 racquetball courts, lap pool, whirlpool, ten-station Nautilus room, aerobics room, steam baths, saunas, croquet court, ski trails, Alpine ski center, horseback riding, biking, hiking, fishing

Dress Code: Casual; jackets customary and encouraged in dining room; blue jeans, T-shirts, and swim shorts not permitted on golf course or tennis courts

Weddings: Can be arranged

Rates/Packages: $189–$589 per couple; $129–$248 during value season; add $66 per person per day for MAP; Classic Romance: $672 per couple, includes 2 nights' accommodations, breakfast daily, 1 dinner for two, champagne, and special gift. Tennis, golf, and ski packages available.

Payment/Credit Cards: Most major

Deposit: Two-night deposit to confirm reservation. Refunds will be issued only if cancellation is received 1 week before your scheduled arrival date. Cancellations are subject to a $15 processing fee.

Government Taxes: 7 percent Vermont rooms and meals tax

Service Charges: Not included

THE GREENBRIER
West Virginia

The Greenbrier, a venerable bastion of Southern gentility and great golf, is a destination in itself— a place to come for golf, tennis, hiking in the great outdoors, and other gracious pleasures, such as afternoon tea, carriage rides, late-night hot chocolate, croquet, and horseback riding. Mineral baths, an array of spa treatments, good food, and dancing in the cocktail lounge are all part of the scene here.

Grooms will have to pack their ties and jackets and brides will get to wear their favorite fancies. At the Greenbrier tradition reigns, and dressy attire is required for dinner at two of the resort's six restaurants. Black tie is also acceptable.

When the rich and famous traveled here in the mid-1800s to revive themselves in the famous mineral waters and socialize with their peers, they told their friends they were going to the "Old White." The guest book of this stately grande dame includes such historical greats as Dolley Madison, Andrew Jackson, Thomas Edison, and John F. Kennedy. At least twenty-six presidents have come here to take in the fresh mountain air and Southern hospitality.

The original 400-foot-long building is gone, but in its place a majestic Georgian-style structure with pillars and rows of windows sits like a great European castle in the midst of a sea of green pine. Most impressive.

This is not exactly a place you'd describe as intimate or cozy. Any resort that claims to sit on 6,500 acres is major stuff. However, accommodations such as the cottages and suites give you all the privacy you want along with a generous dash of luxury.

The public and private rooms are truly grand. The designer Carleton Varney orchestrates all the interior decoration, including the creation of new fabric and wallpaper designs every year. Each of the hotel's 739 rooms and suites has its own unique decor. Yards and yards of brightly flowered fabric, richly swagged and draped around the high windows; bed canopies and pillows; upholstered chairs and chaises; and bedspreads create surprising riots of fresh color against walls and carpets of reds, emerald greens, and yellows. No fainthearted application of color here! Furnishings are a combination of traditional period antiques and antique reproductions, along with gilt-framed mirrors, paintings, and Oriental carpets.

In the lofty lounge, in spite of the dramatic black-and-white marble floor and high columns, chairs and tables have been arranged in intimate, inviting groupings conducive to a quiet chat, a game of backgammon, or afternoon tea, to the accompaniment of chamber music.

If you want to hide away in your own cottage, ask for accommodations in one of the guest houses. The cottages are airy and roomy, and each has its own porch, fireplace, oversize tub, wet bar or kitchen, separate parlor, and dressing room.

With the staff of 1,800 outnumbering the guests, you can be totally decadent and do nothing but allow yourself to be pampered. If your journey here has been a long one, perhaps the first place you should visit is the Spa. In addition to a Greek-inspired, Olympic-size pool ringed with pillars and patterned tile work, you'll find whirlpool baths, saunas, herbal wraps, and massages— over twenty different treatments.

For the more energetic there are aerobics classes, exercise equipment, and other instruments designed for hard labor. There are guided hiking excursions along the miles of mapped and unmapped trails on the Greenbrier grounds and on nearby Kate's Mountain and plenty of tennis courts, indoors and outdoors, along with three great golf courses. Winding through the rolling countryside at the base of the starkly beautiful Allegheny Mountains, these courses give golfers a visual gift as well as a challenge. Newer golfers may prefer the picturesque, gentle-on-your-score Lakeside course. The more competent links mavens can tee off on the championship Nicklaus layout or the Greenbrier, a traditional favorite.

Golf packages are one of the better deals here, giving you unlimited golf, use of a practice range, a professional clinic, and daily club cleaning and storage as well as breakfast and dinner. It is quite a bargain, as the cost to a nonguest for just playing the course is more than $300 with cart.

For a special romantic day, Greenbrier's Romantic Rendezvous takes you on a Victorian carriage ride on the

grounds and ends at their gazebo, where a waiter serves you lunch. The cost for this treat is $216 per couple.

When it comes time to eat, you have a lot of choices. The Main Dining Room, the largest of the eateries, is an elegant affair with chandeliers, pillars, and ornate plasterwork. Meals, featuring continental and American cuisine, are served with a flourish. The presentation is a work of art. Be sure to save room for the chocolate truffles.

The Drapers Cafe is fun, colorful, and informal. Here you can get breakfast, lunch, and dessert and good things from the soda fountain. For a cozy, intimate meal, try the Tavern Room, which specializes in American food, seafood, and rotisserie selections. (Although rates include breakfast and dinner, you'll pay a surcharge to eat here.)

If you are coming from the golf course, you can stop at Sam Snead's for fine dining in a casual setting. You can also catch the latest sports events on TV along with afternoon food and beverages at Slammin' Sammy's, adjacent to Sam Snead's.

There is also the Greenbrier Club for cocktails and dancing and the Rhododendron Spa Cafe. In other words, there are plenty of places to eat, suitable for whatever mood you're in.

Many of the vegetables and fruits come from the local markets, and there are local specialties such as fresh trout. The Tavern serves its own ice cream, made daily. Especially popular at breakfast are the warm, homemade muffins and buckwheat cakes. And if you're into watching what you eat, the Greenbrier has introduced its Greenbrier Spa Cuisine, with one-third the calories and low-fat.

You won't have to go very far if you want to shop. There is a major shopping arcade right in the main building, with stores like Orvis and the Sam Snead Collection Shop. There is also another group of craft shops on the grounds, selling some really good handicraft items.

The Greenbrier

Location: On a 6,500-acre estate in the Allegheny Mountains, in White Sulphur Springs, West Virginia

Romantic Highlights: Victorian carriage ride followed by private lunch in gazebo; sleigh rides in the Allegheny foothills; fireplaces

Address/Phone: White Sulphur Springs, WV 24986; (304) 536–1110; fax (304) 536–7834

Web Site: www.greenbrier.com

U.S. Reservations: (800) 624–6070

Owner/Manager: Ted J. Kleisner, president and managing director

Arrival/Departure: Amtrak offers train service to The Greenbrier from New York and Chicago, with intermediate stops in Philadelphia, Wilmington, Baltimore, Washington, D.C., Indianapolis, and Cincinnati.

Distance from Greenbrier Valley Airport, in Lewisburg: 12 miles (15 minutes)

Distance from Washington D.C.: 250 miles southwest

Accommodations: 739 rooms, 33 suites, 96 guest houses

Most Romantic Room/Suite: Guest houses (Paradise Row or Spring Row) or Garden suites

Amenities: Air-conditioning, hair dryer, clock radio, minibar, toiletries, bathrobes, wet bar or kitchen in some suites, TV, fireplace in guest houses

Electricity: 110 volts

Sports and Facilities: 3 golf courses; 10 indoor and outdoor tennis courts; indoor and outdoor swimming pools; mountain biking; falconry academy; horseback riding; trap and skeet shooting and sporting clays; croquet; whitewater rafting trips; hiking, jogging, and fitness trails; fishing; bowling; sleigh rides; Golf Academy and Land Rover Driving School; 43,000-square-foot spa

Dress Code: Casual by day; jacket and tie for dinner, except in golf club restaurant

Weddings: Can be arranged

Rates/Packages: $167–$339 per person (double occupancy), including breakfast and dinner. Honeymoon packages are $546 per couple per night, including breakfast, dinner, champagne, and a photo. However, if you're into golf or tennis, you'd do better to take the golf or tennis packages, which are priced from $300 and $270 per person daily, respectively, and give you breakfast, dinner, unlimited golf or plenty of tennis plus a clinic and some balls.

Payment/Credit Cards: Most major

Deposit: $300–$600, depending on time of reservations.

Government Taxes: 6 percent sales tax; 3 percent occupancy tax

Service Charges: $25 per person per day

AMANGANI
Wyoming

The minute you enter the expansive lobby area at Amangani, a feeling of peace takes over. This is fitting, since the name Amangani means "peaceful home." The resort faces west, with sweeping views of the Snake River and Teton mountain ranges from virtually every vantage point.

Everywhere you go a zenlike atmosphere permeates, managing to convey both rusticity and elegance at the same time. Large openings lead from one high-ceilinged room to the next, with few doors blocking the flow of movement and energy. Rawhide chairs cushioned in faux fur, original Western art, and pine stumps that serve as cocktail tables fill the common areas.

Suites are spacious with stone, remote-controlled fireplaces; cowhide chairs with simulated wolf fabric; and modern, sleek furnishings. The expansive bathrooms feature twin vanities, separate toilet and shower rooms connected by a deep soaking tub big enough for two, all with stunning views of the mountains and the valley. Floors are delightfully soft cedar.

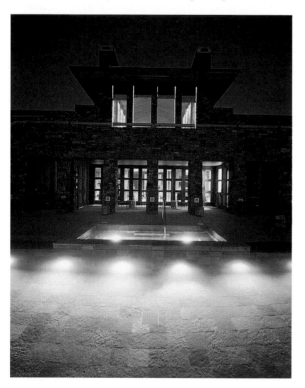

A separate, open dressing area includes twin benches and robes and slippers. The shower is trimmed in slate and faces the mountains. In fact, there's very little you can do at Amangani where you are not in sight of the mountains.

Sliding glass doors lead to a large deck complete with iron outdoor furniture and a sculpture designed by a Western artist (each deck features a different design). A large window seat flanked by pillows and a chenille blanket presents a cozy spot to read your favorite novel. Pull up the silk gauze shades and gaze up at the stars. Better yet, during the spring and summer (and even in the winter if you don't mind the chill) take the telescope that's provided in every room and head out to the deck for stargazing. With few lights and the town of Jackson on the other side of a bend in the road, you'll have no trouble spotting the constellations.

At night take advantage of the "peaceful pillow" placed by your bed. Made of flaxseeds and relaxing lavender, the soothing eye pillow is sure to help you nod off.

Because of its location, Amangani showcases some stunning sunsets. Take it all in while relaxing in the lounge with its two-story window wall and wood-burning fireplaces, or go to the adjacent library where you'll find a huge collection of books on Native American culture and Western art as well as CDs, videos, and games.

The main deck leads to a heated outdoor pool and whirlpool with—you guessed it—views of both the Snake River range and the Tetons. Radiant-heat floors in the deck areas ensure snow melts instantly, allowing you to walk barefoot comfortably from pool to whirlpool.

Amangani's only restaurant, the Grill, serves breakfast, lunch, and dinner. The mood is comfortable elegance as you dine amidst specially commissioned artwork and slate and black terrazzo furnishings. The menu changes seasonally and offers regional cuisine that features venison, elk, and buffalo. Everything is made from scratch at the Grill, with the country's freshest vegetables brought in from California. Vegetarian options are always available.

In the health center there are four treatment rooms where you can enjoy everything from a hydrating salt glow to an herbal wrap. There's also a small fitness center and studio (one-on-one classes and trainer sessions are available), and ladies' and men's locker rooms, each with a steam room and showers.

The stone steam room is one of the best we've seen. The harsh sound of the steam as it permeates the room is

Amangani

Location: Atop a butte in Jackson Hole, Wyoming, with meadows and grazing land below, the Snake River Range to the southwest, and the Grand Teton Range to the north

Romantic Highlights: En suite fireplaces, expansive outdoor decks in every suite, heated outdoor pool and whirlpool, awe-inspiring views of the mountain ranges

Address/Phone: 1535 North East Butte Road, Jackson Hole, WY 83001; (307) 734–7333

E-mail: amanganireservations@rmisp

Web Site: www.amangani.com

U.S. Reservations: (877) 734–7333

Owner/Manager: Monty Brown, general manager

Arrival/Departure: Daily service available to Jackson Hole Airport, Jackson, Wyoming, from several major U.S. hubs. Amangani provides complimentary shuttle service to and from the airport to all guests.

Distance from Jackson Hole Airport: 15 miles (25 minutes)

Distance from Jackson: 5 miles (10 minutes)

Accommodations: 29 superior rooms, 8 deluxe suites, and 3 Aman suites including the Grand Teton Suite

Most Romantic Room/Suite: The Grand Teton Suite, with a wraparound deck and views of both the Snake River Range and the Grand Tetons

Amenities: Air-conditioning, hair dryer, telephone, cable TV, VCR, CD player, ironing facilities, robes, toiletries, 24-hour room service, minibar, fireplace, sports equipment storage, complimentary shuttle service to and from the airport and to and from Jackson Hole

Sports and Facilities: Outdoor heated pool and whirlpool, health center, downhill and cross-country skiing, ski skating, snowshoeing, snowboarding, dogsledding, sleigh rides, snowmobiling, ice skating, hiking, mountain biking, horseback riding, white-water rafting, canoeing, kayaking, hot air balloon rides, golf, tennis, fly-fishing, gift shop

Dress Code: Comfortably elegant

Weddings: Depending on the season, weddings can be arranged for guests anywhere on the property.

Rates/Packages: From $675 per room per night year-round.

Payment/Credit Cards: Most major

Deposit: Secure with credit card; first and last nights' deposit paid at least 15 days before arrival

Government Taxes: 6 percent sales tax

Service Charges: 10 percent

drowned out by soft, New Age music, and a squirt bottle filled with eucalyptus is available should you want your steam bath to have a hint of mint. Some treatments can be performed in the privacy of your suite.

When it's time to venture out, there's a vast array of activity at your beck and call. During the winter, both Jackson Hole and Grand Targhee Ski areas offer some of the best Alpine skiing in North America. In Teton Village at the Jackson Hole ski resort, you'll find a private ski lounge exclusively for Amangani guests. Enjoy a cocktail or a cup of hot cocoa after a long day of skiing. Half- and full-day snowmobile tours to Granite Hot Springs give you the chance to explore the abundant wildlife and natural surroundings; then relax in a 105-degree natural pool.

A trip to the National Wildlife Art Museum includes a tour of thirteen galleries and the chance to ride a horse-drawn sleigh through the National Elk Refuge just across the street. The refuge is home to thousands of elk during the winter, so be sure to bring your camera.

During the summer, the nearby Snake River is perfect for rafting, kayaking, and fly-fishing. A wildlife safari through Jackson Hole with a naturalist guide provides the chance to see hundreds of bird species including bald eagles.

Like the other properties in the Amanresorts collection—Amangani is the only U.S. property—the staff is impeccably trained, the service superb. The staff ratio at Amangani is three per room, which means you'll enjoy a nice combination of individualized attention and a respect for privacy. With a cocoonlike ambience of peace and tranquility and an ecosystem waiting to be explored outside the door, it's easy to see why so many Amanresorts guests keep coming back for more.

SNAKE RIVER LODGE & SPA
Wyoming

The brand-new Snake River Lodge & Spa offers a quiet respite from the hustle and bustles just outside your door where a wealth of mountain activities await, from skiing and snowshoeing in winter to hiking and kayaking in two of the country's best national parks in summer.

Within the resort, the elegant Avanyu Spa is an oasis of relaxation. Enter the spa's grand double doors and the first thing you'll find is a heated pool surrounded by rock formations. During the winter, jump in, swim underneath the divider, and you'll find yourself outdoors surrounded by gorgeous snowy mountain scenery without feeling a pinch of cold. Follow the outdoor heated pathway past the cascading waterfalls and enjoy a soak in the outdoor hot tub.

The 17,000-square-foot spa features men's and ladies' lounges each with saunas, steam rooms, and awe-inspiring views of the Grand Tetons. After indulging in an Avanyu Rock Massage, which uses hot and cold stones to relax you and relieve stress, head back to your lounge for a soak in the oversized whirlpool and watch the skiers (or paragliders, depending on the season) as they glide down the mountain. For die-hard sports fans, the men's lounge boasts its own oversize whirlpool with a giant-screen TV set right in front of it.

Winter visitors will appreciate the only ski-in, ski-out service in the area complete with overnight ski valet service. Head down to the valet each morning to pick up your gear and you'll find boots that are not only dry but warm and toasty, too. The Saddlehorn Nordic Center is right across the street from the lodge and serves as the village's one-stop shop for everything from cross-country ski lessons to snowshoe rentals and dogsledding excursions. Summer brings trips to Grand Teton and Yellowstone national parks where you can bike, hike, or go on a safari

Snake River Lodge & Spa

Location: Nestled in the heart of Teton Village, Jackson Hole's premiere ski resort, with the famous Teton Mountain Range as a backdrop; both Grand Teton and Yellowstone National Parks nearby

Romantic Highlights: Couples' massages with views of the Grand Tetons; indoor/outdoor hot tubs; heated indoor/outdoor pool with cascading waterfalls; en suite fireplaces

Address/Phone: 7710 Granite Loop Road, Teton Village, WY 83025; (307) 732–6000

E-mail: Through the Web site (use the link on the site)

Web Site: www.snakeriverlodge.com

U.S. Reservations: (800) 445–4655

Owner/Manager: Kent Coleman, manager

Arrival/Departure: Daily service available to Jackson Hole Airport from several major U.S. hubs; taxi and car rentals available at airport

Distance from Jackson Hole Airport: 25 minutes

Distance from Jackson: 12 miles (15 minutes)

Accommodations: 88 hotel rooms, 40 luxury suites/condominiums

Most Romantic Room/Suite: Any third- or fourth-floor luxury king-size room or junior suite for best views.

Amenities: Air-conditioning, hair dryer, telephone, cable TV, ironing facilities, robes, toiletries, 24-hour room service, minibar, kitchen, fireplace in suites

Electricity: 110 volts

Sports and Facilities: Lobby bar, indoor and outdoor heated pool, hot tubs, sauna, spa and fitness center, ski-in/ski-out and ski valet service, downhill and cross-country skiing, ski skating, snowshoeing, snowboarding, dogsledding, sleigh rides, snowmobiling, heli-skiing, ice skating, hiking, biking, horseback riding, white-water rafting, canoeing, kayaking, hot air balloon rides, golf, tennis, fly-fishing

Dress Code: Casual

Weddings: Can be arranged

Rates/Packages: $120–$350 for rooms, $350–$1,200 for suites/condominiums; winter packages include Ski Wyoming, starting at $341 per person for two and including 3 nights' luxury accommodations, 2 one-day ski passes, transfers, and taxes; True West, starting at $1,150 per person for two including 7 nights' luxury accommodations, breakfasts, 10 one-day ski passes, transfers, and taxes; other seasonal packages available.

Payment/Credit Cards: Most major

Deposit: First night within 10 days of booking, full payment within 30 days of arrival during peak seasons (winter and summer); prepay in full within 7 days before arrival during shoulder seasons

Government Taxes: 6 percent sales tax

Service Charges: 3 percent resort fee

and get up-close views of the animals as they emerge from their winter hibernation.

The lodge's only restaurant, Gamefish, happens to be one of the best in town, open for breakfast, lunch, and dinner. The menu features local fish and wild game along with Wyoming-raised Angus steaks. If you'd rather venture out, Teton Village has numerous restaurants all within walking distance. Spend one evening in the town of Jackson (shuttles available from the lodge) where you'll find a slew of restaurants and nightspots.

Stop in at the Cowboy Bar and learn to two-step, or head to the Jackson Hole Hat Company and get a custom hat-fitting from owners Marilyn and Paul Hartman. The pair crafted those used in Broadway hits including *Annie Get Your Gun* and *Oklahoma.*

Back at the lodge you'll find the entire property reflects its earthy mountain setting. Oversized brown and deep-red leather sofas and chairs, wood tables, and whimsical hand-carved bears dot the lobby and bar area.

Rooms are simple but elegant with large windows; soft, overstuffed down comforters, and locally made wood furniture. Bathrooms have granite countertops, marble-tile floors, and jet tubs. By far the best feature of the rooms is the bed with a perfectly chosen mattress, not too hard, not too soft. It was so comfortable, we even peeked to see if we could find out who made it. No luck. Along with soft, delicious linens, Snake River's bedding provides a haven for sweet dreams.

Snake River Lodge & Spa is for those whose idea of a perfect resort is one where a location offering an endless array of year-round activity is coupled with a world-class, in-house spa and a five-star-worthy restaurant.

CANADA

THE FAIRMONT BANFF SPRINGS
Alberta

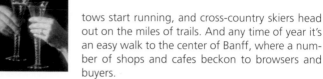

Modeled after a Scottish baronial castle, the Fairmont Banff Springs reigns over the majestic mountains and hills that surround it. This massive stone hotel—with its steeply pitched green roofs and gables topped by finials of gold and its gray granite walls, turretlike wings, and arched passageways—would be right at home perched in the Alps. Built in 1888 by the Canadian Pacific Railroad to provide its passengers with an oasis of opulence, it has enough rooms to accommodate a king, a queen, and their entire court.

Called "Castle in the Rockies," grand features include king-size fireplaces, massive wrought-iron chandeliers, and print fabrics in deep rich tones. The Fairmont Banff Springs invites you to have it both ways: the wilderness experience—trail rides, hiking, and biking—along with luxuries like a full-service spa, fireplaces, minibars, and tons of shops. Certainly its appeal has attracted its share of notables over the years, including Clint Eastwood, Wayne Gretzky, Ivana Trump, and Tina Turner.

A truly four-seasons resort, in the summer flowers overflow in hanging baskets and thrive happily in the gardens, golfers head to the tees, hikers and bikers hit the trails, and white-water rafters swoosh down the swollen rivers.

In the winter the fireplaces get cranked up, the ski

tows start running, and cross-country skiers head out on the miles of trails. And any time of year it's an easy walk to the center of Banff, where a number of shops and cafes beckon to browsers and buyers.

Rooms and suites located in the main building and in the adjacent Manor House are furnished in mostly Victorian style in deep reds, greens, and browns. Unique heritage accessories such as glass bottles, leather-bound books, and brass candlesticks are placed here and there. Views are of the mountains, the pine forests, and the golf course.

A recently completed $75 million restoration and renovation program has resulted in a stunning grand lobby, expanded kitchen facilities, new restaurants, public areas, and shops. Guest rooms have been refurbished and a new arrivals entrance welcomes visitors in grand style. On the picturesque twenty-seven–hole golf course, which winds along the valley at the base of the mountains and along the Bow River, wildlife often calls the shots. Elk are at times as plentiful as geese. This is especially true in the fall, rutting season, when the big guys get all charged up and herd together all the females they can bully. Rangers are called almost on a daily basis to shoo the elk to the sidelines. (A word of caution: Heed posted warnings and don't try to approach an elk with a camera or a club. The bulls can get testy.)

If you want to kick back and head into the hills, Holiday on Horseback offers hourly and two- to six-day overnight pack trips from its base near the hotel. After a four- to five-hour ride through some pretty spectacular countryside, you'll reach Sundance Lodge, a two-story log house with a wide veranda. The lodge has several bedrooms. Beds are very comfortable and food is plentiful—perhaps a ham or roast beef with all the trimmings and homemade pie. In the evening guests gather around the campfire to swap tales and roast marshmallows. The lodge is solar heated and remarkably warm and cozy. Farther up the trail is Halfway Lodge, for folks who want something even more rustic and a longer trip.

The Fairmont Banff Springs participates in the Heritage Mountaineering and Interpretive Hiking Program, offering hikes led by certified mountain guides and naturalists.

At the end of a day's hiking or riding, or just anytime for that matter, the full-service European-style Solace Spa and Fitness Centre, a $12 million dollar 35,000-square-

The Fairmont Banff Springs

Location: Nestled in the mountains at the confluence of the Bow and Spray Rivers in the Canadian Rockies

Romantic Highlights: Castlelike features; awesome views; fresh mountain air; fireplaces; spa treatments and massages for two

Address/Phone: P.O. Box 960, Banff, Alberta T0L 0C0, Canada; (403) 762–2211; fax (403) 762–5755

Web Site: www.fairmont.com

U.S. Reservations: (800) 441–1414

Owner/Manager: Edward T. Kissane, regional vice president and general manager

Arrival/Departure: Shuttle service available from Calgary Airport

Distance from Calgary Airport: 80 miles (1½ hours)

Distance from Calgary: 80 miles

Accommodations: 770 rooms and suites

Most Romantic Room/Suite: Tower rooms featuring a spiral staircase leading to a loft, which may have a round bed, a Jacuzzi, and great views of the valley

Amenities: Coffee/teamaker, minibar, TV, radio, hair dryer, bathrobes, iron/ironing board, toiletries; some with fireplaces, parlors, oversized whirlpools, saunas

Electricity: 110 volts

Sports and Facilities: Solace Spa and Fitness Centre features cascading waterfalls, mineral whirlpools, indoor and outdoor saltwater pools, solaria, steam rooms, saunas, and various treatments; 27 holes of golf, 5 tennis courts, hiking, biking, horseback riding, bowling, rollerblading, whitewater rafting, canoeing, fishing, interpretive walks, rock climbing, mountaineering, skiing, heli-skiing, snowboarding, ice skating, dogsledding, tobogganing, horse-drawn sleigh rides, curling, hockey. A revamped retail shopping area contains 15 speciality and boutique stores.

Dress Code: Resort casual; jacket and tie requested in the Rob Roy Room during summer months

Weddings: Can be arranged

Rates/Packages: Canadian Rockies Experience package includes accommodations, meals, unlimited sports, gratuities, and sight-seeing. Summer package is priced from $671 per room per day; winter from $865. Outdoor activities include golf, canoeing, cycling, fishing, hiking, Heritage Mountaineering and Interpretive Hiking Program, sleigh rides, ski lift tickets.

Payment/Credit Cards: Most major

Deposit: By credit card

Government Taxes: 12 percent

Service Charges: Sometimes included

Entry Requirements for U.S. Citizens: Passport and photo ID

foot facility, pampers you with aromatic wraps, refreshing facials, scrubs, baths, and hour-long massages. There is a sauna, Jacuzzi, inhalation room, and steam room as well as a 105-foot saltwater pool divided into lanes for doing laps. In another area mineral water cascades in silvery sheets into three massage pools heated at different temperatures; from there you can step into a larger therapeutic mineral pool and then relax on the cushioned lounges.

Outside there is another heated pool open year-round and a large Jacuzzi. Solace also boasts a fully equipped cardio- and strength-conditioning fitness center and an aerobics theater where daily classes are scheduled. Views of mountains and dense stands of pine all around complete the blissful picture.

Relax in the new lobby where 20-foot windows overlook the Sulphur Mountain Range and extensive skylights frame mountains and sky. Or try the new Rundle Room (formerly the hotel lobby), which has been transformed into an elegant guest parlor with vaulted ceilings, huge windows, and antique furnishings. With seventeen restaurants and lounges including Rob Roy; Banff Shire Club featuring gourmet cuisine in a private club-style setting; Grapes, a European bistro and wine bar; and Samurai, where you can make a meal out of their California rolls— the only decision you have to make when it comes time to eat is do you turn right or left out of the elevator.

You can spend a week, a month, or more at the Fairmont Banff Springs and never tire of things to do or see.

THE FAIRMONT CHATEAU LAKE LOUISE
Alberta

Built in 1913 this white stucco resort is huge, with sweeping vistas of the snow-topped mountains that cradle a stunning glacier-fed turquoise lake. Even at night the lake glows, a shimmery, glassy surface framed by the jagged steep cliffs, pine-clad hills, and striated rock formations that have shifted over thousands of years to slant toward the water. Dark blue velvet skies ringed by patches of misty clouds sparkle with stars. The resort twinkles with tiny white lights, creating an outdoor wonderland. Then daylight. The lake, not large, is a watercolor of reflections fanning out from the narrower end, where the glacier lies receding in the distance.

From the beginning the Fairmont Chateau Lake Louise was built to appeal to guests with outdoor interests. Its orientation to one of the most beautiful lakes in North America and its setting of manicured lawns and gardens surrounded by densely forested mountains laced with hiking, biking, skiing, and horseback riding trails, rock faces to climb, and rivers to conquer hold enough interests and

challenges to appeal to people of all skill levels.

Some come simply to soak up the scenery and enjoy a variety of dining experiences. Famous guests have included Queen Elizabeth II, Mary Astor, John Barrymore, Cary Grant, Prince Rainier of Monaco, and many of today's Hollywood celebrities.

With close to 500 rooms and suites, the Fairmont Chateau Lake Louise could hardly be called your cozy inn in the Rockies. Yet within its walls there are intimate spaces, comfortable sofas, warm-paneled wood lounges, and fireside groupings. Built to celebrate the outdoors, the hotel has immense arched windows that frame the mountain peaks and paths that lead to the water's edge and along it.

Rooms and suites are spacious and oriented toward the lake or the mountains. Some have balconies and over-size whirlpool tubs. High ceilings, rich, thick carpets in greens and reds, hand-painted folk art on each guest room door, chandeliers, brass fixtures and wood paneling are featured in public rooms and guest accommodations. Special touches include such items as books, glass bottles, and candlesticks. A shopping arcade sells everything from Canadian sweaters and fleeces to jewelry and Irish goods, including wool capes, sweaters, and crystal.

Restaurants include Walliser Stube, specializing in Swiss Alpine cuisine—the fondue and raclette are excellent. For casual dining there is the Poppy Room, serving breakfast, lunch, and dinner, and the Glacier Saloon, where the Old West comes alive. The Edelweiss Dining Room features world-class cuisine, and in the Victoria Dining Room you can experience grand dining in a European atmosphere punctuated by beautiful chandeliers, linens, and china. Backpackers can stock up at the Chateau Deli on water, sandwiches, soups, and desserts; cocktails are available in the Lobby Bar.

Recalling the time one hundred years ago when Swiss guides arrived in the area, greatly boosting the hiking and mountain climbing activities, the Fairmont Chateau Lake Louise has launched its Heritage Mountaineering and Interpretive Hiking Program. There are hikes for all levels, from those just moderately fit to the highly experienced. Certified mountain guides and naturalists take you on a wonderful journey of from four to ten hours.

"Prepare to leave civilization," cautions naturalist guide Bruce Bembridge in a hushed tone. The snow continues to fall through the trees, the ice on the path melts into dark wet patches. Snow clings to spiderweb threads hanging from pine branches like Christmas tree icicles. You continue walking down the hill, finally reaching the wide open grounds that lead to the entrance of the hotel. You have left the tiny blue flowers poking through the snow, the views high up and through the spruce and firs of Lake Louise, the teahouse perched on a mountain peak, the chipmunks gathering and cracking nuts. It's all so breathtakingly beautiful.

The Fairmont Chateau Lake Louise

Location: In Banff National Park in the Canadian Rockies

Romantic Highlights: Awesome views of crystal-clear lake and mountains; horse-drawn sleigh rides; fireplaces; moonlight skating

Address/Phone: Lake Louise, Alberta T0L 1E0, Canada; (403) 522–3511; fax (403) 522–3111

Web Site: www.fairmont.com

U.S. Reservations: (800) 441–1414

Owner/Manager: David M. Bayne, general manager

Arrival/Departure: Shuttle service available from Calgary Airport

Distance from Calgary Airport: 120 miles (2½ hours)

Distance from Banff: 36 miles

Accommodations: 487 rooms, including 83 suites; 26 rooms with whirlpools; 4 split-level suites with balconies

Most Romantic Room/Suite: Junior Suites on upper floors with sitting areas and lake views; the Belvedere Suites, two-level accommodations with balconies overlooking lakes and mountains; Room 303 with its coffered ceiling, wide balcony, and wood paneling is especially grand; Number 536, decorated in the Victorian style, with an elegant living room, balcony, fireplace flanked by bookcases, and a bathroom and powder room

Amenities: Minibar, hair dryer, TV, dressing table, toiletries, coffee/tea facilities, iron/ironing board, robes, fan

Electricity: 110 volts

Sports and Facilities: Recreation center with indoor pool, whirlpool, steam rooms, weights and exercise equipment; walking, hiking, canoeing, tennis, fishing, mountaineering, rock climbing, dogsledding, Alpine and cross-country skiing, ice skating, river rafting, golf, guided snowshoeing expeditions, snowboarding, heli-skiing, horse-drawn sleigh rides, curling, hockey, broom ball, guided trail rides and overnight horseback adventures, arcade and video room, art classes

Dress Code: Resort casual; jacket and tie required for Edelweiss Dining Room

Weddings: Can be arranged

Rates/Packages: Canadian Rockies Experience package includes accommodations, meals, unlimited sports, gratuities, and sight-seeing. Summer package is priced from $791; winter rates are from $576. Outdoor activities include canoeing, cycling, fishing, hiking, Heritage Mountaineering and Interpretive Hiking Program, sleigh rides, ski lift tickets.

Payment/Credit Cards: Most major

Deposit: By credit card

Government Taxes: 12 percent

Service Charges: Sometimes included

Entry Requirement for U.S Citizens: Passport and photo ID

THE FAIRMONT JASPER PARK LODGE
Alberta

It began as an eight-bungalow wilderness retreat at the turn of the century in the 4,200-acre Jasper National Park, a place where people could escape and reconnect with nature. And they came: the Kennedys, John Travolta, Marilyn Monroe, Bob Newhart, and many others who could afford the best.

Today Jasper Park Lodge has grown: more cottages, more facilities, a wonderful main lodge with enormous lounges, shopping arcade, dining rooms, swimming pool, golf clubhouse, and outdoor Jacuzzi. Still, although it now has close to 450 rooms and seven places to eat and drink, it has emerged with its integrity intact. It continues to appeal to anyone who appreciates cool mountain air, walking along lakeshore paths, going to bed hearing the plaintive calls of elk, skipping stones across a white-blue translucent lake, sitting in front of a crackling fire drinking hot chocolate, and heading out to the golf course, ski trails, or other outdoor pursuits for fresh air and exercise.

The Fairmont Jasper Park Lodge, a comfortable enclave of log cabins and cedar chalets, features spacious, well-appointed rooms with all the amenities you could wish for, including padded hangers, minibars, TVs, down duvets, king-size beds, large picture windows, pine armoires, and colorful burgundy, green, and brown print fabrics. Some rooms open onto decks or patios; some have fireplaces and oversized whirlpool baths. One thing

is certain, you may be stomping around the grounds and surrounding mountains in your wool socks and hiking boots, but when it comes time to eat or hit the sack, you'll find nothing rough about your accommodations.

Cottages range in size from three bedrooms, each with private bath, to Milligan Manor, with eight bedrooms, nine baths, and a 900-square-foot living and dining room. The Point and Overlook, older cabins loaded with charm, feature several well-appointed bedrooms, lofty living room, kitchen, and dining room (Bill Gates and his family rented one of these on a recent vacation). Since all rooms in these multibedroom cabins are complete in themselves, with en suite baths and outside entrances, they can be rented singly but are also ideal for a group of couples who desire private bedrooms but the use of a central living, dining, and kitchen area.

Those seeking privacy can book their own one-bedroom cabin that sits on a bluff overlooking the water and comes with a separate living room, fireplace, and a whirlpool tub-for-two. Other options include the Whistler king suites, featuring enormous vaulted-ceiling living rooms with fireplaces and kitchens; French doors open onto decks overlooking the lake.

Golfers will find the Stanley Thompson–designed golf course challenging but very playable. Tees on the course,

The Fairmont Jasper Park Lodge

Location: On 903 acres in Jasper National Park, one of North America's largest wilderness areas

Romantic Highlights: Awesome views; fresh mountain air; fireplaces; wildlife all around

Address/Phone: P.O. Box 40, Jasper, Alberta T0E 1E0, Canada; (780) 852–3301; fax (780) 852–5107

Web Site: www.fairmont.com

U.S. Reservations: (800) 441–1414

Owner/Manager: Kevin Toth, general manager

Arrival/Departure: Shuttle service available from Calgary Airport

Distance from Calgary Airport: 256 miles (4 hours)

Distance from Edmonton: 225 miles

Accommodations: 446 rooms, suites, cabins, and chalets

Most Romantic Room/Suite: Number 467 (Athabasca) known as the "Honeymoon Cottage"; Whistler king lakeside suites also good

Amenities: Bathrobes, coffeemaker, minibar, TV, radio, hair dryer, iron/ironing board, umbrellas, scale, toiletries, turndown service; some with fireplaces, oversize whirlpool baths

Electricity: 110 volts

Sports and Facilities: Walking, hiking, fishing, mountaineering, rock climbing, dogsledding, Alpine and cross-country skiing, ice skating, river rafting, biking, heli-hiking, canoeing, sleigh rides, canyon ice crawling, snowmobile tours; 18-hole golf course, 4 tennis courts (hard surface); game room and fitness center with exercise equipment, steam room and whirlpool, year-round heated outdoor pool, Miette hot springs; billiards; guided snowshoeing expeditions, trail rides, and overnight horseback adventures

Dress Code: Resort casual

Weddings: Can be arranged

Rates/Packages: Canadian Rockies Experience package includes accommodations, meals, unlimited sports, gratuities, and sight-seeing. Summer package is priced from $697; winter packages from $475, per room per day. Outdoor activities include golf, canoeing, cycling, fishing, hiking, Heritage Mountaineering and Interpretive Hiking Program, sleigh rides, ski lift tickets.

Payment/Credit Cards: Most major

Deposit: By credit card

Government Taxes: 12 percent

Service Charges: Sometimes included

Entry Requirements for U.S Citizens: Passport and photo ID

which meanders along the shores of Lac Beauvert, are oriented to mountain peaks and some holes require driving over water. All but three of the holes are fenced to keep elk off the fairways and greens.

Restaurants range from the elegant Edith Cavell Dining Room, serving gourmet cuisine, to the Tent City Sports Pub, a sports bar offering billiards and shuffleboard and pub-style food. When dining at the Edith Cavell, be sure to try the mushroom chowder; it's the best. Also good is the filet of Alberta beef tenderloin on a Yukon Gold potato cake, the fresh lemon curd flan, and the birch and apple cider–basted British Columbia salmon filet. Fresh herbs and vegetables grown in Jasper's greenhouse are used in food preparation; breads and pastries are freshly baked.

All the mountain-oriented sports and activities are available at Jasper, including the Heritage Mountaineering and Interpretive Hiking Program and horseback riding. For a memorable adventure arrange a rafting trip with Mount Robson Whitewater Rafting, about forty-five minutes from the hotel in Valemount, B.C. Operated by the Cinnamon family, this company has more than twenty years' experience in taking venturesome travelers down the spectacular Fraser River, the longest river in British Columbia. At the end of the trip, chow down on some of the best veggieburgers or hamburgers you'll ever taste—the recipe is a secret.

The Fairmont Jasper Park Lodge is a peaceful place. Listen carefully as you walk along the paths and through the pines. Shhh. You may be able to hear the soft tread of the eclectic group of early adventurers who explored the land and climbed the mountains.

AUBERGE WILD ROSE
New Brunswick

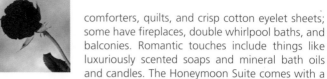

On a recent trip to New Brunswick, I discovered a wonderful inn just outside Moncton, a small city about 100 miles northeast of St. John just twenty minutes from the coast. A real find I thought, for anyone who loves the outdoors, brisk fresh air, and still at the end of the day desires a romantic comfortable place to sleep along with a superb meal. With rates beginning at $52 with breakfast, the Auberge Wild Rose is a great bargain as well.

Set on rolling lawns in a peaceful grove of fruit trees and gardens showcasing wild roses, the inn offers luxurious comforts such as down duvets, Egyptian cotton towels, candlelight dinners, whirlpool baths, and delicious food. This red clapboard house is designed in the traditional colonial style and features highly polished hardwood floors, antique and traditional reproduction furniture, fireplaces, and French doors leading out to the back deck where in the fall, the trees are heavy with pears, apples, and cherries. I'm told you can even pick them.

The sixteen individually decorated rooms are large, airy, and well appointed with Egyptian cotton towels, comforters, quilts, and crisp cotton eyelet sheets; some have fireplaces, double whirlpool baths, and balconies. Romantic touches include things like luxuriously scented soaps and mineral bath oils and candles. The Honeymoon Suite comes with a king-size bed, large-screen TV and VCR, double whirlpool, mini-fridge, microwave, chaise lounge, wing-back chairs, and in-room access to the balcony. Another good choice is one of the suites with a fireplace.

Meals served in the cheerful dining room focus on sumptuous gourmet breakfasts and dinners featuring home-grown vegetables and fruits. A typical dinner might start with fricassee of wild mushrooms or escargots in Cognac followed by a salad of baby greens with poppy seed dressing. The main course could be shrimp and scallops au Pernod with fresh mushrooms and green onions, or pork tenderloin Dianne sautéed with green onions and fresh mushrooms and topped with a brandy sauce. Dessert (this was really great) might be a raspberry crème brûlée.

Whatever is on the menu, according to the enthusiastic innkeeper, Diane Logan, "You won't find any deep-

fried items here. We really stress fresh, healthy cuisine. We also offer barbecues some evenings on the deck."

The inn is an excellent base for exploring New Brunswick and enjoying outdoor pursuits such as hiking, biking, whale-watching, camping, and kayaking. Golfers need only go next door to the eighteen-hole Lakeside Golf Course and it's just a twenty-minute drive to Parlee Beach, which claims to have the warmest waters north of Virginia Beach.

New Brunswick is a place where you can enjoy natural beauty without bumper-to-bumper traffic. You can devour fresh lobster, clams, and sweet shrimp by the bucket, go out to sea for whale-watching, walk for miles on endless beaches, play golf by the sea, and kayak through Hopewell Rocks, huge rock formations that only that morning you could walk around.

Heading south to St. John (100 miles), you can get drenched on a thrilling Reversing Falls jet boat as your craft spins and charges in the turbulence created by the harbor pushing over a waterfall into the St. John River that kicks up high waves and whirlpools as the two bodies of water meet.

Going north to the Acadian Peninsula, it's a good day trip along the coast with lots of driving, but the route along the coast past Kouchibouguac Park (where you can stop for a look at their interpretative center and stretch your legs along the seaside boardwalk) is magnificent.

The only thing not French about the Acadian Peninsula is the electrical current. Signs are in French and Acadians speak English with a French accent. But it's more complex than that. Ask people from this area, the northernmost part of New Brunswick, what they are and they will quickly tell you they are Acadian. Which is not English nor is it French. Not exactly.

To understand the whole thing better, visit the Village Historique Acadian near Caraquet. Much more than a recreation or historical site, the houses are real, brought from other areas, carefully dismantled part by part down to the original pegs and nails, then each piece numbered and meticulously reconstructed on the new site.

Life here has been replicated as it once was: Wool is sheared from the farm's sheep, cleaned, carded, spun into yarn, dyed with natural colors—onion skins, indigo, and so on—woven on looms into cloth for clothing and knitted into sweaters and socks. Flax is grown on the property and made into linen garments and cloth. Bread is baked in beehive ovens; cedar shingles are split from logs and planed into shakes for the roofs. And there's a restaurant where you can eat the kind of food the Acadians ate, prepared in the old methods.

Another place worth seeing is Le Pays del la Sagouine, an Acadian cultural village based on Antonine Maillet's fictional story "La Sagouine."

Then at the end of your day, return to the Auberge Wild Rose for a four-course candlelight dinner and a night of bliss.

Auberge Wild Rose

Location: Set on 37 acres in the countryside just outside the city of Moncton

Romantic Highlights: Large rooms with down duvets and fireplaces; candlelight dinners in the "Couples Only" dining room; picnic lunches in nearby parks; incredible outdoor adventures without the crowds

Address/Phone: 17 Baseline Road, Lakeville, Westmoreland County, New Brunswick, E1H 1N5, Canada; (888) 389–ROSE (7673) or (506) 383–9751; fax (506) 383–9751

E-mail: wildroseinn@hotmail.com

Web Site: www.wildroseinn.com

U.S. Reservations: Available at the Web site

Owner/Manager: Fred and Dianne Logan

Arrival/Departure: Transportation to and from the Moncton Airport can be arranged. For those who come by car, the inn is just off the Trans Canada Highway (Route 2) at exit 465. Go north on Route 134 for 1 mile, then right onto Baseline Road.

Distance from Moncton Regional Airport: 5 miles (8 minutes)

Distance from Moncton: 7 miles (10 minutes)

Accommodations: 16 rooms: 2 full suites, 4 honeymoon suites, 5 junior suites, 5 standard rooms

Most Romantic Room/Suite: Full suites, honeymoon suites, and junior suites all with fireplaces and double whirlpool baths; 3 of the honeymoon suites with large (7 feet by 5 feet) whirlpools in the bedroom area

Amenities: Air-conditioning, TV, hair dryer, terry robes, toiletries, telephone, in-room coffee/tea service, some with large TV with four-head VCR and large whirlpools

Electricity: 110 volts

Sports and Facilities: Game room with snooker table, golf next door. The region offers many options from kayaking to biking and hiking.

Dress Code: Casual

Weddings: Can be arranged if wedding party books all the rooms

Rates/Packages: From $52.00 to $76.25 (per couple); Honeymoon suites are $99.95 and full suites are $120.00. Rates include full breakfast.

Payment/Credit Cards: Most major

Government Taxes: Harmonised sales tax is extra at 15 percent but is refundable upon application by U.S. citizens.

Service Charges: Not included

Entry Requirements for U.S. Citizens: Passport and photo ID

Note: The staff is bilingual and the inn happily advertises that it offers a smoke-free environment. Not suitable for children under 12.

LA PINSONNIÈRE
Quebec

This small inn, which lies between the Laurentian Mountains and the tidal flats of the St. Lawrence River, is a real find for those honeymooning in Canada. La Pinsonnière, which means "house of the finches," sits about 200 feet up a bluff overlooking the river, which at this point is wider than one of the Finger Lakes is long. This sprawling white manor house, with its pointed towers and garden setting ringed by tall trees, would seem equally at home on the Loire River in France's château country.

The personal involvement of owners Jean and Janine Authier, who purchased the mansion several years ago and converted it into an inn, is just one reason this property is so special. The Authiers, along with their daughter, Valérie, La Pinsonnière's manager, are committed to providing their guests with an exceptional place to stay and dine. Their restaurant, with its French-trained chef, has already received a number of awards and has gained a reputation for serving some of the finest cuisine in Canada.

In addition to the hotel business, the Authiers have an avid interest in the arts. Contemporary paintings by Quebec artists, many for sale, hang in the dining room and in other places throughout the inn.

Each of the rooms has a personality all its own; several have been recently redecorated. For example, one has a king-size brass bed, fireplace, private sauna, and large whirlpool tub. Another is a vision of romantic Victoriana, with white wicker and rattan furniture, a white marble bath, lace duvet cover, and puffy white cushions.

Some rooms are decorated in muted traditional colors and feature Queen Anne–style furniture, brass lamps, and wing chairs; others are light and airy, decorated in soft sea colors with rattan and pine furniture and French doors leading to terraces overlooking the river.

Large marble baths with designer soaps, fluffy down duvets, classical music, and chairs you can really sink into and fall asleep in, add up to accommodations that are comfortable but not obtrusive.

La Pinsonnière is located in the Charlevoix region, an area known for its rugged cliffs, rolling hills, coves, and exceptional river views. A late afternoon pleasure for the inn's guests is to sit on the terrace of the hotel's lovely large patio and watch the sun set over the tops of the tall cedar, spruce, and birch trees. You can also follow the path that leads down through a cedar forest to the inn's private, rugged beach, a great place for a picnic. Going down the 226 steps is easy. Going up you'll find rustic benches where you can stop and rest or just sit for a while.

The inn may be small, but it still offers a lot of choices for active couples. There is a tennis court, indoor pool, and massage therapists who can pamper you with a variety of soothing treatments.

In the warmer months, you can hike on the trails in the surrounding hills, take a whale-watching cruise, and play golf at nearby Murray Bay. Cruise up the Saguenay Fjord, the world's southernmost fjord, and marvel at the spectacular scenery of sheer rocky cliffs plunging dramatically down to the river. Or visit the artists' town of Baie Saint Paul, a pleasant drive from the inn, where you can browse through about twenty galleries featuring Charlevoix and Quebec painters. There are also many summer theater productions and concerts held nearby.

If you come in the winter, you can cross-country and

La Pinsonnière

Location: On the banks of the St. Lawrence River, in the picturesque Charlevoix region north of Quebec City

Romantic Highlights: Private fireplaces; terraces above the river; whirlpool baths for two

Address/Phone: 124 Saint-Raphael, La Malbaie (Cap-à-l'Aigle), Charlevoix, Quebec G0T IB0, Canada; (418) 665–4431; fax (418) 665–7156

E-mail: pinsonniere@relaischateaux.fr

Web Site: www.lapinsonniere.com

U.S. Reservations: (800) 387–4431; Relais & Châteaux, (800) RELAIS–8

Owner/Manager: The Authier family

Arrival/Departure: There is a very small airport, St.-Irenée, about 3 miles from the inn; free pickup can be arranged.

Distance from Quebec International Airport: 95 miles

Distance from Quebec City: 90 miles

Accommodations: 25 rooms, including 1 suite

Most Romantic Room/Suite: Room 312, which has a rosewood king-size bed, whirlpool bath for two, and sauna with a spectacular view of the St. Lawrence River; Room 211, a creamy white confection with king-size bed, white lace duvet cover, double whirlpool, fireplace, marble bath, and deck

Amenities: Hair dryer, toiletries, fireplace (some rooms), TV, telephone, robes, ceiling fans, air-conditioning, and classical music

Electricity: 110 volts

Sports and Facilities: Indoor pool, hiking, beach, tennis, kayaking, skiing, skating, sauna, whale-watching, massage therapy

Dress Code: Casually smart; no jackets required for dinner

Weddings: Can be arranged

Rates/Packages: Can$115–$450 (U.S.$73.74–$288.55) per couple per night (low season); Can$145–$460 (U.S.$92.98–$294.97) (high season—warmer months and holidays); Can$65 (U.S.$41.68) breakfast and dinner

Payment/Credit Cards: Most major

Deposit: 50 percent of total cost of stay required; balance due on arrival;. refundable if canceled 15 days or more prior to date of arrival

Government Taxes: $2.00 per night; 7 percent federal; 7.5 percent provincial

Service Charges: Included

Entry Requirements for U.S. Citizens: Passport and photo ID

downhill ski at Mont Grand Fonds, go snowmobiling, ice skating, and dogsledding and at the end of the day curl up in front of a crackling fire in your room or in the lounge.

Want an adventure? In the warmer months you can climb into a red isothermic suit and head off by boat for the world of the belugas and blue whales that inhabit the Saguenay Marine Arctic Park.

Vistas from La Pinsonnière's restaurant, as well as from most of the rooms, are expansive. Large windows afford marvelous views of the rivers, hills, and trees. Dining by candlelight at a beautifully appointed table is a special pleasure. Cuisine centered on continental fare with an emphasis on French cooking includes dishes such as ravioli croustillants de crabe en velouté de cidre, foie gras de canard poelé aux poires confites, and wild mushrooms served in a delicate sauce. In 2001 the restaurant was awarded the Table d'Or du Quebec as the best restaurant in the province. A prix-fixe dinner is about $35 (U.S.) for three courses, $50 for five course, $65 for seven courses, plus tax and service charges. The Authiers' 13,000-bottle wine cellar is impressive, and you are invited to participate in frequent wine tastings. A new a la carte menu has been added.

An exquisite romantic hideaway, the inn is a member of the prestigious Relais & Châteaux group.

THE CARIBBEAN, BAHAMAS, AND BERMUDA

CAP JULUCA
Anguilla

Cap Juluca's dazzling white towers, turrets, and arches, set against the dense greens of the foliage and clear turquoise of the Caribbean waters, create a fairy-tale village straight out of *Arabian Nights*. Nothing but brightly hued blossoms of bougainvillea and waving palm fronds comes between you and your view of the sea from your oversize terrace or turret patio. Set on 179 acres, all rooms and villas are just steps away from the white, sugary sand crescent beach; no building is higher than the palm trees.

The exteriors of the buildings, with their parapets and domes, are dramatic enough, but wait until you get inside. Rooms are really large—at least 16 feet by 16 feet—and one-bedroom suites go up to 2,200 square feet. Villas, with up to five bedrooms, have private pools set in an enclosed red-tiled garden courtyard. You can rent bedrooms and suites in the pool villas, or you can rent the entire villa yourself for complete privacy.

Bathrooms are outrageously opulent, with tons of marble, double sinks, showers, and bidets. Some have double-size bathtubs with headrests; some open onto a private walled solarium furnished with chaises and a table. Louvered windows let the sea breezes slip through, yet preserve your privacy. You can lie back and catch the sun wearing as little as you want or nothing at all.

Rattan furniture with thick cushions, king-size beds, fine linens, potted palms in clay pots, dark Brazilian walnut doors and trim, white walls, and ceramic tile floors in various muted colors provide a sumptuous setting for romance. Unique accessories, such as wooden bowls and sculpture, leather, and clay, as well as beautiful area rugs, inlaid mirrors, and artwork, many imported from northern Africa, are found in some rooms; others lean toward a more European feeling, with traditional period furnishings and accessories.

There are three tennis courts, and the pro schedules round-robin tournaments every week. There is also a fitness center and a croquet court set up British style. Complimentary water sports include waterskiing, sailing, and sailboarding. You can also go scuba diving (this is extra), or if you want to set off on your own "True Love" cruise, you can charter a yacht.

No one will intrude on your privacy, even while you're on the beach—unless, of course, you plant a red flag in the sand. This means you would like someone to come over and see what you want, whether it be a clean towel or another Sea Breeze. Intimate "garden rooms," partitioned with hedges, are located around the pool. If you want service, just ring a bell.

Cap Juluca's beaches are long and very walkable. The main beach stretches along Maunday's Bay for about a mile. Go around the eastern end of the headland and there is another 2-mile beach running along Cove Bay. In the center of Maunday's Bay beach is an Olympic-size pool, which is surrounded by white market-style umbrellas and tables along with many lounge chairs—a popular gathering place.

Many guests, especially those who have terraces with great sea views, prefer to have breakfast brought to their room. Fresh fruits and juices, muffins and banana bread, and steaming coffee or tea are beautifully set up on your patio table complete with linen and china. You also get a summary of the latest news from the *New York Times* faxed that morning from the States (just in case you've missed it).

One night you may wish to order a West Indian dinner served on your patio. Linger over a bottle of wine from the resort's extensive wine cellar, and see if you can spot the lights of St. Martin or tiny Saba twinkling across the water.

Cap Juluca has two open-air restaurants: the casually elegant Pimms and the more informal George's. Pimms is tucked into the corner of the protected eastern end of the cove and sits just 6 feet from the water's edge. George's is located midway along Maunday's Bay beach and is open all day for casual dining.

After dinner kick off your shoes and walk hand in hand back to your room along the moonlit beach and be lulled to sleep by the sound of waves rolling up on the shores. Or linger at your table at George's for some dancing under the stars.

When you come to Anguilla, don't expect a roaring nightlife. After all, an island where the 30-mile-an-hour speed limit is reinforced by a series of speed bumps and the airport allows only prop planes to land is not a swinging place. Come here if you like to picnic on an uninhabited island or drift away in a hammock in a garden perfumed with the scents of frangipani, jasmine, and orchids.

Cap Juluca

Location: Along Maunday's Bay, on the southern coast of Anguilla

Romantic Highlights: Sugar-white crescent beach; palatial bathrooms, some with private solarium; massages for two en suite

Address/Phone: P.O. Box 240, Maunday's Bay, Anguilla, Leeward Islands, British West Indies; (264) 497–6666; fax (264) 497–6617

E-mail: helen@capjuluca.com

Web Site: www.capjuluca.com

U.S. Reservations: (888) 8–Juluca; fax (305) 935–3780

Owner/Manager: Cap Juluca Holdings, Inc., owner; Dion Friedland, chairman of the board; Eustace Guishard, general manager

Arrival/Departure: Anguilla is reached via scheduled air service from San Juan (50 minutes) or St. Martin (5 minutes) or via ferry from Marigot in French St. Martin (25 minutes). Guests are met on arrival.

Distance from Wallblake Airport: 8 miles (15 minutes)

Distance from Marigot, St. Martin: 8 miles (25 minutes by ferry); 5 miles from the valley

Accommodations: 58 luxury rooms and junior suites; 7 suites; 6 pool villas

Most Romantic Room/Suite: For privacy try the end units: Pool Villa 19 and a room or suite in Villa Building 12.

Amenities: Air-conditioning, ceiling fans, private walled terrace, toiletries, refrigerator, stocked minibar, kitchen in villas

Electricity: 110/220 volts

Sports and Facilities: 3 Omni-surface tennis courts (2 lighted), croquet, sailboarding, waterskiing, snorkeling, scuba diving, Hobie-Cats, Sunfishes; Olympic-size pool, 6 villa pools, 3 miles of beach; extra charge for use of 32-foot motor cruiser; massages

Dress Code: Casually elegant and sophisticated; no jacket or tie required

Weddings: Can be arranged

Rates/Packages: $420–$1,820 per couple (spring/fall); $325–$935 (summer); $735–$2,115 (winter); includes continental breakfast on your patio, tennis, water sports, entertainment, use of fitness center, tea.

Payment/Credit Cards: Most major

Deposit: Three-night deposit within 14 days

Government Taxes: 8 percent (except for package where tax is included)

Service Charges: 10 percent (except for package where service charge is included)

Entry Requirements for U.S. Citizens: Return ticket and proof of citizenship required; passport best

Closed: Early September–late October.

CURTAIN BLUFF
Antigua

If there is a pot of gold at the end of one of Antigua's most winding, bumpy roads, it has to be Curtain Bluff. It's worth every torturous mile it takes to get you to this superb little resort, which seduces you from the moment you arrive. Consistently rated as one of the best resorts in the Caribbean for almost forty years, Curtain Bluff rises from a narrow peninsula between two beaches, marking the place where the Caribbean and Atlantic meet, and giving you nonstop ocean views from every room. Bougainvillea, hibiscus, oleander, royal palms, and every other tropical flower you can think of line walkways, hug buildings, and fall in great clouds of blossoms from trellises and walls. And wherever you go, you never lose sight of the sea.

Some of the two-story buildings are spread out along the beach whereas the villa suites climb gently up the slope of the peninsula. At the top of the bluff sits the home of the owner, Howard Hulford. It's the crown to Curtain Bluff's string of pink and white buildings and the site of weddings as well as cocktail receptions honoring Curtain Bluff's guests.

There was nothing much on the land when Hulford bought the property, but he brought seeds and cuttings from plants he liked from everywhere, started his own nursery, and soon had the grounds flourishing with palms, flowering shrubs, and other tropical plants. Today Hulford says he enjoys spending at least an hour a day tending to his fledgling seedlings and newly grafted shrubs. This attention to detail by a man who once flew planes for a living is just part of the story and helps explain the beauty and seductive influence Hulford and his beautiful wife, Chelle, have created at Curtain Bluff.

All the rooms and suites are decorated with impeccably good taste by Chelle in soft pastels and natural textures—clay pots, baskets filled with flowers, red tile, and an abundance of plants and real art. Rooms are airy and large with spacious patios, rattan furniture, puffy pillows, and natural fiber rugs on the Italian-tile floors. Large sliding doors, which glide like butter, open onto a spacious, well-furnished seaside patio. Ceiling fans (even in some bathrooms) along with louvered side windows let the sea breezes slip in and keep the rooms fresh and pleasantly cool. There is no air-conditioning, nor is it needed.

White walls and high, vaulted cedar ceilings distinguish the executive multilevel suites. In addition to the seaside patio, there is another, flower-filled open-air patio with walls just high enough to give you total privacy. A roomy hammock big enough for two is slung across a corner. A dining area, bedroom, bath, and another patio are located on the top level.

All the suite bathrooms are large and luxurious, with lots of tile and marble. They boast twin vanities, endless shelf space, a bidet, a walk-in, no-curtain shower, and a large tub.

Dining is on an open terrace, where a band plays every evening. Dance under a spreading tamarind tree and a canopy of stars. Chef Christophe Blatz is adept at preparing delicious American and European cuisine. Ingredients are the freshest you can find in the Caribbean: Fish is delivered every day and is filleted right on the property.

Curtain Bluff has an impressive 25,000-bottle cellar. Dust off a bottle of 1983 Louis Roederer Cristal and toast your bride, or try a bottle of '83 Dom Perignon or an '81 Taittinger Brut Reserve.

On Wednesdays you can warm up to reggae at the beach party, which is held at the bay beach. Lunch is served at the beachfront restaurant, where a lavish buffet

tempts you with salads, fish, pasta, and meat dishes. Or, if you want to eat in the privacy of your room or on your patio, just order room service. It's all included in the price.

Straddling the peninsula, the two beaches offer something for everyone. The waters off the ¾-mile beach on the Caribbean side are calm, gentle, and great for swimming. You can sailboard, snorkel, sail, or just laze away the hours on the beach. On the other side the Atlantic stirs up more surf and the winds beckon to sailors and those looking for a little more excitement. A swimming pool, overlooking the bay beach, has a seating area in the water.

Tennis is big here, with four superbly maintained Laykold courts. Lessons, clinics, round-robins, tournaments, and just friendly play keep the action rolling. There's a good-size stadium for spectators to watch their favorite players as well as a squash court and a croquet field.

The fitness center is well equipped with Trotter treadmills, steppers, and the latest in health and fitness equipment. Aerobics classes are held on an adjacent deck.

There are no TVs in the rooms, but there is Television House, perched high on stilts near the tennis courts and fitness center. Guests gather here to watch events like the Super Bowl and the Kentucky Derby.

The ages and interests of guests range from older, well-heeled traditionalists to active, younger couples. You'll see a lot of Brits here, especially during January and February.

At first glance Curtain Bluff may seem a bit pricey at $4,500 to $6,000 for a week (in the deluxe rooms). But everything is included (except wine by the bottle), even the scuba diving and the deep-sea fishing. Curtain Bluff is for those who love a beautiful, warm place by the sea where they can get away and totally unwind while a superb, dedicated group of people see to it that nothing interferes with this vision of what paradise should be.

Each year Curtain Bluff closes down for five months in order to refurbish and refresh. Perhaps this is one reason nothing here ever looks tired or worn. A recent addition on the beach contains glamorous suites.

Curtain Bluff

Location: Situated on Antigua's south shore, on a private peninsula jutting out into the water

Romantic Highlights: Dancing under the stars; hammocks for two on your own private patio (executive suites)

Address/Phone: P.O. Box 288, Antigua, West Indies; (268) 462–8400; fax (268) 462–8409

Web Site: www.curtainbluff.com

U.S. Reservations: (888) 289–9898 or (212) 289–8888

Owner/Manager: Howard W. Hulford, owner and chairman, board of directors; Robert S. Sherman, managing director; Calvert A. Roberts, general manager

Arrival/Departure: Taxi to and from airport. Local regulations prevent hotel from sending drivers.

Distance from V. C. Bird International Airport: 15 miles (35 minutes)

Distance from St. John's: 9 miles

Accommodations: 63 rooms and suites with king-size beds, all with terraces and all overlooking the sea: 51 deluxe rooms, the Terrace Room with four-poster king-size bed, 5 one-bedroom suites, 1 junior suite, and 5 executive/deluxe rooms, as well as a Presidential Suite

Most Romantic Room/Suite: The Terrace Room, with its huge terrace, and the one-bedroom suites

Amenities: Hair dryer, wall safe, ceiling fans, bathrobes, telephone, fresh flowers daily, minibars in suites

Electricity: 110 volts

Sports and Facilities: 4 tennis courts, squash court, putting green, swimming pool, fitness center; waterskiing, sailboarding, scuba diving, snorkeling, sailing, croquet, deep-sea fishing, swimming, aerobics (land and water)

Dress Code: Ties for men, even in peak season, are optional at dinner. Jackets are required except on Sunday and Wednesday at peak season.

Weddings: Can be arranged

Rates/Packages: All-inclusive rates include accommodations, 3 meals daily, all bar drinks, afternoon tea, hors d'oeuvres, tennis, weekly beach party, entertainment, mail service, and water sports including scuba diving. $750–$1,525 per couple per night (mid-December to mid-April); $555–$1,055 per couple per night (mid-October to mid-December and mid-April to mid-May).

Payment/Credit Cards: American Express, Visa, MasterCard, personal check, traveler's check

Deposit: 3-night deposit

Government Taxes: 8.5 percent

Service Charges: 10 percent

Entry Requirements for U.S. Citizens: Passport

Closed: mid-May–late October

HYATT REGENCY ARUBA RESORT & CASINO
Aruba

When you get to Aruba, don't bother trying to find a weather report in any local newspaper or on the TV. You won't find one, because the weather never changes. All they need to do is to put up a permanent sign: ABOUT 82 TO 83 DEGREES. CLEAR BLUE CARIBBEAN SKIES WITH AN OCCASIONAL PUFFY WHITE CLOUD SHAPED LIKE POPCORN FLOATING BY, WINDS ABOUT 16 MILES PER HOUR; AND NO RAIN. IF ANYTHING'S GONNA CHANGE, WE'LL CALL YOU. This is just one reason Aruba is one of the more popular island destinations.

There are a lot of hotels here, most of them lined up along the broad, white Palm Beach, which stretches along the southwestern coast for several miles. An all-around good choice for romantics is the Hyatt Regency Aruba Resort & Casino. It's got a lot going for it.

As you check in and feel Aruba's famous trade winds blowing through the expansive, open-air lobby, you'll feel you've wandered back to a classic time of luxury and elegance. There are magnificent chandeliers, wooden beams, Oriental rugs, and frescoes on the walls and ceil-

ings. A sense of Aruban history pervades this relatively new resort: The architecture of the Hyatt borrows from the 1899 Gold Smelting Works of Balashi and Bushiribana on the North Coast of Aruba. The grounds, more lush than the rest of this desert island, do not disappoint.

Just off the lobby, walkways curve down toward the beach along waterfalls and the hotel's cascading, three-tiered pool—check out the two-story water slide. There's also a 5,000-square-foot pool stocked with tropical fish, and there are large aviaries of exotic birds. Here in this lush landscape, you'll find plenty of secluded areas in which to bask in the sun as well as larger patios if you wish to mingle.

The Hyatt's pools end where Aruba's white, sandy Palm Beach begins. The trade winds keep the temperature at a comfortable level, allowing you to loll in the sun with a tropical drink from one of the Hyatt's outdoor bars or to enjoy the shade at one of the resort's thatch-umbrella tables. If you want to be more active, you can join in a game of beach volleyball or go parasailing, scuba diving, sailboarding—something Aruba is known for—or simply float on a raft in the 80-degree Caribbean Sea.

In addition to offering the usual water sports, the hotel's Red Sail Sports Center also features Balia catamaran cruises, canoe rentals, scuba diving, and sunset cruises.

While the turquoise water welcomes visitors with its gently rolling waves on this side of the island, you should pay a visit to the northeastern coast, where rough waves crash in, carving out craggy cliffs. Here the remains of the island's original inhabitants, such as tools and hieroglyphics left in chalk caves, together with twisting rock formations, lend a historical, desert-island feel to Aruba. The windswept, native divi divi trees lean over in 45-degree angles like giant bonsai trees; iguanas perched on rocks, and cacti complete the picture. Land tours of the island are readily available and can be arranged through the Hyatt.

A sporting way to explore the desert landscape is to play a round of golf on Aruba's newly built Tierra del Sol, a championship golf course designed by Robert Trent Jones Jr. Located at the base of the island's California Lighthouse, the course is distinctly Aruban in its landscape. All but three holes offer a panoramic view of the Caribbean as you play this challenging course. Built to complement the terrain, the roughs can be nasty. Errant balls find trouble in the form of cacti, divi divi, and native desert grasses; hit it straight and you'll land in wonderfully

Hyatt Regency Aruba Resort & Casino

Location: On Aruba's historic Palm Beach, known for its white, sandy beaches and turquoise waters, on the southwestern coast of Aruba, 14 miles off the coast of Venezuela

Romantic Highlights: Terraces overlooking the Caribbean; walking along the white-sand beach under the moonlight; Sunset Service (watching the sun go down while you're served hors d'oeuvres and wines by a tuxedoed waiter)

Address/Phone: L. G. Smith Boulevard, Number 85, Palm Beach, Aruba; 2978–61234; fax 2978–61682

U.S. Reservations: (800) 233–1234

Owner/Manager: Barry Kaplan, general manager

Arrival/Departure: Taxis and car rentals available at airport

Distance from Queen Beatrix Airport: 7 miles

Distance from Oranjestad: 2 miles

Accommodations: 360 rooms, including 17 suites, 1 Regency Club floor, and 1 Governor's Suite

Most Romantic Room/Suite: Suites overlooking the Caribbean

Amenities: Air-conditioning, ceiling fans, minibar, cable TV, direct-dial telephone with voice-activated dialing, in-room safe, coffeemaker, radio, hair dryer, toiletries, room service

Electricity: 110 volts

Sports and Facilities: Sailing, snorkeling, sailboarding, deep-sea fishing, 2 lighted tennis courts, volleyball, golf, beach, pools, health and fitness club

Dress Code: Casual

Weddings: Can be arranged

Rates/Packages: $400–$500 per room (winter); $215–$335 (spring, summer, and fall). "Honeymoon Romance" package (per couple): $1,275, 4 days, 3 nights; $2,507, 8 days, 7 nights, including accommodations, champagne, breakfast for two on first morning, sunset cruise, massage for two, jeep rental for 1 day, snorkel/sail with lunch on 53-foot catamaran, gratuities included for food and beverage items, service charges, taxes, and clothing discount at Red Sail Sports; scuba-diving packages also available

Payment/Credit Cards: Most major

Deposit: Reservations must be secured with deposit within 14 days of verbal confirmation; refundable if cancellation received in writing no later than October 1 for arrivals during Christmas season, 14 days in advance for all other periods

Government Taxes: 6.5 percent, included in honeymoon plan

Service Charges: Included for items on honeymoon plan

Entry Requirements for U.S. Citizens: Proof of citizenship; passport best

lush, watered fairways. The Hyatt offers reserved tee times for guests, and clubs can be rented at a reasonable fee.

Dining at the Hyatt gives you a number of options for a variety of tastes. There's Cafe Japengo, an island hot spot serving nigri sushi and rolls, maki, temaki sushi, sa Res, and other Asian-inspried food and drinks; Cafe Piccolo, an Italian cafe specializing in regional cuisine; Ruinas del Mar, featuring continental cuisine; and Palms, a casual restaurant serving Caribbean cuisine. Especially appealing is to dine at one of the cozy tables located out among the fountains and weeping walls of the Spanish-influenced hotel building—perfect for special romantic evenings.

Nightly entertainment is not forgotten. The resort's lively Casino Copacabana beckons to those who want to try their hand at blackjack, roulette, craps, or the slots. Bands play for dancing, and entertainment is regularly featured.

With 360 rooms, this is not your small, intimate hotel. It is, however, a superb choice if you're looking for lovely accommodations in a tropical sun and sand destination. It's one of Hyatt's winners.

With a reputation for being squeaky-clean and safe, Aruba is popular among honeymooners. Only those bent on finding an island with a colorful, native culture with lots going on locally (politics, industry, working farms, sugar and banana plantations, etc.) may be disappointed. Aruba's main business is tourism; its hotels and casinos are where you'll find most of the action.

OUR LUCAYA
Freeport, The Bahamas

Our Lucaya, which lives like three smaller resorts on one "campus," is breathing fresh air into the resort scene on Grand Bahama Island. Until about the late 1990s, Grand Bahama Island, which lies north of the smaller, more populated island of New Providence, home of Nassau and Paradise Island, appeared to be stuck in the '60s when most of the hotels were built. Although attempts had been made over the years to renovate properties like the Lucayan, Grand Bahama was rather like a thirtieth class reunion trying hard to hold in its stomach. Still, it was popular with cruise passengers for its duty-free shopping, gamblers who could have cared less if the sun never came up, and golfers who enjoyed playing a handful of good courses.

Recently I came here again, this time to check out a highly touted new $400 million resort, Our Lucaya, along with a new golf course designed by Robert Trent Jones Jr. From the time I checked in at the gracious colonial-style Manor House reception area and slid the plastic card into the slot to open the door to my bright, cheerful room, I was impressed. Our Lucaya is indeed a brand new resort that promises to raise the bar when it comes to resorts on Grand Bahama Island.

Our Lucaya is part of a huge development project by Hutchinson Whampoa Limited, a Hong Kong–based, multinational conglomerate, to turn the island into a major resort destination. In addition to the resort and new golf course, there is the well-established Lucayan Country Club, within a five-minute shuttle of the resort.

Our Lucaya is big; in fact it's largest resort in the Caribbean. It sits on 372 acres on the site once occupied by the Lucayan Beach Hotel, the Grand Bahama Beach Hotel, and an adjacent vacant beachfront site. Its 1,350 rooms are located in three building clusters spread out along the Atlantic coastline. (Technically, the chain of the Bahamas islands, which starts off the eastern coast of Florida, is located in the Atlantic, not in the Caribbean, even though for marketing reasons, the islands are often identified with the latter.)

At the southern end of the broad white-sand beach is Reef Village, a low-rise complex with a child-friendly pool, waterfall, and kids' club—definitely the place where most of the families stay. Reef Village rooms are decorated in bright greens, yellows, oranges, and blues and many have views of the sea.

Next door is Breakers Cay, a pyramidal high-rise building containing the most rooms (579). The decor is cheerfully bright but a bit toned down in color intensity from the Reef. Most rooms have balconies, some very large. Next up the beach is a group of twenty-five lanai suites that fan out toward the beach. Decorated in tasteful neutrals with plenty of marble and natural woods, these accommodations, the most luxurious of all and the most expensive, are popular for romantic getaway vacations.

At the northern end of the property, Lighthouse Pointe is for folks who desire more privacy, quieter quarters, and nonstop water views. The 25,000-square-foot Senses Spa and Spa Cafe are located here along with the extensive exercise facilities. A variety of treatments include submerged massages, rain massage, sports massage, and hydro baths. A stunning infinity pool parallels the beach just steps away.

The Fitness Center is equipped with treadmills, bikes, elliptical machines, and spinning V bikes. Personal trainers are on hand to assist guests with fitness routines.

Throughout the resort, there are various restaurants and lounges, fourteen in all, ranging from the elegant Churchill's Chophouse offering gourmet fare and the seaside China Beach to the Havana Cay Cigar Bar and the Prop Club, an outdoor sports bar and club. Barracudas is a '50s-themed eatery, and Arawak offers fine continental and Bahamian cuisine.

I was especially impressed with Willy Broadleaf's, a world marketplace buffet medley where several stations feature cuisine from Mexico, Italy, Africa, and other world destinations. There's no way you can go there even for breakfast and stick to the basics. I started with my usual yogurt, fruit, and juice and went back for cheese quesadillas, falafel, fried plantains, a freshly made omelet loaded with goodies, a bowl of oatmeal that someone said was the greatest (I love oatmeal), and a small helping of spicy cubed potatoes fried with veggies. And, oh yes, some beignets hot from the kitchen. You'd think after all that I'd skip lunch. No way. The menu at Portobello's, an Italian/Mediterranean bistro, was just too tempting.

The newest addition to the resort, a 30,000-square-foot casino with thirty tables including baccarat, black-jack,Caribbean stud poker, and roulette plus 400 slots and sports gaming.

Everything is beautifully integrated by gardens, ribbons of winding paths, and covered walkways. You have a choice: Sit on the beach and swim in the ocean or splash around in one of a trio of stunning pools.

Throughout my stay, I saw no one running out before breakfast to throw a towel on a lounge to save it, no buffet lines, no panic to reserve a favorite spot at the pool. Our Lucaya has enough deck space, enough chairs, and places to eat to accommodate everyone comfortably.

While you are on the island, I recommend a dolphin encounter with The Underwater Explorers Society (UNEXCO). You get to the protected harbor where the dolphins hang out by boat. As your boat approaches the cove you may see, close by, a smaller boat running alongside. Suddenly two dolphins rise out of the water and perform a high arc in perfect unison in the air before splashing back into the water. It whets your appetite for more dolphin fun. Arriving at UNEXCO's Sanctuary Bay, you'll get a crash course on dolphins and enter the water where you can stroke the animals, who seems to like a good rub as much as people do. The more daring can swim with the dolphins holding onto the flippers while they pull you into shore. Divers also have the opportunity to dive with dolphins in the open Atlantic.

Grand Bahama is a much quieter place than Nassau; in fact, outside Our Lucaya, there isn't much going on unless you want to shop, kayak through the mangroves at Gold Rock Creek, or explore limestone caves at the Lucayan National Park.

Our Lucaya

Location: Sprawled along a 7½ mile ribbon of white sandy beach, 55 miles east of Miami on Grand Bahama Island, one of the largest of the 700 Bahamian islands

Romantic Highlights: Views from rooms and balconies of white sand and water

Address/Phone: Royal Palm Way, F42500 Freeport, Grand Bahama Island, Bahamas; (242) 373-1333; fax (242) 373–8804

E-mail: reservations@ourlucaya.com

Web Site: www.ourlucaya.com

U.S. Reservations: (877) OUR–LUCAYA

Owner/Manager: Hutchinson Whampoa Limited, owner; Peter Schmidt, general manager

Arrival/Departure: Jet service and commuter flights offered by several carriers; just a 35-minute flight from Miami International Airport; 2½ hours from New York

Distance from Grand Bahama International Airport: 25 minutes

Distance from Freeport: In Freeport

Accommodations: 1,350 rooms and suites: 550 in Reef Village; 579 in Breakers Cay; 221 rooms and 25 Lanai suites in Lighthouse Pointe

Most Romantic Room/Suite: Lanai suites. Then there is the two-story Lucaya Suite that comes with a personal butler, a wraparound veranda, and a price tag of $5,500 per night.

Amenities: Air-conditioning, hair dryer, refrigerator, dataports, in-room safe, telephone, TV, toiletries

Electricity: 110 volts

Sports and Facilities: Senses Spa & Fitness Center, 2 golf courses, 3 freshwater pools, snorkeling, water skiing, kayaking, sailing, 4 tennis courts, basketball, sand volleyball, and horseshoes; UNEXSO dolphin encounters can be arranged

Dress Code: Resort casual

Weddings: Can be arranged

Rates/Packages: From $140 per room, per night; a romance package priced from $499 per couple including 2 nights' accommodations, breakfast, champagne, candlelight dinner, tax and service charges, and room upgrade if available

Payment/Credit Cards: Most major

Deposit: Credit card

Government Taxes: $18 departure tax at airport

Service Charges: Included

Entry Requirements for U.S. Citizens: Proof of citizenship; passport best

SANDALS ROYAL BAHAMIAN RESORT & SPA
Nassau, The Bahamas

It's couples-only at this European-style Sandals where the elegance factor in this pink-and-white confection has been turned up several notches with huge Palladian windows, tons of marble, chandeliers, frescoed ceilings, fountains, and pillars everywhere.

If all those pillars that seem to float on the water and the huge, rather fearsome statue of Neptune that greets you at the entrance seem a bit excessive, the overall impression is nevertheless one of opulence and grandeur. Hard to argue with that.

Sandals Royal Bahamian has three large pools and two private minipools. Located in the middle of every-

thing, the heated main pool comes with Jacuzzis, waterfalls, a swim-up bar, and even Neptune himself, spouting a stream of water out of his mouth. For cooling off you can sit under the misting pool.

Work up a sweat in the Fitness Center on the penthouse level using snazzy exercise equipment like Lifecycles, exercise bicycles, stairclimbers, treadmills, and Cybex/Universal weights, and show up for poolside aerobics classes.

Although the resort is located on the sea and has a moderate-size beach, the best beach is found on Sandals Cay, a private island reached by water shuttle just a half mile offshore. Besides the wonderful white sand, there is

a pool with a swim-up bar, a Jacuzzi, and the Cafe Goombay. Sandals also offers a full range of water sports, including scuba diving.

Accommodations range from beachfront rooms in The Manor House to villas and suites. You can choose from twelve different styles of rooms and suites. The ultra-luxurious Beachfront Royal Windsor Suite features a separate living room, oversize vanity, 27-inch color TV, Roman soaking tub, Italian-tile floors, and incredible views of the beach from the balcony. Some suites even come with 24-hour butler service and a VIP Rolls Royce limo ride to and from the airport.

Furnishings are traditional and elegant, with hand-carved mahogany four-poster king-size beds, flowing flowered fabrics, and comfortable upholstered chairs. Many rooms have balconies or patios.

There will be no need to go off the property when it comes to dining choices: Sandals Royal Bahamian has eight restaurants, ranging from the dazzling crystal room and French-inspired Baccarat restaurant to Spices, serving a medley of Caribbean and Mediterranean-inspired dishes. And there is the popular and casual Cricketers. If Cricketers looks like an authentic English pub, that's because it is; much of the interior was brought here piece by piece from Great Britain.

For late-nighters there is entertainment and a disco. The brash, neon-lit Carnival Resort and Casino, just down the road, is far enough away not to impinge on the romantic mood, yet close enough for those who want a night out to gamble.

For total pampering you can head to the 6,000-square-foot spa, where you'll find a wide choice of European-style services and treatments. Kur baths, Finnish saunas, reflexology, aromatherapy, deep-cleansing facials, and much more are offered here and are about the only items not included in Sandals's all-inclusive price.

Sandals Royal Bahamian Resort & Spa

Location: Cable Beach, Nassau, Bahamas

Romantic Highlights: Nonstop activities; one super spa; cooling off under the misting pool; sipping a deliciously wicked "Sex-on-the-Beach" at the resort's private island; free weddings

Address/Phone: P.O. Box CB-13005, Cable Beach, Nassau, Bahamas; (242) 327–6400; fax (242) 327–6961

U.S. Reservations: (800) SANDALS

Owner/Manager: Stephen Ziadie, general manager

Arrival/Departure: Sandals guests are met at the airport and escorted to the resort.

Distance from Airport: 15 minutes

Distance from Nassau: 5 minutes

Accommodations: 406 rooms, suites, and villas

Most Romantic Room/Suite: Grande Luxe Oceanfront rooms in The Manor House

Amenities: Air-conditioning, king-size beds, ceiling fans, hair dryer, generous kits of lotions and shampoo, telephone, clock radio, color TV, and safe; suites also with fully stocked wet bars, terry robes, and *New York Times* faxes

Electricity: 110 volts

Sports and Facilities: 3 freshwater pools, 2 mini-pools, 5 whirlpools, 2 tennis courts, fitness center, scuba diving, snorkeling, sailboarding, sailing, paddleboats, canoes, kayaks, golf (nearby), pool/billiard tables, volleyball, shuffleboard, croquet, waterskiing, full-service spa (services and treatments are extra)

Dress Code: Casual

Weddings: On-site wedding coordinators arrange all the details, including taking care of the paperwork, leading the couple through the process of getting the marriage license, flowers, music, and reception. "WeddingMoons"—Sandals's term—can be as intimate as a couple getting married in a horse-drawn carriage or under a gazebo with a best man and attendant "borrowed" from the Sandals staff, or it can be an even more elaborate affair, with a reception for a couple's family and friends. Stay 5 nights or more and weddings are free.

Rates/Packages: All-inclusive rates start at $335 per person

Payment/Credit Cards: Most major

Deposit: Guarantee with credit card

Government Taxes: Included

Service Charges: Included

Entry Requirements for U.S. Citizens: Proof of citizenship; passport best

OCEAN CLUB
Paradise Island, The Bahamas

From the moment you are greeted with a bubbling glass of fine champagne by warm, hospitable people, you know your honeymoon at this small, intimate resort on Paradise Island is off to a good start.

Once part of billionaire Huntington Hartford's holdings, the Ocean Club just continues to get better without losing its sense of intimacy and elegance.

Since Sun International acquired the property in 1995, this little jewel has seen some changes including a new seaside restaurant, Dune, as well as a new spa, championship golf course, and ongoing room renovations, all costing a cool $100 million. Always fresh and quietly exclusive, the Ocean Club continually burnishes its reputation for providing guests with superb service and luxurious accommodations appealing to those seeking European ambience in a tropical setting.

Whether you are staying in one of the oceanfront rooms or suites in the new Crescent Wing, a room in the Hartford Wing, or one of the spacious villas, youa re sure to be pampered by the kinds of services and amenities Croesus would have desired. Regal, king-size beds, softly colored pastel linens and fabrics, sink-in-your-toes carpeting, noiseless central air-conditioning, designer ceiling fans, stocked minibars, and 27-inch TVs are just the beginning. Bathrooms have state-of-the-art appointments with imported marble, tile vanities, bidets, scales, and many other features you'd expect to find in fine European hotels, right down to the customized toiletries and bottled water. And something you probably wouldn't find across the "pond"—irons and ironing boards!

But that's not the total picture. Add twenty-four–hour room service, a maid who cleans your rooms three times a day, complimentary shoeshines, free shuttle transportation on Paradise Island, use of the bicycles, and a wonderful fruit basket in your room and you have a pretty good idea of what's yet to come.

One of the unique features of the Ocean Club is the terraced Versailles Gardens flanked by beautiful old trees, tropical flowers, and shrubs that are tiered like a wedding cake up a gentle hillside. At the top is a thirteenth-century

French cloister that was imported from Europe and rebuilt stone by stone by Hartford. With its marble columns, arches, and statues, it is a lovely place to relax and enjoy the beauty of the gardens and the sea. (It's also a great place to have a wedding ceremony.)

For tennis players there are nine Har-Tru courts, lighted for night play and free to guests, a teaching pro, and a well-equipped pro shop. For pool loungers there is a pool adjacent to both the tennis courts and a delightfyul open-air restaurant serving lunch and cocktails. The soft, white, sandy beach, one of the prettiest in the Bahamas, is set in a protected cove lined with palms and tropical plants. A new full-service spa offers a varitey of rejuvenating treatments.

With the opening of the totally rebuilt Ocean Club golf course at the end of 2000, golf in the Bahamas was brought to an entirely new level. When Tom Weiskopf designed his brilliant links-style course, he made sure the crystalline sea was hardly ever out of sight. Here water, sand, and wind play key roles. Cart paths snake through the fairways, tall palms poke up into the sky, and bunkers with deep, soft, white sand lie in wait everywhere.

Breakfast, lunch, and dinner are served in the chic new Dune beachfront restaurant created by Internationally renowned chef and restauranteur Jean-Georges Vongerichten. Serving as a focal point, the kitchen is encased in transparent blue glass, reflecting and mirroring the blue of the sky and the water and geometrical designs around the room. The cuisine makes good use of the fresh local produce and seafood as well as herbs grown on the property. Menu choices reveal a Pacific Rim influence but are international in scope.

You couldn't ask for a more seductive place to dine than the Courtyard Terrace restaurant, an outdoor venue where tables are arranged around fountains and gardens. With such a setting you'd almost be willing to accept the most mundane of meals. But this is not necessary here. This restaurant is known for serving some of the finest cuisine in the islands. The a la carte menu features items such as Beluga caviar, homemade soups, lobster medallions with a warm sauce surrounded by local vegetables, chateaubriand for two, and a superb chocolate mousse.

For a casual drink by the sea, there is a bar set into the hill overlooking the beach.

Because Sun International owns about 75 percent of Paradise Island, you are close to the action, glitter, and glitz of the megasize Atlantis, located less than a mile down the road. At the Atlantis there are twelve different restaurants and a 30,000-square-foot casino complete with Las Vegas–style shows. The casino is open twenty-four hours a day for the slot machines and from 10:00 A.M. to 4:00 P.M. for the gaming tables. If you crave some action, this is the place to come, courtesy of the Ocean Club, which runs a free shuttle every half-hour until midnight.

Ocean Club

Location: On Paradise Island off the northern edge of Nassau, New Providence Island

Romantic Highlights: Terraced Cloister Gardens; seaside dining in the Dune; massages in the open-air oceanfront pavilion; hammocks for two; fountains and gardens

Address/Phone: P.O. Box N4–777, Nassau, Bahamas; (242) 363–2501; fax (242) 363-2424

E-mail: info@oceanclub.com

Web Site: www.oceanclub.com

U.S. Reservations: Sun International, (800) 321–3000

Owner/Manager: Sun International Bahamas, Ltd., owner; Jean Luc Naret, general manager

Arrival/Departure: Paradise Island Airlines leaves from Miami, Ft. Lauderdale, and West Palm Beach twice a day and lands 5 minutes from the Ocean Club. Delta, Kiwi, American, and United also fly into Nassau. Transfers can be arranged.

Distance from Paradise Island Airport: 1 mile (5 minutes); Nassau International Airport, 15 minutes

Distance from Nassau: 3 miles (10–15 minutes)

Accommodations: The Crescent Wing features 40 beachfront rooms and 10 suites; the Hartford Wing features 50 rooms, 4 suites, and 5 two-bedroom garden villas.

Most Romantic Room/Suite: Suites overlooking ocean

Amenities: Hair dryer, toiletries, central air-conditioning, ceiling fans, iron and ironing board, 27-inch TV, DVD/CD player, bathrobes, scales, safe, bidet, minibar; 24-hour room service, laundry and valet service

Electricity: 110 volts

Sports and Facilities: 9 Har-Tru lighted tennis courts, 18-hole golf course, spa, sailing, swimming, snorkeling, Aquacat sailing, kayaking, cycling, croquet

Dress Code: Casual day; jackets required for dinner at Courtyard Terrace

Weddings: Can be arranged

Rates/Packages: $450–$975 per room, per night; $750–$1,750 for suites; $900–$1,390 for two-bedroom villas.

Payment/Credit Cards: Most major

Deposit: 2 nights' room rate deposit; cancellation 15 days or more prior to arrival, no charge

Government Taxes: 10 percent room tax; $15 departure tax at airport; ask about honeymoon packages

Service Charges: $3 housekeeping gratuity

Entry Requirements for U.S. Citizens: Proof of citizenship; passport best

COBBLERS COVE
Barbados

Not quite as opulent as some of its more pricey neighbors on Barbados's western coast, still Cobblers Cove is a jewel of a place: small and casual, yet lovely enough to be wildly romantic. It's the kind of place couples look for when they want to get away and simply enjoy each other for a serene few days. Cobblers is very British in feeling; not slick, not elaborate, just an easy, laid-back kind of place. It offers water sports as well as tennis, but although you'll find Cobblers to be very friendly, no one tries to organize your time or urge you to play volleyball.

The hotel is located on only three acres, and you don't have to go very far to find anything. Water sports? A quick snack or the resort's famous bar drink, the Cobbler's Cooler? Everything's right there.

Each of the ten two-story, pink-and-white cottages has four suites with sitting rooms and louvered-window walls that open onto terraces or patios. The cottages and the main reception building and restaurant sit amid tropical gardens near the sea. Each suite, decorated in cheery colors, comes with a kitchenette, bamboo and contemporary white furniture, and good-size closets. Although many of the suites are not right on the water, it's still hard to find a "bad" room here. For the most privacy ask for the rooms to the left of the clubhouse (as you're facing the water). Those on the other side mostly overlook the gardens and lawns, where some people like to sit and sunbathe. The upper suites have peaked ceilings and better views.

If you really want to splurge, book the Camelot Suite, which is aptly named. This bilevel little spot of heaven, appropriately decorated in blues and whites, has a massive white four-poster king-size canopied bed; a spacious sitting room; a huge bathroom with whirlpool tub; twin sinks; white marble floors; and luxurious, upholstered chaise and chairs. Climb the spiral stairway to your private pool on the furnished deck above, where you'll also find a wet bar and nonstop views.

The 1,780-square-foot Colleton Suite, located in the west turret of the Plantation House, delivers total luxury. It has a huge bathroom with a Jacuzzi and neck massage facility, separate sitting room, and bedroom with canopied Empress-size bed. French doors lead onto an expansive sun terrace, where the views are what dreams are made of.

The resort's kidney-shaped pool is not large, so if you find it a little too populated for your taste, all you have to do is walk about eight steps to one of the loveliest and quietest beaches in Barbados. For the more active there are complimentary tennis, waterskiing, sailboarding, sailing, and snorkeling right off the beach. The hotel will also make arrangements for you if you want to go deep-sea fishing, play golf, or take an island excursion.

Jennen's at Cobblers Cove is right by the sea. Here you can enjoy some of the best cuisine on the island, if not the Caribbean. You'll have meals to write home about—guaranteed. European-trained chefs offer new choices every day. The emphasis is on Caribbean specialties with lots of fresh fish, fruits, and vegetables. You can sit on the open-air terrace right by the water and watch the sunset. Music and other entertainment are provided on various nights during the week.

Cobblers Cove

Location: On west coast of Babados

Romantic Highlights: Friendly, laid-back ambience; lovely beach

Address/Phone: Road View, St. Peter, Barbados; (246) 422–2291; fax (246) 422–1460

E-mail: cobblers@caribsurf.com

U.S. Reservations: Relais & Châteaux (800) RELAIS–8 or (212) 856–0115; fax (212) 856–0193; Karen Bull Associates, (800) 890–6060; fax (404) 237–1841

Owner/Manager: Hamish Watson, general manager

Arrival/Departure: Arrangements can be made for transfer from the airport for a fee; it's included in some package rates.

Distance from Barbados International Airport: 18 miles (45 minutes)

Distance from Bridgetown: 12 miles (25 minutes)

Accommodations: 40 suites, including 2 multilevel luxury suites with pools

Most Romantic Room/Suite: The Colleton Suite and the Camelot Suite are to die for; otherwise go for the Sea View, second-story suites.

Amenities: Air-conditioning, ceiling fans, direct-dial telephone, stocked minibar, hair dryer, bathrobes, drying rack, toiletries, ice service, in-room safe; radio and TV can be arranged on request; room service from 8:00 A.M. to 9:00 P.M.

Electricity: 110/220 volts

Sports and Facillities: Tennis, sailboarding, waterskiing, snorkeling, swimming at pool or beach, Sunfishes, and a new Keep Fit exercise room; extra charge for deep-sea fishing and scuba diving; gift shop

Dress Code: Casually elegant; jeans, shorts, and swimwear not allowed in bar after 7:00 P.M.

Weddings: In the staff's own words, "We help arrange it all, the ceremony, the champagne, and the cheers."

Rates/Packages: Suites $306–$459, no meals, plus $94 per person for breakfast or lunch and dinner (April–September); $371–$517, speciality suites $987–$2,115 (October–December).

Payment/Credit Cards: Most major

Deposit: Three-night deposit required in winter and spring; one-night deposit, summer and fall

Government Taxes: 7.5 percent VAT on accommodations; 15 percent VAT on food and beverages

Service Charges: Not included

Entry Requirements for U.S. Citizens: Return ticket and proof of citizenship required; passport best

CAMBRIDGE BEACHES
Bermuda

Cambridge Beaches, located on the western end of the island, has five Bermuda-pink pristine beaches and numerous little coves to discover that are tucked into the rocky ledges of the peninsula. With water on three sides, the resort's pink-and-white limestone cottages nestle into the nooks and crannies of the well-manicured tropical gardens above and along the shoreline. White roofs and louvers, mellow stone walls and steps that turn golden in the late-afternoon sun, and lush, flowering oleanders and hibiscus that have had many years to mature transform Cambridge Beaches into a magical world where dreams are made and fulfilled.

It's truly one of the world's premier hideaway resorts and one of Bermuda's most exclusive properties. There is a variety of rooms and suites, most with king-size beds and sitting areas, others with fireplaces, vaulted beamed ceilings, and French doors leading to large terraces and spectacular views of Long Bay, the Atlantic Ocean, or Mangrove Bay, dotted with sleek yachts riding at anchor, their stays slapping masts with low-pitched tings.

Rooms are individually decorated with cheerful English chintz fabrics in warm pinks, sunny golds, and blues; traditional Queen Anne furniture; and marble baths. Some of the larger suites feature charming antique pieces and extended grassy terraces; most have whirlpool tubs. Attractive scenes of Bermuda decorate the walls. You have your own terrace, where you can enjoy a cozy, private breakfast or dinner, and from your door it's only a short walk to the beaches.

The 275-year-old Great House, overlooking Mangrove Bay, shelters a gracious lobby furnished with Bermuda and English antiques—it has that comfortable "been here a long while" feel, yet decor is light and pleasant. An adjacent library is filled with books and English tea is served in the living room each afternoon.

Downstairs you'll find the elegant Tamarisk Restaurant, where the food is a work of art. The chef, Jean-Claude Garzia, has won the prestigious MOF (Meilleurs Ouvriers de France), awarded to just eighteen French chefs worldwide every five years. Your plate may be decorated with fans of fresh fruit, delicate lacy butterflies of chocolate, or swirls of raspberry sauce in a pool of vanilla custard. The menu also includes island-style items such as baby shrimp curry pie with a light banana sauce, bouillabaisse, and pan-fried tenderloin with a Chambertin red wine and truffle sauce—all superb, as are the pastries, breads, and ice cream, which are made in Cambridge's own Pastry Shop.

The recently redecorated Port O'Call Bar, with its cozy

fireplace, is a perfect spot to hide out when the weather is cool. A cable TV provides news and sports fans with the latest broadcasts.

For lunch and more casual dining, the Mangrove Bay Terrace invites you to dine and dance under trees and night sky. Wrought-iron chairs and tables are set on the stone terrace, where you can see the harbor from just about anywhere you sit. The resort's exchange dining program invites you to eat at five other properties at no extra charge.

Enjoy casual fare alfresco at the new Long Bay Cafe right on the water's edge at Long Bay Beach. Deep, burnished sunsets, endless stargazing, and soft surf make this a perfect place for special nights.

Water sports activities at the resort's private marina are a short stroll form the Main House. Rent a boat and explore the private islands just off the coast or head to nearby Turtle Cove beach, pick up the phone at the bottom of the steps, and order "room service." The resort has a number of boats you can use, including kayaks, sailboats, and motorboats. Cruise on a luxurious yacht, and watch the sunset while sipping a Sea Breeze.

Want to be pampered? Then treat yourself to a massage or facial at the Ocean Spa, where you can indulge in a choice of more than one hundred treatments and services. There's even a "His and Her" massage plus a special session designed for couples who wish to learn the art of massage. Relax by the lovely Ocean Spa pool, which is built under a retractable glass room—perfect for those cooler days or swim against the current in the Swimex spa pool.

If you can bear to leave the beach, check out the shops, art galleries, and other attractions in Hamilton. A free Cambridge Beaches ferry shuttles you to the city three times a week. You can explore Dockyard, located at this end of the island, or take a romantic horse-and-buggy ride in the nearby town of Somerset. Rent a moped or bicycle and ride off to discover the beauty of Bermuda. The speed limit on the island is 20 miles per hour, so you can really enjoy an easy, carefree spin.

At Cambridge Beaches entertainment is not forgotten. There is music for listening and dancing every evening in season. Apparently, the magic works. A big board, outside the dining room is filled with names of repeat guests. One couple came to Cambridge on their honeymoon in 1947 and have been coming back ever since; in all they've returned seventy-six times.

Cambridge Beaches

Location: On a 25–acre peninsula on Bermuda's western coast, near Somerset Village

Romantic Highlights: Dancing under the stars; boat ride to a private island for a picnic; 5 pink beaches to sink your toes into; couples' massage; private breakfasts in your cottage

Address/Phone: 30 Kings Point Road, Somerset, MA 02, Bermuda; (441) 234–0331; fax (441) 234–3352

E-mail: cambeach@ibl.bm

Web Site: www.cambridgebeaches.com

U.S. Reservations: (800) 468–7300

Owner/Manager: Michael J. Winfield, president; Romana Heeg, manager

Arrival/Departure: A 45-minute taxi ride from the airport costs approximately $44.

Distance from Bermuda International Airport: 18 miles

Distance from Somerset: ½ mile

Accommodations: 94 rooms and suites in cottages,18 of which were brand new in 2001. All older ones have been refurbished.

Most Romantic Room/Suite: Cambridge Suites, which have a bedroom and separate living room with panoramic water views; suites with water views also good. Sunset Suite is superb.

Amenities: Air-conditioning, ceiling fans, telephone, bathrobes, hair dryer, whirlpool, toaster, safe, mending kit, room service, free shuttle to Hamilton, cable TV

Electricity: 110 volts

Sports and Facilities: 3 tennis courts, croquet, heated indoor and outdoor pools, 5 beaches, snorkeling, scuba diving, sailing, sailboarding, kayaking, fishing, motorboating; Ocean Spa; golf nearby

Dress Code: In the dining room 3 evenings are casually smart; 4 evenings jackets are requested (no tie required)

Weddings: Can be arranged

Rates/Packages: Per couple per night $460–$1,450 (mid-April to end of October); $330–$1,200 (November); $260–$1,015 (December–end of February), including breakfast, tea, dinner, use of sports facilities. Romance Package from $3,800 including water-view room, breakfast in bed, afternoon tea, dinner, 1 private candlelight dinner, "His and Hers" massage, massage lesson, special picnic lunch, private sauna, and airport transfers.

Payment/Credit Cards: Visa or MasterCard

Deposit: Two-night deposit at time of booking

Government Taxes: 7.25 percent goverment tax; 4 percent surcharge

Service Charges: $13.50 per person per night

Entry Requirements for U.S. Citizens: Proof of citizenship; return ticket; passport best

THE REEFS
Bermuda

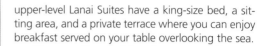

The Reefs, one of Bermuda's most romantic honeymoon resorts has been consistently rated as one of the best on the island for a number of years, and it just got even better following a $5 million renovation program that added eleven new suites, including three spectacular Pointe Suites, a new arrivals area, and a porte cochere. Sitting high above the beautiful pink beach and coral reefs below, the salmon-hued low-rise lanai cottages ramble over the landscaped, terraced grounds. All have great views of the sea from the balconies.

Rooms are attractively furnished with rattan chairs, sofas, tables, and bed; bright tropical prints; area rugs on red-tiled floors; and cheery prints of Bermuda scenes. The upper-level Lanai Suites have a king-size bed, a sitting area, and a private terrace where you can enjoy breakfast served on your table overlooking the sea.

The reception building houses an attractive lobby, comfortable lounge-bar, dining room, and tropical conservatory, where you dine under a glass roof. In the warmer months, you can enjoy a candlelit dinner outside on the terrace under the stars, and there is often music for dining and dancing. The Reefs's delicious international cuisine is included in your room rate.

If you want to dine outside while the surf rolls in nearby, try eating at the Ocean Echo Terrace Grill or the casual, thatched-roof Coconuts, the beach-level restaurant (warmer months only).

The Reefs has a new infinity pool and hot tub that overlooks the water and two all-weather tennis courts. There's a wonderful pink beach—one of Bermuda's best—and more to discover if you walk around the big black boulders that lie at the ends of the beach. Here you'll come upon more delightful small beaches tucked into coves, which continue along the shoreline. And, yes, the sand is really tinged pink from the bits of pulverized coral that have been mixed in over the years. In the summer, an activities director is on hand to help you plan your days.

The Reefs is located within walking distance of the Sonesta Beach Hotel, so if you are in the mood for an evening show, some lively entertainment, or some spa treatments, simply walk next door. You can also rent a moped or go by bus or taxi to nearby Hamilton for some serious shopping.

The Reefs' traditions, such as serving tea each afternoon, are grounded in the British way of doing things, but the hotel is more informal than many other Bermuda hotels. Although the resort certainly appeals to a solid group of over-fifties who come back year after year, its lively mix of nightly entertainment, water sports, and fresh tropical decor attracts a large number of well-heeled young couples, as well.

The Reefs

Location: In Southampton, on the south shore of Bermuda

Romantic Highlights: Hillside rooms overlooking the sea; breakfast on your private balcony; private pink beach

Address/Phone: 56 South Shore Road, Southampton SN 02, Bermuda; (441) 238–0222; fax (441) 238–8372

E-mail: reefsbda@ibl.bm

Web Site: www.thereefs.com

U.S. Reservations: Islands Resorts Reservations Ltd., (800) 742–2008

Owner/Manager: David Dodwell, managing director; Neal Stephens, general manager

Arrival/Departure: A 25-minute taxi ride from the airport costs approximately $26 weekdays, $35 weekends.

Distance from Bermuda International Airport: 11 miles

Distance from Hamilton: 7 miles

Accommodations: 67 rooms and 8 one- and two-bedroom cottages

Most Romantic Room/Suite: Pointe Suites; Number 316, a premier lanai, with wraparound views

Amenities: King-size bed, refrigerator, bathrobes, hair dryer, in-room safe, umbrella, air-conditioning, daily newspaper, in-room beverages. New suites have TV/VCR/DVD players.

Electricity: 110 volts

Sports and Facilities: 2 tennis courts, pool, beach, hot tub, fitness center, shuffleboard, croquet, cycle rentals, snorkeling, scuba diving; helmet diving and glass-bottom boats

Dress Code: Casual during day; men required to wear jackets in Clubhouse dining room except for Sunday, Monday, and Thursday, which are casual

Weddings: Can be arranged

Rates/Packages: Rates are $226–$1,274 per couple per night and include breakfast and dinner, local phone calls, in-room beverages, and use of sports facilities. Romance Package, $3,170–$5,266, includes 6 nights' accommodations, all the above inclusions, plus champagne, dinner for two, transfers, three-day bus and ferry pass, picnic lunch for two, taxes and service charges. Rates are 20 to 35 percent less during the winter

Payment/Credit Cards: Most major

Deposit: Two-night deposit at time of booking

Government Taxes: 7.25 percent of nightly rate; included in Romance Package

Service Charges: 10 percent; included in Romance Package

Entry Requirements for U.S. Citizens: Proof of citizenship; return ticket; passport best

PETER ISLAND RESORT AND YACHT HARBOUR

Peter Island, British Virgin Islands

Peter Island is an easy, twenty-minute boat ride from the Beef Island Airport on Tortola, just long enough for you to stretch travel-weary limbs and bask in the warm sun and fresh salt air. As you pull up to the resort's pier, you'll see deserted white sandy beaches, coconut groves, and low hills covered with cactus and bougainvillea.

There aren't a lot of buildings here, and what structures do exist are so unobtrusive, you have to look hard to find them. There are only fifty-two rooms and two villas (Hawks' Nest and Crow's Nest), along with two restaurants, a lounge, library, reception area, fitness center, and dive shop, on the entire 1,200-acre island. You'll find no Club Med sorts of "playmakers," no casino, no disco. What you will find is the opportunity to do pretty much what you want when you want to do it. If you like beaches, sun, and water sports, this island can be your nirvana. Like to sail? You can choose from a 42-foot yacht, Hobie Cats, 19-foot Squibs, and Zumas along with kayaks and sailboards. There are also power boats that can be chartered for deep-sea fishing.

If you feel a little green about sailing a Sunfish by yourself, don't worry. The instructor keeps an eye on everyone. "I've never lost anyone yet," he'll tell you with a smile as he helps you push your boat into the water.

Peter Island is an excellent place for snorkeling and scuba diving as well as sailing. Snorkeling gear is free to guests, and just offshore the main swimming beach is a reef where you can see a wonderful assortment of colorful fish, shellfish, corals, and aquatic plants. All you have to do is to wade out, don your mask and fins, and paddle off.

Scuba lessons and dives are available for all levels. One of the most popular dive sites is the wreck of the *Rhone*, a nineteenth-century British mail ship and the site of the filming of Peter Benchley's *The Deep*.

If you like to go exploring, you can climb the rocks at the end of the main beach, follow the fitness trail and see who is the most flexible and the strongest, and walk to the really isolated Reef Bay Beach around the corner, where you can find lots of shells, coral, and bits of sea glass. Take along a blanket and a picnic lunch and enjoy a few hours on your own.

Peter Island has four Tru-flex tennis courts along with a small tennis center. A pro is available (high season) to give you lessons or arrange partners if you're looking for a set of doubles. Also located at the tennis center is a paperback book exchange library.

One of my criteria for a great beach resort is a place where you can go from your room to the beach in twenty paces and walk on that beach (and others) for miles. Peter Island passes the sand test. But there's more: king-size beds, attractive decor in the island mode, plenty of thirsty towels, lights bright enough for night reading, and a great view of the sea. You also have a minibar, a sitting area, a shower that looks into a small private garden, a double sink, a large walk-in closet, and lots of louvers that you can open to let in the breezes and the sounds of waves. Patios or balconies are furnished with beautiful teak lounge chairs. There are CD players in all rooms, but if you want to watch TV, you'll have to head to the library, tucked between the pool and the sea.

Great water views are revealed from the Tradewinds Restaurant and patio. For casual, beachfront dining, there is The Deadman's Beach Bar and Grill. Peter Island gets its fish daily from local fishermen, and the chef knows how to cook it! Especially good is the grilled tuna served with a homemade pineapple chutney. The resort also makes its own desserts and pastries. Fresh muffins in the mornings, great cookies with white chocolate chunks and macadamia nuts, and Key lime pie made the traditional way are all delicious.

For entertainment there is music by local bands for dancing or listening almost nightly on the open-air patio. Excursions to neighboring islands such as St. Thomas, Jost

Peter Island Resort and Yacht Harbour

Location: A private 1,200-acre island in the British Virgin Islands

Romantic Highlights: Private honeymoon beach; deserted beaches to explore on your own

Address/Phone: P.O. Box 211, Road Town, Tortola, B.V.I.; or P.O. Box 9409, St. Thomas, U.S.V.I. 00801; (800) 346–4451, (284) 495–2000; fax (284) 495–2500

Web Site: www.peterisland.com

U.S. Reservations: (800) 346–4451; fax (770) 476–4979

Owner/Manager: Wayne Kafcsak, managing director; Jeff Humes, general manager

Arrival/Departure: Those arriving at the Beef Island Airport are taken by private launch to Peter Island.

Distance from Beef Island Airport: About 4 miles by sea

Distance from Tortola: 4 miles

Accommodations: 52 rooms and suites: 32 with ocean or harbor view, 20 junior suites on beach; 2 villas

Most Romantic Room/Suite: Go for the newly redecorated beachfront suites.

Amenities: Air-conditioning, ceiling fans, minibar, coffeemaker, double sinks, hair dryer, bathrobes, umbrellas

Electricity: 110 volts

Sports and Facilities: Sunfish, sailboard, kayaks, floaters, snorkeling gear, dive center, and fishing charters; 4 Tru-flex tennis courts (2 lighted); fitness trail; pool

Dress Code: Casual by day; casually elegant by night. No tie required at dinner, but collared shirts, pants, and shoes are required.

Weddings: Can be arranged

Rates/Packages: $615–$1,100 per couple per night, including meals, transfers, water sports, bicycles, tennis, and ferry transportation to Tortola; seven-night land-and-sea packages from $4,955 per couple, including meals. Romance package: per room, $2,406–$4,130 for 4 nights; $3,835–$6,852 for 7 nights including accomodations, meals, champagne, couples' massage, vintner dinner, day trip to neighboring island, unlimited use of island activities, sports facilities, transfers, and unlimited ferry service to and from Tortola.

Payment/Credit Cards: Visa, MasterCard, American Express

Deposit: Full payment required within 5 days of booking. No refunds on unused portions. Refunds available no later than 4 weeks prior to scheduled arrival.

Government Taxes: 7 percent

Service Charges: 10 percent

Entry Requirements for U.S. Citizens: Proof of citizenship necessary. Passport best.

Van Dyke, and Tortola are also offered.

The resort's rates include breakfast, lunch, and dinner, a good thing since Peter Island's restaurants are the only game in town. For the best of both worlds, cruise around the British Virgin Islands aboard the resort's luxurious 41-foot sailing yacht *Silmaril* and spend the rest of the time on Peter Island.

Peter Island is for those who love beautiful beaches and water sports and don't need a lot of high-level activity. You're on your own here, with all the toys at your disposal.

BITTER END YACHT CLUB
Virgin Gorda, British Virgin Islands

Don't let the name turn you off. This "Bitter End" could be your "Sweet Beginning." Artfully tucked into a cove on the northernmost tip of Virgin Gorda, one of the most picturesque of the British Virgin Islands, Bitter End Yacht Club (BEYC) is a perfect place for newlyweds who love to sail. You can combine your passion for a romantic setting with a few days' cruise aboard a bare boat or crewed yacht, exploring the neighboring islands. Or you can spend all your nights at the resort and venture out onto the gentle seas during the day.

World-class yachtsmen have known about this place for many years, and people like Jean-Michel Cousteau and Mel Fisher have rendezvoused often at this unique tropical haven, which has seventy deepwater moorings, two restaurants, and a host of water sports activities—all first-class from beginning to end.

Protected by coral reefs and beach-fringed cays, this secluded, idyllic spot can most easily be reached by boat. The white-sand beach, fringed by gnarled sea grape shrubs and palms, frames a lagoon that seems more like a large, clear, turquoise lake dashed with flashes of the bright-colored sails of sailboarders.

From the time of your arrival at Virgin Gorda's tiny airport—hardly large enough to hold your luggage—everything is handled by the Bitter End staff with great style. After you've gathered your luggage, you're whisked up and over the steep hills to a landing area about twenty minutes away. Then it's a five-minute boat ride across a brilliant Caribbean-blue lagoon, where you are met by a smiling staff member at the dock. (Those landing at Tortola come to BEYC via high-speed water taxi.)

Native stone lines the walkways and roads, and flowers and tropical plants, including fragrant frangipani, bougainvillea, hibiscus, oleander, and sea grape, wind along the paths and up the hillside. Colorful nautical flags fly from the rafters of the bar, from poles along the walkways, and just about everywhere. Buildings are decorated with whimsical gingerbread trim and iron grillwork and are connected by a series of garden courtyards. Blue-and-white-painted wrought-iron tables and chairs sit on brick-paved patios accented by tiered fountains and flowering plants. All very Mediterranean.

As the sun sets, you'll soon become aware that the lighting throughout the resort is seductively low. (Can this be due to the Caribbean-style electrical power or is it planned for romantics like you?) As you walk along the seaside paths to the dining room, you'll find the tiny flashlight you got at check-in extremely useful.

Because BEYC is actually the marriage of two different resorts, the styles of accommodations are quite different. There are rustic beachfront bungalows that blend into the hills, with their thatched roofs and weathered wood exteriors, and there are the more contemporary hillside North Sound Suites. The bungalows are much closer to the water than the suites—some are right on the beach—and are very Caribbean in feeling. You won't have a room key, because there are no locks. Nor are they needed. Open wraparound, palm-thatched verandas, ceiling fans, large walk-in showers, bamboo furniture, a tiled dressing area, and native art and quaint knickknacks lend a homey island feeling to the bungalows. Since most come with twin beds, request ahead to have them put together.

The deluxe 600-square-foot North Sound Suites, perched high over the water, are more spacious and luxurious, with vaulted ceilings, balconies, air-conditioning, two queen-size beds, and a very large marble inside/outside garden shower room. Connected by wooden walkways much like jungle catwalks, the suites have wood peaked ceilings and glass doors leading out to balconies, and they are attractively decorated in rich fabrics, native art, and grass-cloth walls.

The North Sound Suites and bungalows come equipped with a refrigerator and coffeemaker, and each has telephone service to the front desk and a comfortable sitting area. The choice is yours: Lie in luxury overlooking the harbor or pick a casual, native-style beachfront villa.

When it comes to water sports, you're in sailing heaven. There are enough Mistral sailboards, Sunfish, Lasers, Hobie Cats, Rhodes 19s, J-24s, and outboard-powered skiffs to get the whole guest population of the resort out on the water at the same time.

There are daily escorted snorkeling trips, scuba lessons, dive trips, and lots of regattas. There is also the full-service Sailing School, a great way for new sailors to

learn how to tell a *jib* from a *ready-about*. If you want to explore nearby shores, you can take one of the skiffs and chug over to other parts of the island for a picnic or a visit. For landlubbers a lovely pool and patio area is located on the eastern end of the resort, near the suites.

Well worth seeing is Anegada, known as Shipwreck Island. Also be sure to visit The Baths, giant granitelike boulders on the southwest coast. Take your bathing suit and swim in the pools located in, under, and around the huge rocks, some as high as 40 feet.

If you want the best of both worlds, you can live aboard one of the resort's Freedom 30s, fully outfitted, sporty yachts that you can sail into the sunset for a few days or a few hours, returning to your home base for the evening. All meals are included, whether you eat on board or ashore.

BEYC has two restaurants. The Clubhouse, on the shore, serves breakfast, lunch, and dinner. You can eat inside, on the tree-shaded terrace, or on the veranda. The terrace bar, poised on the edge of the water, is a popular gathering place for guests to enjoy morning coffee or a late-afternoon cocktail.

Nearer the North Sand Suites is the dining room of the English Carvery, which is open four nights a week for intimate candlelight dinners and dancing. You can also grab a quick snack or a light lunch at the English Pub at the Emporium, which serves pizza, hot dogs, and fish burgers.

Bitter End Clubhouse attracts top-notch Caribbean "jump-up" entertainers, and there is more romantic dinner music at the Carvery. Bitter End's steel band plays several nights a week, and there are beach barbecues and sunset and moonlight cruises.

With close to 200 staff for just eighty-five rooms, Bitter End gives you all the attention you want and need, but one of the best things of all is that it's done in a totally unobtrusive manner. You can wash your hair, take a walk on the beach, and when you return find a fresh towel in your room. Beds are turned down every night, and the beaches are raked every morning.

Although you will be surrounded by tempting things to do, you can find your own quiet spot on one of the secluded beaches and just sit back under a palm tree and watch a yellow finch eat sugar from your outstretched hand.

Bitter End Yacht Club

Location: Covers 25 acres along a mile of beach and waterfront on the North Sound of Virgin Gorda—the most protected and secluded deepwater harbor in the Caribbean

Romantic Highlights: Magnificent sailing; thatched-roof bungalows on the beach; opportunity to combine a yacht cruise with an island stay; sunset sail

Address/Phone: North Sound, Virgin Gorda, B.V.I.; (809) 494–2746; fax (809) 494–4756

E-mail: binfo@beyc.com

Web Site: www.beyc.com

U.S. Reservations: (800) USA–BEYC, (800) 872–2392, or (305) 468–0168; fax (305) 468–0156

Owner/Manager: Owned by the Hokin family for over 25 years; Coastal Hotel Group Management, managers

Arrival/Departure: Transfers from Beef Island Airport, Tortola, or Virgin Gorda Airport included in 5-day package; otherwise $20 per couple charge for transfer

Distance from Virgin Island Airport: 30-minute drive or bus ride plus 10-minute boat ride

Distance from Spanish Town: 30 minutes

Accommodations: 85 rooms and suites, ranging from beachfront villas to North Sound Suites and live-aboard Freedom 30 yachts

Most Romantic Room/Suite: Beachfront bungalows for beach lovers; North Sound Suites for those who prefer luxury and a bird's-eye view of the water

Amenities: Air-conditioning (North Sound Suites only), ceiling fans, garden shower, hair dryer, coffeemaker, refrigerator, VCR (in suites), turndown service, shops and convenience store

Electricity: 110 volts

Sports and Facilities: Water sports galore: Mistral sailboards, Sunfish, Lasers, Hobie Cats, Rhodes 19s, J-24s, and outboard-powered skiffs; snorkeling, scuba diving, swimming pool, 3 beaches, fitness trail, marina, Blue Water Excursions

Dress Code: Very casual. Leave your cocktail dresses and sports jackets at home

Weddings: Can be arranged

Rates/Packages: From $430 per couple per night (spring–fall); $585 (winter); includes 3 meals and use of water sports equipment. A Honeymoon Package, 8 days/7 nights, is $3,010–$5,390 per couple. A package combining 5 nights on a yacht and 4 nights in the resort is priced from $3,870 per couple.

Payment/Credit Cards: Most major

Deposit: 3 nights; cancel 30 days prior to arrival date for refund (by October 1 for Christmas season)

Government Taxes/Service Charges: 15 percent

Entry Requirements for U.S. Citizens: Proof of citizenship; passport best

LITTLE DIX BAY
Virgin Gorda, British Virgin Islands

One of the most consistently appealing Caribbean resorts, Little Dix Bay was established over thirty years ago by Laurance S. Rockefeller, who visualized an ecological preserve and wilderness resort where privacy and solitude were paramount. Today Little Dix remains extremely romantic and seductive. It sits on 500 acres and has a lovely 1/2-mile crescent-shaped beach. The rooms and public areas are designed to blend into the surrounding gardens of flowering shrubs, sea grapes, and palms. Cottages containing two to eight rooms all face the sea. Some are on stilts and have cone-shaped roofs; others are more conventional. All have louvered-window walls designed to catch the cooling trade winds.

Coral reefs and a cove create a calm, safe "harbor" for swimming and water sports. In 1993 Rosewood Hotels & Resorts took over the operation of the resort, giving the property a major facelift, with new furniture and custom-designed fabrics, new lighting, telephones, redesigned bathrooms, and the addition of air-conditioning in all the rooms. To lend a Polynesian ambience, bamboo beds and other interesting furniture pieces were imported from Asia,

and unique touches were added, such as wicker baskets and artwork. Throughout the renovation, great care and sensitivity were taken to preserve the harmonious pact Little Dix has had with nature.

Cottages are constructed of native wood and stone with peaked wooden ceilings, circulating fans, and tile floors. Bamboo king-size beds; rattan furniture, including chaises roomy enough to hold two; and natural fiber area rugs are low-key yet elegant enough to satisfy the most discerning of guests. Rooms are located in clusters of cottages, some on ground level.

With more than 300 on staff, the hotel provides excellent, yet not overpowering, service. They pay attention to the little things, like replenishing your ice bucket daily and providing an abundant supply of fresh towels.

Little Dix has three restaurants. The open-air Pavilion, which has four dramatic Polynesian-style pyramid roofs and a stone terrace, offers international and Caribbean specialties, lunch buffets, afternoon teas, and candlelight dinners. Rack of lamb, fresh salmon, red snapper, and grouper are served grilled or with wonderful light sauces. Guests often gather on the terrace early in the evening for cocktails as the sun sets. After dinner a band plays music for dancing under the open skies. The romantic Sugar Mill gives you the opportunity to get dressed up for a really lovely evening of good food, wine, and romance—the kind of night you always dreamed about.

The Sugar Mill menu, which reflects both Asian and Indian cuisine, offers all organic food and incorporates as many locally available fresh foods as possible. The entree might be tempura-fried prawns in tomato and lime relish served with saffron-scented cilantro-ginger emulsion. A particularly interesting soup is Anegada Lobster Cappucino flavored with lemongrass and topped with curried foam.

Should you want to dine under the stars on the beach surrounded only by tiki torches, rustling palms, and the sound of gently lapping water, you can order from the Sugar Mill selections.

The open-air, ocean-view Beach Grill, where you can get light lunches and dinners, has been recently renovated in the low-key, elegant Little Dix style with floors made from locally quarried stone. Everything from fish to burgers to salads is served. Eat on the terrace or take your lunch to the beach.

At Little Dix the beach is right in your "front yard." Float the afternoon away on a rubber raft, or sit under an umbrella of palm fronds. Take a box lunch and umbrella

and climb aboard the resort's water taxi, which will shuttle you to a secluded beach. Snorkel in Devil's Bay and explore Mosquito Island. Ask the boatman to drop you near the famous Baths, and spend a few hours climbing above, under, and around the huge boulders that create this unique natural phenomenon. Swim in the grotto pools and climb the path that leads from the beach to a hilltop restaurant/bar.

Guided snorkel tours are offered four times a week, and you can take Sunfish lessons, aerobic exercise, and even a tour of the gardens with the resident horticulturist. The tennis center offers complimentary clinics and round-robins twice a week, and movies are shown every evening in the large, open-air lounge.

Your honeymoon package includes a sunset cocktail sail on the resort's trimaran Pond Bay and a ride on a Boston Whaler to Spring Bay for a picnic. Full-day sails to nearby areas as well as scuba diving, fishing charters, and beauty treatments are also available as optional choices.

Well-heeled guests have been coming here for years, appreciating the easy ambience and the excellent service—they treat it rather like their personal island club. During the winter months the guests tend to be on the more mature side. But in the spring—honeymoon season—the resort is popular with newly married young couples, many of whom have learned about the resort from their parents. (But beware: Christmas and Easter attract families.) Spring, summer, and fall are great times to come to Little Dix. Prices are lower, and the weather is great.

Little Dix Bay

Location: Northwest corner of Virgin Gorda, just off the Sir Francis Drake Channel

Romantic Highlights: Beachfront setting; dining and dancing under the stars; hammocks for two; secluded beaches

Address/Phone: P.O. Box 720, St. John, U.S.V.I. 00831-0720; (284) 495–5555; fax (284) 495–5661

Web Site: www.rosewoodhotels.com

U.S. Reservations: (800) 928–3000; fax (214) 758–6640

Owner/Manager: Managed by Rosewood Hotels & Resorts; Peter Shaindlin, general manager

Arrival/Departure: Virgin Gorda can be reached via San Juan, Puerto Rico, Tortola, and St. Thomas. Shuttles are also available to and from St. Thomas and Caneel Bay.

Distance from Virgin Gorda Airport: 1 mile

Distance from Spanish Town: 2 miles

Accommodations: 98 rooms and 4 one-bedroom suites all facing the sea.

Most Romantic Room/Suite: Newly created beachfront suites with oversize soaking tubs and showers and separate bedroom and living room, or the elevated hexagonal rooms on the west side, near the beach

Amenities: Air-conditioning, ceiling fans, hair dryer, telephone, TV, minibar, refrigerator

Electricity: 110 volts

Sports and Facilities: Tennis day or night, scuba diving, snorkeling, sailboarding, sailing, Sunfish, kayaking, water-skiing, aerobics, fitness room

Dress Code: Informal during day; although jacket and tie are not required, most guests usually wear elegant attire when dining at Sugar Mill and long pants are required for men

Weddings: Can be arranged

Rates/Packages: $450–$1,650 per couple (winter); $375–$1,100 (spring/fall); $275–$800 (summer); seven-night honeymoon package (per couple): $3,600-$7,500 (summer); $4,700-$9,000 (spring/fall); $5,900-$14,000 (winter); includes accommodations, meals, trimaran day sail, sunset cocktail cruise, Spring Bay afternoon picnic, champagne and fruit, transfers, tennis, water sports, afternoon tea, water taxis to nearby beaches, guided snorkeling tour, Sunfish lessons, aerobic exercise, and massage for two.

Payment/Credit Cards: Most major

Deposit: 50 percent of package, due 14 days from date of booking. If booking 30 days prior to arrival, credit card deposit required within 24 hours of booking.

Government Taxes/Service Charges: 7 percent room tax and 10 percent service charge. Meal plans, food, and beverages are subject to a 15 percent service charge.

Entry Requirements for U.S. Citizens: Proof of citizenship; passport best

HYATT REGENCY GRAND CAYMAN
Grand Cayman, Cayman Islands

Basking in the sun, playing golf on a unique championship course, and enjoying a side order of super scuba and snorkeling are all part of the honeymoon experience at the Hyatt Regency Grand Cayman. Entering the resort's palm-lined driveway, you quickly leave the hubbub of life back home far behind. The Hyatt's British-inspired, low-rise colonial buildings are surrounded by lush green foliage and a rainbow of tropical flowers. The Caribbean is just across the way, where the Hyatt recently built 53 new beachfront suites.

The pastel colors of the buildings, all offset by the brilliant blue sky, set the mood. After checking in, couples who have requested the Honeymoon Package are escorted out of the reception area past a stunning reflecting pool and tropical garden—the centerpiece of the Hyatt's courtyard—to a luxurious guest room, where a chilled bottle of champagne awaits. Rooms are typically Hyatt with a light tropical twist, but every amenity you could wish for is there, including, for some, a garden Jacuzzi. Regency Club rooms, located in a separate building, are extra special and offer more amenities, a private concierge, and complimentary continental breakfast and evening cocktails. The new suites are smack on the beach.

As you walk through the courtyard and gardens, all beautifully manicured, at every turn along the path you'll find romantic little enclaves. Whether it's a bench set in an alcove by a pond or a bridge over a stream running through the property, the setting seems designed for couples in love. The one-third-acre free-form pool has a great swim-up bar, which serves some fabulous frozen drinks.

The Britannia Beach Club will be high on your exploration list. Located across the street, on Hyatt's pearl-white sand strip of Seven Mile Beach, it is here where you may encounter your toughest dilemma. What to do? Lie back and relax at the edge of the crystal-clear Caribbean with a dark rum and orange juice from the Britannia Beach Club's bar, or choose from the almost overwhelming number of activities available through Red Sail Sports—sailboarding, parasailing, Waverunners, and more.

After unwinding for a few days, if you crave some adventure, try scuba diving. Not certified? No problem. A resort course is available for beginners. You'll learn to dive in one day, and at the end of it all, you'll understand why the Grand Cayman is called the underwater capital of the Caribbean.

For a unique experience, don't miss the 20-foot dive to Stingray City, where you'll feed the stingrays and perhaps catch a glimpse of Psycho, the dive master's "friendly" pet eel! Even if you don't dive, take the trip with your snorkeling gear and watch the scene from on top of the water. But don't think you'll avoid an encounter with the stingrays, as the dive master usually coaxes the rays to the top for a closer look at guess who? You.

A dive along the famous North Wall is a fascinating Cayman exclusive—one sure to provide scuba enthusiasts with new thrills. For those nondivers who don't want to miss the sights, Atlantis Submarines offers several unique services. Choose from a personal submarine trip for two (with a captain) or a voyage aboard one of its larger subs. Both submerge to depths of over 100 feet. Through the Cayman's crystal-clear waters (there's a minimum $500,000 fine for dumping anything into the water), you'll see every type of tropical fish you've ever seen in an aquarium and then some. The corals and underwater "road" systems may even give you that needed push to

Hyatt Regency Grand Cayman

Location: Directly across from Seven Mile Beach

Romantic Highlights: Seven Mile Beach at sunset; tropical walkways laced through the property; sunset sail on the 65-foot *Spirit of Ppalu* catamaran

Address/Phone: Seven Mile Beach, Grand Cayman, B.W.I.; (345) 949–1234; fax (345) 949–8528

U.S. Reservations: Hyatt Resorts, (800) 55–HYATT

Owner/Manager: Ellesmere Britannia of Canada, owner; Hyatt Hotels & Resorts, operator; Mark Bastis, general manager

Arrival/Departure: Taxis available at airport; transfers can be arranged (are not included in the Honeymoon Package)

Distance from Owens Roberts Airport: 5 miles (8 minutes)

Distance from Georgetown: 2 miles

Accommodations: 289 rooms and suites in 6 buildings; 53 new beachfront suites on Seven Mile Beach, 44 Regency Club rooms, 2 bilevel suites, and 50 villas offering one to four bedrooms with kitchen and laundry facilities

Most Romantic Room/Suite: Bilevel Governor's and Georgetown Suites

Amenities: Air-conditioning, minibar, satellite TV, direct-dial telephone, in-room safe, hair dryer, 24-hour room service, lotions, shampoos, and bath gels

Electricity: 110 volts

Sports and Facilities: Red Sail Sports has 2 locations on the Hyatt property and offers every water sport imaginable. Special activities include scuba/snorkeling trips to Stingray City and parasailing over Seven Mile Beach. The resort's golf course is designed by Jack Nicklaus.

Dress Code: Beach attire during the day; casual attire for evenings

Weddings: Can be arranged

Rates/Packages: Honeymoon Package includes accommodations, champagne, special Britannia honeymoon breakfast for two delivered to your room on the first morning (when meal plan is purchased), jeep rental for 1 day (minimum age, 25), sunset sail on the *Spirit of Ppalu*, massage for two, and a round of golf. Rates per couple: 4 days/3 nights from $1,152; 8 days/7 nights from $2,012.

Payment/Credit Cards: Most major

Deposit: 1 to 2 nights' room rate required 14 days after verbal confirmation; refundable on advance cancellation received in writing no later than October 1 for arrivals during the Christmas season, or 14 days in advance for all other periods

Government Taxes: 10 percent

Service Charges: 10 percent

Entry Requirements for U.S. Citizens: Proof of citizenship is required for U.S. and Canadian citizens.

try the one-day resort scuba course to get a closer look at this magnificent underwater world. Look carefully and you may spot some sea turtles!

After the excitement of Stingray City, all you may be up for is finding a lounge chair and watching the sun sink in the horizon while Calypso music plays in the background.

By this time you've probably worked up quite an appetite. The award-winning Hemingway's, located at the Britannia Beach Club directly on Seven Mile Beach, provides a wonderful setting for a romantic dinner for two. With some of the best cuisine on the Island, Hemingway's specialty is, of course, Caribbean cuisine, including fresh fish and seafood. The swordfish and crab cakes are a must-try! At the Bamboo Lounge, you can enjoy sushi and even learn how to prepare it. Bamboo has an extensive "sake-tini" menu as well.

If you have any time left for other activities, try golf. The Hyatt offers a unique Jack Nicklaus–designed layout. Says Victor Lopez, divisional vice-president for Hyatt Hotels & Resorts, "The course configuration varies depending upon where the tees are located, so the forty-acre course can be played three ways: regulation golf, executive course golf, or Cayman ball." It's a challenge any way you play it.

For pure luxury in a tropical setting, with appealing activities and dining options, the Hyatt Grand Cayman delivers.

CASA DE CAMPO
Dominican Republic

Casa de Campo! It's big. Very big and most of it has been completely renovated and redecorated following a hit by Hurricane George in 1998. There are new rooms, new restaurants, and new features.

Casa de Campo offers a mind-boggling list of things to do, and it's got all the ingredients those looking for sun, sand, and sea require: pools galore, a private beach, and lots of water toys, plus thirteen tennis courts, an equestrian center, a fitness center, plenty of places to eat and drink, thousands of acres, a world-class shooting facility, splendid accommodations, and room service. What more could a body ask?

Want privacy? You've got it. There are 300 newly redecorated rooms and 150 villas, which may sound like a lot, but when they're spread out over 7,000 acres planted with all sorts of tropical things, you can be assured of finding your own very special private places.

There are shuttle buses running regularly throughout the property, but you may want to pay $27 to $35 a day and rent your own golf cart. It's a great way to get around.

Casa de Campo, which is Spanish for "house in the country," has a variety of rooms and suites. Within the mix of accommodations are hotel rooms and hacienda-like villas. The superspacious hotel rooms are located in one- and two-story clusters overlooking the golf links, which wind through the property. Stone and adobe rooms come with balconies, tile floors, louvered shutters, and designer furnishings. Two-, three-, and four-bedroom villas each have a living room, dining room, kitchen, terrace, gardens, and maid service. They may also come with private pools or Jacuzzis. All are exquisitely furnished.

Golfers will think they died and went to heaven, given the thirty-six magnificent holes to tee off on. This includes the world-class Teeth of the Dog course, which has been consistently ranked by Golf Digest in the "Top 100 in the World." Designed by Pete Dye, the course has eight holes that hug the rugged coastline, offering smashing views and teeth-rattling shots. Wait until you get those sand bunkers in your sights: Overshoot the bunkers and you're likely to hit either the rocks or more sand—the beach.

And speaking of beaches, "lounge lizards" will be blissfully happy. There are three beaches, including the lovely, private Minitas Beach. Coconut palms and thatched umbrellas provide shade on the wide, white stretch of sand. Water sports include just about anything you can think of, from sailboarding to scuba diving. Package rates include some sports, but you may have to pay extra for things like scuba and deep-sea fishing.

Each of the fourteen pools is unique in design and patio landscaping; all are so inviting you'll want to plant yourself in a different one each day.

Play tennis and you won't wear yourself out chasing an errant ball. Casa de Campo's tennis staff includes a number of people who will run and fetch for the players. The pro will give you private lessons, or you can participate in the clinics and round-robins that are routinely scheduled.

Also located on the grounds is a shooting center, the finest of its kind outside England. It has a 110-foot tower and a variety of sport-shooting options.

There is an extensive equestrian center where you can learn to ride or practice skills you already have. There are also an active polo operation, dude ranch, and rodeo arena.

Sitting atop some cliffs above the winding Chavon River is a must-see—the Altos de Chavon. This replica of a sixteenth-century Italian village, designed by the Italian film-maker Roberto Copa, was constructed entirely by hand by local craftsmen. Cobblestone paths, stone carvings, arches, plant-shaded walks, and weathered stone buildings with red-tile roofs look very Old World, indeed. Although you

Casa de Campo

Location: On 7,000 acres, on the southeastern coast of the Dominican Republic

Romantic Highlights: Moonlit horseback rides; vast tropical areas to explore

Address/Phone: P.O. Box 140, La Romana, Dominican Republic; (809) 523–3333; fax (809) 523–8548

E-mail: res@pwmonline.com

Web Site: www.casadecampo.cc

U.S. Reservations: (800) 877–3643 or (305) 856–5405; fax (305) 858–4677

Owner/Manager: Ana Lisa Brache, managing director

Arrival/Departure: Transfers can be arranged; Excel Club (a premium accommodations category) guests receive complimentary transportation from airport to resort

Distance from Santo Domingo Airport: 1½ hours; La Romana Airport, 5 minutes

Distance from Santo Domingo: 1½ hours

Accommodations: 300 rooms, 150 two-, three-, and four-bedroom villas

Most Romantic Room/Suite: Go for a room nearest the location of your interests, such as a golf course or the beach.

Amenities: Air-conditioning, ceiling fans, minibar, coffeemaker, TV, clock radio, in-room safe, hair dryer. Excel Club guests also get private maid service, breakfast, Dominican Bar, and more.

Electricity: 110 volts

Sports and Facilities: 3 championship 18-hole golf courses (1 for members only), Tennis Center with 13 Har-Tru courts (10 lighted), free weights and exercise equipment, shooting center, 14 pools, equestrian center, polo, marina, hiking, full range of water sports, fishing

Dress Code: Casually smart

Weddings: Can be arranged

Rates/Packages: $155–$285 per couple per night (summer and fall); $235–$700 (winter); Honeymoon Inclusive package includes 3 nights' accomodations: $1,562 (summer and fall); $2,084–$2,720 (winter) with extra nights available.

Payment/Credit Cards: Most major

Deposit: Secure with credit card

Government Taxes: Rooms, 12 percent; food, 12 percent

Service Charges: 10 percent

Entry Requirements for U.S. Citizens: Proof of citizenship; passport best

might think it all a bit contrived, somehow it works.

Here you'll find a church, a museum of archaeology, an art gallery, an art school, craft shops, boutiques, and four restaurants. There is a large outdoor Roman amphitheater, which has been the venue for a number of name-brand concerts and performances, drawing stars like Frank Sinatra and Julio Iglesias.

When you stay at Casa de Campo, you'll have a choice of restaurants, running the gamut from gourmet candlelight dinners to barefoot-casual. Go Italian at La Piazzetta and Cafe del Sol; try Latin and gourmet options at the eateries in the new marina complex; or sample Dominican specialties at Cafe el Patio. Fresh fish like grouper, tuna, and red snapper along with quality meats and locally produced vegetables and fruits are artfully prepared. Try the banana milkshakes in the open-air, thatched Lago Grill or have dinner prepared for you in the privacy of your villa. So many options.

Your best bet is to choose the Honeymoon Inclusive package, providing you with accommodations, sports, food, and beverages. Villas are very pricey, and who needs to pay for an extra bedroom!

SPICE ISLAND BEACH RESORT
Grenada

Sure it's on the quiet side—it doesn't have a disco or a casino. It also doesn't have activity leaders. But if being smack on a great beach, having your own private pool in a walled garden courtyard, and enjoying a large Jacuzzi tub for two interests you, then you should definitely check out the Spice Island Beach Resort. Here the white towels are thick and fluffy, the king-size bed is dressed in high-thread-count linens, and the beach chairs under the wind-sculpted sea grape trees are just too inviting to pass by.

Spice is a well-seasoned beach resort that has been honed and perfected by its Grenadian owners, headed by Royston Hopkin, CMG, and his brother, Arnold. The Hopkin family has been in the hotel business for many years and really knows how to do it right. The resort has a high repeat guest business, and heaven help the Hopkins if they decide to make any major changes: They'll really hear it from their guests, who are happy with things just as they are. And who can complain?

Set on 1,600 feet of wide, white beachfront are two meandering rows of one- and two-story cottages huddled under palms and sea grapes. The one-story whirlpool beach suites, where you literally step from your patio right into the sand, have large Jacuzzis illuminated by a skylight, a sitting area, a bath with supersize shower, and two twin or double beds. There is also a terrace where you get unobstructed views of the water and the picturesque capital of St. George's in the distance. If being on the beach is a top priority, these rooms should do it. But you will have to put up with guests walking back and forth right in your "front yard," as they go to, from, and along the beach.

The private pool suites are much more secluded, especially the older ones on the northern end of the property, which have larger pools (about 16 feet by 20 feet) and raised garden terraces that give you excellent views of the sea through wide breaks in the row of whirlpool beach suites. The pool, the terrace, and a large garden are all enclosed by an 8-foot wall that ensures your privacy. Your terrace comes with two lounges, an umbrella, a round table, and two chairs. Walls are draped with passion flowers, bougainvillea, hibiscus, and other flowering plants.

The private pool suites on the other side of the reception area are newer and perhaps even a bit more private. They are also smaller, and when you sit on your terrace, although the beach is only twenty steps away, you really can't see it. You can also choose one of the whirlpool garden-view suites. These are located on the second story over the newer pool suites and have vaulted ceilings and wide, tiled terraces. Water views and sea breezes are superb from here.

All rooms have whirlpool bath; some have full-size hot tubs with all the bells and whistles. Most baths have bidets, and rooms are furnished with rattan furniture, original paintings by Grenadian artists, and tropical print fabrics. Floors are ceramic tile, and there are lots of louvers to open for cross-ventilation, unless you want to crank up the mother of all air-conditioners; it's a big one. Spice's new royal private pool suites are not only very private, they're the most luxurious accommodations of all. A private sundeck, a canopied fitness area with a sauna and exercise bike, lush gardens, and a pool set the mood outside, while inside you can enjoy your marble bath, king-size bed, minibar, TV, music center, and lots of other amenities.

The property is well landscaped with a variety of tropical flowers and palms. Trellises, walls, and wood-slat roofs support lush vines, many covered with flowers like the showy, yellow buttercups.

The open-air bar and restaurant are adjacent to the beach, and entertainment is provided in the bar or courtyard several nights a week. Cuisine includes fresh local specialties and international dishes.

At the water sports center, you can arrange for complimentary snorkeling, kayaking, and Hobie-Cats, and there is a tennis court that provides racquets if you need them. Lessons are extra. The new Janissa's Spa on site provides massages and other pampering treatments and two boutiques are located on the property.

Spice is located near St. George's and is thus close to "the action," but Grenada is not a place you come to for a lively nightlife. There are a couple of local clubs, such as Fantasia 2001 and Le Sucrier, nearby, and a weekly Rhum Runner Cruise, where it is party time big time, but in general you will have to be content with dancing to Spice's band, walking in the moonlight on the beach, sitting on your patio as the sun sets, and taking midnight swims in the sea or your own pool.

Grenada has a lot to offer in the way of hiking, scuba diving, and just sheer beauty. Its people couldn't be friendlier; its waters, more inviting. Still relatively undiscovered by Americans, Grenada gives you a lot for your money. For those who love the beach and privacy, Spice is a real winner.

Spice Island Beach Resort

Location: On Grand Anse Beach

Romantic Highlights: Private garden patios with pools; Jacuzzis for two; patio a step away from the sand

Address/Phone: P.O. Box 6, Grand Anse Beach, Grenada, W.I.; (473) 444– 4258; fax (473) 444–4807

E-mail: spiceis@caribsurf.com

Web Site: www.spicebeachresort.com

U.S. Reservations: (800) 223–9815 or (212) 476–9444

Owner/Manager: Royston Hopkin, CMG, chairman and managing director; Arnold Hopkin, deputy chairman

Arrival/Departure: 10-minute taxi ride from the airport (about $15)

Distance from Point Salines International Airport: 3 miles

Distance from St. George's: 6 miles (10 minutes)

Accommodations: 66 rooms: 4 royal private pool suites, 6 luxury private pool suites, 7 private pool suites, 36 whirlpool beach suites, 10 whirlpool ocean-view suites, and 3 whirlpool garden-view suites

Most Romantic Room/Suite: Royal Private Pool Suites

Amenities: Whirlpool tub for two or hot tub, bidet, hair dryer, air-conditioning, ceiling fan, AM/FM clock radio, coffee and tea bar, minibar, in-room safe, bathrobes, plush towels, telephone with Internet access

Electricity: 220 volts

Sports and Facilities: Swimming at the main pool and beach, snorkeling, sailing, kayaking, fitness room, tennis court (lighted for night play); scuba diving nearby

Dress Code: Casual elegant (no shorts at dinner)

Weddings: Wedding coordinator on premises; wedding package available.

Rates/Packages: $570–$990 per couple per night (winter); $470–$780 (spring–fall), including meals, beverages, and house wine. Passion in Paradise, from $3,950 per couple, includes 7 nights' accommodations, all meals and drinks (except wine and champagne), dinners served by candlelight on the couple's private patio, flowers, massages, sunset cruise, water sports, bicycles, tennis, use of fitness center, a basket of spice-scented oils, snorkeling trip, greens fees, taxes, service charges, and sunset cruise.

Payment/Credit Cards: Most major

Deposit: One-night deposit during summer months; three-night deposit in winter.

Government Taxes: 8 percent

Service Charges: 10 percent

Entry Requirements for U.S. Citizens: Proof of citizenship; passport best

GRAND LIDO SANS SOUCI
Jamaica

According to legend, the natural mineral springs located on the grounds of Grand Lido Sans Souci will fill the hearts of couples who take a dip with the power of the forbidden, passionate love secretly shared by an English admiral and a Spanish maiden. All this aside, you won't need much inducement to feel the romance at this seaside property, which combines the elegance of a bygone era with the comforts you look for today.

After going through several ownership and management changes over the years, Grand Lido Sans Souci is now part of the all-inclusive SuperClubs family. At this upscale and quietly elegant resort, you can now enjoy the benefits of package pricing. Everything—even name-brand liquors, meals, golf fees, and scuba-diving instruction—is all rolled into one price, paid before you come. Even weddings are complimentary.

Grand Lido Sans Souci enjoys a wonderful beachfront setting; part of it is tucked into the cliff at one end of the property, which drops to a white-sand beach where the newest suites are located. The resort's pinky beige, three-story buildings are cheerfully accented with white gingerbread trim and terraces. One of the oldest resorts in Jamaica, it has been drawing people since the 1700s to partake in the curative powers of the natural mineral springs, which still flow down the rocks to the sea.

In the 1960s Sans Souci established itself as a holiday residential community for wealthy Brits who purchased apartments on the grounds. In the 1980s new owners renovated the entire place, turning the apartments into guest quarters. Recently an entire new group of buildings was constructed on the 400-foot beach at the west end of the property.

Over the years the gardens, one of the most charming aspects of Grand Lido Sans Souci, have had plenty of time to grow and mature. Follow the winding walks, which eventually lead to the spa, pool, and beach, and take in the beauty of the hibiscus, bougainvillea, red tulip trees,

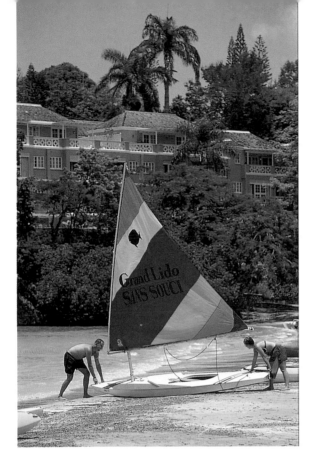

Grand Lido Sans Souci

Location: Ocho Rios, on Jamaica's north shore
Romantic Highlights: Adults-only resort; private Jacuzzi; dancing under the stars alongside the beach
Address/Phone: P.O. Box 103, Ocho Rios, Jamaica, W.I.; (876) 994–1353; fax (876) 994–1544
E-mail: info@800gosuper.com
Web Site: www.superclubs.com
U.S. Reservations: (800) GO–SUPER
Owner/Manager: John J. Issa, chairman; Pierre Battaglia, general manager
Arrival/Departure: Transfers included in rate
Distance from Donald Sangster International Airport, Montego Bay: 70 miles (1¾ hours)
Distance from Ocho Rios: 2 miles (5 minutes)
Accommodations: 146 suites
Most Romantic Room/Suite: Beachfront suite with Jacuzzi
Amenities: Air-conditioning, hair dryer, double vanities, whirlpool tub (most), direct-dial telephone, TV, AM/FM clock radio/CD player, mini-refrigerator, in-room coffee and tea, 24-hour room service, laundry, valet, and dry-cleaning services
Electricity: 110 volts
Sports and Facilities: 4 tennis courts (lighted for night play), 4 pools, 2 Jacuzzis, 2 beaches; sailboarding, Sunfish sailing, waterskiing, snorkeling, kayaking, glass-bottom boat rides, scuba diving with resort certification, Hobie-Cats, watertrikes, mineral whirlpool tub, natural mineral spring pool, beach; Ping-Pong, basketball, volleyball, shuffleboard, bocce ball, darts, croquet; bicycling, morning walks, golf, aerobics, aquacize, fitness center
Dress Code: Tropically casual
Weddings: "Super-Inclusive" weddings are complimentary and include marriage license, minister, witnesses, flowers, music, champagne, and cake. The ceremony can take place in the seaside gazebo, on the beach, or in the gardens.
Rates/Packages: $840–$1,340 per couple per night (January 1–late March); $395–$1,200 (late March–end of June); $740–$1,150 (July 1–December 31).
Payment/Credit Cards: Most major
Deposit: Guarantee with credit card
Government Taxes: Included
Service Charges: Included
Entry Requirements for U.S. Citizens: Proof of citizenship; passport best

palms, and exotic flowering shrubs planted all along the way. In addition to the main beach, there is a clothes-optional beach.

Rooms and suites that overlook the ocean are spacious; most have separate sitting areas and large balconies. The newer suites on the beach are decorated in soft, light colors and have French doors that separate the bedroom from the living room area. Baths are natural-colored tile and marble with double sinks, and many have Jacuzzis.

You have a choice of three restaurants, including the casual Ristorante Palazzina, an indoor/outdoor eatery serving breakfast, lunch, and dinner; Casanova featuring gourmet cuisine and the most formal of the restaurants, perfect for romantic dining under the stars; and the Beach Grill offering snacks and local specialties.

If you want to be active, there are plenty of water sports as well as tennis, golf, croquet—you name it. You can also relax at Charlie's Spa: Get a massage, facial, manicure, pedicure, body scrub, and reflexology. At night there is music for dancing under the stars, and local entertainers often perform on the Terrace.

In French Sans Souci means "carefree." Once you spend a few days here, you'll understand why the name is so apt.

HALF MOON GOLF, TENNIS, AND BEACH CLUB

Jamaica

Half Moon Golf, Tennis, and Beach Club enjoys one of the most romantic settings in the Caribbean. Put this together with one of the best managers in the Caribbean, Heinz Simonitsch, part owner and managing director of Half Moon since 1963, and it's no wonder that this resort attracts a sophisticated, international clientele, including Sean Connery, the Beatles, Prince Charles, and George Bush. Set on 400 acres of manicured gardens bordering a mile-long, white crescent beach, most of Half Moon's stark-white, two-story, plantation villas and beach houses are quietly arranged along the edge of a lovely, palm-fringed beach. Gardens are interspersed among the buildings, which serve as a brilliant backdrop for the red and orange bougainvillea that climbs up the walls and hugs the arches. Some of the rooms open onto wrought-iron balconies; first-floor rooms have arched Palladian windows with French doors that open onto a seaside terrace. The villas are really superb, with private pools and gardens.

Golfing couples will enjoy the excellent par 72 championship golf course designed by Robert Trent Jones, and racquet players can challenge their partners on the squash or tennis courts and meet other couples at the tennis pavilion. There is a full-service health center with Nautilus and life fitness equipment as well as aerobics classes, and there are biking, horseback riding, and paths for walking. Swimmers and sunbathers have a choice of several freshwater pools, located throughout the grounds, or they can head to the beach. You don't even have to get up when you want a drink poolside or on the beach. Waiters will scurry to bring drinks and refreshments right to your chair. Snorkeling, scuba diving, sailing, sailboarding, and deep-sea fishing are readily available, and if you want to totally relax you can try a sauna, a massage, or even an herbal wrap.

Your choice of accommodations includes deluxe rooms, suites, and villas, most strung along the beach and some set in the gardens. Rooms are airy and spacious, and most have sitting areas. They are furnished with white wicker and Queen Anne–inspired pieces made out of Jamaican mahogany. Black-and-white-tiled floors, sisal throw rugs and Oriental carpets, English flowered chintz, and authentic Jamaican art create an elegant yet exuberant mood, somewhat different from the usual Caribbean style. Worth considering are the Royal Beachfront Suites, which are enclosed in their own garden courtyard with two pools and a central lounge reserved exclusively for Royal Suite guests, where continental breakfast and evening cocktails are served each day.

Half Moon has six outstanding restaurants, the open-air Seagrape Terrace, the Sugarmill Restaurant, Il Giardino, La Baguette, Sakura, and the Royal Stocks. Guests can select over one hundred different kinds of wines from several countries at any of the restaurants. The Seagrape specializes in Caribbean cuisine, and diners can sit on the tree-shaded seaside patio and enjoy dining by candlelight under the starry skies. If you're in the mood for chicken marinated in lime and fresh herbs, *duckanoo* (sweet potato dessert), or breadfruit vichyssoise, this is the place to come. During and after dinner there is a resident band for dancing well into the evening and a discotheque for late-night fun.

Under the direction of the Austrian chef, Andreas Rauscher, the Victorian-style Sugarmill Restaurant is located on the grounds of—surprise—a sugar plantation, where you'll find the remains of a 200-year-old water-powered mill. Here diners are treated to dishes such as freshly made pastas, prime rib, flambéed entrees, and shrimp stuffed with ripe bananas and cooked in coconut batter. You can dine on the open-air terrace or inside while enjoying live music for listening and dancing.

For a change of pace, you can order room service and indulge in a lazy morning with breakfast in bed. Try the coconut waffles, fresh fruits, and Blue Mountain coffee. A Night Owl menu is available from 10:00 p.m. to 1:00 a.m. Beach parties, floor shows with native entertainers, and steel drum bands are scheduled on various days. As if there weren't enough places to hang out, there is also the breezy, beachside bar.

Since the choices and quality of food at Half Moon are among the best in Jamaica, if not the Caribbean, take one of the plans that includes food as well as the various sports activities. The Imperial Plan is the most comprehensive, followed by the Platinum Plan. There are also programs that allow you to dine around at sister properties (Round Hill, Coyaba, Dragon Bay, and Jamaica Inn).

Half Moon Golf, Tennis, and Beach Club

Location: On 400 beachfront acres in Montego Bay

Romantic Highlights: Clusters of villas and suites, some with private pools; candlelight dining under the stars

Address/Phone: Montego Bay, Jamaica, W.I.; (876) 953–2211; fax (876) 953–2731

E-mail: reservations@halfmoonclub.com.jm

Web Site: www.halfmoon.com.jm

U.S. Reservations: Charms, (800) 742–4276

Owner/Manager: Heinz W. Simonitsch, managing director

Arrival/Departure: Transfer complimentary with Imperial, Golf, Spa, and Platinum Plans

Distance from Donald Sangster International Airport, Montego Bay: 6 miles

Distance from Montego Bay: 7 miles

Accommodations: 419, including rooms, suites, cottages, and villas; many with private pools

Most Romantic Room/Suite: Imperial Suites, Royal Suites, or beachfront cottages

Amenities: Air-conditioning, ceiling fans, hair dryer, minibar, cable TV, radio, double sinks (villas and Royal Suites)

Electricity: 110 volts

Sports and Facilities: 18-hole championship golf course, putting green; 9 tennis courts; 4 squash courts; scuba diving, snorkeling, sailboarding, sailing, paddleboats, glass-bottom boat, deep-sea fishing; horseback riding, bicycles; saunas; aerobics classes; 3 large pools, 1 children's pool

Dress Code: Casually smart

Weddings: A wedding package, priced at $850, includes marriage officer, witnesses, flowers, champagne, video, cake, and photos.

Rates/Packages: The Platinum Plan, $270–$745 per person per night, includes transfers, champagne, meals, bar drinks, minibar drinks, room service bar, dine- and lunch-around program, tennis, golf, watersports, sauna, use of gym, bicycles, squash, horseback riding, government tax, and service charge. Imperial Plan, $345–$820 per person per night includes everything in the Platinum Plan plus private car transfers, tours, wine and champagne, golf cart, caddy fees, club and shoe storage, club rental, golf clinic, spa service and health and fitness programs. European Plan, spa, and golf packages also available.

Payment/Credit Cards: Most major

Deposit: 3 nights required for confirmation

Government Taxes: Included

Service Charges: Included

Entry Requirements for U.S. Citizens: Valid passport, or birth certificate with raised seal along with two recent photo IDs

SANDALS RESORTS

Jamaica

Sandals Resorts packages romance with a capital "R." Starting in Montego Bay, Jamaica, with the first property, Sandals now has more than a dozen (and growing) spread out over several other islands, including St. Lucia, Antigua, and the Bahamas. The resort company's all-inclusive, couples-only concept continues to score a "ten" with honeymooners for a number of reasons.

For starters, their ultra-inclusive plan, whereby you pay one price up front for virtually everything, is a real winner. Accommodations, meals, snacks, bar beverages including name-brand liquors, water sports, tennis, golf, tips, and just about anything else you can think of are all rolled into the package. Since many young couples have a set amount to spend, knowing there will be no surprises when they check out provides a high level of emotional comfort. It also eliminates the "Do we have enough cash to eat here tonight?" kind of discussion. But no matter how good an idea, this wouldn't work unless the resorts themselves were really romantic and special. They are.

Guided all along the way by its dynamic founder and chairman, Gordon "Butch" Stewart, Sandals has attained a well-deserved reputation for consistently delivering what it promises: a "no problem" romantic holiday with all the bells and whistles. Standard with Sandals are king-size beds, beautiful decor, a whole range of sports and fitness facilities, every water sport you can think of, including scuba diving, and a staff that radiates as much good cheer as kids on their first day of summer vacation.

The fact that you can walk up to any of the bars and order a drink or food at will without having to sign a chit or pull out your wallet is a big plus. This also goes for the restaurants. You can eat at the same one every night or eat around. You can order anything on the menu—wine, beer, mixed drinks—whatever you're in the mood for, and it's all part of the package.

There is a huge list of activities available to guests, all complimentary. On hand to keep the mood upbeat and arrange special activities and parties are the energetic Playmakers. If you like to be on the go from dawn to dusk waterskiing, hiking, or playing tennis or golf at the Sandals Golf and Country Club, you can pig out on the vast array of activities on tap at any of the Sandals properties. And if you tire of the scenery where you're staying, you can hop on a shuttle and spend the day or evening at one of the other Sandals resorts as part of their Stay at One, Play at Six, Enjoy All concept.

You'll find many other young newlyweds to exchange wedding stories with on your honeymoon at Sandals, and since the resorts operate exclusively for couples, you won't have to share your pool space with any kids. Many couples marry here and go on to make friendships that may last a lifetime.

Each of the Sandals properties offers the same quality of services and amenities. Where you choose to stay, however, will depend on what is really important to you. Each place has its own unique allure.

Sandals Montego Bay, the oldest of the properties and one of the most intimate, enjoys a wonderful beach. Its 245 rooms and suites are located in two-story buildings and two-unit cottages that are literally a stone's throw from the sand. The lobby is not as elegant as those of the other properties, and the resort's location close to the airport can be a distraction. However, the staff and guests cheerfully make light of the occasional jets that zoom in and out by waving to them—a Montego Bay tradition. And being so close to the airport means you can land, clear customs, and be on the beach inside about a half-hour. The beachfront suite with separate sitting room, marble bath, four-poster bed, and patio with a private pool is wonderful. And especially good here are the restaurants.

The 190-room **Sandals Royal Caribbean** is also close to the airport and is set on seventeen acres fringed by a series of six white, sandy beaches. The rooms, which are located in two- and three-story pink-and-white buildings, are designed in the spirit of a traditional Georgian great house and are elegantly furnished with four-poster beds, English flowered chintz drapes and bedspreads, and classic mahogany furniture. The buildings, arranged around three nice little pools, are named after homes owned by British royalty and look to the sea.

If you love white sandy beaches and don't mind being a bit out of the way, try the 223-room **Sandals Negril Beach Resort & Spa**. Ask for the loft suites, which are set into the palms and gardens along a 7-mile, powdery, white-sand beach. It's about a ninety-minute ride from the airport and has a more laid-back ambience than the other Sandals resorts.

Set in a virtual Garden of Eden, **Sandals Ocho Rios Resort & Golf Club** is a botanical wonderland of flowers, trees, and shrubs. Hammocks are hidden in little glades, small streams bubble through the ferns and grasses, and bridges span the waterways. Two pools are action centers for high-energy sports like water volleyball and swimming races. There is also a smaller pool, hidden in the dense "jungle," where you can escape and simply loll around. If you're looking for a long stretch of white-sand beach, you may be disappointed; the beach here is small. The views from your oceanside room are great, though, and the satisfaction level of the property's guests is high.

Sandals Dunn's River Golf Resort & Spa, one of Sandal's newest resorts in Jamaica, resembles a posh establishment on the Italian Riviera. Rooms are located in two large, red-roofed, two- and six-story buildings facing the sea. Here the grounds have been sculpted, molded, and planted to the nines, creating a playground of plea sure. The largest pool in Jamaica, with its own waterfall—a replica of Dunn's River Falls—and swim-up bar, along with seaside gazebos, Jacuzzis, bridges, and a piano bar are spread out over a large area. Rooms are elegantly furnished, and the beach is good.

You might assume, since the food is already included and paid for, that a place like Sandals could get away with providing rather average restaurants. Not so. At Sandals the restaurant side of the resort operation is first-rate. Dinners feature a la carte menus, and couples can dine alone or with other couples. Breakfast and lunch are buffets, but a nice Sandals touch is the "white glove" service—a waiter carries your tray to your table. Each resort averages four restaurants, and all offer a distinctly different dining experience, ranging from informal to elegantly casual. Most of the restaurants are oriented to the sea, and the Bali Hai restaurant at Sandals Royal Jamaican is actually on its own little island.

If you like Italian food, you can head to Cucina Romana, at Sandals Montego Bay, where you can dine on a freshly made pasta of your choice while enjoying the sunset view from your table on the open-air deck. Next door, at Sandals Royal Jamaican, the Courtyard treats its

diners to fresh-grilled specialties. If the flair and flourish of a teppanyaki Japanese restaurant is tempting, you can try Kimonos at Sandals Negril. Here you'll dine on exotic Oriental entrees prepared right in front of you.

Sandals went all the way to Holland to find an authentic Indonesian chef for Bali Hai. Since the restaurant is located just offshore from Sandals Royal Jamaican, getting there via the resort's private launch is part of the fun. Once you arrive at the entrance of the ornate, carved-wood building, a hostess wraps a colorful silk scarf around you, your "costume" for the evening. Diners sit at long tables where hot and spicy as well as mild dishes (for more timid

palates) are placed in the center for everyone to sample.

In the elegant category, Sandals Montego Bay's Oleander Room, brainchild of Horace Peterkin, the resort's enterprising general manager, has stenciling on the ceiling and a warm coral decor accented with brass lamps, chandeliers, and Palladian windows overlooking the sea. Most romantic. This is your chance to try some tasty Jamaican specialties.

Get hungry between meals? Each Sandals resort has an "anytime grill," open well into the night, offering snacks as well as made-to-order meals.

Dollar for dollar, the Sandals resorts offer a lot of value and a lot more unexpected pleasures.

Sandals Resorts

Location: Montego Bay, Negril, and Ocho Rios

Romantic Highlights Couples only; nonstop activities and quiet hideaway places; romantic restaurants; Stay at One, Enjoy All program—use all the Sandals resorts at no extra charge

Address/Phone: In Jamaica, W.I.: Sandals Montego Bay, P.O. Box 100, Kent Avenue, Montego Bay, St. James; (876) 952–5510 or 952–5515; fax (876) 952–0816; Sandal's Royal Caribbean, Mahoe Bay, Box 167, Montego Bay, St. James; (876) 953–2231 or 953–2232; fax (876) 953–2788; Sandals Negril, P.O. Box 12, Negril; (876) 957–5216 or 957–4217; fax (876) 957–5338; Sandals Ocho Rios, P.O. Box 771, Ocho Rios, St. Ann; (876) 974–5691; fax (809) 974–5700; Sandals Dunn's River, P.O. Box 51, Ocho Rios, St. Ann; (876) 972–1610; fax (876) 972–1611

U.S. Reservations: (800) SANDALS

Owner/Manager: Gordon "Butch" Stewart, chairman of the board; Horace Peterkin, general manager, Sandals Montego Bay; Carl Hendricks, general manager, Sandals Royal Caribbean; Baldwin Powell, general manager, Sandals Negril; Michael Darby, general manager, Sandals Ocho Rios; Louis Grant, general manager, Sandals Dunn's River

Arrival/Departure: Sandals guests are met at the airport and escorted to their resort.

Distance from Donald Sangster International Airport, Montego Bay: Driving time: Montego Bay 5 minutes; Ocho Rios 1¾ hours; Negril 1½ hours

Accommodations: Rooms, suites, bungalows: Sandals Montego Bay, 245 rooms and suites in nine categories; Sandals Royal Caribbean, 190 rooms in six categories; Sandals Negril, 223 rooms in six categories, including loft suites; Sandals Ocho Rios, 237 rooms in five categories; Sandals Dunn's River, 256 rooms and suites in five categories

Most Romantic Room/Suite: At Sandals Montego Bay, the Presidential or Prime Minister Suites or the beachfront suite with the private pool (shared only with adjacent suite); Sandals Royal Caribbean, Grand Luxe Honeymoon Beachfront or Beachfront Royal Suites; Sandals Negril, Beachfront Honeymoon Suite or Beachfront Honeymoon One-Bedroom Loft Suites; Sandals Ocho Rios, Penthouse Honeymoon Ocean-View Suite; Sandals Dunn's River, the Penthouse Honeymoon Suite or the one-bedroom Oceanfront Suite. These accommodations will run you approximately $500 more (for 7 nights) than the most inexpensive room but are worth it if you care to splurge a bit.

Amenities: Air-conditioning, king-size bed, ceiling fans, hair dryer, generous kits of lotions and shampoo, telephone, clock radio, TV, minibar, and safe deposit box

Electricity: 110 volts

Sports and Facilities: Tennis day or night, scuba diving, snorkeling, sailboarding, sailing, Hobie-Cats, paddleboats, canoes, kayaks, racquetball, golf, pitch-and-putt golf, volleyball, basketball; pool tables, shuffleboard, horseshoes, croquet, Ping-Pong, aquatriking, squash, and waterskiing (except Ocho Rios); "Fit-Shape" program, exercise rooms, aerobics classes

Dress Code: Casual

Weddings: Over 500 weddings are performed annually at the various Sandals properties. On-site wedding coordinators arrange all the details, including taking care of the paper work, leading the couple through the process of getting the marriage license, flowers, music, and reception. "Wedding-Moons"—Sandals's term—can be as intimate as a couple getting married at the beach or under a gazebo with a best man and attendant "borrowed" from the Sandals staff. Or it can be a more elaborate affair held at one of the Sandals villas with a reception for the couple's family and friends.

A Sandals wedding costs $750 (or is free with a stay of 5 nights). The package includes preparation of documents, best man/maid of honor (if needed), wedding announcement cards, services of a justice of the peace or clergy, tropical flowers, wedding cake, champagne, personalized candlelight dinner, and wedding video. Options include special treats such as sunset cruise, reception, gift baskets, and upgraded villa accommodations.

There are many places a couple can choose to be married. Most popular are places like the gazebo at Sandals Montego Bay and the beach or the gardens in Sandals Ocho Rios. Brides can bring their own dresses or use one provided by Sandals. One bride who got married in Sandals Dunn's River wore a white, two-piece swimsuit with her veil, gloves, and garter. The groom wore a pair of white shorts, a bow tie, a cummerbund, and a boutonniere attached to one of his shirt garters. Taking a quick dip in the Caribbean after the ceremony was "no problem."

Rates/Packages: All-inclusive rates for 7 nights start at $1,715 per person

Payment/Credit Cards: Most major

Deposit: Guarantee with credit card

Government Taxes: Included

Service Charges: Included

Entry Requirements for U.S. Citizens: Proof of citizenship; passport best

SWEPT AWAY NEGRIL
Jamaica

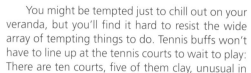

Swept Away's romantic beachfront setting, gardens, and spacious veranda suites along with its exceptional health and fitness complex have been wooing romantics ever since the resort opened just a few years ago. The luxurious suites, which sit amid tropical gardens overlooking the turquoise sea, are as tastefully decorated as they are comfortable. Jamaican in style and character, the decor is designed to complement the natural colors of the outdoors with the use of local woods, rattan chaises and chairs with puffy cushions, king-size beds, red-tile floors, and upbeat, pink-and-white fabrics. Your bedroom opens onto a very large veranda where you can enjoy the views of the gardens and sea. Rooms are air-conditioned, but you will probably find that the louvered-window walls along with a gently turning ceiling fan will keep you cool.

You might be tempted just to chill out on your veranda, but you'll find it hard to resist the wide array of tempting things to do. Tennis buffs won't have to line up at the tennis courts to wait to play: There are ten courts, five of them clay, unusual in the Caribbean, where courts are most often of the hard-surface variety. Swept away has a 25-meter pool, complete with lap lanes, air-conditioned racquetball and squash courts, an easy-on-your-feet aerobics floor, a par-course fitness circuit, and even a basketball court. If you want to work out, you can head to the gym, which has all the latest equipment. Unlimited golf at the Negril Hills Golf Club, five minutes away, is included in your package.

Sitting on a twenty-acre piece of pristine beachfront on the western end of Jamaica, Swept Away has a boatload of water sports, such as sailing, kayaking, sailboard-

ing, and waterskiing. Certified scuba divers get two free dives daily, and you can join others for a game of beach volleyball—always a good way to meet other guests.

Swept Away earns kudos for its cuisine, which tastes as good as it looks. Since the resort stresses a healthy lifestyle, you'll find a lot of choices on the menu that are low in fat, yet very tasty. There are a fruit and veggie bar on the grounds and a beachside grill where you can get things like fresh fruit and vegetable juice concoctions, pita sandwiches, and fish sandwiches. When it comes to serious eating, you can dine in either the alfresco Sea Grape beachside restaurant, featuring Jamaican specialties, or Feathers Restaurant, which offers gourmet cuisine. Be sure to try the pumpkin soup and fresh red snapper.

When night falls, you can dance under the stars to the music of a resident band or you can sit back and relax in the piano lounge.

Newlyweds are invited to a special party just for honeymooners, where they can win a one-week return stay at the resort, a dinner for two at a nearby restaurant, a catamaran cruise, horseback rides, or a 30 percent discount at the boutique.

You can be as active—or as lazy—as you want to be. No one coaxes you to do anything. One of the most difficult choices you may have to make is just what you want to do first. Do you want to dawdle in bed in the early morning and have room service bring you breakfast? Do you want to settle into a comfy chaise on the beach or by the smaller seaside pool, or do you feel up to the early morning beachfront power walk?

Swept Away packs a lot of value in its all-inclusive package, even a special massage class, where you can learn techniques to reduce and relieve stress in your mate. Just about the only thing you'll have to pay extra for are the services provided by the new full-service spa and salon facility, where you can get massages and beauty treatments.

Swept Away Negril

Location: Located on 20 acres on Long Bay in Negril, at the western tip of Jamaica

Romantic Highlights: Superb sports and fitness complex; white-sand beach; large ocean-view balconies

Address/Phone: Long Bay, Negril, Jamaica, W.I.; (876) 957–4061; fax (876) 957–4060; U.S. address: 4944 LeJeune Road South, Coral Gables, FL 33146

E-mail: info@couples.com

Web Site: www.couples.com

U.S. Reservations: (800) COUPLES

Owner/Manager: Paul Pennicook, president and CEO, Issa Hotels and Resorts

Arrival/Departure: A representative from the resort will meet you at the airport for transfer to the resort.

Distance from Donald Sangster International Airport, Montego Bay: 60 miles (1½ hours by car); 2 miles (5 minutes) from Negril Airport

Distance from Negril Center: 5 minutes

Accommodations: 134 Caribbean-style veranda suites in three categories: garden, atrium, and beachfront

Most Romantic Room/Suite: Beachfront suites

Amenities: Hair dryer, telephone, in-room safe, ceiling fan, toiletries, air-conditioning; room service for continental breakfast, coffeemaker, umbrella, robes, iron/ironing board

Electricity: 110 volts

Sports and Facilities: 10 lighted tennis courts (5 hard, 5 clay), pool tables, 2 pools, bicycles, jogging track, golf course, basketball court; watersports; gym; aerobics; racquetball, squash, volleyball; saunas, Jacuzzis

Dress Code: For daytime dining women are requested to wear coverups and men, shirts; resort casual in Main Dining Room; in Feathers men required to wear collared shirt

Weddings: Complimentary with any package are minister's fee, marriage license, flowers, wedding cake, and champagne.

Rates/Packages: All-inclusive packages include accommodations, transfers, all meals, 24-hour food service, unlimited drinks, water sports, use of fitness facilities, afternoon tea, entertainment, clinics, and golf. $510–$840 per couple per night. Honeymoon and wedding packages available.

Payment/Credit Cards: Most major

Deposit: One-night deposit for three- to seven-night stay, three-night deposit for stays over 7 nights

Government Taxes: $27 departure tax

Service Charges: Included

Entry Requirements for U.S Citizens: Proof of citizenship required; passport best

FOUR SEASONS RESORT NEVIS

Nevis

Once you hear the rustle of the swaying palms, feel the gentle breezes crossing the beach, and see the flourishing tropical rain forest from your private veranda, you will no doubt believe that you have landed in paradise.

Four Seasons Resort Nevis, which is part of the Four Seasons group of prestigious, upscale resorts in exotic locations around the world, lives up to its reputation for providing a bundle of services and luxurious appointments, such as the large marble baths and the Evian water sprayed gently on your face by attendants to cool you while you lounge on the beach or by the pool. But beware: This resort also delivers high prices and can make a serious dent in your budget.

One of the best things Four Seasons has going for it is its location—really spectacular, with a long, golden sand beach lined by what seem to be hundreds of tall, graceful palm trees that blend into the hillside beyond.

It also has an impressive, 6,725-yard, eighteen-hole Robert Trent Jones II golf course that climbs from sea level up the volcanic slopes of Mt. Nevis to the fifteenth hole, where, from your perch at about 1,000 feet above sea level, you will see some incredible views of the sea and craggy hills. The course takes you up and down the mountainside, over deep ravines, and along the ocean. What more could a golfer want! Perhaps a pro shop? Of course. Nothing is left to chance here.

Tennis players have a fancy complex of ten courts, a pro shop, and organized lessons and clinics. And if this isn't enough, there is a fully equipped health club, a complete water sports center, two pools, Ping-Pong, croquet, hiking paths, and myriad other activities that may pull you away from your lounge on one of the most beautiful beaches in the Caribbean.

Occasionally even those with a passion for *plein air* find it necessary to come inside. Because the restaurants and lounges have been designed to ensure maximum exposure to the outdoor environment, even when you are technically indoors at the resort you can still enjoy a mag-

nificent view, trade-wind breezes, and the sound of lapping waves.

Most of the public rooms are located in the sumptuous Great House, the heart of the resort. Many public rooms are open-air, with patios and terraces leading to gardens of tropical Nevisian flowers. The Library Bar is enclosed, cozy, and could have come straight from England—it even has a fireplace and paintings of tall ships. On the rare occasions when the sun is not shining, this is a wonderful place for cocktails before and after dinner.

The two-story bungalow buildings that stretch along the beach have rather uninspired architectural designs, but the interiors of the rooms and suites are spacious and decorated to the nines. Deep chestnut-brown armoires, carved headboards, brass lamps, and botanical prints contribute to the British ambience. The use of rattan chairs, tropical-colored fabrics and prints, and tile floors keep the rooms from looking too heavy. Fresh flowers and potted palms also help lighten it all up.

The bathrooms will really knock your socks off. They're simply superb, with lots of marble, double vanities, attractive lighting, and plenty of fluffy towels. The Four Seasons toiletries are especially fine.

There are two gourmet restaurants that serve Caribbean-inspired meat, fish, and seafood dishes and fresh fruits and vegetables: the more formal Dining Room, with its French doors, high ceiling and chandeliers; and the casual, open-air Grill Room La Cabana, which serves Mediterranean specialties and brick-oven pizzas. The Ocean Terrace overlooks the pool and the beach, and there is the Tap Room, with a game area and entertainment lounge for children and teens, and a sports pavilion.

Evenings you will be able to enjoy dancing and listening to local bands, including a steel drum group.

So if you don't mind blowing a lot of cash, be prepared to revel in one of the most ultraluxurious megaresorts in the islands.

Four Seasons Resort Nevis

Location: Set on 2,000 feet of beachfront on Nevis's leeward coast

Romantic Highlights: Catamaran cruise to private beach; candlelight dinners on your veranda

Address/Phone: P.O. Box 565, Pinney's Beach, Charlestown, Nevis, W.I.; (869) 469–1111; fax (869) 469–1112

Web Site: www.fourseasons.com

U.S. Reservations: (800) 332–3442

Owner/Manager: Robert Whitfield, general manager

Arrival/Departure: Most fly to San Juan for a quick flight to St. Kitts, where guests are met by a hotel representative and whisked to the private dock in Basseterre to board a boat for the 30-minute ride to the resort. Prior to boarding you complete check-in formalities and enjoy some refreshments. From Antigua and St. Martin you can fly direct to Nevis via regional carriers.

Distance from St. Kitts Airport: 20 minutes by boat; 6 miles by land

Distance from Charlestown: 1½ miles

Accommodations: 196 rooms and suites, each with a large veranda ranging from 120 to 160 square feet, overlooking the ocean, Nevis Peak, or the golf course. There are also 20 exquisite villas and homes for rent.

Most Romantic Room/Suite: The oceanfront Nelson and Hamilton Suites

Amenities: Air-conditioning, ceiling fan, toiletries, telephone, TV, VCR, clock radio, ice maker, minibar, hair dryer, twin vanities, separate shower and tub, magnifying mirror, bathrobes, bath scale, 24-hour room service

Electricity: 110 volts

Sports and Facilities: 10 tennis courts (3 lighted), 18-hole championship golf course; health club, massage therapies; beach, pool, snorkeling equipment, sailboards, kayaks, sailboats, sea cycles, catamarans, waterskiing, fishing, scuba diving; croquet, volleyball, shuffleboard, and hiking

Dress Code: Casually elegant

Weddings: Can be arranged

Rates/Packages: Romance in Paradise package, $3,815–$7,455 per couple, includes 7 nights in deluxe oceanfront accommodations, flowers, champagne and truffles, candlelight dinners, unlimited golf and tennis, massage for two, transfers, and half-day catamaran cruise to private beach.

Payment/Credit Cards: Most major

Deposit: Three-night deposit applied toward first and last nights' stay (if staying for a week); refundable if canceled 3 weeks or more prior to arrival date.

Government Taxes: 8 percent

Service Charges: 10 percent

Entry Requirements for U.S. Citizens: Proof of citizenship; passport best

NISBET PLANTATION BEACH CLUB
Nevis

You come here for the peace and the waves washing up on shore, the sound of which mingles with the rustling coconut palms. Cone-shaped mountain peaks rise like soft-pointed hats into the mist; a few lazy cows trespass across manicured rolling lawns; you walk barefoot in the sand as the sun sets. Isn't this what the Caribbean is all about? You expect an island of just 36 square miles with a population of about 9,000 to be quiet and laid back. It is.

If you want to experience the "real" Caribbean, try Nisbet Plantation Beach Club. It all starts with your arrival at the little island airport just barely large enough for a small counter and desk. Already the warm tropical air is blowing away the travel kinks.

I arrived at Nisbet just in time for tea accompanied by thinly sliced salmon sandwiches, pumpkin bread, and chocolate chip cookies. Sitting at an umbrella-shaded table on the outdoor patio of the Great House, I had an unobstructed view right down to the sea, a promise of things to come.

Staggered from the Great House along either side of a wide, grassy, palm-studded way leading to the sea are one- and two-story yellow cottages with four-sided, pointed roofs (Nevis, by law, has no buildings more than two stories high). Hibiscus, oleanders, crotons, and a variety of other brilliant tropical flowers and shrubs hug the buildings and walkways. A tennis court is tucked into a corner of the property, and an open-air beachfront restaurant and bar sits at the water's edge.

Cottages are airy and beautifully appointed with tropical fabrics, rattan chairs, white-tile floors, and plump cushions. Most have high ceilings, walk-in closets, screened porch, and king-size beds. All have patios or balconies and air-conditioning as well as louvered windows, fans, and constant ocean breezes guaranteed to keep you cool.

What surprises at Nisbet are the details. There's a faucet to rinse the sand off your feet just outside your entrance, reading lamps by your bed at just the right height, a drying bar for wet suits, a minibar, a full-length mirror, double vanities, straw carpets in the screened sitting area, plenty of tables and chairs, a coffeemaker, umbrellas, and even a flashlight and a can of bug spray. (Yes, the Caribbean does have an occasional bug or two.) Cool blue-and-white seersucker bathrobes are a refreshing change from the traditional terry. Half shutters between the two rooms in the suites allow air and light to come into the bedroom without sacrificing privacy.

At night the property is lit not with neon-colored floods into the trees, but naturally, softly. It feels like a plantation (which it was in its former life). There are few concrete walkways, mostly you walk on grassy or gravel paths (leave your heels at home). There are rows of palms heavy with clusters of coconuts, banana trees, and room to play croquet.

The beach is wide and long and there are plenty of chaises to go around. Hammocks are strung between palms, and there is a seaside pool and terrace.

What makes it all work is the husband-and-wife management team, Kathie and Don Johnson. They're young and energetic but certainly not inexperienced. Each has more than twenty years in the hotel industry. And it shows.

From ensuring that their guests are met at the airport to being on hand to make sure everything runs smoothly—from a guest who requests a fan to coffee being served promptly at the beachfront restaurant—they oversee every detail. Kathie and Don are "people people." They like to talk to their guests to hear how things are going. To make sure they are happy.

Nisbet has three restaurants: the romantic, candlelit Great House, with its open terrace, high tray ceiling, and arched windows; Coconuts, the casual poolside restaurant open for breakfast and lunch; and the beach bar where guests can enjoy lunch with a view by the water. The food does not disappoint. The executive chef uses as much fresh local ingredients as he can get his hands on. The menu changes each night, revolving around what he can get that morning: fresh fish, poultry, meat, vegetables, and fruits are skillfully and creatively cooked into dishes that combine the flavors of the Caribbean and more traditional tastes. There is always a vegetarian dish.

Nisbet Plantation Beach Club

Location: On Nevis's reef-protected north shore

Romantic Highlights: Private cottage; hammocks for two; in-room massages

Address/Phone: St. James Parish, Nevis, W.I.; (869) 469–9325; fax (869) 469–9864

E-mail: nisbetbc@caribsurf.com

Web Site: www.NisbetPlantation.com

U.S. Reservations: (800) 742–6008; e-mail: irr@worldnet.att.net

Owner/Manager: David Dodwell, owner; Kathie and Don Johnson, managers

Arrival/Departure: Round-trip transfers provided from St. Kitts

Distance from St. Kitts: About 5 minutes by Nevis Express; 45 minutes by ferry; Puerto Rico about 1 hour by air

Distance from Charlestown: 10 miles; distance from St. Martin about 25 minutes by Winair or Nevis Express

Accommodations: 38 rooms and suites in plantation-style cottages

Most Romantic Rooms/Suites: Deluxe Suite with a separate living room; Premier Suites with living room, wet bar, and open patio

Amenities: Hair dryer, fans, minibar, TV, coffee bar, *New York Times* fax, some rooms with air-conditioning

Electricity: 110 volts

Sports and Facilities: Pool; walking, hiking, boating, tennis, snorkeling, massages, golf, horseback riding, plantation tours, ecotours, guided hikes, scuba diving, biking, deep-sea fishing nearby.

Dress Code: Resort casual. About the only one who wears a tie around here is Patterson, the maître d' who claims to own more than 700 unique ties.

Weddings: Can be arranged; wedding package $993 for ceremony, private massage for bride and groom, champagne, flowers, cake, photographer, wedding coordinator, license, registration and minister's fee

Rates/Packages: $290–$645 per room per night, including breakfast and dinner, tennis, snorkeling, laundry service, transfers from Nevis Airport, local telephone calls, and postage. Island Intimacy Romance Package: from $3,629 per couple, including 6 nights' accommodations, breakfasts, dinners, tea, champagne, car rental for 2 days, service charges, taxes, transfers, private massages, private picnic on Lover's Beach, and a sailing cruise or kayaking trip.

Payment/Credit Cards: Most major

Deposit: Three-night deposit at time of booking

Government Taxes: 9 percent

Service Charges: 10 percent

Entry Requirements for U.S. Citizens: Proof of citizenship; passport best

Chilled avocado and passion fruit soup, fresh mahimahi fillet with almond and banana crust served with a lemongrass sauce and steamed purple potatoes; smoked butternut squash ravioli served with artichokes and shiitake mushrooms in a sun-dried red pepper cream sauce with fresh Parmesan cheese; and chocolate truffle torte are typical choices.

In the evening Kathie and Don greet their guests with complimentary hors d'oeuvres in the Great House lounge before dinner. Once a week, Nisbet's popular beach barbecue features an array of fresh fish and other items. Local bands play in the lounge most evenings.

Nisbet is not a place to come if you want to party all night, ride madly on Jet Skis, or play volleyball in the pool. Rather, you come to soak up the enticing aromas of the flowers and the views of the sea and hills, poke down roads overgrown with grasses to an abandoned sugar mill, pack a picnic and drive to a secluded beach for lunch, or just hang out on the beach with a piña colada.

Above, the palms' feathery fronds gently nudge the sea breezes. Cooling and soothing. Peace.

HORNED DORSET PRIMAVERA HOTEL
Puerto Rico

The elegant Horned Dorset Primavera Hotel, which is hidden away on Puerto Rico's western shore, focuses more on relaxation than recreation and offers only a few facilities. The resort attracts solitude-seeking guests who want a small hotel with plush European standards. Located 2½ hours from San Juan, the Horned Dorset isn't the easiest of places to find. But once you do, you may never want to leave. And that is just part of its mystique.

Its name sounds like a weird kind of English pasta, but the hotel, directly on the pounding surf, is named after a breed of sheep raised on the grounds of the owner's upstate New York inn. No sheep are in sight; still, the setting is bucolic.

The grounds are lavishly landscaped with exotic plants. A recently built Spanish colonial hacienda with a curving split staircase brings you to the stunning, tiled-floor breezeway/lobby and an open porch cantilevered over to catch the sea spray. Below is a courtyard with a gigantic fountain, and beyond that is a large swimming pool with a wide lounging deck set up with Japanese umbrellas.

Off the lobby is a smaller, open dining terrace for breakfasts of warm banana bread, local fresh-ground coffee, finger bananas, papaya, and pineapple from local fields. Light lunches might feature fresh, grilled fish and a yummy salad. Drinks are served in the charming, wicker-furnished library, home to Pompideau, a pampered macaw in a huge cage.

The walk up the hacienda's stairway to dinner, with the tree frogs chirping a chorus, brings you to the second-floor dining room, where you are served a six-course, prix-fixe dinner by candlelight. A member of the elite Relais & Châteaux group, the resort serves fine, French-inspired cuisine. A typical dinner might include Carrot Soup, Lobster and Grilled Vegetable Salad, Passion Fruit Granité, Roasted

Sierra with Red Wine Sauce, Radicchio and Celery Salad, Cheeses, and Papaya Soufflé with Lemon Sauce.

As you dine, romantic ballads are softly played in the background by a classical guitarist. You can sit by French doors that open onto a balcony overlooking the ocean and the tiny beach.

The tropical grounds are extremely quiet. No pets, no TVs, no radios, and no children are allowed on the property. What to do? How about lazing by the pool or reading a novel from the library? Fishing, whale-watching, and golf are only thirty minutes away and can be easily arranged. Or walk along an almost deserted beach for a couple of miles past a small fishing settlement.

Temptation in this languorous, lush bit of paradise lurks behind the mahogany-shuttered windows of well-appointed suites that match the plush public rooms in quality. There are handwoven rugs over tile floors, louvered and mullioned windows, roomy armoires, and large, lavish European baths with quirky features like big, old-fashioned tubs and brass antique shower fixtures.

Woodwork is from island artisans, and four-poster beds, claw-footed tubs, and some of the only bidets on the island are unexpected amenities. All units have individual air-conditioning, queen-size sofa beds in sitting areas, and furnished balconies looking out on the water and beach.

An ultraluxurious unit housing eight suites with plunge pools was finished in 1995, and in Spring 2002, twenty-two 1,400-square-foot duplex suites were added. These stunning new suites all face the ocean and come with private plunge pools. Along with the new Mirador Villa, they are the most superb accommodations.

The Horned Dorset is located in a part of Puerto Rico you may not even have a clue exists: quiet, quiet, and, yes, quiet. No casinos, no discos, no glitz. Just the Straits of Mona separating you from another island far across the water.

Horned Dorset Primavera Hotel

Location: On 4 acres, tucked away on the west coast of Puerto Rico

Romantic Highlights: Small, intimate inn by the sea; cocktails on seaside veranda as the sun sets

Address/Phone: Rincon, Puerto Rico 00677; (787) 823–4030; fax (787) 823–5580

E-mail: PGH@coqui.net

Web Site: www.horneddorset.com

U.S. Reservations: (800) 633–1857

Owner/Manager: Harold Davies and Kingsley Wratten

Arrival/Departure: Transfers can be arranged from the San Juan or Mayaguez Airports.

Distance from San Juan International Airport: 120 miles (2½ hours); Mayaguez Airport, 6 miles (10 minutes)

Distance from Rincon: 5 miles

Accommodations: 52 suites and the Mirador Villa

Most Romantic Room/Suite: New suites with plunge pools

Amenities: Air-conditioning, hair dryer, marble bath, toiletries, ceiling fans, ice service, room service (breakfast)

Electricity: 110 volts

Sports and Facilities: Pool; water sports and golf nearby; scuba and deep-sea fishing can be arranged

Dress Code: Semiformal, evenings

Weddings: Can be arranged

Rates/Packages: $190–$290 per person per night (winter), $140–$230 per person (summer); Mirador Villa, $400 per person per night (winter), $325 per person (summer); $80 per person includes breakfast and dinner; Romance package, $3,350–$4,130 per couple (summer), includes 7 nights' accommodations, breakfast, dinner, transfers, and champagne.

Payment/Credit Cards: All major

Deposit: Credit card deposit for 4 nights (winter); 1 night (summer); for refund cancel within 45 days of arrival date (winter); 15 days (summer)

Government Taxes: 9 percent

Service Charges: 15 percent on food and beverages; 3 percent for general service

ANSE CHASTANET
St. Lucia

There are no televisions, no room phones, nothing really to break the spell of tropical moonlight, refreshing sea breezes, and the scent of frangipani in this dense, green, jungly paradise that is the idyllic setting for Anse Chastanet. Your room may be wide open to lofty views of the blue-green pyramidlike peaks of the Pitons and the variegated blue sea. And this is exactly what Nick Troubetzkoy had in mind when he created Anse Chastanet.

Nick, an architect, and his wife, Karolin, have carved into the thick tropical forests on this remote hillside one of the world's most unique and romantic resorts. In the premium rooms there are no walls at all, so that you can easily hear the birds, the waves, and the rustling of palms. Waking up to see the cones of the two Pitons framed by the arches of your octagonal "tree house" can blow you away.

There are only forty-nine cottages, partially camouflaged by the foliage that rises like a thick green carpet from a lovely, coconut-palm-fringed beach. Thirty-seven of the cottages are staggered up the hillside, and twelve are located at the beach level. As you walk up the hillside to your cottage, you may wonder if the climb is worth it. It is. The higher you are, the better the view and the privacy.

Each room is fun and dramatically different not only in decor but in shape. Standard hillside rooms are rectangular and slightly smaller than the superior rooms, which are octagonal or rectangular in shape and feature two twins or one king-size bed. Beachside rooms are spacious, with either two double or one king-size bed, a bath with two sinks, a shower, and a large balcony or patio. Although these are just steps from the beach and probably the best choice for those who can't or don't want to climb the hill, they have garden, not ocean, views. It is the premium rooms located high up the hill that are so spectacular.

Even the showers are worth writing home about; many are as large as a garage. Ginger (number 14B) has a gommier tree growing right through it. Some open onto gardens, others to the sea. Most have no curtains or doors.

It's not just that the rooms are superspacious—7B is roughly 30 feet by 30 feet—it's the way they blend into the surroundings. Mahoe (number 14A), for example, is totally open on two sides. The only creatures that will share your private moments are the birds (which you'd expect would fly in and out, but they don't). You have mosquito netting, but you really don't need it.

Red-tile or wood floors, original art by Reina Nieland, a Dutch-Canadian artist who works in burlap and mixed media to create superb abstract collage, and woodcarvings by Lawrence Deligny, a St. Lucian artist, are located throughout the rooms and public areas. Simple but effective basket lamp shades with yellow insect repellent bulbs hang around the perimeters of the rooms, balconies, and restaurants.

If you can tear yourself away from your room, you'll find there's plenty to do here if you like water sports, hiking, or a massage. Located in a new beachfront building is the spa, Kai Belté ("house of beauty" in patois), where you can enjoy facials and body scrubs using natural fruits like mango and coconut. Professionally trained therapists offer a variety of massage treatments and reflexology at the spa or in your room. Also available at the spa are other beauty and body treatments, including body polishes, waxing, facials, pedicures, and manicures.

Among the resort's new toys are fifty Cannondale bikes with all the accessories, which can be rented for a half or full day. Ten miles of trails lace the 500-acre property.

There is a palm tree or palm-roofed umbrella for every guest who wants some shade on the picturesque, volcanic sand beach, which seems to sparkle with diamond dust in the sun. At one end of the beach, you'll find the casual Trou-au-Diable restaurant and bar, two boutiques, and the scuba center.

Two other restaurants, a bar, and a reception area are located midway up the hill. Dining up in the Tree House Restaurant, you look through foliage and flamboyant trees down to the beach and the turquoise waters. Breakfast is served at the Piton Restaurant, on the same level as the Tree House.

Food is excellent, especially the fresh-grilled catch of the day, which might be red snapper or grouper. Fresh fruits and vegetables such as breadfruit and christophine as well as curries are very tasty. And be sure to try the banana pancakes, a house specialty.

One of the Troubetzkoys' major commitments is to the crafts of St. Lucia. A woodcarver has his own workshop area at the northern end of the beach; a pottery shop has been established on the grounds. The work of local and international artists is represented in many of the rooms.

For scuba enthusiasts the waters off the beach are brilliantly clean and clear, and a reef on the southern end of the beach was recently declared a marine preserve.

Michael and Karyn Allard, managers of the Scuba St. Lucia Dive Center, maintain a staff of seven fully qualified dive instructors and offer a complete range of courses. Dive trips operate daily to sites around the island.

A must-do while you're here is an excursion with Menau, Anse's resident horticultural guide. He will take you to the ruins of an eighteenth-century French sugar plantation located off the resort's Anse Mamin Beach.

A complimentary water taxi, *Peace on Earth*, takes you to Anse Mamin and Soufrière. Or charter the resort's 37-foot yacht for a sail and snorkeling tour.

If you must have quick access to phones, TVs, and faxes, keep in mind the only public phones are found in the reception area midway up the hill and there's a fax machine in the office. That's it.

Anse Chastanet

Location: Situated on 600 hillside acres on the southwestern coast of St. Lucia

Romantic Highlights: Dramatic open rooms with spectacular views; huge open showers; candlelight dining and dancing

Address/Phone: P.O. Box 7000, Soufrière, St. Lucia, W.I.; (758) 459–7000 or (758) 459–7554; fax (758) 459–7700

U.S. Reservations: Ralph Locke Islands, (800) 223–1108 or (310) 440–4225; fax (310) 440–4220

Owner/Manager: Nick Troubetzkoy, owner and managing director; Karolin Guler Troubetzkoy, director of marketing and operations

Arrival/Departure: Pickup can be arranged at the airport

Distance from Hewanorra International Airport: 18 miles (1 hour); Virgie Airport, 30 miles (1¾ hours)

Distance from Soufrière: 1½ miles

Accommodations: 49 rooms: 4 open-style, Premium rooms on hillside, with dramatic Piton views; 12 large, open Deluxe hillside rooms; 12 Deluxe beachside rooms with a garden view; 17 Superior hillside rooms with wraparound balconies; 4 Standard hillside rooms

Most Romantic Room/Suite: Room 7F, huge and open on two sides; 14B, wide-open room with a tree growing in the shower; 14A, four-poster bed and wide-open vistas

Amenities: Hair dryer, refrigerator, tea and coffee bar, ceiling fans, supersize baths (most), bidets (some)

Electricity: 220 volts

Sports and Facilities: Scuba diving; snorkeling, kayaking, sailboarding, Sunfish sailing, hiking, swimming; spa; tennis; table tennis; mountain biking; yacht charters

Dress Code: Men requested to wear long slacks or long-cut Bermuda shorts at Tree House Restaurant

Weddings: Can be arranged. Wedding package priced at $695, with a number of options.

Rates/Packages: Double room, including breakfast and dinner, $440–$790 (winter); the breakfast and dinner plan is optional in the shoulder and summer seasons and is available at $60 per person per day; double room $245–$540, meals not included (spring and fall); $210–$485 (summer)

Payment/Credit Cards: Most major

Deposit: 3 nights in winter; 2 nights in summer and shoulder seasons; all weekly packages must be prebooked and prepaid in full.

Government Taxes: 8 percent

Service Charges: 10 percent

Entry Requirements for U.S. Citizens: Proof of citizenship; passport best

SANDALS ST. LUCIA GOLF RESORT & SPA
St. Lucia

Sandals has brought its couples-only, ultra-all-inclusive concept to St. Lucia, with Sandals St. Lucia Golf Resort & Spa. Getting to the resort can be an interesting experience depending on the airport you fly into. Coming into the Hewanorra, the larger airport, guarantees you a one-hour trip through winding mountain roads. It allows you views of banana plantations, the rain forest, the Pitons, and the island's volcanic attraction. For a closer look you can book tours of the island through the resort. The trip from the airport may be enough, however, since the resort offers plenty of things to keep you busy.

The first thing one couple I spoke to said you should do when you get to the resort—"even before the obvious honeymooner thing"—is to make dinner reservations. Said this newly married couple, who spent their June honeymoon there, "While we certainly never experienced a shortage of food at the resort, we found that there was limited seating at the specialty restaurants, especially the French place, La Toc, and Mario's, the Italian restaurant at the Halcyon resort." (At Sandal's St. Lucia you're allowed full access to the other resort on the island, Sandals Halcyon St. Lucia; a free hourly shuttle runs between the resorts.)

They said they loved Sandals St. Lucia for a number of reasons: "Here you don't have to deal with kids and singles. If you do feel like socializing with others, you have something instantly in common with the other guests—you share the same wedding date. So not only is everyone in the best mood of their lives, but you can feel free to trade wedding stories from what went perfectly right to where Uncle Ralph's hairpiece flew during the Electric Slide." They added, "If you feel like making a party out of it, you can join others with the Sandals' 'Playmakers,' who organize everything from aqua aerobics to beer-chugging contests."

The couple added, "One extra that we did indulge in was a sunset cruise. It's one of the few things you have to pay extra for, arranged through Sandals. It was a three-hour cruise on a large catamaran fully equipped with a stocked bar, a guitarist you can sing along with if you choose to, and a breathtaking view of the island at sundown. It turned out to be one of the most memorable parts of our honeymoon."

The larger and more luxurious of the company's two properties on the island, Sandals St. Lucia sits on 155 acres and boasts a huge, sprawling pool (the largest on the island), with waterfalls, a swim-up bar, whirlpool baths, bridges, and a pavilion. The property has 329 rooms, offering twelve categories in various locations and configurations including 56 new villas on Sunset Bluff. Two-story town houses, with a living room and patio upstairs and a bedroom downstairs, are set high along a bluff at one end of the property and come with marble baths, minibars, four-poster beds, and sitting areas; some also come with private plunge pools. Other rooms and suites are located closer to the ½-mile beach and near the golf course. Some of the villas are two-story; some also have plunge pools. Although the villas are more private, if you want to be near the action, go for the Grande Luxe Beachfront rooms and suites.

Sandals St. Lucia has several restaurants and bars, two pools, a fitness center, and a whole boatload of sports options, including golf on the premises, as well as a disco and nonstop other activities.

With five restaurants on the property and the opportunity to use three more at the second Sandals property, you can stay a week and dine at a new place every night. You can choose from the elegant La Toc restaurant, where the emphasis is on French cuisine, or try Japanese food at Kimonos, steak and ribs at Arizona, or Caribbean and Creole items at the Pitons Restaurant. You can eat inside by candlelight; outside, under the stars by the sea or by the pool. At night entertainment kicks in with

theme parties, disco dancing, billiards, and a piano bar.

Although you may find little impetus to leave the property, if you do decide to explore, there's much to see. St. Lucia, with its starkly beautiful Pitons, reminiscent of upside-down ice cream cones, is blessed with more than 19,000 acres of verdant rain forest. Reminiscent of Fiji or Kauai, with its steep hills and valleys carpeted with rich tapestries woven of palms, banana trees, bamboo, flowering plants, and other tropical foliage, St. Lucia is cut by streams and waterfalls plunging into deep pools curtained with giant ferns and fringed by golden sand. Dark volcanic-grained beaches sparkle like diamonds in the sun.

Most visitors make a trip to the famous La Soufrière volcano and Sulphur Spring. The last eruption here took place 200 years ago, leaving a smoking crater with more than twenty-one bubbling black pools of water that resemble liquid tar. Hydrogen sulfide, a stinky but non-poisonous gas smelling like rotten eggs, continually rises from somewhere deep in the earth, creating these boiling pools that are thought by some to have health benefits (when cooled down sufficiently, of course).

The whole scene is like a set from *Star Wars*. As you peer over the top of the rim and look down over this most inhospitable landscape, you can occasionally see someone bravely trekking over the grayish ground and rocks. (Don't try it—that stuff is hot.)

At Morne Coubaril Estate, a fifty-acre working plantation and museum, you can stroll through the attractive gardens and see reconstructed houses similar to those the original plantation workers lived in, small cramped affairs with mud floors and walls papered with newspaper. Here you can see how cocoa is harvested, dried, pulverized, and molded into chocolate sticks; you can also watch workers at the coconut "factory," where coconuts are processed and every part is put to some practical use, including the fiber of the shell, which is used in mattresses.

Sandals St. Lucia Golf Resort & Spa

Location: On a ½-mile stretch of white sandy beach in Castries on St. Lucia's northwestern coast

Romantic Highlights: Couples only, all-inclusive plan, non-stop activities and quiet hideaway places, romantic restaurants, secluded villas with private plunge pools; Stay at One, Play at Two program gives you use of Sandals Halcyon St. Lucia Beach restaurants and facilities at no extra charge

Address/Phone: P.O. Box 399, Castries, St. Lucia, W.I.; (758) 452–3081; fax (758) 452–1012

U.S. Reservations: (800) SANDALS

Owner/Manager: Konrad Wagner, general manager

Arrival/Departure: Sandals guests are met at the airport and escorted to their resort.

Distance from Virgie International Airport: 10 minutes; Hewanorra International Airport, 75 minutes

Accommodations: 329 rooms, suites, villas in 12 categories

Most Romantic Room/Suite: One-Bedroom Sunset Oceanview Suites (with private pools) and Grande Luxe Beachfront Suites

Amenities: Air-conditioning, king-size bed, ceiling fans, hair dryer, generous kits of lotions and shampoo, telephone, clock radio, color TV, safe; suite concierge service also includes terry robes, upgraded amenity kit, fully stocked wet bar, sitting area, mahogany four-poster bed, daily *New York Times*, fax, and services of dedicated suite concierge

Electricity: 110 volts

Sports and Facilities: 3 freshwater pools, 3 whirlpools, fitness center, tennis, scuba diving, snorkeling, sailboarding, sailing, Hobie-Cats, aquatriking, waterskiing, paddleboats, kayaks, golf, pool, volleyball, darts, shuffleboard, table tennis, lawn chess

Dress Code: Casual

Weddings: On-site wedding coordinators arrange all the details, including taking care of the paperwork, leading the couple through the process of getting the marriage license, flowers, music, and reception. "WeddingMoons"—Sandals's term—can be as intimate as a couple getting married at the beach or under a gazebo with a best man and attendant "borrowed" from the Sandals staff.

Rates/Packages: All-inclusive rates for 7 nights start at $2,170 per person

Payment/Credit Cards: Most major

Deposit: Guarantee with credit card

Government Taxes: Included

Service Charges: Included

Entry Requirements for U.S. Citizens: Proof of citizenship; passport best

WINDJAMMER LANDING VILLA BEACH RESORT & SPA
St. Lucia

You can reach Windjammer by land or by sea. Either way, you'll be impressed with this little seaside "village" of white villas with red roofs and white adobe turrets and arches reminiscent of Mykonos in the Greek islands. Narrow, winding brick paths, which meander up the hillside to the villas, are lined with a profusion of flowering bougainvillea, hibiscus, and oleander. Since the villas are clustered together comfortably, there is room on this 55-acre resort to explore: to poke around the nooks and crannies defined by the villas, gardens, pools, restaurants, and beaches.

An open-air car with a fringed top shuttles you up and down the hill to and from your villa to the beach, pools, and restaurants. But you'll find it tempting to laze away the day at your own private plunge pool, which is set in a tiled courtyard surrounded by flowers. From here the views of the sea and the hills in the distance are magnificent.

The one-bedroom villas, with 1,200 to 1,300 square feet of space, are a perfect choice for a romantic hideaway. The living rooms are large and airy, furnished with wicker furniture with pastel fabric cushions that contrast nicely with the red-tile floors and thick, round arches and windows. Cocoa straw mats, hand-painted tiles, and original art along with fresh flower arrangements add splashes of color to the white plaster walls, and lofty ceilings are light, pickled pine. There is a lovely tiled terrace with a dining area as well as a good-size kitchen. Baths are spacious and some have tubs and showers open to the sky. Taking a shower together while gazing out to a sailboat far out to sea can be a real turn-on. It does rain occasionally allowing some water to seep into the tub/shower area, but that only enhances the sense of being outdoors that (in my estimation) far outweighs being totally dry-docked.

If you hate air-conditioning—I'm in that camp—you can open the door to your patio as well as the louvered windows to allow the ever-present breezes to waft through. Still, for those who must be mechanically refreshed, Windjammer's AC works very well and is amazingly quiet.

Water sports on the grounds are complimentary, including an introductory scuba lesson. You can join in the aerobics, participate in the waterskiing contest, go on a snorkeling trip, or take part in a sailing regatta. There are fashion shows, games in the main pool, beach volleyball, water polo, and calypso lessons. Tennis courts are lighted for night play.

Windjammer has five restaurants and two cocktail lounges, along with a mini-mart, boutique, and on-site car-rental office. One of the most popular restaurants, Jammers, carries you into the world of the South Seas with its Polynesian decor. Its sprawling, open-air veranda, covered with a thatched roof, is a great place to enjoy breakfast, lunch, and dinner. Seafood, grilled fish, and fresh island vegetables are superbly prepared by the resident chef. Try a cocktail of mango shrimps dressed in honey and ginger vinaigrette.

The Mango Tree adjacent to Jammers serves a la carte dinners by candlelight; the two-tiered Josephine's Restaurant serves breakfast and Sunday brunch with occasional extra guests on board: Audaciouis little birds are forever poised to swoop down and nip off with the slightest stray muffin crumb.

A wood-fired oven set into the wall is a feature of Papa Don's Taverna, where you can enjoy a variety of healthy items in keeping with the resort's new spa. (And you can still order a pizza and have it delivered to your room.)

Want a very private dinner for just the two of you? Just ask the kitchen staff to prepare and serve a special meal on your terrace. Start with Chilled Breadfruit Vichyssoise and follow it up with a Mille-Feuille of Fresh Mahimahi with a Saffron Cream Sauce and a Panache of Vegetables.

Windjammer Landing Villa Resort & Spa

Location: Set on a hillside on Labrelotte Bay, on the northwestern coast of St. Lucia

Romantic Highlights: Private dinner on your garden terrace overlooking the sea; your own plunge pool

Address/Phone: P.O. Box 1504, Labrelotte, Castries, St. Lucia, W.I.; (758) 456–9000; fax (758) 452–9454

E-mail: reservations@windjammer-landing.com

Web Site: www.windjammer-landing.com

U.S. Reservations: (800) 743–9609; L.R.I. (Loews Representation International), (800) 223–0888

Owner/Manager: Marc Joinville, general manager

Arrival/Departure: Round-trip transfers included in Honeymoon package

Distance from Hewanorra International Airport: 32 miles (1¾ hours); 5 miles (20 minutes) from George Charles Airport

Distance from Castries: 5 miles

Accommodations: 232 rooms and suites in 114 villas: 31 one-bedroom villas; 28 two-bedroom villas; 27 three-bedroom villas; 3 four-bedroom villas; 21 standard rooms; 21 deluxe rooms; 4 estate villas

Most Romantic Room/Suite: One-bedroom villas (2 have private Jacuzzis overlooking the bay)

Amenities: Hair dryer, air-conditioning, cable TV, ceiling fans, bathrobes, in-room safe; villas have fully equipped kitchen, microwave, blender, and coffeemaker

Electricity: 110 volts

Sports and Facilities: 4 pools, Serenity Health Spa, beach, PADI scuba program, snorkeling, waterskiing, sailboarding, fitness center, aerobics; golf nearby

Dress Code: Casually elegant

Weddings: Windjammer's wedding package, $650 per couple

Rates/Packages: Lovers' Paradise, $2,230–$4,150 includes 7 nights' accommodations, candlelight dinner, sparkling wine, sunset cruise or day's car rental with gourmet picnic, tennis, watersports, and transfers.

Payment/Credit Cards: Most major

Deposit: Three-night deposit at time of booking.

Government Taxes: 8 percent

Service Charges: 10 percent

Entry Requirements for U.S. Citizens: Passport

Note: With an extensive children's program, Windjammer is understandedly popular with families. So if having kids around on your quiet romantic interlude is not on your wish list, I would suggest you check with the hotel as to what weeks are for the most part kid-free.

LA SAMANNA
St. Martin

After setting a standard for the ultimate in luxury resorts in the Caribbean since the mid-1970s, La Samanna went through a period of decline in the late eighties. In 1996 Orient-Express Hotels purchased the hotel and began a multimillion-dollar renovation.

The decor is light, elegant, and airy with lots of wicker, bamboo, and wood. Furniture upholstery and cushions are covered in blues, yellows, and oranges. Custom-designed wood and natural hemp headboards, large hand-carved bedside chests, limestone-topped dining tables on bamboo bases, and majavey-wood director's chairs for dining on the terrace provide guests with a comfortable, attractive environment. Appointments include hand-blown glass candle cylinders and a unique collection of contemporary artwork. Suites have oversize sofas, mahogany desks and chairs, and tiled kitchen counters.

The stark, white buildings, softened by the brilliant colors of bougainvillea, hibiscus, and other tropical flowers and the cerulean blue doors, stand at one end of a pristine beach, which you can see from just about every spot on the property. Very Mediterranean in style, with white arched windows and doors and terra-cotta tile floors, your room's terrace or patio opens onto the beach. The twisted shapes of wind-sculpted sea grape trees frame patches of bright turquoise sea just outside your room.

While at La Samanna you'll be pampered with a number of special services. For example, you can opt for express checkout service, whereby your exit documents are processed quickly—no long lines to deal with.

Cuisine is French-inspired, although you will also find some regional Caribbean dishes on the menu. You can dine in the main restaurant or al fresco on the terrace. The bar, with its multihued Indian wedding tent ceiling, is furnished with comfortable cushioned wicker chairs—a lovely place to sip a chilled glass of champagne while you enjoy the cooling sea breezes.

There is also a new rotisserie grill located at the poolside bar where you can order lunch and beverages. Want to take a picnic and have lunch at a secluded beach? All you have to do is ask and everything will be arranged.

The pool is a serene haven for those who simply want to lie back on their cushioned teak lounges and enjoy the sun.

Water sports available at La Samanna include sailing, sailboarding, snorkeling, waterskiing, and swimming. You can also play tennis or exercise in the Fitness Pavilion. The spa is world class and offers a range of pampering treatments.

Indulge in a little shopping spree in the picturesque seaside village of Marigot, just ten minutes away. Here you'll find a number of upscale designer boutiques along with some trendy restaurants. La Samanna has recently added two boutiques and three new suites and has renovated most accommodations and beachfront villas.

La Samanna

Location: On 55 acres of beachfront property on the French side of St. Martin

Romantic Highlights: Spectacular ocean views; private terraces opening onto a pristine, white-sand beach; superb spa

Address/Phone: P.O. Box 4077, 97064 St. Martin CEDEX, F.W.I.; 590–87–64–00; fax 590–87–87–86

U.S. Reservations: Orient-Express Hotels, (800) 854–2252

Owner/Manager: John Volponi, general manager

Arrival/Departure: A La Samanna representative greets guests at the airport and has a prearranged taxi service waiting for a prompt transfer to the resort. Transfer is included with package; others pay $15 each way.

Distance from Juliana International Airport: 6 miles (10 minutes)

Distance from Marigot: 5 minutes

Accommodations: 81 ocean-view accommodations include traditional guest rooms, one- and two-bedroom suites, and three-bedroom villas, all with living rooms, dining areas, and private patios or terraces. Recently second-floor balconies were added to some units; stairs give direct access to the beach.

Most Romantic Room/Suite: Baie Longue Suite and beachfront villas

Amenities: Hair dryer, air-conditioning, robes, ceiling fan, toiletries, telephone, stereo with CD player, minibar, vanity mirror, nightly turndown service, 24-hour room service, daily newspaper, welcome amenity and departure gift; VCR and video library available, including all Academy Award–winning films

Electricity: 220 volts

Sports and Facilities: Spa, 3 tennis courts, infinity pool, snorkeling, sailboarding, waterskiing, fishing; deep-sea dive boat and sailboat rental; fitness center, massages, and beauty treatments

Dress Code: Casually elegant

Weddings: Can be arranged

Rates/Packages: Passion in Paradise package 7-nights, $3,465–$8,255 includes accommodations, transfers, dinner for two, massages, rental car for 2 days, bathrobes, and picnic cruise to private island

Payment/Credit Cards: Most major

Deposit: Three-night deposit; balance due 30 days prior to arrival; full refund if canceled 30 days or more prior to arrival date

Government Taxes: 5 percent

Service Charges: Not included

Entry Requirements for U.S. Citizens: Proof of citizenship; passport best

POINT GRACE
Turks and Caicos

The elegant stone work of the intimate Point Grace casts a faint pink glow against the wide-open azure blue sky. In front, within view of the terraces of the oceanfront suites, 12 miles of sandy beach fan out in either direction along an impossibly clear turquoise sea.

Inspired by British colonial and planters' estate homes, Point Grace, with its balustrades and wide, sweeping stairways reflected in the garden pool, is simply stunning. Apparently no expense has been spared in the creation of these side-by-side twin palaces with their blush-hued domes, green shutters, columns, and lofty spacious suites. Details tell all.

The resort has thirty-two spacious suites housed in two four-story beachfront buildings along with a few cottages that face the pool area. Accommodations range from a 1,080-square-foot one-bedroom cottage to two- and three-bedroom suites and the penthouse. Much of the hardwood and hand-carved teak furniture, as well as the silk, cotton, and linen fabrics, has been imported from Bali, Java, and other exotic places. Special features include Turkish marble floors and hand-carved mahogany doors along with much original artwork and antiques such as 200-year-old wall hangings from India, Indonesian wedding chests, and leather-bound books.

In addition to air-conditioning, ceiling fans, direct dial telephone—things you'd expect— these villas come with cable TV with DVD and CD player, safe, kitchen with granite counters and Sub-Zero refrigerator, washer and dryer, two bathrobes per person (a thick Frette terry cloth

and a light Indonesian cotton), and king-size beds that are lavishly dressed in Frette linens.

Then there are the little niceties. Like when you arrive back in your room after dinner and find your bed turned down and an oil lamp glowing softly on the bureau, or opening your fridge to find it stocked with juices, water, and soft drinks. Or the excellent selection of CDs and books in the bookcase. And, oh yes. There are secretarial services, in-room fax machines, baby-sitting, additional maid and butler services, private in-room chefs, and personal fitness trainers.

The entire property is lushly landscaped with palms, tropical shrubs, and flowers, some quite unusual. There is a Monkey Nut Tree that produces small pink trumpetlike flowers, several traveler's palms, a cacti garden, yuccas, Alexander Palms, and Chinese Fan Palms as well as brightly colored bougainvillea and hibiscus.

Breakfast and lunch are served on the terrace or patio gardens just off the main reception area and there is an espresso machine where you can help yourself to a variety of coffees at any time of day. Dinner is in Grace's Cottage where the chef has created quite a stir on the island with his creative and tasty cuisine. I'm not sure which I liked best: the carpaccio of tuna with poached scallops, dry vermouth, and a leek fondu or the hot chocolate soufflé with homemade chocolate ice cream.

The $2.5 million penthouse—the 7,200-square-foot, four-bedroom "Nonsuch"—simply knocks your socks off. An Indonesian *bale* bed on one of the suite's two roof terraces, custom-made Mandalay lamps (brass floor lamps with fans) in the Grand Salon, a grand piano, computer-operated sunshades, a cabinet crafted from a canoe, a tented bed bathed in muslin, silk pillows—the opulence goes on and on. There is even a massage room and a dressing room with mahogany cabinets and custom-made Indonesian brass work. And all for just $4,500 per night!

Point Grace is about in the middle of the beach. Club Med is a forty-minute speed walk away at one end; the frenetically busy all-inclusive Sandals Beaches resort, where I saw enough kids to fill a day care center, is a thirty-minute walk in the other direction. In between, except for a few low-key resorts, private homes, and empty spaces, there really isn't much going on. So aside from walking the beach, water sports including incredible diving opportunities and snorkeling off Smith Reef and Coral Garden, and soaking up the sun, there's not a whole lot of action on the island. There is just one small casino

and a handful of small clubs where local bands entertain. Of course you can visit the Conch Farm, play golf at the Provo Golf Club for about $120 a round (a five-round pass is $450); or grab your binoculars and go bird-watching. But if you're looking for a happening nightlife, this is probably not your cup of tea.

For others, it may be just perfect. One couple fulfilled a dream by getting married on the beach at Point Grace. They walked down an aisle created by flower-filled conch shells and exchanged marriage vows and red roses just as the sun raked its streaks of orange and red across the skies. Thanks to help from the resort's staff in the months prior to the event, everything went like a Swiss watch (Point Grace was the result of the vision of a Swiss developer, after all).

To choose the menu for the small reception, sample menus had been exchanged via e-mail, a picture of what the bride wanted for her bridal bouquet was scanned and e-mailed to a Turks and Caicos florist, a cake was chosen, and legalities were reviewed. After the couple agreed on the guest list—only a handful of close friends and family would be invited—invitations were sent out.

In order to comply with island laws, the couple arrived three days before the wedding date (the law requires forty-eight hours residency). In that time, Pamela Ewing, Point Grace's wedding coordinator, helped the couple get their wedding license, went over the ceremony with the minister, and met the couple's guests who arrived on Thursday. The couple was married on Saturday and after the guests returned home on Monday, the newlyweds stayed on at Point Grace for a two-week honeymoon in their oceanfront suite (a complimentary upgrade by Point Grace).

The honeymoon was everything they dreamed it would be. "We weren't looking for nonstop activities. We simply wanted to relax and unwind in a beautiful place. We really enjoy each other's company," said the bride.

Point Grace

Location: Set in the center of a spectacular, wide white-sandy crescent along Grace Bay, in Providenciales

Romantic Highlights: Stunning views of beach from stone balcony; returning after a candlelight dinner to find your bed turned down, an oil lamp glowing softly on the bureau

Address/Phone: P.O. Box 700, Providenciales, Turks and Caicos Islands, B.W.I; (888) 682–3705, (649) 946–5096; fax (649) 946–5097.

E-mail: pointgrace@tciway.tc

Web Site: www.pointgrace.com

U.S. Reservations: (888) 682–3705

Owner/Manager: Duncan MacArthur, general manager

Arrival/Departure: Transfers can be arranged

Distance from Providenciales International Airport: 15 minutes

Distance from Providenciales Center: 10 minutes

Accommodations: 32 oceanfront suites and cottages

Most Romantic Room/Suite: Oceanfront villas

Amenities: Air-conditioning, ceiling fans, cable TV with DVD and CD player, hair dryer, safe, kitchen with refrigerator, washer and dryer, bathrobes, king-size bed

Electricity: 120 volts

Sports and Facilities: Pool, beach, Hobie Cats, kayaking, windsurfing, snorkeling, 26-foot Chris-Craft for island tours; complimentary membership (and shuttle) to nearby Provo Country Club where golf and tennis are available

Dress Code: Resort elegant

Weddings: The basic ceremony including legal fees and minister, cake, champagne, dinner for two, flowers, CD music, photograph, and services of the wedding coordinator averages about $850.

Rates/Packages: Rates start at $345 per night including gourmet continental breakfast, daily cocktail hour, use of the business center, transfers, shuttle to golf and tennis club, and nonmotorized water sports. A Romantic Retreat package at $2,155 per couple includes 5 nights/6 days with breakfasts, champagne and chocolate-covered strawberries, 3 dinners for two, spa/beauty treatment, boat ride with picnic for two on a remote island beach, and transfers.

Payment/Credit Cards: Most major

Deposit: 50 percent required within 10 days of booking; balance due 30 days prior to arrival

Government Taxes: 9 percent plus $15 departure tax

Service Charges: 10 percent

Entry Requirements for U.S. Citizens: Passport or birth certificate and photo ID such as a driver's license

Closed: Three weeks in September

CANEEL BAY
St. John, U.S. Virgin Islands

With 5,000 acres of tropical jungle around you, there is plenty of room to spread out on Caneel Bay, one of Laurance Rockefeller's most beautiful creations. He discovered this pristine, jungle-covered island in 1952 when he was on a sailing trip. After purchasing a good portion of the island, he set about to personally oversee the building of Caneel Bay, insisting that it be a low-key, ideal vacation resort for those who wanted to escape to a peaceful, natural retreat.

Over the years many couples have started their married lives here, and their children have come after them on *their* honeymoons. It's traditionally been ranked as one of the best honeymoon resorts in the world, the kind of place "old money" likes—elegance without the glitz or bells and whistles.

In 1993, the upscale Rosewood Hotels & Resorts took on its management and undertook a multimillion-dollar renovation project, redecorating just about everything except the scenery.

The cottages, which are constructed of natural stone and weathered wood, are spread out along the fringes of the beaches and in the gardens and manicured lawns.

Designed to blend into the lush tropical plants and trees that surround them, the cottages have louvered windows that let in the cooling sea breezes and wonderful views of the beaches or gardens.

For those who prefer a more controlled environment, air-conditioning has recently been installed in all cottages. The new decor emphasizes a palette brought in from the outdoors, including corals, blues, and greens. Accessories and furniture also echo nature's design in clay, cane, bamboo, and local hardwood. There are six categories of rooms: courtside, tennis garden, ocean-view, beachfront, and premium as well as Cottage 7, a luxury villa popular with visiting bigwigs.

On the whole, the rooms are not superluxurious, nor are the baths mega-marble marvels. But with Caneel's setting and amazing natural assets, who can complain?

If you come here for a week's honeymoon, you will be able to plunk yourself on a different beach every day, but the alluring Honeymoon Beach may seem most appropriate. At Caneel your day spreads out before you like a sybaritic feast of wonderful things to do and see. If you love nature, you'll have miles of trails to follow that wind through the 5,000-acre Virgin Islands National Park. At night you can take walks along the pathways, which are softly lit with low mushroom lights to aid hikers, joggers, and strollers. Need to relax? The Self Centre, a spa for physical and mental well-being sits high atop Honeymoon Beach and offers yoga, Pilates, t'ai chi, m'ai chi (water aerobics eastern-style) and for couples, "The Rhythms of Relationships" course featuring yoga, touch, and meditation exercises designed to heighten each other's connection as well as their physical and mental needs. This one is perfect for newlyweds.

Feel adventurous? Then take a jeep or boat to other islands or to Caneel's sister property, Little Dix Bay on Virgin Gorda. Ask Caneel to pack a picnic lunch for you, and spend a relaxing day on your own. You can also head to Cruz Bay for shopping and browsing. There are several excellent shops in this little town along with some good restaurants.

Tennis players will be in racquet heaven, with eleven courts surrounded by tropical gardens in the terraced Tennis Park. The resort offers complimentary clinics and private lessons, and there is an on-staff pro and a fully stocked shop.

Water sports abound. Stop at the Beach Hut and get a Sunfish or sailboarder and sail off into the calm waters in the bay. You can go snorkeling either by yourself or with a guide or charter a boat for deep-sea fishing. The

best snorkeling is off the north end of Caneel Beach, where you can see bright green parrot fish, funny-looking needlefish, and sinister moray eels tucked into crevices of coral. The brilliant world underwater also comes to life through the eyes of Lucy Portlock, the staff marine biologist, who personally escorts guests on weekly snorkel tours through the island's undersea treasures.

More than 1,400 different kinds of plants and trees flourish on Caneel's property. The resort's horticulturist, Oriel Smith, will take you on a tour of the grounds.

Caneel's three restaurants and terrace lounge look out over the sea. Turtle Bay, a gourmet restaurant reminiscent of a grand plantation house, invites you to enjoy open-air all-day dining while looking out over gardens to the deep turquoise sea beyond. At the Caneel Beach Terrace, a casual, open dining room along the beach, you can indulge in a sumptuous lunch buffet every day. From your table in the Equator, which is set in the ruins of an ancient sugar plantation, you can see the twinkling lights of St. Thomas across the water; the Breezeway and Terrace provide a casual, comfortable place to meet friends and relax with a cool rum punch.

Meals are included in the romance and other packages. Those on daily rates should budget for the meal plan: $90 per person per day for breakfast and dinner; $110 for all meals.

At night there is live music for dancing under the stars while the torches set in the lush foliage turn the resort into a tropical wonderland.

Caneel Bay

Location: Situated on a private, 170-acre peninsula on St. John

Romantic Highlights: A different beach for each day; natural splendor of a national park surrounding the resort; candlelight dining amid flower-bedecked ruins

Address/Phone: P.O. Box 720, Cruz Bay, St. John, U.S.V.I. 00831-0720; (340) 776–6111; fax (340) 693–8280

Web Site: www.rosewoodhotels.com

U.S. Reservations: Rosewood Hotels & Resorts, (800) 928–8889; fax (212) 758–6640

Owner/Manager: Rosewood Hotels & Resorts, management company; Brian Young, general manager

Arrival/Departure: Caneel Bay can be reached via San Juan, Puerto Rico, and St. Thomas. Caneel Bay's regular ferry service operates between downtown St. Thomas and Caneel Bay several times each day.

Distance from Cyril E. King Airport: 12 nautical miles (40 minutes)

Distance from Cruz Bay: 3 miles

Accommodations: 166 rooms and cottages. All have terraces; many have king-size beds.

Most Romantic Room/Suite: Secluded Cottage Point area

Amenities: Ceiling fans, air-conditioning, minibar, hair dryer, bathrobes, TV, in-room safe

Electricity: 110 volts

Sports and Facilities: 11 tennis courts (5 lighted), pool, boating, sailing, snorkeling, and swimming

Dress Code: Casual during the day; men required to wear slacks, collared shirts, and closed-in footwear in evening; jackets required during height of winter season for dinner in Turtle Bay restaurant

Weddings: Can be arranged

Rates/Packages: $300–$1,100 per couple per night includes use of nonmotorized boats, snorkeling gear, shopping trip to St. Thomas, tennis and weekly clinics, scuba clinic, and garden walk. Pure Romance package: $4,700–$11,525 per couple also includes 7 nights' accommodations, champagne meals, sunset cruise, transfers, massage for two.

Payment/Credit Cards: Most major

Deposit: Three-night deposit; balance due 30 days prior to arrival.

Government Taxes: 8 percent on room rate only; packages subject to a 15 percent surcharge, which covers all room tax, service charges, and meal-plan gratuities

Service Charges: 7.5 percent

Entry Requirements for U.S. Citizens: Proof of citizenship required when traveling between the United States and the British Virgin Islands

MEXICO

MAROMA
Cancun

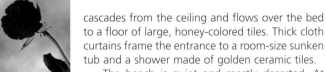

From the time you arrive at the small, elegant Maroma, you are completely pampered and left alone. Yet the Maroma "family" makes you feel as though anything is possible; all you have to do is ask. And for the most part, it's true!

Marked by a plain wooden gate off the Yucatán Peninsula's main corridor, a rutted, single-lane path winds through jungle, past flowering trees and around iguanas sunning themselves. In a small clearing is a cobblestone driveway, at the end of which is an elegant whitewashed hacienda. A small reflecting pool and an assortment of honking geese and ducks greet you.

Upon entering the open-air, tiled foyer, you are welcomed by a charming hostess and a frosty Maroma margarita (with a delicious secret ingredient). The hostess asks if you have any special requests and tastes: When would you like your fresh coffee, juice, and pastries to arrive in the morning? What are your favorite foods and drinks? What special activities would you like arranged?

A quiet, secluded estate of loosely linked suites and elegantly lighted walkways set around a pretty blue-tiled swimming pool fed by a gurgling fountain, Maroma is a collection of one- and two-story buildings, some topped by thatched palapa roofs made of native palm fronds.

Past the pool is the large, breezy main building, El Sol, with high ceilings, winding staircases, and terra-cotta tile floors. Inside are a small bar and a casually elegant dining room, flanked by a slate terrace with a large Jacuzzi and steps leading to a beach of fine, soft white sand.

Your room, designed to appeal to the senses, is furnished with handsome Mexican colonial furniture, rich fabrics, and original artwork. A silky, translucent netting

cascades from the ceiling and flows over the bed to a floor of large, honey-colored tiles. Thick cloth curtains frame the entrance to a room-size sunken tub and a shower made of golden ceramic tiles.

The beach is quiet and mostly deserted. At one end of the mile-wide cove is a secret sulphur spring that feeds into the shallows. Find it by digging your toes in the talc-soft sediment. You'll know you're there when you smell the pungent sulphur. The jungle that surrounds Maroma is home to monkeys, anteaters, possum, foxes, and a variety of exotic birds.

Maroma, Spanish for "somersault," is named for the swirling currents beyond the offshore reef, a mixing of tidal currents and upwellings that first bedeviled Mayan seafarers trading along the coast and at the nearby island of Cozumel. It's odd that such a quiet, serene place like this should be named after a turbulent waterway.

La Maroma, the namesake ocean current, however, poses no problem for the snorkeler or swimmer. The water sports concession is run by Jean-Claude, a Frenchman, and Michael, his teenage son. They are expert guides to the local waters and are both full of exuberant French charm and a love of this area.

Charles, the relaxed restaurant host, chats easily with all the guests, recommending things to do and telling stories about Maroma. Under his laid-back but attentive eye operate a cast of smiling, expert servers. Not quite an employee but surely part of the Maroma family is Pierre, a small, beautiful jungle cat that Charles raised from a kitten. Pierre spends his afternoons lounging on the wood beams under the palapa roof of the beachfront bar.

The menu at Maroma clearly caters to an international crowd. The elegant but pricey fare includes appetizers like lobster in filo on balsamic-perfumed tomato compote and duck mousse with green peppercorns and entrees such as mosaic of fish and shellfish with caviar, beef tenderloin medallions with Roquefort, and an array of chicken, pork, lamb, and duck dishes. If you have a taste for heat, ask for the *chnee-pek*, Mayan for "dog's nose." This salsa—a combination of onions, habañero chiles, and tomatoes— will spice up any meal.

Charles and the servers will encourage you to use your imagination and ask for whatever dish you're in the mood for. If the ingredients are in the kitchen, they'll be happy to make you a custom meal. Another tip: When it's not busy, ask to have a flambéed coffee drink prepared for you and taken up to the Mirador, a private rooftop alcove with

Maroma

Location: On the east coast of the Yucatán Peninsula, 20 miles south of Cancun

Romantic Highlights: Small, intimate property with 520 acres (much of it jungle); a secluded beach; king-size beds draped with silky netting; private terrace with hammock

Address/Phone: P.O. Box 51, Cancun, Quintana Roo, 77500, Mexico; 52–998–28200; fax 52–998–28220

E-mail: reservations@maromahotel.com

Web Site: www.maromahotel.com

U.S. Reservations: Contact the hotel directly

Owner/Manager: Jose Luis and Sally Moreno

Arrival/Departure: Complimentary transfers are provided in a comfortable, air-conditioned Maroma car.

Distance from Cancun Airport: 30 minutes

Accommodations: 9 premium rooms, 24 suites; 1 junior suite; 1 one-bedroom suite; 1 two-bedroom suite; 1 three-bedroom villa

Most Romantic Room/Suite: The one-bedroom suite on the 3rd floor overlooking the ocean and jungle

Amenities: Hair dryer, toiletries, telephone, 24-hour room service, bottled water

Electricity: 110 volts

Sports and Facilities: Snorkeling, Hobie-Cat sailing, sailboarding, scuba diving, deep-sea fishing, horseback riding; library with TV and VCR; boutique; Jacuzzi, massage; beach bar; golf courses nearby. Visits to Tulum, Cozumel Island, and Xcaret theme park and day and overnight excursions to Chichen Itza, Sian Ka'an Biosphere Reserve, Merida, and Tikal.

Dress Code: Casually elegant

Weddings: Can be arranged

Rates/Packages: Rates including breakfast, transfers, and 1 snorkeling trip, $333–$1,602 per couple, per night; seven-night honeymoon/anniversary packages, $3,404–$4,787 including ocean-view room, champagne, breakfast, dinner with wine, snorkeling trip, couples' massage, spa session, archeological tour, sunset cruise, and transfers.

Payment/Credit Cards: Most major

Deposit: Guarantee with credit card; cancel within 7 days of arrival to avoid a one-night penalty charge in low season. In high season 15 days are required and the penalty is 2 nights. At Christmas, New Year's, and Easter, a twenty-one-day cancellation is required and the penalty is 2 nights.

Government Taxes: 10 percent IVA, 2 percent hospitality tax

Service Charges: 10 percent, rooms; 15 percent, restaurant

Entry Requirements for U.S. Citizens: Passport or original birth certificate

sweeping views of the moonlit beach. For lunch the strip steak with Oaxaca cheese and roasted poblano chilies is hearty and delicious. Breakfast is leisurely and lovely and offers all kinds of choices, ranging from the compote of pineapple marmalade, dripping with honey and spiked with cinnamon, to custom egg dishes and pancakes with bananas and pecans. As the sun is fading on the beach, order margaritas, chips, and the incredible guacamole.

If you're looking for a real traditional Mexican meal, you're best off heading to a restaurant in nearby Playa del Carmen. About twenty minutes south on the main strip, this is the shopping and nightlife hub of the area. Playa's shopping district is filled with roaming European backpackers and tourist couples from the occasional cruise ships that dock there. Along the main drag, wall-to-wall shops sell jewelry, clothes, hammocks, and all manner of gifts and souvenirs. Music trickles out from bars and eateries. Several of the restaurants have mariachi bands that wander through the outdoor tables—a Mexican-vacation must.

But some guests never feel the urge to leave Maroma. And it's not hard to understand why. Like the peacocks that roam the walkways prowling for bugs, like the ducks and geese that have made their home at Maroma, and like little Pierre taking his afternoon naps at the Beach Bar, honeymooners at Maroma may find that it's really quite pleasant to stay just where they are.

THE RITZ-CARLTON, CANCUN

Cancun

Cancun, with its very large hotels and booming commercial areas, may not be everyone's margarita, but anyone who appreciates luxury, pampering, and just the finest in accommodations and service can totally "get into" this superb resort. Once you step onto the marble floors of the elegant lobby, check in, and see where you'll be spending the next few nights, you may find you'll have little desire to do much more than lounge on the beach or by the two sparkling pools. You could take a day to visit the Mayan ruins at Chichen-Itza or Tulum. And you could go shopping. That is if you can drag yourself away from all the good things at the Ritz.

The Ritz-Carlton, Cancun has received a lot of awards for everything from service to overall excellence since its opening more than six years ago. You really can't go anywhere on the property without feeling special. In addition to soft corals and golds, sparkling chandeliers, sweeping drapes, Oriental carpets, and highly polished traditional furniture, there are flowers everywhere.

Rooms are beautifully furnished in traditional French furniture upholstered in light brocades and prints. They come with marble baths and full-length French doors lead to spacious balconies overlooking the sea.

On the patios and dining terrace, the cobalt blue market umbrellas are offset by red-tile floors and white chairs and lounges. The cobalt theme is subtly repeated in the crystal water goblets in the dining room, where plushly upholstered chairs in coral fabrics and beautiful appointments such as Chinese vases and original art help create a quietly elegant place for that special dinner.

The coral and cream hotel may have 365 guest rooms and suites; still its design, roughly in the shape of a "U" facing the sea, with the public areas in the center, makes it feel like an intimate boutique hotel. You can get from your room to the beach in no time at all. The elevators are zippy; everything works.

There are four restaurants: The Caribe Bar & Grill, offering light meals and tropical drinks; The Club Grill, featuring regional specialties; El Cafe Mexicano, for casual dining including meals on the oceanfront terrace; and the elegant Fantino, the most formal of the four places to eat. Fantino's white-and-gold brocade chairs and beautiful china and crystal set the mood. The Lobby Lounge with its white wicker chairs, puffy cushions, potted palms and ornate marble floors, almost Moroccan in style, provides a pleasant place for cocktails and entertainment.

At the Ritz, you'll find yourself looking forward to your next meal. Everything is so good, so beautifully presented—starting with breakfast, where you may choose, for starters, fresh papaya, oranges, berries, mango, and pineapple served in a half shell of coconut or the Papaya Smoothie, a meal in itself.

For dinner you might have risotto of lobster, apple and foie gras Napoleon with black pepper and honey vinegar, savory bread soufflé with tequilla sauce, and porcini with white truffle butter. Certainly a dessert like warm black and white chocolate almond cake will satisfy the most demanding sweet tooth.

For those who want to get in on the latest craze, check out the new Cigar Lounge, which, by the way, is as popular with women as with men. Here you can select your smoke from a fine selection of Cuban cigars as well as sip a variety of tequilas, ports, and cognacs. The decor—burgundy leather chairs, wood paneling and original oil paintings—simply adds a bit of humph, humph to the whole scene.

If tequila is one of your passions, you'll have plenty of opportunity to indulge. Thirty of Mexico's finest tequilas can be found at the Lobby Lounge, many quite rare. Want to learn more about this national beverage? The Ritz's "tequiller" holds daily tasting sessions where you can get the scoop on its history and production.

The Ritz-Carlton, Cancun is a perfect setting for romance. You can arrange a private candlelight dinner for two on the beach or on your terrace; wake up late and have breakfast in bed; or sit under a beach cabana and enjoy some quiet time. But be warned: you may never want to leave.

The Ritz-Carlton, Cancun

Location: On 7½ acres along the Caribbean Sea at the tip of the Yucatán Peninsula in Cancun

Romantic Highlights: Private candlelight dinner on the beach or poolside; massage on the beach; private patios overlooking the sea

Address/Phone: Retorno del Rey #36, Zona Hotelera, Cancun, Quintana Roo, Mexico; 52–9881–0808; fax 52–9885–1015

E-mail: ritz-carlton-cancun@rc-cancun

Web-Site: www.ritzcarlton.com

U.S. Reservations: (800) 241–3333

Owner/Manager: Tony Franzetti, general manager

Arrival/Departure: Arrangements can be made for pickup at the Cancun Airport.

Distance from Cancun International Airport: 15 minutes

Distance from Cancun: In the hotel zone

Accommodations: 365 rooms including 50 suites and 57 Ritz-Carlton Club rooms.

Most Romantic Room/Suite: A suite on the Ritz-Carlton Club floor; Executive Oceanfront Suite also great

Amenities: Air-conditioning, hair dryer, telephone, toiletries, 24-hour room service, two-line telephone with fax connection, TV, minibar

Electricity: 110 volts

Sports and Facilities: 2 outdoor pools, whirlpool; 3 tennis courts, health center, saunas, water sports, massage therapy, gym, golf nearby

Dress Code: Casually elegant

Weddings: Can be arranged

Rates/Packages: $249–$550 per room per night; three-night honeymoon package from $1,224

Payment/Credit Cards: Most major

Deposit: Guarantee with credit card

Government Taxes: 10 percent federal tax; 2 percent lodging tax

Service Charges: Not included

Entry Requirements for U.S. Citizens: Proof of citizenship; passport best

LAS BRISAS RESORT IXTAPA
Ixtapa

It creeps up on you. At first this monolithic structure of high ceilings and ochre-colored concrete walls pierced by patterns of square and rectangular openings, which let in light and air, seems strangely stark. Plain. Even ugly, to some. The reception area is softened only by a few pieces of simple, sturdy, varnished wood tables and a long bench reminding one of the sitting area in a railroad station. Look up and see geometric splashes of bright canary yellow and magenta. Clay pots, looking much like relics from an archaeological dig, sit in clusters on the pitted quarry tile floor. Giant stone marbles of various sizes sit in a corner of the lobby. Strange place, this.

Then, just about the time you're pulling out your credit card, you start to feel the breezes. No matter how hot it is just outside in the glaring Mexican sun, you are cooled and soothed. The architect, Ricardo Legorreta, who designed the hotel, built it without actual windows—just open spaces to take full advantage of the building's cliff-side location on the edge of the sea. Unless you actually get out on the water, you can't really see the entire structure, which is constructed in the shape of a pyramid, its balconies climbing up the receding sides. All rooms have spectacular views and capture the refreshing breezes coming in from the Pacific.

At the base of the resort is a lovely cove beach that belongs exclusively to Las Brisas Resort Ixtapa; unlike the other resorts just around the bend, which are lined up side by side along the 2-mile stretch of Palmar Beach, guests at the La Brisas need not share their sand with anyone else. You get down to the beach by elevator, or you can take an ecowalk along paths lined with rain forest–like tropical foliage.

When he created this hotel, Legorreta, one of Mexico's most renowned architects, produced an excellent example of the minimalist style of Mexican architecture, in this case, reminiscent of an Aztec pyramid. Corridors are

lit by open squares cut into the ceiling; large-scale contemporary art hangs on walls in both the public areas and guest rooms. Nothing is frivolous here.

The most romantic accommodations are the junior suites, located on the top floor. You have a sitting room, a bedroom, a roomy marble bath with granite-topped vanities, and two patios, one with a Jacuzzi. You can sit in the Jacuzzi under the stars and gaze out at the sea or relax in your hammock.

Furnishings are understated and very classy: cobalt blue glass–based lamps, three-dimensional wall murals, Mexican red-tile floors, blue-tiled headboards, flowers in wonderful pots and vases, and lots of space. Beds are covered with brightly colored cotton spreads and pillows.

These are not suites you want to leave. Sofas have double-thick cushions covered in brilliant Mexican woven fabrics in magenta, yellow, and turquoise. Closets, in keeping with the natural look, have nets instead of doors.

There are four pools, one just for adults; all sit on a hill overlooking the sea. The adjacent solarium serves light meals, including fresh seafood, and Les Fuentes is the place to go for drinks.

Restaurant selections include El Mexicano, a romantic, hacienda-like eatery with an inner garden courtyard; Portofino, serving gourmet Italian cuisine; Bella Vista, where you eat outdoors on a covered terrace looking out over the Pacific and enjoy international fare; and La Brisa, a snack bar on the beach.

At dusk the Las Brisas glows warmly as the golden rays of the sinking sun turn the hotel into a temple of gold.

Las Brisas Resort Ixtapa

Location: 120 miles northwest of Acapulco, on Mexico's western coast

Romantic Highlights: The only large hotel in Ixtapa on its own beach; magnificent suites; lobby bar is *the* place to be for sunset

Address/Phone: Playa Vista Hermosa 40880, Ixtapa Zihuatanejo, Gro., Mexico; 52–755–321–21; fax 52–755–31031

E-mail: ixtapa@brisas.com.mx

Web Site: www.brisas.com

U.S. Reservations: (888) 559–4329

Owner/Manager: Francisco Garcia, general manager

Arrival/Departure: The Ixtapa-Zihuatanejo Airport is 20 minutes away by taxi (56 pesos, about $7.00); transfers by van can be arranged.

Distance from Ixtapa Zihuatanejo International Airport: 10 miles (20 minutes)

Distance from Ixtapa Center: 3 minutes

Accommodations: 428 rooms and suites, each with patio

Most Romantic Room/Suite: Go for the junior suites on the top floor, or the master suites, which have private pools.

Amenities: Air-conditioning, ceiling fans, king- or queen-size bed, toiletries, TV, radio, cotton bathrobes, real hangers, hammocks; hair dryer in suites; refrigerator and telephones in master suites, some have whirlpools or minipools; laundry and valet service, 24-hour room service

Electricity: 110 volts

Sports and Facilities: 4 lighted tennis courts, gym, 4 pools, beach, Jacuzzis, most water sports, health club, golf 5 minutes away

Dress Code: Casual

Weddings: Can be arranged

Rates/Packages: $99–$230 per couple per night (low season) $189–$315 per couple (high season)

Payment/Credit Cards: Most major

Deposit: Two-night deposit; cancel 7 to 14 days prior to arrival date (depending on season) for refund.

Government Taxes: 15 percent plus 2 percent state tax

Service Charges: 15 percent suggested

Entry Requirements for U.S. Citizens: Proof of citizenship; passport best

HACIENDA KATANCHEL

Merida

The clackety-clack of wheels rolling over the corrugated-like path announces the arrival of guests brought to the front door of their suite in a small cart pulled by Margarita, the horse. So begins another memorable stay at one of Mexico's most unique resorts, the Hacienda Kantanchel.

Much like Sleeping Beauty was awakened after a long deep sleep, so, too, was Hacienda Katanchel, a restored seventeenth-century, 741-acre country estate in the heart of Mexico's Yucatan. When Monica Hernandez and her architect husband, Anibal Gonzalez, were looking for a vacation home near Merida, the jumping-off point for those visiting ancient Mayan archeological sites, they learned about a special place in the jungle a few miles east of town. Driving onto the property thick with rampaging jungle vegetation, they knew they had arrived at the main house when the bumper of their Suburban hit the bottom step of the staircase leading up to the front door. They ducked under the vines that were held up by chicken wire, went up the stairs, and were met by a caretaker and four dogs. Incredibly they walked into a sparkling-clean room. Although the wealthy owner had not visited the property for more than thirty-five years due to ill health, the caretaker had maintained the living quarters in case the owner were to return.

"We knew immediately this was for us," said Monica, awed by the beauty of the rooms. Spanish colonial in style, the Hacienda seemed perfect. As they set about cleaning and restoring the building and grounds, they discovered small houses also covered in rampant jungle growth that

had once been residences for the local workers. It was a bit overwhelming. So many houses, thirty-three in all, were discovered hidden in the tall underbrush that had grown unchecked for more than thirty years.

When they realized that this complex would make a wonderful hotel, Monica and Anibal plunged into the venture, restoring and transforming the small houses into guest cottages they called pavilions. They furnished the rooms with all their favorite things bringing in interesting furniture pieces from everywhere, including antiques, Ralph Lauren damask bed linens, and pillows Monica personally head tested. "I love good pillows" she said.

Six more guest accommodations were created from rooms in the original Hacienda. In addition to the banana trees, papaya, and other fruit trees on the grounds, other precious trees were planted, such as mahogany, rosewood, and the regional fruit-bearing ciricote. Each pavilion got its own plunge pool filled with invigorating mineral water pumped in by turn-of-the-century windmills from the seventeen wells also found on the property. Terraces were added to the pavilions and furnished with hammocks and comfortable lounges. Gardens were planted for every cottage, following the ancient Maya custom of combining four types of plants: decorative, fragrant, edible, and medicinal.

Rooms are quietly dramatic, decorated in the elegant minimalist style. Lots of white. White iron king-size beds, white sheets, white blankets, towels, linens, Egyptian cottons, and furniture fabrics—all set against a backdrop of rich jewel-like wall colors in peaches, melons, and reds. Rooms are spacious with brilliant Mexican tile floors. Each item used in the decor, from the artwork on the walls to the antiques and lamps, is carefully placed. Nothing in these rooms is superfluous.

The lofty Casa de Maquinas, with its polished hardwood floors, high arches, and fine wood tables and chairs, is a perfect setting for elegant dining, the result of an extensive renovation project. Casa de Maquinas also has a new bar, boutique, lounge, and billiard room. For more casual dining there is the open-air terrace. Much of the food is prepared using produce grown right on the property. Meals, which can best be described as light cuisine with a touch of Mayan or "Mayan Novelle," are delicious and include fresh seafood.

The Tienda de Raya, once an on-premise general store, now houses a library and meeting rooms. A large

swimming pool is enclosed by trees and lounge areas.

Even the toiletries are special, natural: papaya shampoo, handmade soaps, and a citrus-based insect repellant that smells good to everyone but the bugs. There are virtually no mosquitos because of the balance established between nature and the food chain. If the birds don't nail the mosquitos, the frogs or bats will.

There is no TV, no radio, no clock. Yet you do have a phone and a fax, and Internet access is available in reception. There is no air-conditioning, nor is it needed. Anibal designed the pavilions to take full advantage of the cool jungle breezes. Ceiling fans help things along and portable air-conditioners are available on request.

With all this natural beauty, there is no need to do anything beyond relax in the gardens, get a soothing massage, and swim in the pool. However, for those who love nature, guided walks are richly rewarding. Maybe you'll spot a rare white-fronted parrot or Green Breasted Mango. The region is filled with more than one hundred species of exotic birds, animals, and plants. Pink clouds of flamingos can be found in wildlife preserves on the coast.

There are out-of-the-way archeological sites and better-known places like Chichen Itza, Uxmal, and Ake. You can bike along trails and swim in the crystalline waters of the jungle's cenotes, deep sinkholes that are blue, blue, blue. If you're daring enough, you can swim through the underground caves carved into the cavernous limestone.

Certainly you will want to visit nearby villages, which seem to belong to another century, places where people work in crafts passed down for generations. Some work in henequen (sisal) and jipijapa, a method of fine straw weaving used to make hats, baskets, and other items; some weave hammocks and embroider tablecloths and *huipil* (traditional smocks). Hand-painted pottery is also locally made. The resort's sedans or vans with English-speaking driver-guides are available to take you to visit charming pastel-colored colonial villages and historic haciendas located in the area.

Hacienda Katanchel is a place for those who love nature and quiet and things from another time. And luxury.

Hacienda Katanchel

Location: Built on the grounds of an ancient Mayan settlement near Merida in the heart of the Yucatan

Romantic Highlights: Private pavilions surrounded by exotic jungle flowers and foliage; personal plunge pools; swimming in jungle pools; guided hikes to archeological sites

Address/Phone: about 15 miles east of Merida, Highway 180, (just off Merida-Cancun Highway), Yucatan, CP 97470 Mexico; 52-999-923-4020; fax (888) 882-9470

E-mail: hacienda@mda.com.mx

Web Site: www.hacienda@katanchel.com

U.S. Reservations: Fax hotel directly at toll-free number above, or call Small Luxury Hotels, (800) 525-4800

Owner/Manager: Monica Hernandez and Anibal Gonzalez

Arrival/Departure: Arrangements can be made for pickup at airports in Merida and Cancun. A 2.4-mile private driveway leads from the highway to the property entrance.

Distance from Merida Airport: 15 miles

Distance from Merida: 15 miles (2½-hour drive from Cancun)

Accommodations: 40 rooms and suites

Most Romantic Room/Suite: Honeymoon Suite with king-size bed and plunge pool; Presidential Suite with a good-size private pool

Amenities: Telephone, toiletries, ceiling fans, fancy natural papaya soaps and shampoo; hair dryer on request

Electricity: 110 volts

Sports and Facilities: Large main pool, several plunge pools; hiking, swimming, aerobics, yoga, massage therapy, spa treatments, nature walks, bird-watching, excursions to ruins

Dress Code: Casually smart

Weddings: Can be arranged

Rates/Packages: Room rates from $200 with breakfast (summer); Honeymoon Suite $300 (summer with breakfast), $350 (winter)

Payment/Credit Cards: Most major

Deposit: Guarantee with credit card; for refund cancel 7 days or more before scheduled arrival date

Government Taxes: 17 percent

Service Charges: 10 percent

Entry Requirements for U.S. Citizens: Proof of citizenship; passport best

HOTEL VILLA DEL SOL
Zihuatanejo

It's only 6 miles from Ixtapa, but this small gem is quite different, indeed, from Ixtapa's large chain of hotels. It has a beauty of a beach sheltered by a dense canopy of palms and framed by a carpet of tropical foliage that begins at the edge of the beach, rising up into the hills behind. Nestled in this greenery are fifty-four suites in adobelike two-story casitas. Six new luxury Lagoon Suites and a two-bedroom Presidential Suite were added in 1999. Winding stone walkways lead from the cottages to the two palapa-roofed bar/restaurants and the beach. Water runs in a meandering channel from the main fountain, along the paths, and into the pool.

Once you've had time to let the magic of Villa del Sol sink in, you'll be hooked. From the time you step up into the rather unpretentious yet charming tiled reception area and pass through to the gardens just beyond, you've entered the Mexican version of the Garden of Eden, and in this garden everything works: from the high-tech faucets that glide open like butter to the attractive lights that line the walkways. Created by Helmut Leins, who came to Mexico several years ago from Germany, Villa del Sol combines the casual and colorful ambience of Mexico with the superb service-oriented traditions of Europe.

Passionate about details, Helmut says he sleeps in every room at least once a year. This way he knows if everything is as it should be. It's only when you stay here that you notice how well thought out it all is—subtle things like soap dishes, towel bars, and shelves are all perfectly placed.

Helmut's charming French wife, Muriel, oversees the room decor and goes to great lengths to get just the right accessories and furnishings. Each of the fifty-four suites is unique and appointed with authentic Mexican artifacts, such as wooden masks, terra-cotta pots, and ceramic birds. One-bedroom suites have king-size beds; two-bedroom suites have one king-size and one queen-size bed. Suites come with separate sitting areas, terraces or balconies, and luxurious baths with large walk-in showers. Rooms are decorated in rich, Mexican-loomed fabrics and enhanced by colorful handmade Mexican tiles. Terra-cotta and white ceramic tile floors are accented by area rugs; beds are draped in filmy white gauze; and a hammock is strung in a corner of each patio, providing a pleasant retreat for an afternoon siesta.

Villa del Sol's beachfront suites are about as romantic as it gets. The problem is, once you've seen them, you'll not want to leave. These suites are pure Mexican magic at its best. Each has a large patio smack on the beach with a hammock for two as well as a table and chairs; you can wake up slowly there to fresh coffee and croissants each morning. Sitting areas open onto a wide deck with a blue-tiled plunge pool. A lounge for two, padded and comfortable, is the perfect place to catch a snooze. King-size canopied beds and extra-large baths and views of orange-flamed sunsets take the romance level up another notch. Red-tile floors, fresh flowers, shelves, and roomy closets all add to the wonderful ambience.

If one wants to nitpick (and that's all it is): A few of the bungalows are a bit on the dark side, especially those that front the gardens. The heavy tropical vegetation overhanging the roofs tends to keep sunlight at bay. But this is a minor thing and will soon be forgotten once you settle in. The majority of suites including the beachfront suites are quite open and spacious.

A large round palapa-thatched roof, which looks much like a giant sombrero, houses an open-air bar and restaurant. Orlando's Bar, named after the affable master of the bar, whose wit and diplomacy are legendary, is also housed under its own thatched roof. Repeat guests always look forward to swapping stories with Orlando,

who will serve you exotic drinks such as coco loco, margaritas, and a mean martini.

The white-sand beach, shaded by palms and palm-frond umbrellas, is set up with comfortable lounges with thick cushions, where you can crash and snooze. Want a frosty margarita and some freshly made guacamole and tortilla chips? Just signal the beach attendant, and it will be brought to you in speedy fashion. Generally the waters off La Ropa, unlike the rougher beach areas in neighboring Ixtapa, are very swimmable. When the surf kicks up, however, you can cool off in one of the resort's four pools including a stunning new infinity pool overlooking the beach.

There are two lighted tennis courts, which, like everything else on the property, are well maintained. If you're looking for a game of tennis and your spouse isn't up to it, ask Helmut if he'd like a set or two. A fitness center is equipped with basic exercise equipment.

Dining at the Villa del Sol under the palapa roof is just about everything you could want: excellent, well-prepared food, candlelit tables by the sea, and warm smiles from those who serve you. Mediterranean fare is served at La Cantina Bar & Grill. Eat at the bar, on the large wooden deck, or inside near the open kitchen. Each Friday, enjoy a Mexican Fiesta featuring a sumptous buffet and live entertainment.

Just outside the resort entrance lies the picturesque village of Zihuatanejo. Still very much a sleepy fishing village in spite of the tourism influx at nearby Ixtapa, here you can still watch the fishermen bring in their daily catch, and you can stroll down decorative brick-paved streets past small shops and cozy little restaurants. If you crave a bit of lively nightlife, you can head to one of the large hotels on Ixtapa's Palmar Beach. But then, who really wants to leave the Villa del Sol for very long?

Hotel Villa del Sol

Location: On palm-lined La Ropa Beach in the quaint village of Zihuatanejo, 150 miles northwest of Acapulco on the Pacific Coast

Romantic Highlights: Lovely white crescent-shaped private beach; private terrace with hammock; garden mini-pools; dinner on the beach

Address/Phone: P.O. Box 84, Playa La Ropa, 40880 Zihuatanejo, Gro., Mexico; 52–755–554–2239 or 52–755–554–3239; fax 52–755–554–2758 or 52–755–554–4066

E-mail: hotel@villasol.com.mx

Web Site: www.hotelvilladelsol.net

U.S. Reservations: (888) 389–2645

Owner/Manager: Helmut and Muriel Leins, owners; Peter M. Koehler, general manager

Arrival/Departure: Taxis are available at the airport (about $7.00 each way per car)

Distance from Ixtapa-Zihuatanejo International Airport: 15 minutes

Distance from Zihuatanejo: 5 minutes; from Ixtapa, 10 minutes

Accommodations: 56 individually designed rooms and suites, including 18 luxury suites

Most Romantic Room/Suite: Beachfront suites, each with a private terrace with ocean view, double chaise lounge, extra-large hammock, and mini-pool

Amenities: Air-conditioning, ceiling fans, king-size bed, in-room safe, TV, refrigerator, terrace, hammock, telephone, laundry and valet service. Suites have a living room area, minibar, bathrobes, private fax, satellite TV, stereo, and CD player. Some have whirlpool or mini-pool. Services include room service, *New York Times*, fax, massages, and beauty salon.

Electricity: 110 volts

Sports and Facilities: Beach, waterskiing, snorkeling, sailboarding, sailing, 4 freshwater pools; 2 lighted tennis courts; two 18-hole golf courses 10 minutes away; scuba diving, deep-sea fishing, and horseback riding can be arranged

Dress Code: Casual; casually elegant for dinner

Weddings: Can be arranged

Rates/Packages: From $170 (summer); from $240 (winter). During winter the meal plan for breakfast and dinner is mandatory ($60 per person per day in summer). No children under 14 during winter months.

Payment/Credit Cards: Most major

Deposit: Two-night deposit

Government Taxes: 15 percent; 2 percent lodging tax

Service Charges: 10–15 percent suggested

Entry Requirements for U.S. Citizens: Proof of citizenship; passport best

LA CASA QUE CANTA
Zihuatanejo

La Casa Que Canta, "the house that sings," is one of those rare finds in Mexico, a small, intimate, five-star inn perched atop a cliff overlooking the Pacific. The clusters of pink-hued adobe-like casitas with terraces and thatched roofs that look like giant mops atop little blockhouses are staggered down the hillside so that you get a great view of the sea from each room.

Eclectically and creatively furnished with authentic Mexican artifacts and furniture, the suites have chairs with arms that are brightly painted to resemble birds and legs carved like feathers. A colorful striped animal (could it be a pig or a tapir?) sits on the floor balancing a carved bird on its back. A large terra-cotta bird with real, brightly colored feathers sits on a table, one of the many cleverly designed lamps scattered here and there in the public areas and suites. Furniture painted by well-known Mexican artists such as Frida Kahlo and Diego Rivera, mermaids, and ceramic angels along with tons of plants and Mexican tapestries and paintings add beauty and a sense of fun to La Casa Que Canta.

Your suite, with its bedroom, sitting room, and separate patio, is home to a number of valuable and whimsical art pieces: hand-painted desks, folk art from Erongaricuaro and *equipale* chairs. All these wonderful things are set against a background of creamy white walls and bed linens and red-tile floors edged with shiny, polished pebbles. Wood louvered doors open out to the terraces, which are partially thatched and have two extra-long lounge chairs, colorfully painted wrought-iron tables and chairs, a cushioned sitting area, lamps, and hammocks. In the harbor below you'll see a scattering of beautiful yachts—picture-postcard stuff. Don't look for a TV: There isn't one—but who needs it, with such views? (If you really need a quick catch-up on the world outside, there's a TV in the "theater room.") Your bath has a granite counter with double vanity, a pink-marble walk-in shower, a walk-in closet, separate toilet with bidet, and oversize bath towels.

Other resorts might be able to duplicate the decor (although I doubt it, unless the designers are prepared to spend years searching for interesting Mexican art and furniture pieces), but a more stunning setting would be hard to find. Your terrace, the pool, the dining room, the various terraced rooms tucked into the descending hillside—everything—sits over the sea, which continually crashes into the wet, dark, jagged rocks at the base of the cliff. There is a saltwater pool as well as a Jacuzzi cut into the rocks near the bottom of the cliff. The freshwater pool, near the top of the cliff, is constructed so that the water

seems to simply slip over the side of the pool down to the sea. You can quite happily while away the entire day sitting on the patio here, enjoying the scenery and sun.

In the evening when you come into your room, you'll find a floral surprise waiting for you: an elaborate pattern of flower petals on your bed, perhaps shaped into a heart. You also might find flowers tucked into washcloths, in soap trays, and on your bedside table.

La Casa Que Canta is but a two-minute walk to Playa La Ropa, a lovely white sandy beach with good swimming.

Meals are served outdoors overlooking the bay or in a palapa-palm-frond–thatched structure, where you'll also find a reception area, lounge, and bar. Dining hours are relaxed. You can eat anytime after 8:00 A.M., and Mexican specialties, salads, and grilled items are offered at both pool terraces. Like tequila? The resort features twelve different brands. Try a frosty and yummy quanabana margarita, or go for a cold Corona, the local beer, which goes great with the bar's new selection of Mexican tapas at the Terrace Bar.

Enjoying cocktails and dinner on the terrace at night is about as romantic as it gets: The soft, yellow lights play on the lofty, palm-thatched ceilings, and endless views of the sea are punctuated by the winking lights of Zihuatanejo in the distance. Light peeks through the holes of large round terra-cotta pots and gently glows from hanging wicker shades; there are enough private cozy sitting areas tucked here and there for couples who want their own space.

Just five minutes away is Zihuatanejo, a charming fishing village nestled into the curve of a bay cut sharply into the hills. Small white houses with red-tile roofs, a variety of fishing vessels anchored in the bay or pulled up on the shore, and a small population of happy, easygoing people make this a fun place to visit. If you crave some modern-day action, the beach resort area, Ixtapa, is just a ten-minute drive around the corner.

This all may seem familiar if you saw the movie *When a Man Loves a Woman*, starring Meg Ryan and Andy Garcia, which was filmed here. A glance at the guest book says it all: A honeymoon couple writes, "La Casa Que Canta was the best place to start the first day of the rest of our lives." Another says simply, "Wow! Pure magic."

La Casa Que Canta

Location: On a cliff above Zihuatanejo Bay adjacent to Playa La Ropa, near the center of Zihuatanejo

Romantic Highlights: Views, view, views; intimate suites with private plunge pools; wonderful small terraced places where you can drink or dine

Address/Phone: Camino Escenico a la Playa la Ropa, 40880 Zihuatanejo, Gro., Mexico; 52–755–47030, (888) 523–5050; fax 52–755–47040

E-mail: lacasaquecanta@prodigy.net.mx

Web Site: www.lacasaquecanta.com

U.S. Reservations: (888) 523–5050 or Small Luxury Hotels, (800) 525–4800

Owner/Manager: Jacques Baldassari, owner; Teresa Arellano, Marcos Ramirez, and Anna Maria Frias, management committee

Arrival/Departure: Transfers from Ixtapa/Zihuatanejo Airport can be arranged

Distance from Ixtapa-Zihuatanejo International Airport: 12 miles (20 minutes); 35-minute flight from Mexico City

Distance from Zihuatanejo center: 5 minutes

Accommodations: 24 suites, each with its own living room and terrace; suites range in size from 800 to 1,733 square feet; 10 suites have private pools

Most Romantic Room/Suite: Private pool suites

Amenities: Air-conditioning, fans, bidet, large walk-in shower, magnifying mirror, toiletries, hair dryer, telephone, in-room safe, minibar, bathrobes; room service, massages available

Electricity: 110 volts

Sports and Facilities: 2 pools (1 freshwater "infinity" pool, 1 saltwater), saltwater Jacuzzi, new well-being center with 4 treatment rooms for massage therapy, most water sports, horseback riding; golf and tennis nearby

Dress Code: Casually elegant

Weddings: Can be arranged

Rates/Packages: $330–$415 (high season); $285–$375 (low season) per couple per night; Master Pool Suite, $600 (high season), $525 (low season).

Payment/Credit Cards: Most major

Deposit: Two-night deposit; refund if canceled 30 days prior to arrival date (60 days for Christmas and Easter)

Government Taxes: 17 percent

Service Charges: 10 to 15 percent suggested

Entry Requirements for U.S. Citizens: Proof of identity; passport best

EUROPE

HOTEL GOLDENER HIRSCH
Austria

The Hotel Goldener Hirsch is pure Austrian, from the puffy duvets to the quaint, wrought-iron folk art lamps that decorate the rooms. If you are coming to Austria for your honeymoon and want a historic inn in the heart of Salzburg, try this one. You'll know you're there when you spot among the many beautifully wrought hanging signs along the narrow street the one with a gold deer atop an ornate golden circle—Goldener Hirsch stands for "gold deer." From the time you check in at the elaborately carved front reception desk and follow the bellman to your room on a rather circuitous route, you'll begin to realize that this is indeed a unique place.

The Goldener Hirsch is not just one building but a combination of interconnected buildings that stand smack on one of the most elegant streets in the baroque, historic heart of Salzburg. The Getreidegasse is lined with trendy boutiques and antiques shops, and just down the street is Mozart's birthplace; close by is the Festspielhaus (Theater).

Each of the sixty-nine rooms and suites is individually furnished with cozy sitting areas, a conglomeration of antiques, and masterpieces of rural art. On the beds are those wonderful creations of European refinement—goose-down duvets and fine, soft linens. Headboards, desks, tables, and bureaus are likely to be mellowed orange pine. The baths are modern, and rooms come with comfortable amenities such as telephone, TV, radio, and minibar.

There is no way you can spend a night here and not be touched in some way by the rich heritage of this fine old inn. Its character and place in the world are due in part to the work of a very special lady, Countess Walderdorff. She is the one who rescued the centuries-old structure from its sad state of disrepair and began its reconstruction during the difficult years following World War II. During the renovations the countess supervised every detail of the hotel's rebirth, from the hand-wrought iron light fixtures to the specially made china.

Hotel Goldener Hirsch

Location: In the heart of Salzburg, on elegant Getreidegasse

Romantic Highlights: Antique beds; Old World charm in fifteenthth-century inn; the magic of Salzburg

Address/Phone: Getreidegasse 37, A–5020, Salzburg, Austria; 43–662–80840; fax 43–662–843–349

E-mail: welcome@goldenerhirsch.com

Web Site: www.goldenerhirsch.com

U.S. Reservations: (800) 325–3535; fax (800) 325–3589; Leading Hotels of the World (LHW), (800) 223–6800

Owner/Manager: Johannes Walderdorff, director

Arrival/Departure: Taxi from airport or train station

Distance from Munich International Airport: Approximately 84 miles (2 hours); 3 miles (10 minutes) from Salzburg Airport

Distance from Salzburg: Located in heart of town

Accommodations: 65 rooms, 4 suites

Most Romantic Room/Suite: Room 23 with its antique painted bed is charming; suites are roomier

Amenities: Hair dryer, minibar, TV, telephone, radio, toiletries, air-conditioning, room service, valet service

Electricity: 220 volts

Sports and Facilities: Guest privileges at Gut Altentann Golf & Country Club with payment of greens fees; other sports nearby include tennis, swimming, skiing, squash, and horseback riding

Dress Code: Informal by day; jacket and tie for men appreciated for dinner

Weddings: Can be arranged

Rates/Packages: From €390 (U.S.$368) per couple per night, including taxes; Luxury Romance Package, €509 (U.S.$480) per couple per night, includes breakfast, taxes, service charges, champagne, and late checkout

Payment/Credit Cards: Most major

Deposit: Guarantee with credit card

Government Taxes: Included

Service Charges: Included

Entry Requirements for U.S. Citizens: Passport

Almost from the first day it opened its doors, the Goldener Hirsch became known as the "in" place for notables to stay and be seen when they came to Salzburg. Heads of state and the elite of the world have come to overnight and sup at this famous hostelry, among them the Duke and Duchess of Windsor, Herbert von Karajan, and Leonard Bernstein.

Today it's the lady's son, Count Johannes Walderdorff, who heartily welcomes guests from near and far places. Enjoy a quiet cocktail at the bar before sitting down to dinner. You can try local specialties and delicious draught beer in the rustic Herzl-Taverne, with its attractive inner courtyard. Indulge in all kinds of good things at the hotel's Goldener Hirsch restaurant, one of the best in Austria. Ask Count Walderdorff to recommend his favorite dishes and he may suggest that you try the goose liver and *tafelspitz* (a boiled beef dish). Top it all off with a delectable caramel soufflé and caramel and walnut pancakes. "I tried twenty-eight versions of this recipe until I got it right," said the Count.

The Goldener Hirsch is not a particularly elegant place, nor is it one that offers much in the way of entertainment or activities. It doesn't need to. It's friendly and charming, and imagine: The whole wonderful city of Salzburg is right outside your door, with just about everything within easy walking distance. There are museums to explore, concert performances to attend, romantic little restaurants to try out, shops to browse, and endless, interesting streets to discover.

THE FEATHERS HOTEL
England

At the bottom hem of the Cotswolds, in the back-yard of Blenheim Palace, birthplace of Sir Winston Churchill, is the small market town of Woodstock. The first time I was in Woodstock, I was with a tour en route to visit a number of gardens and homes in the region. We zipped right through town, bypassing the village center and barely hesitating long enough for the driver to shift gears. This is not unusual. Except for those who go directly to Blenheim, Woodstock is not a usual stop on the tourist route. Which makes Woodstock all the more desirable to any who want to explore the Cotswolds but escape at the end of the day to a more serene place than its more famous neighbors over the hills.

Still, Woodstock has to be one of England's prettiest towns. Many of its buildings, which are constructed largely of mellow Cotswold stone, date back to the twelfth century.

In the center of this historic village, within walking distance of the Triumphal Arch leading into the palace grounds and just down the street from Chaucer's house and some wonderful old pubs, is the seventeenth-century Feathers Hotel. The Feathers Hotel, composed of four adjacent but separate houses, is grand without being pretentious. Thanks to the congenial general manager, Peter Bate, and his staff, you feel relaxed, welcome.

Richly furnished rooms, filled with antiques, gilded mirrors, original paintings, leather, and fabrics, all contribute to an ambience of timeless tradition and privilege. Yet, whether you're staying for one night or one week, it doesn't take very long for you to feel quite at home.

Sofas and chairs are so comfortable, you're tempted to put your feet up on the highly polished coffee table (wouldn't suggest it however) and sink into the plump cushions for a snooze or read one of the books or maga-zines provided in the library (by all means).

Tea is served in late afternoon in the study; after dinner, coffee and cordials are offered. On cooler evenings a log fire radiates good cheer and warmth. The holidays are a particularly cheery time; the public rooms are decorated with Christmas trees and hot mulled wine is served.

In summer the Courtyard Garden, filled with flowers and shrubbery, is a perfect place for a light lunch, tea, or a drink. There is also the Whinchat Bar, a cozy place to unwind and perhaps sip a Pimms or brandy. A unique feature of the Whinchat is its display of stuffed birds in glass boxes: During the Victorian period these pieces were very much in vogue and today are collector's items.

Each of the twenty rooms and suites is different, starting with the names. Continuing the "feathers" theme, each room is named after a bird; e.g. partridge, barn owl, peacock. Canopied beds, carved mahogany headboards, flower bedspreads, flowing drapes, balloon curtains, traditional wallpapers, and a mix of period reproductions and antique furniture are skillfully incorporated into the decor. One room decorated in navy blue and white has a high, pitched ceiling with the original heavy beams; another with a king-size bed is decorated in deep reds, beautifully setting off the mahogany armoire and headboard. In still another room, French doors lead out to a private courtyard.

Some rooms have fireplaces; suites come with sitting rooms and a second tv. The rooms are continually being redecorated and updated—you'll certainly not find these accommodations stuffy or tired.

Antique paneling and walls of bookshelves create a unique setting for the restaurant. The cuisine, prepared by David Edwards, is beautifully presented and served. As much as possible, Chef Edwards uses local produce, meats, and fish, successfully marrying classical cuisine with innovative touches.

In addition to an a la carte menu, there is a table d'hôte lunch menu of two or three courses. Almost 250 kinds of wines in a variety of price ranges are offered to complement the meal.

The Feathers Hotel is an excellent base for exploring the Cotswolds. It is also close to many walking paths and the river, where you can try punting (with a chauffeur). Other leisure pursuits available locally include helicopter lessons, rally driving, golf, shooting, fishing, horseback riding, walking, and ballooning!

The Feathers Hotel

Location: In a small market town on the edge of the Cotswolds near Oxford

Romantic Highlights: Fireplaces; elegant town house style rooms; intimate candlelit restaurant

Address/Phone: Market Street, Woodstock, Oxfordshire OX20 1SX, England; 44–1993–812–291; fax 44–1993–813–158

E-mail: enquiries@feathers.co.uk

Web Site: www.feathers.co.uk

U.S. Reservations: Josephine Barr, (800) 323 5463

Owner/Manager: Peter Bate, general manager

Arrival/Departure: Car rentals available at London's Heathrow and Gatwick Airport; transportation can be arranged by the hotel

Distance from London Heathrow International Airport: 60 miles (1¼ hours)

Distance from Oxford: 8 miles

Accommodations: 20 rooms and suites

Most Romantic Room/Suite: The Peacock, a spacious suite with a garden patio and separate sitting area; Goldcrest Suite, with two baths (one with a power steam shower)

Amenities: Hair dryer, telephone, TV, toiletries; some have air-conditioning, fax machine

Electricity: 240 volts

Sports and Facilities: Walking, hiking, golf, shooting, fishing, horseback riding, and ballooning nearby

Dress Code: Informal, but no jeans or shorts please

Weddings: Can be arranged for up to 50 people

Rates/Packages: £135–£290 (U.S.$199–$428) per couple per night including full English breakfast, tea and VAT; £185–£340 (U.S.$273–$502) including breakfast, dinner, tea, and VAT. Special packages available.

Payment/Credit Cards: Most major

Deposit: Guarantee reservation with credit card

Government Taxes: Included

Service Charges: Included

Entry Requirements for U.S. Citizens: Passport

HARTWELL HOUSE
England

Just because it looks like it would cost a king's ransom doesn't mean it actually does. In fact, Hartwell House, though certainly appealing to the well-heeled, is one of the more reasonably priced Grand Estate–style hotels I've come across. Apparently King Louis XVIII thought so, too. Exiled from France when Napoleon was flexing his muscles, King Louis leased the estate in 1809 at a grand sum of £500 per year.

Large enough to accommodate more than 130 people who came with him to keep him company, Louis made Hartwell House his residence for the next five years. Since that time Hartwell House has been altered by three architects, damaged by fire, and used as a school. Today, after a meticulous restoration by Historic House Hotels, Hartwell House stands as one of Europe's most gracious country house hotels.

Located about an hour's drive from London's Heathrow Airport, Hartwell House lolls in contented splendor amid rolling manicured lawns accented by topiary. Beyond these grounds cows graze peacefully, held back from nibbling the lush lawns by a ha-ha, an "invisible," ditchlike barrier.

Rooms and suites are in the main building as well as in Hartwell Court, a group of charming eighteenth-century coach houses that also contain the Hartwell Spa and a series of meeting rooms.

Although every room is different, each has a sitting area. Some rooms have four-poster canopy beds. Some have fireplaces. All have marvelous bathrooms with all the expected amenities.

Louis's former bedroom, now called the King's Room, looks out over the south lawns and pastures and is almost too opulent to leave. You can perch on the sofa, pour two glasses of sherry from the decanter on the coffee table, sit back, and gaze out over the bucolic scene just outside your high bay windows. Cows find shelter from the sun under groves of trees; two children dash across the lawns to hide behind one of the tall, chipped yew hedges—probably not unlike the scene Louis himself viewed when he had time to muse.

History permeates this room, for peering down on you from their lofty perches on the walls are the life-size oil paintings of some very important-looking aristocrats from King Louis's days.

Although Hartwell's Georgian interiors date from the 1740s, with much use of the ornate rococo style, I did not find the house to be dark or imposing. Decorators have lightened the look with soft pastel colors.

Large mullioned windows let in plenty of light, and ceilings and walls are high. Superb plasterwork details include leaves and flowers in ivory against pale pastel backgrounds on walls and ceilings, and balusters on the unique Jacobean staircase create interest with their wood-carved, not-so-flattering figures of influential people.

The Great Hall, a masterpiece of English baroque design, features an elaborate carved fireplace. Just a few steps away is the oak-paneled bar, where you can sip your Pimms while gazing at original paintings of the eighteenth-century gardens of Hartwell by Spanish painter Balthazar Nebot.

There are three dining rooms, decorated in soft golds and greens, with artfully designed ceilings, chandeliers, and draperies. The library at Hartwell is appointed with many antiques and period pieces, including some objects that were in the original house.

Cuisine, created by Chef Daniel Richardson, includes imaginative dishes such as layered terrine of home-smoked duck and chicken with globe artichokes and truffle dressing; filet of Scottish beef with creamed spinach and celeriac, confit shallots and garlic, a parsley puree, and a Cabernet Sauvignon jus; and three apple puddings: tarte tatin, apple and cider mousse, and crispy apple dishes with sorbet served on lemon custard.

For something more casual there is the Spa Buttery, open for breakfast, lunch, and afternoon tea, and the Spa Bar, open daily until 7:00 P.M.

At Hartwell there is plenty to keep you busy without leaving the grounds. Take time to stroll through their

Hartwell House

Location: Set on 90 acres in the Vale of Aylesbury, Buckinghamshire, 50 miles northwest of London

Romantic Highlights: Gracious country estate; fireplaces; elegant dining; gardens; serpentine walkways; lake; wonderful spa

Address/Phone: Oxford Road near Aylesbury, Buckinghamshire HP17 8NL, England; 44–1296–747–444; fax 44–1296–747–450

E-mail: resarc@relaischateaux.fr

U.S. Reservations: (800) 260–8338; Relais & Châteaux, (212) 856–0115

Owner/Manager: C. A. Jonathan Thompson, director and general manager

Arrival/Departure: Guests can be met by prior arrangement at London Heathrow Airport; nearest rail stations are Aylesbury and Thame & Haddenham Parkway

Distance from London Heathrow International Airport: 35 miles

Distance from London: 50 miles

Accommodations: 30 rooms and suites in the main house; 16 rooms and suites in Hartwell Court

Most Romantic Room/Suite: King's Room (Number 15); Queen's Room (Number 12); in Hartwell Court (Number 3), a ground-floor suite opens onto a private garden

Amenities: Hair dryer, telephone, TV, bathrobe, toiletries, magnifying mirror, pants presser

Electricity: 240 volts

Sports and Facilities: The Hartwell Spa with pool, whirlpool spa bath, steam room, sauna, treatment rooms, and gym; 2 tennis courts, jogging track

Dress Code: Gentlemen requested to wear jacket and tie evenings in the dining room

Weddings: Small wedding receptions can be arranged

Rates/Packages: Room rates from about £340 (U.S.$502) per couple with early morning tea, service, and VAT. Winter and Spring Champagne Breaks, £290–£410 (U.S.$428–-$605) per couple per night (minimum 2 nights), including room, early morning tea, breakfast, dinner, champagne, service, and VAT; Historic House Summer Breaks from £290 (U.S.$428) per couple, including all of the above plus admission to one of the historic properties in the area, such as Blenheim Palace. Spa packages also available. (The hotel welcomes children 8 years of age and older.)

Payment/Credit Cards: Visa, MasterCard

Deposit: Guarantee with credit card

Government Taxes: Included

Entry Requirement for U.S. Citizens: Passport

lovely park. It features a number of pavilions and monuments, including a statue of Hercules and an obelisk.

The Hartwell Spa, modeled after an orangery, is just 100 yards from the main building. It has a swimming pool, a steam room, a whirlpool bath, saunas, and a gym, along with the bar and small restaurant—a great place to relax with coffee, breads, and the London *Times* after an early morning workout. The pool is surrounded by an arcade furnished with comfortable lounges. Treatments include facials, massages, reflexology, aromatherapy, and detoxifying algae wraps.

The rococo-style Morning Room, the Drawing Room, and the Library overlook the gardens. The sunny roof terrace, once used by King Louis's buddies for growing vegetables and keeping rabbits and chickens, gives you a great view of the countryside. Or on a cool day, after a brisk walk, you can retreat to the warmth of the Great Hall and the comfort of the highly plumped couches in front of a crackling fire while you sip a glass of brandy or sherry or a cup of tea. Highly civilized.

Hartwell House makes an excellent base for exploring the English countryside. Within easy driving distance are places like Blenheim Palace, Waddesdon Manor, Claydon House, Windsor Castle, and Stowe Landscape Gardens. The Vale of Aylesbury is picnic country. Ask the hotel staff to pack a picnic lunch for you. They can fill your hamper with good things like smoked salmon and lemon, avocado and prawns, fruits, lobster salad, strawberries and cream, scones, and wines and champagne.

Lord Byron, thinking Louis a bit foolish to leave Hartwell, even if it was to assume his throne, wrote, "Why wouldst thou leave calm Hartwell's green abode . . . Apician table and Horatian Ode?" And the spa wasn't yet built in Louis's day!

LE MANOIR AUX QUAT' SAISONS
England

Those who dream of honeymooning in a centuries-old stone manor house and have the wherewithal to pay the bill should head to Le Manoir aux Quat' Saisons. England has a lot of wonderful castles and estate hotels, but you'd have to look far and wide to find a place with as much going for it as this one: romantic rooms, idyllic setting, superb service, convenient location near the Cotswolds and London, plus one of the best restaurants in all the kingdom.

Once a favorite country retreat of Lord Coventry, trusted servant of James I, and a refuge for public officials in high standing, this magnificent estate became a hotel in 1984 when Raymond Blanc opened Le Manoir. During the past few years, the property has been totally refurbished, and a garden wing and two glass conservatory dining rooms have been added.

One of the most unique accommodations, the Michael Priest Suite, is located in the fifteenth-century dovecote, a round, stone tower with a conical pointed roof. The bathroom has a huge antique tub on feet that has been painted with fanciful pink and white doves and flowers. A great shower gives you the option of steam superjets coming at you from all sides. A wide, soft pink–carpeted staircase winds up to the second level, where a queen-size bed is topped by "garlands" of white-and-pink fabric swags held aloft by white doves suspended from the ceiling by invisible wires. The thick walls of the tower are painted in a warm yellow and decorated with pretty pictures hanging from wide pink ribbons. There are also a skirted dressing table, a cabanalike pink-and-white-striped tented "closet," and a small leaded window opening onto the gardens. The only downside of this blissful romantic bower is its size—it's a bit tight; other suites are roomier. But for sheer romance this is a honeymoon favorite.

Hollyhocks is in the main building and was the bedroom of one of the former owners of the estate. It is extremely spacious, furnished with a couch, chairs, dressing table, desk, coffee table, and large, canopied bed. A number of leaded windows open onto the courtyard. Also popular are the two-story garden suites, which have a sit-ting room on the lower level along with a furnished patio; the bedroom is upstairs. All are exquisitely decorated with a combination of traditional English furniture, antiques, artwork, chintz, and French accents.

New rooms arranged around a garden courtyard combine clean contemporary lines with antique accents. Broad bands of off-white textures wrap around walls; mirrored tables and twentieth-century artwork complement hand-hewn beams and geometrical tapestry carpets.

Flowers are lavishly spread through the public areas and guest rooms. An in-house florist has her own cutting garden and flower house tucked into the corner of the property. A recent addition to the hotel, a Japanese garden, may seem a bit out of sync with the English gardens, but somehow it fits. A delicate mist of water falls from hidden places between the trees that overhang the pond, and a Japanese teahouse welcomes those who want to stop and be soothed.

Throughout the grounds you'll find a number of original sculptures. A bronze work of birds rising through the reeds is particularly appealing. Many are for sale, as the gardens serve as an excellent showcase for artists such as Judith Holmes Drewry and Lloyd Le Blanc. Prices range from about $300 to over $50,000.

Walk through the three acres of vegetable gardens and you'll begin to understand why the food here is so good. The thirty or so chefs who prepare the meals each day use only the freshest of ingredients. Baby zucchini picked just minutes before serving, with blossoms still attached (to stuff with crabmeat and truffles); beetroot, runner beans, artichokes, leek, spinach, tomatoes—more than one hundred varieties of vegetables, herbs, and fruits planted here supply the hotel with most of its produce. Meat comes from a local butcher just down the road. The hotel has expanded its kitchen and restaurant facilities, adding a patisserie and bakery, a new cookery school, and a cocktail bar. Take a peek in the kitchen, and on the shelves you'll see huge glass jars filled with plums, cherries, raspberries, and other fruits.

But having the right ingredients is just the beginning of the road leading to a Michelin two-star rating. It takes a great chef like Raymond Blanc to complete the picture: Blanc's list of credits fill a page and more. Each of his creations not only looks like a work of art; it titillates taste sensations you never knew you had. Your meal may also seem to be priced like an art object (hors d'oeuvres such as pressed duck confit and foie gras in a truffle gelée costs about $36; entrees such as pan-fried wild salmon fillet on a sorrel sabayon will set you back about $47; homemade sorbets on a waffle "painter's palette" cost around $23), but look at it this way: Sure it costs a lot, but here you're not just paying for dinner, you're investing in a delectable memory guaranteed to last a lifetime. If you come to the hotel and can't afford to try the restaurant, you might as well go somewhere else.

Meals are served in three different dining rooms: the original one and two new conservatory rooms, which are pleasant and pretty year-round.

Lest you be tempted to simply loll on the grounds and take in the never-ending vistas of pure English countryside, there is a croquet court and a garden courtyard, enclosed by hedges. You can go biking, walking, or fishing or arrange with the concierge to play golf or go horseback riding. And Le Manoir is in a great location for exploring the Cotswolds, Oxford, and other historic and interesting places, such as Blenheim Palace, the Royal Shakespeare Theatre, and Windsor Castle.

Le Manoir aux Quat' Saisons combines the country charm of merry old England, the cuisine of France, and the technical expertise of today's engineering: a real winner! Now if the price of a room here in 1474—about 95 cents for a week—could be matched today, you'd really be in heaven.

Le Manoir aux Quat' Saisons

Location: In a small country village between the Chilterns and the Cotswolds

Romantic Highlights: Cocktails on the terrace overlooking the meadows and gardens; a stroll through the tranquil Japanese gardens; sleeping in a round, stone, medieval dovecote

Address/Phone: Church Road, Great Milton, Oxford OX44 7PD England; 44–1184–427–881; fax 44–0184–427–8847

E-mail: info@blanc.co.uk

Web Site: www.manoir.co.uk

U.S. Reservations: Relais & Châteaux, (800) RELAIS–8

Owner/Manager: Raymond Blanc, chef-patron; Philip Newman-Hall, general manager

Arrival/Departure: Pickup at London's airports can be arranged; from Heathrow via private limousine (about $135 per car); from Gatwick Airport (about $235); helipad on grounds

Distance from London Heathrow International Airport: 40 miles (under 1 hour); Gatwick, 55 miles (1½ hours)

Distance from Oxford: 8 miles south

Accommodations: 32 rooms and suites

Most Romantic Room/Suite: The two-story Michael Priest Suite, built in a fifteenth-century dovecote; Hollyhocks, a spacious room with a four-poster bed in the main building; and the two-story suites in the new garden wing

Amenities: Hair dryer, TV, telephone, radio, terry robes, sewing kit, heated towel bar, bidet, double sinks, toiletries, magnifying mirror, full-length mirror, padded hangers, trouser press; daily newspaper, fresh fruit, Madeira, mineral water, 24-hour room service, fresh flowers, VCR on request

Electricity: 220/240 volts

Sports and Facilities: Latex tennis court, croquet, pool, bicycles, walking trails, fishing; riding and golf nearby

Dress Code: Country elegant

Weddings: Can be arranged; gardens and terraces make lovely setting

Rates/Packages: £425–£825 (U.S.$627–$1,218) per couple per night for a suite; £245–£395 (U.S.$361–583) per couple per night for a room; rates include a French breakfast.

Payment/Credit Cards: Most major

Deposit: $150 per couple per night; cancel 2 weeks prior to arrival date for full refund

Government Taxes: Included

Service Charges: Included

Entry Requirements for U.S. Citizens: Passport

RADISSON EDWARDIAN HAMPSHIRE HOTEL
England

You couldn't be more in the middle of all the London action if you pitched a tent in the center of Leicester Square. The Radisson Edwardian Hampshire Hotel sits right on the square and is within easy walking distance of theaters, Covent Garden, Piccadilly Circus, Chinatown, the National Gallery, SoHo, and many trendy restaurants and nightclubs; the Hampshire's Penthouse overlooks Trafalgar Square. Elegant and intimate, the Hampshire stands on ground once occupied by seven private houses built in the late 1600s by the Earl of Leicester, who saw this area as a great social center for his wealthy country friends.

All you have to do is walk through Leicester Square on a warm, balmy day and see that this part of London is still a beehive of activity. Street entertainers draw crowds around them, people stand in small groups talking, and many come and go, in and out of the restaurants and stores surrounding the square. The entrance to the tube is steps away. It's a happening place.

The building that is today the Hampshire started life as the Royal Dental Hospital around 1900. In 1987 Radisson Edwardian Hotels bought the structure and, after an expensive and expansive redo, opened the Hampshire in 1989 as a five-star hotel. Furnished in the style of English country houses, each of the 124 guest rooms is different (and each is buffered from outside buzz by triple-glazed windows).

The decor recalls the Edwardian period, a bit difficult to define, since this "style" is actually a mixture of many cultures. This style was fashionable during the Edwardian period (1901 until the death of King Edward VII, in 1910). At this time wealthy travelers returned to England with furniture and artifacts from their grand trips to faraway places like the Orient and the Middle East. They used their money garnered from the booming Industrial Revolution to fill their homes with things like Persian carpets, Chinese porcelain, Indian tapestries, Japanese paintings, and delicately carved wood pieces.

It is this eclectic mix of English fabrics and wood paneling accented by selected pieces and colors of other countries that makes each of the 124 rooms in the Hampshire so unique. Yet everything works splendidly together, the decor sending out a message of elegance with soft creams, light greens, and corals. Beds have romantic canopies, fabric crowns, or other interesting treatments—the decorators used yards and yards of material both for the beds and for the drapes. Many rooms have built-in armoires, and lovely moldings accent the ceilings, windows, and doors throughout the hotel.

Little touches like a chandelier in the elevator and the glimpse of an inviting lounge let you know before you even enter your room that your accommodations will be special. The Lynhurst Suite (Number 705) for example, decorated in light creams and greens, has a beautiful four-poster bed and a sitting room. The Winchester Suite is very roomy, with a wonderful shower. And Number 116 is especially appealing. You can check out all the activity in Leicester Square through your huge arched windows, but no one from the outside can see you, for the window

Radisson Edwardian Hampshire Hotel

Location: In the heart of the West End, London, on the south side of Leicester Square

Romantic Highlights: Four-poster beds; one-way arched windows overlooking Leicester Square let you see out, but those you're looking at cannot see you

Address/Phone: Leicester Square, London WC2H 7LH England; 44–207–839–9399; fax 44–207–930–8122

U.S. Reservations: Radisson Edwardian Hotels, (800) 333–3333

Owner/Manager: Paul Mansi, managing director; Shahdad Jahanban, front-of-house manager

Arrival/Departure: Limousine service available from airport; Underground from Heathrow or Gatwick takes you within 1 block of the hotel (take Piccadilly Line to Leicester Square)

Distance from Heathrow and Gatwick Airports: About 15 miles

Accommodations: 124 rooms and suites

Most Romantic Room/Suite: Junior suites, Four-Poster King suites; 3rd floor rooms/suites with large one-way windows; and Hallmark rooms also good choices

Amenities: Air-conditioning, TV, minibar, tea- and coffeemaker, hair dryer, toiletries, room service, no-smoking rooms, 24-hour room service, trouser press, fax machines, terry robes and slippers (some rooms); in-room safes in deluxe rooms

Electricity: 220 volts

Sports and Facilities: Fitness studio; golf can be arranged through the concierge

Dress Code: Casually smart; jacket requested for dinner at the main restaurant

Weddings: Can be arranged; Penthouse provides beautiful setting overlooking London

Rates/Packages: From $284 "Go! London" package including VAT and breakfast. Rates are guaranteed in U.S. dollars and are per room per night.

Payment/Credit Cards: Most major

Deposit: Guarantee with credit card one-night deposit

Government Taxes: 17.5 percent VAT

Service Charges: Included

Entry Requirements for U.S. Citizens: Passport

glass is one-way. In fact most rooms on the third floor have arched one-way windows overlooking the square.

The Hampshire "Hallmark" rooms, though designed to appeal to business travelers since they feature work areas, fax machines, and two telephones, still have amenities that would be welcome to those on a romantic getaway: bathrobes and slippers, king-size beds, and express check-in and check-out. These rooms also tend to be larger, with sitting areas. The Hampshire's Apex Restaurant serves modern British food; the Apex Bar is cozy, comfortable, and a good place to unwind any time of the day or evening. For lighter meals try the Terrace Brasserie, an informal eatery right on Leicester Square. All restaurants serve pre- and posttheater menus. You can even eat dinner early, see a show, and come back for dessert and coffee, then sit quietly by the fire or in a private alcove or brush shoulders with the locals in the Crescent Bar on the lower level.

The Hampshire is a great base for those who love theater and lots of things to do, all within shouting distance.

TYLNEY HALL
England

It's hard to believe that a hotel that now has accommodations for 110 once belonged to just one family. Tylney Hall belongs to another era, one of privilege and status, when those who came here didn't have to worry much about asking for vacation time. Driving past the hedge-enclosed gardens and fountains to the entrance of this imposing red-brick Elizabethan Tudor-style estate with its chimneys, gables, arches, balustrades, and banks of small-paned tall windows, you know you are at the start of a splendid adventure where you can let your imagination turn to a time when the rich and the noble were honored guests.

There has been a house on the property since 1561, but Tylney Hall as we know it today was built about 1900 by Lionel Phillips, a baronet. Over the years, the hall has served as a private home, a hospital (during World War I), the headquarters for Lord Rotherwick's shipping line, a school, and, since 1985, a hotel and restaurant.

More impressive features include the reception area, with its black-and-white-tiled marble floor and massive oak stairway and the Italian Lounge featuring walnut-panelled walls, a stone fireplace, and an Italian walnut ceiling brought in sections from the Grimation Palace in Florence.

Tylney Hall spreads out over several acres with rooms and suites located in the main building and in separate houses and wings. Several of the rooms are located in the main building overlooking a variety of gardens. Rooms in the Orangery overlook the water gardens and other rooms are found in the garden wing. One of the most enchanting suites opens onto a private furnished patio covered by a trellis wound with the dense vines of passion flowers that scent the air sweetly.

As you might expect, everything is presented grand scale: Ceilings are high, lofty; fireplaces, huge; drapes have enough material to keep Scarlet in ball gowns for years; and furnishings are lavish with a lot of damask, silk, velvet, and tapestry. There are chandeliers, wood panelling, hand-painted borders, gilt reliefs, mirrors, and solid traditional furniture. This is not to say the rooms are heavy or glooomy. On the contrary, most are light and airy, decorated in sunny yellows, whites, and soft pastels.

Special room features include four-poster canopy beds, Jacuzzi baths, fireplaces, sitting areas, wood panelling, and window alcoves. Some rooms have two levels or stories.

The Oak Room restaurant is, no surprise here, richly panelled in oak. It features a distinctive glass dome ceiling and a large fireplace that is lighted on cooler nights. The tables are appointed with linen tablecloths and napkins, fresh flowers, and candles. Through the many windows, you get wonderful views of the gardens. The cuisine features an international menu accompanied by an excellent selection of wines.

The comfortable Library Bar is a good place for a before- or after-dinner cocktail. It has a fine coffered ceiling and a fireplace big enough to roast an ox in.

Surrounded by a vast carpet of green grass bordered by formal and informal flower gardens and six ponds, guests at Tylney have many delightful places to wander. From the back terraces, vistas are wide and sweeping. A ha-ha, a sort of ditch with one steep side—the uniquely British solution to keeping livestock in their place without spoiling the view with fences—marks one of the boundaries.

Garden mavens should be particularly interested in the fact that many of the gardens were originally laid out by Gertrude Jekyll, one of the best-known garden designers in history. Stroll around the Italian Garden, Rose and

Tylney Hall

Location: About an hour west of London in the rolling countryside of Hampshire

Romantic Highlights: Strolling through the many gardens; dining in baronial splendor the Oak Room; four-poster beds with regal canopies

Address/Phone: Rotherwick, Hook, Hampshire RG279AZ, England; 44–1256–764–881; fax 44–1256–768–141

E-mail: reservations@tylneyhall.co.uk

Web Site: www.tylneyhall.com

U.S. Reservations: (800) 525–4800

Owner/Manager: Elite Hotels, owners; Rita Mooney, manager

Arrival/Departure: Many arrive by car via the M3 out of London. Transfers from Heathrow or Gatwick airports can be arranged.

Distance from London Heathrow International Airport: 40 minutes

Distance from London: 40–60 minutes

Accommodations: 110 rooms and suites

Most Romantic Room/Suite: #101, a two-story suite at the end of the gardens with its own large trellis-covered patio; four-poster junior or master suites

Amenities: Air-conditioning, telephone, hair dryer, TV, radio, modem connection, safe, trouser press, 24-hour room service, toiletries

Electricity: 220 volts

Sports and Facilities: Billiards, outdoor pool, indoor pool, whirlpool, fitness room, sauna, snooker, 2 tennis courts, croquet, bicycles, jogging trail, room service; golf next door

Dress Code: Jacket and tie in Oak Room for evening

Weddings: Can be arranged with several venues including 12 magnificent rooms, the gardens, or by the lake

Rates/Packages: Nightly room rates from about $225; Romantic Break, about $300 per couple per night, includes accommodations, champagne, chocolates, flowers, a full English breakfast, newspaper, service, and VAT. Other packages available.

Payment/Credit Cards: Most major

Deposit: By credit card

Government Taxes: Included

Service Charges: Included

Entry Requirements for U.S. Citizens: Passport

Azalea Garden, Dutch Gardens, Water Garden, and Kitchen Garden. There is a greenhouse as well as an orchard, boathouse, lake, and tea house.

There is a large outdoor pool with plenty of comfortable chairs and lounges and an indoor glass-covered pool. Other on-site sports include archery, tennis, billiards, and clay pigeon shooting. The fitness center offers the latest in equipment and, for a special treat, early morning balloon rides over the countryside can be arranged. A golf course is adjacent to the property.

Cultural events, which are held throughout the year, have a grand setting. For example, a black-tie evening, "A Night of Operette," with dinner featured renowned opera singers Marilyn Hill Smith and Ian Caddy accompanied by Rebecca Holt

Because of its grandeur, you might think Tylney Hall could be a tad on the pretentious side. I did not find it so. The staff was helpful and friendly without being over imposing.

CHÂTEAU DE LA CHÈVRE D'OR
France

For pure romance you can't beat it. Perched on the rocks of the ancient hilltop village of Eze, this Relais & Châteaux property is a jewel. Château de la Chèvre d'Or appears to be carved into the rocky side of a cliff, suspended between sea and sky and awash in romance and mystery. From your balcony poised 1,200 feet above the sea, you can see far out to the Mediterranean. To your right are the lights of Nice, and the beaches and misty piece of land, long a playground of the smart and stylish, called Cap Ferrat; somewhere out to the left is Monte Carlo. It all spreads out below you, this feast of international chic, which is, in fact, but a few minutes down the hill.

But caught up here in your own hideaway away from it all, you may never want to leave this little piece of heaven.

The hotel is not far from the entrance to Eze Village, which is a good thing since no cars are allowed in the small town. You'll park (or take a taxi) to the entrance and walk up to the hotel with help from the staff with your bags.

From its lofty rock pedestal, Eze, a twisty, rocky, little place that 1,000 years ago was designed for horse and donkey traffic and quite certainly not for cars, consists of narrow cobblestone alleys banked by artsy little shops, multilevel terraces, clouds of bougainvillea tumbling over the rocks, and brilliant seascapes framed by ancient stone arches.

The furnishings and appointments of the Chèvre d'Or are far from medieval. Canopy beds, fireplaces, Oriental carpets, heavy beamed ceilings, crystal chandeliers, wrought-iron trim, and French doors opening onto private terraces or balconies cast their spell.

Each of the thirty-three rooms and suites is different. Some are located in the mansion itself, others are tucked away in separate buildings that, with their rugged stone

Château de la Chèvre d'Or

Location: In the medieval hilltop village of Eze above the Mediterranean between Nice and MonteCarlo

Romantic Highlights: Views, views, views; private balconies overlooking the French Riviera; soaking in a Jacuzzi tub looking out to sea

Address/Phone: Côte d'Azur (Moyenne Corniche), Rue du Bani, 06360 Eze-Village, France; 33–492–106–666; fax 33–493–410–672

E-mail: reservation@chevredor.com

Web Site: www.chevredor.com

U.S. Reservations: (800) RELAIS–8 (735–2478)

Owner/Manager: Thierry Naidu, general manager

Arrival/Departure: By taxi available at airport

Distance from Nice Côte d'Azur Airport: About 12 miles (30 minutes)

Distance from Nice: 10 miles (15 minutes)

Accommodations: 33 rooms and suites

Most Romantic Room/Suite: La Suite, an elegant gold-and-white confection with glass window walls and marble whirlpool for two overlooking the sea, marble floors, Oriental carpets, and hand-painted ceilings; suites overlooking sea

Amenities: Air-conditioning, toiletries, hair dryer, TV, telephone, minibar, safe, bathrobes

Electricity: 220 volts

Sports and Facilities: 2 pools, fitness center, free access to the Borfiga Tennis Club (five-minute walk), golf and beaches nearby

Dress Code: Casually elegant; jackets preferred for men at dinner in La Chèvre d'Or restaurant

Weddings: Can be arranged

Rates/Packages: €260–€1,500(U.S.$245–$1,415) low season—March, April, November; €350–€2,400 (U.S.$330–$2,265) high season—Easter and from May to end of October; per couple, including taxes and service

Payment/Credit Cards: Most major

Deposit: 1 night

Government Taxes: 1 euro (U.S.94 cents) per person per day city tax

Service Charges: Included

Entry Requirements for U.S. Citizens: Passport

Closed: Late November–early March

walls, arches, winding steps, tile, and billowing flowering vines, appear to have been here for hundreds of years. Which they have.

Fill your en suite marble Jacuzzi with bubbles, light the candles, open the Cristal, and slip into the water to soak and soothe in sensuous pleasure; gaze out to the sea and the stars and the lights of the Riviera. Later light the fire and cuddle up.

The two swimming pools are set in flower-filled courtyards. Both overlook the sea—pure joie de vivre.

French cuisine reigns at La Chèvre d'Or gourmet restaurant where the food is as special as the mind-blowing setting. Dishes are so artfully presented you won't know whether to eat them or paint them. Rich, sensual chocolate desserts are guaranteed to add to your love handles. For more casual fare try Le Grill du Château for a quick lunch or salad and L'Oliveto d'Or for Mediterranean and Italian fare. The bar-lounge features stone walls, large fireplace, and a lovely medieval-style beamed ceiling.

The whole world of the French Riviera is minutes away. Try your luck at the Monte Carlo casino, swim and sun on the beach at Nice, shop in the stylish boutiques and speciality shops, play golf, tour the palace of Monaco's royal family, and visit towns along the Riviera and in Provence like Antibes, Mougins, Cagnes sur-Mer, and Vence. It's magic.

CHÂTEAU DU DOMAINE ST. MARTIN
France

As you approach the unassuming entrance to the Château du Domaine St. Martin after a rather heady ride through narrow, loopy roads, a break in a lush, thick, clipped hedgerow takes you into the quaint complex of charming old buildings with roots dating back to A.D. 350. Once the residence of the Knights Templar, this serene place is a haven for those who love history and peace, graciousness and good food.

Several rooms in the château itself are beautifully appointed with antique furniture, Persian and Flemish carpets, original art, and fresh flowers that set a mood of timeless elegance. There are also six *bastides*, one, two or three bedrooms each with en suite bathroom, sitting room, and a whole lot of privacy. Enjoy the sunset while sipping a glass of fine French champagne from your private terrace and look out over the tops of the trees and old stone houses staggered down the hill to the sea beyond. In the vivid late afternoon light, this shimmering vision conjures up a page from a romantic novel.

Wander into the gracefully landscaped lawns and gardens, where you'll find chairs and tables for relaxing; head to the tennis court for a bit of exercise or to the swimming pool, where there are lounges, umbrella tables, and chairs. During the summer months you'll also find a grill restaurant that serves fine Mediterranean cuisine.

The restaurant is known for its fresh fish, which in all likelihood has been purchased by the chef the same morning from local fishermen. The skillful use of herbs and preparation of vegetables and fruits harvested from the Domaine's own gardens are what has given this restaurant a reputation as one of the best in the region. Homemade pasta and soups, rack of lamb, superb soufflés, and chef specialties are hard to resist. The hotel's selection of regional wines is also excellent.

The Domaine is ideally situated to serve as a base for exploring the excitement of Cannes and Nice as well as Monaco, not far away. Also nearby are some extraordinary art galleries, such as the Maeght Foundation, where you'll find Miró, Calder, Chagall, Kandinsky, and Matisse paintings and sculptures. Several large sculptures are also located on the beautiful, sprawling grounds.

A short drive away is the medieval town of Vence, which has preserved its old ramparts and has some wonderful little shops and streets. It is also home to the Matisse chapel. Not far from Vence is Cagnes-sur-Mer, where you'll find Les Collettes, once the home and studio of Renoir. It's with a sense of reverence that you see the chair he sat in when he painted, the brushes he used, the lounge with its fragile silk covering where his models lay, and the old shed and twisted old olive trees that appear in many of Renoir's best-known works.

Visit one of the loveliest fortified medieval towns in Europe, St. Paul de Vence, less than 2 miles away. It sits high on a hilltop and is still partially ringed by ancient stone walls. Wander through the narrow, twisting, cobbled streets; watch the men play a game of *boules* in the village square; and browse through the many antiques shops. Among the prize souvenir items you'll find here are the miniature ceramic house "blocks" by Jean-Pierre Gault and other artists, which replicate the French houses in these medieval towns.

And after you've been out exploring the countryside and small villages, you can return to spend the rest of the day and evening amid the quiet elegance of Château du Domaine St. Martin. Magnifique!

Château du Domaine St. Martin

Location: Centrally located in the center of the Fren[ch R]iera in a 32-acre park overlooking the Mediterranean a[nd] the quaint village of Vence

Romantic Highlights: Cottages with private terraces looking out to the sea; serene setting steeped in history

Address/Phone: Avenue des Templiers-BP 102, 06140 Vence CEDEX, France; 33–493–5802–02; fax 33–493–24–0891

E-mail: reservations@chateau-st-martin.com

Web Site: www.chateau-st-martin.com

U.S. Reservations: (800) 735–2478 or www.relaischateaux.com

Owner/Manager: Philippe Perd, general manager

Arrival/Departure: Rental cars available in Nice

Distance from Nice Côte d'Azur Airport: 12 miles (20 minutes)

Distance from Nice: 7 miles

Accommodations: 34 junior suites; 6 *bastides* all with private terrace or balcony overlooking the Mediterranean

Most Romantic Room/Suite: Private *bastides*; deluxe junior suites with terraces

Amenities: Hair dryer, toiletries, air-conditioning, bathrobes, TV, telephone, balcony or terrace, room service

Electricity: 220 volts

Sports and Facilities: 2 tennis courts (clay), heated infinity pool, *boules*; golf nearby at Biot, Valbonne, and Mougins

Dress Code: Jacket required for dinner only

Weddings: Can be arranged

Rates/Packages: Per couple: February–mid-April €230–€460 (U.S.$217–$434); mid-April–mid May €395–€695 (U.S.$372–$656); mid-May–mid–October €476–€790 (U.S.$449–$745); Wedding Package, €1,070–€1,360 (U.S.$1,009–$1,283) including 1 night in a junior suite with terrace and sea view, champagne breakfast, use of the chapel or gazebo, champagne and canapes, and gourmet dinner with wine.

Payment/Credit Cards: Most major

Deposit: All reservations must be confirmed with a deposit in accordance to length of stay and for refund must be cancelled within a specified length of time prior to scheduled arrival date. (This varies with time of year.)

Government Taxes: Included

Service Charges: Included

Entry Requirements for U.S. Citizens: Passport

Closed: November, December, January

CHÂTEAU EZA
France

...dary Camelot, Château Eza stands ... medieval hilltop village awash in romance and mystery. But while King Arthur's domain was an invention of British folklore, this exquisite, intimate hotel tucked away in a 1,000-year-old fortress village is very real. Modern-day Lancelots and Guineveres will love this castle of stone, the former residence of the Swedish royal family.

Try your luck at the Monte Carlo casino, spend the day at the Nice beach, shop where the beautiful people shop, play golf, and visit small towns and markets such as Antibes, Mougins, Cagnes-sur-Mer, and Vence.

Narrow stone passages and walkways lead to ten guest. accommodations. All have modern conveniences such as air-conditioning and fine baths, and the rooms are enhanced by charming fireplaces, stone walls, beamed ceilings, balconies, and the pièce de résistance: the views.

Each room is thematically different: There is a quaint room perched on the cliff's edge overlooking the mountains, and there is an intimate, romantic room with a canopy bed, fireplace, and balcony as well as a very grand Louis XVI chamber with a separate dressing area fit for a queen. La Suite du Château, a three-room suite with a floral and ivy theme, has a bedroom with loft, sitting room, separate dressing room, private terrace with garden, and spectacular sea view.

Another suite is especially dramatic, with high ceilings, arches, columns, and an enormous iron bed. Take your pick! All the rooms are elaborately furnished with Oriental rugs, antiques, upholstered chairs, and stunning accessories. Fresh flowers are replaced daily.

Although there are no sports facilities on the property, within the walled city of Eze there is the Jardin Exotique, filled with cacti as well as gift shops, art galleries, and restaurants.

Dinner at Château Eza is served in either the indoor glass dining room or outdoor terrace atop the cliffs. It is considered one of the most romantic dining spots in the world. Chef Christophe L'Hospitalier shops each morning

Château Eza

Location: Situated inside the medieval village of Eze on the Moyenne Corniche between Nice and Monaco, on the Côte d'Azur

Romantic Highlights: Seductive views of the Mediterranean, the stars and lights of the Riviera and Cap Ferrat; regally appointed themed rooms; champagne breakfasts on your balcony; narrow cobblestone pathways winding between ancient stone buildings draped in masses of bouganvillea

Address/Phone: 06360 Eze Village, Côte d'Azur, France; 33–493–411–224; fax 33–493–411–664

E-mail: chateza@webstore.fr

Web Site: www.chateza.com

U.S. Reservations: (800) 507–8250

Owner/Manager: Mr. and Mrs. Terry Giles, owners; Jesper Jerrik, general manager

Arrival/Departure: By taxi, available at airport

Distance from Nice-Côte d'Azur Airport: 12 miles

Distance from Nice: 8 miles (15 minutes)

Accommodations: 4 suites; 6 guest rooms

Most Romantic Room/Suite: Le Suite du Château

Amenities: Air-conditioning, safe, TV, video, telephone, hair dryer, toiletries, bathrobes, flowers, champagne, candy

Electricity: 220 volts

Sports and Facilities: Beach 10 minutes away

Dress Code: Men should wear a jacket at dinner.

Weddings: One of their specialties

Rates/Packages: Rates per couple: about $507–$870; suites $870–$1,015 including breakfast, service charge, and taxes.

Payment/Credit Cards: Most major

Deposit: One-night deposit; for stays 3 nights or more, 50 percent deposit; fifteen-day cancellation notice for full refund

Government Taxes: Included

Service Charges: Included

Entry Requirements for U.S. Citizens: Passport

Closed: Early November–early April

at the Nice market for fresh fruits, vegetables, and meats. Tempting items include foie gras terrine and salad; canard challandais roti (roast duck); filet de loup roti (sea bass); Grand Marnier soufflé; and accompaniments such as wonderful sauces, tapenades, seasonal vegetables and fruits like figs and wild mushrooms.

The wine list is extensive. Although dinner for two with wine is on the high side of $200, a special lunch menu with wine costs about $65.

The staff at the hotel is efficient, friendly, and helpful; restaurant service, excellent.

You would need a time machine to travel back more than a thousand years to the medieval era—unless, of course, you chose to visit Château Eza. Here, on a spellbinding cliff overlooking the Mediterranean, all the romance and chivalry of King Arthur is yours, albeit for the modern-day equivalent of a king's ransom.

Situated midway between Nice and Monte Carlo, Château Eza is conveniently located on the Moyenne Corniche (the middle road running between the two cities), allowing guests easy access to the many attractions of the famous Côte d'Azur—provided they can tear themselves away from the breathtaking views.

HOTEL DE MOUGINS
France

Just down the road from the Provençal town of Mougins, it looks like it has been here forever: an old farmhouse surrounded by four country villas in the midst of fragrant flower gardens. In reality, Hotel de Mougins is new, making it the best of both worlds. Warm terra-cotta stucco walls and arches, red-tile roofs, bougainvillea spilling over trellises, and courtyard gardens lend a sense of timeliness, yet modern amenities like state-of-the-art bath and light fixtures, direct-dial telephones, in-room safes, and coral marble vanities are incorporated throughout this charming boutique hotel.

If quality is in the details, this property is top of the line. Tile floors, white antiqued furniture; Provençal fabrics in yellows, blues, and corals; wicker and wrought iron; French doors leading to balconies; built-in armoires; and white-tiled showers make the rooms extremely pretty and comfortable. From your balcony you see peaks of cypress poking up into the sky, groves of mimosa trees, fig trees, bursts of lavender and rosemary, and stone walls.

There is a lovely pool, a number of gardens, and an outdoor patio under the trees furnished with wrought-iron furniture.

La Figuière offers both superb food and romantic, intimate ambience. You can dine under century-old ash trees, at poolside, or in the blush-colored dining room. Start the day with one of their flaky croissants, fresh fruit, and a cup of café au lait. From here it only gets better. Dinner might be tendresse de filet de boeuf aux mangues en parfum de poivre de Séchuan (beef filet), croquettes de céleri, with crème brûlée aux gousses de vanille for dessert. In

Hotel de Mougins

Location: Set into the hills surrounding Cannes in the residential district of Saint-Basile

Romantic Highlights: The scent of mimosa and lavender drifting over the gardens; views of the countryside over tall cypresses from your terrace; breakfast on your patio

Address/Phone: 205 Avenue du Golf, 06250 Mougins, France; 33–92–92–1707; fax 33–92–92–1708

U.S. Reservations: (800) 888–4747

E-mail: info@hotel-de-mougins.com

Web Site: www.hotel-de-mougins.com

Owner/Manager: Alain Delporte, general manager

Arrival/Departure: Arrangements can be made for pickup at the Nice-Côte d'Azur Airport.

Distance from Nice-Côte d'Azur Airport: 10 miles

Distance from Cannes: 3 miles

Accommodations: 48 rooms, 2 junior suites, 1 suite

Most Romantic Room/Suite: Suites

Amenities: Air-conditioning, hair dryer, safe, pants press, toiletries, minibar, reading lamps, full-length mirror, telephones, satellite TV

Electricity: 220 volts

Sports and Facilities: Tennis, pool, *boules*; golf next door

Dress Code: Informal

Weddings: Can be arranged

Rates/Packages: €148–€221 (U.S.$139–$208) per room; €107–€146 (U.S.$101–137) per person, double occupancy including lunch and dinner; golf packages available

Payment/Credit Cards: Most major

Deposit: Credit card

Government Taxes: Included

Service Charges: Included

Entry Requirements for U.S. Citizens: Passport

the summer there are two bars and Le Pool-house, an outdoor grill by the pool.

Gravel paths lead from the main building, through the gardens, and to the pool and rooms, a bit hard on heels and difficult going for wheelies; still, the pebbles are so in keeping with the area, I'm not sure I would want to see anything different. After all, you can always wear flat shoes and call a valet for your luggage.

There is a tennis court on site and a choice of several excellent golf courses close by. Next door is the celebrated Golf Country Club de Cannes-Mougins, an easily walkable, scenic, rolling course with a sixteenth-century clubhouse occupying what was once an olive oil production facility.

The Royal Mougins Golf Club, a dramatic, newer course with all the bells and whistles, five tee boxes, lots of bunkers, water, and elevations, undulates and rolls with great abandon. Holes with names like Angel's Dive, Le Lac, and Roller Coaster give you a fair idea of what to expect.

One day, make sure you visit Mougins, a lovely, hilly little town filled with delightful restaurants, art studios, craft shops, galleries, and gift stores.

SCHLOSSHOTEL LERBACH
Germany

When you stay at the ivy-covered Schlosshotel Lerbach, once a private castle, you feel much like you are visiting privileged friends in the country. The sprawling grounds, rooted in a setting of gently rolling green hills and meandering streams, are bucolic. Situated in Germany's Bergischesland, east of Cologne, the castle is surrounded by fine old trees, and double stone stairs lead down to a nice garden area and a glimmering fish pond. The Lerbach staff treat you as if you were privileged guests of an old friend, making it easy to settle in here very quickly.

Over the past 600 years, the hotel, once Burg Lerbach Castle, has gone through a lot of changes. Built around 1384, the castle was converted to the classic English manor house style in 1838. After serving as a private palace and later as headquarters for a film company, this magnificent estate was transformed into a stylish hotel just a few years ago.

Each of the fifty-four rooms and suites is individually decorated and distinguished by welcoming touches like books on the shelves and fresh flowers. Some have canopy beds, others brass beds. Many suites are multilevel with nice sitting areas with writing desks. Rooms are furnished with period furniture and artwork, tapestries, Oriental carpets, and interesting accessories like puffy throw pillows, porcelain pieces, and leather-bound books. Bathrooms are large and have tubs and showers.

The castle sits in a park of more than seventy acres. You have plenty of room to find your own private place. For a special treat arrange for a hot air balloon tour of the countryside. Your journey starts in the park and lifts you over the hills, valleys, vineyards, and lakes, which are so beautiful here. Enjoy a delightful picnic later under the trees.

One of the most dreamy places to relax is the pretty terrace, which is set up with wrought-iron tables and perky yellow umbrellas. In good weather you can have your breakfast, lunch, or tea here. For more active souls there is a red-clay tennis court on the grounds as well as a well-equipped health club, the beauty salon, and spa.

Or how about a hiking trip in the Siebengebirge? You start out with a gourmet breakfast in the hotel, then it's off on a guided hike in the mountains, with a picnic lunch served in the countryside.

The hotel has two restaurants: the gourmet Restaurant Dieter Müller, featuring creative modern French specialties such as Homard Rôti Parfumé aux Truffes Exotique Saint-Pierre and Sorbet au Champagne. Dieter Müller has earned a three-star Michelin rating as well as other honors. The more moderately priced but also excellent Schloss Restaurant specializes in regionally influenced new German cuisine. There are also the Hotelbar, showcasing original artwork by famous painters such as Salvador Dali and Max Ernst, a terrace overlooking the park, and a lounge featuring a large fireplace.

Schlosshotel Lerbach is an excellent base for exploring this exceptionally beautiful area of Germany. History buffs will want to visit nearby Cologne, where there is a lot to see besides the famous cathedral, such as an original Roman mosaic floor, museums, and art galleries. Have lunch in an old brewery or take a day cruise on the lovely Rhine River.

Schlosshotel Lerbach

Location: 9 miles east of Cologne, in the wooded valleys of Bergischesland

Romantic Highlights: Relaxing in quiet country setting; ballooning over the countryside

Address/Phone: Lerbacher Weg, D–51465, Bergisch Gladbach, Germany; 49–2202–2040; fax 49–2202–204940

E-mail: info@schlosshotel-lerbach.com

Web Site: www.schlosshotel-lerbach.com

U.S. Reservations: Relais & Châteaux, (800) RELAIS–8

Owner/Manager: Thomas H. Althoff, owner; Hinrik Dollmann, director

Arrival/Departure: Private transfers from airport can be arranged

Distance from Cologne/Bonn Airport: 15 miles

Distance from Cologne: 12 miles (20 minutes)

Accommodations: 47 rooms; 7 suites

Most Romantic Room/Suite: Each is different; ask for a room with a canopy bed.

Amenities: Hair dryer, minibar, TV, in-room safe, music system, telephone; portable fax machine on request; room service, fresh flowers, fruit basket

Electricity: 220 volts

Sports and Facilities: Archery, swimming pool, sauna, solarium, massages, fishing, hiking, jogging trails, tennis, horseback riding (in season), ballooning (arranged), golf nearby

Dress Code: Casual by day; jacket requested in Dieter Müller for dinner

Weddings: Can be arranged

Rates/Packages: €220–€295 (U.S.$207–$278) per couple per night for a room; junior suite, €415 (U.S.$391); suite, €520–€1,300 (U.S.$490–$1,227) including breakfast, minibar, parking, use of swimming pool and sauna, tax, and service

Payment/Credit Cards: Most major

Deposit: Credit card guarantee

Government Taxes: 16 percent VAT included

Service Charges: Included

Entry Requirements for U.S. Citizens: Passport

LONGUEVILLE HOUSE
Ireland

Irish eyes smile on those who stay at Longueville House, a lovely Georgian Heritage manor house hotel encircled by the green and heather-clad foothills of southwestern Ireland. This is off-the-beaten-track countryside living at its best. The property is impeccably furnished and maintained by William and Aisling O'Callaghan, proprietors.

Longueville House, a grand white mansion, sits on 500 wooded acres with streams and ponds, a haven for those who love walking, fishing, and hunting. Dating from 1720, Longueville has a magnificent, sweeping wooden staircase that rises from the entrance hall to the top rooms on the third floor and inlaid mahogany doors with brass locks. Elegant gilt mirrors, chandeliers, Oriental rugs, original artwork, and hand-painted ceilings by an Italian artist enhance the interiors.

The property originally belonged to the O'Callaghans and the ruins of their Dromineen Castle, demolished in the Cromwellian Confiscation, are in full view of the house. Now, some 300 years later, Longueville is once more in O'Callaghan hands. For an interesting photo, you can line up the gray stone ruins of the old home with the imposing Longueville House in the distance.

Perhaps the most charming aspects of the property are the side gardens and the old stone courtyard in the back—often you can hear the cows mooing somewhere beyond the walls.

Attached to one wing of the house is a splendid Victorian conservatory constructed in 1866 by Richard Turner, arguably the greatest ironmaster and designer of glasshouses of the Victorian era. The fountain, which is now located in the lower flower garden, was originally positioned in the semicircular end of the conservatory. Today the conservatory with its white wrought-iron chairs and tables is a lovely place to eat overlooking the river.

Each of the rooms and suites has its own personality. Some have king-size beds with canopies and tufted sofas. Long windows are framed by flowing drapes, and the fabrics, wall coverings, and upholstery are all beautifully fresh and elegant.

As you would expect in an Relais & Châteaux property, the Presidents' Restaurant under the direction of Chef William O'Callaghan, is a winner. The warmly romantic restaurant features salmon-colored walls lined with oil paintings of famous presidents. Crystal, candles, and white linens set the mood.

Chef O'Callaghan draws on as many locally produced ingredients as possible; most come from area farms and rivers and the hotel's own walled garden, which supplies Longueville with fruit, vegetables, and herbs throughout the year. Occupying a space of two and a half acres, the garden is surrounded by a large stone wall that dates back to 1829. In its heyday there were twenty gardeners employed to keep the garden and glasshouses.

Meals are complemented by a a selection of wines from Longueville's 150-vintage wine cellar.

Using Longueville as a base to explore scenic southwestern Ireland, you won't want to miss the Blackwater River Valley, a fisherman's paradise known for its wild salmon and brown trout. Walking trails wind through the property and there are several golf courses nearby including the famous links at Ballybunion, Old Head of Kinsale Golf Links, Lee Valley Golf Course, and Fota Island Golf Club.

Interesting places to visit within easy driving distance include The Foynes Flying Boat Museum, Foynes, County Limerick. Housed in the original terminal building, it tells the story of early airplane flights across the Atlantic.

Tours of Frank McCourt's *Angela's Ashes* hometown, Limerick City, include the street where Frank lived, the school he attended, and St. Vincent DePaul where his mother asked for food.

On the fringe of the busy city of Cork, those with a passion for history will find *Cobh: The Queenstown Story*, a fascinating history of this port city's role in emigration from Ireland to America. It is from here that the *Titanic* left for its fatal voyage and that luxury liners like the *Lusitania* sailed.

I also suggest you take a day to drive the 110 miles around the Ring of Kerry. The road is so narrow, buses are allowed to go only in one direction. So don't think you can zip around, nor should you want to, for then you would miss the stunning views of sea, rocks, and trees.

Besides the wonderful scenery, staying at Longueville House can be one of the most enjoyable aspects of your vacation. You'll stay in rooms furnished with antique mahogany armoires, chaise lounges, dressing tables with silver hand-mirrors; leather-bound books—things that may have been passed down through generations of good living; there are coffee and cordials in the sitting room after dinner in front of a fireplace; and perhaps one or more members of the O'Callaghan family will join you and introduce some Irish songs. The Irish love to sing!

Longueville House

Location: In the rolling countryside 3 miles west of Mallow overlooking the Blackwater River Valley

Romantic Highlights: Dining by candlelight in a Victorian conservatory; long walks through the gardens and the scenic wooded estate grounds; drinks by a log fire in the elegant dining room

Address/Phone: Mallow, County Cork, Ireland; 353–22–47156; fax 353–22–47459

E-mail: info@Longuevillehouse.ie

Web Site: www.longuevillehouse.ie

U.S. Reservations: Josephine Barr, (800) 323–5463

Owner/Manager: The O'Callaghan family, owners and innkeepers

Arrival/Departure: Most arrive by car via the N20 highway; transfers can be arranged.

Distance from Cork Airport: 28 miles (45 minutes)

Distance from Cork: 28 miles (45 minutes)

Accommodations: 20 rooms and suites, including 2 suites, 5 mini-suites, and 13 rooms

Most Romantic Room/Suite: Vineyard Suite, Blackwater Suite

Amenities: Thermostat-controlled heating, hair dryer, iron/ironing board, tea trays, direct-dial telephone, satellite TV, toiletries

Electricity: 220 volts

Sports and Facilities: Walking, fishing, biking, shooting (November–February)

Dress Code: Casually Smart

Weddings: Can be arranged and can accommodate 42 guests overnight and in the restaurant. Current laws do not allow Irish hotels to host wedding services on site, but these can be arranged at a local church or registry office.

Rates/Packages: €168–€336 (U.S.$248–$496) per room per night, including breakfast

Payment/Credit Cards: Most major

Deposit: By credit card

Government Taxes: Included

Service Charges: Discretionary

Entry Requirements for U.S. Citizens: Passport

Closed: Mid-December–early March

EXCELSIOR PALACE HOTEL
Italy

The Excelsior Palace Hotel is a great find, offering excellent value and service in Rapallo, one of Italy's most popular resort areas. The grand turn-of-the-century Excelsior Palace, set on a piece of prime waterfront land on the Italian Riviera, has been restored and is now an excellent choice for those looking for romantic yet reasonably priced accommodations overlooking the Mediterranean. Once a popular gathering place for the international beau monde, it has welcomed Ernest Hemingway, Rita Hayworth, and Eleanora Duse.

Marble halls are punctuated with huge vases of fresh flowers; a grand health club features spacious granite baths; most of the bedrooms and suites boast balconies and a view of the sea through large sliding glass doors; rooms are more spacious than many of the pricier digs in the area. Furnishings are tasteful, understated, and upbeat, with light-colored print fabrics and white-painted French Provincial–style furniture.

The Yachting Bar and dining rooms flow out on the lovely terrace with its white balustrades, candlelight, and

Excelsior Palace Hotel

Location: On the Portofino Coast overlooking the Mediterranean

Romantic Highlights: Seaside balconies; boat trips along the coast; in-room massages for two; Old World elegance

Address/Phone: Via San Michele di Pagana, 8-16035 Rapallo, Portofino Coast (GE) Italy; 39–185–230–666; fax 39–185–230–214

E-mail: excelsior@thi.it

Web Site: www.excelsiorpalace.thi.it

U.S. Reservations: Summit Hotels and Resorts, (800) 457-4000 and JDB Associates (800) 346–5358

Owner/Manager: Michele Zanconato, general manager

Arrival/Departure: Shuttle service available from Genova Airport on request

Distance from Genova Airport: 18 miles; Milan, 90 miles

Distance from Portofino: 3½ miles

Accommodations: 114 rooms; 17 suites; all with sea views

Most Romantic Rooms/Suites: Junior suites

Amenities: Air-conditioning, hair dryer, toiletries, in-room safe, minibar, turndown service, cable TV

Electricity: 220 volts

Sports and Facilities: Beach Club; health and fitness club with indoor heated pool, sauna, steam bath, Jacuzzi, gym, massages, thalassotherapy, beauty treatments, sunbed; beach, water sports; tennis, golf course, horseback riding, boat excursions, and hiking trails within 1 mile of hotel

Dress Code: Resort casual

Weddings: Can be arranged

Rates/Packages: Room rates from €380 (U.S.$358) per couple per night, including breakfast, taxes, and service charges. Sea, Beauty, and Relax and the Green Sea (for golf and tennis) packages available

Payment/Credit Cards: Most major

Deposit: By credit card

Government Taxes: Included

Service Charges: Included

Entry Requirements for U.S. Citizens: Passport

wrought-iron tables and chairs—a perfect place to sip your Pelligrino or Campari while gazing out at the deep blue water and the yachts riding at anchor in Rapallo Bay. Enjoy traditional Italian cuisine in the Lord Byron restaurant and regional and Mediterranean dishes in the Eden Roc. Or venture into historic Rapallo and try one of the many delightfully intimate restaurants; dance the night away at Happening (a disco on the hills above the town) or Villa Porticciolo (a seafront disco); or savor delicious fresh fish at Ristorante Eden.

Hike the trails that wind along the coast and in the national park; take a boat from Rapallo around the peninsula to Camogli, passing Portofino and S. Fruttuoso, and instead of taking the boat back, hike through the park back to the hotel. Explore the caves at Isolona, visit the many shops and galleries in Rapallo and Portofino, and explore ancient castles. The beautiful Ligurian coastline, the Cinque Terre, and Genoa are not far away.

One of the oldest golf courses in Italy is less than a mile from the hotel, and a variety of water sports including waterskiing and scuba diving can be arranged at the Beach Club. For those who want it both ways, you can stay a few days in the hotel and extend your vacation cruising on a chartered yacht stopping at such ports as Naples, Portofino, Capri, Ischia, and Venice.

GRAND HOTEL PUNTA MOLINO TERME
Italy

If the term *romantic* suggests a private hideaway, then the Grand Hotel Punta Molino Terme, overlooking the Bay of Naples, is about as romantic as it gets. This contoured, white-as-snow hotel sits in a vast pine woods park opposite the Aragonese Castle, on the little fisherman's island of Ischia.

The boat to the island takes a little over an hour from Naples and is slow, breezy, and dreamy. You pass the fabled Isle of Capri, and then Ischia appears in the distance, guarded by the picturesque castle on the cliffs.

Ischia (pronounced Iskea) is still undiscovered by tourists, and certainly few Americans know about it. Mention the name even to an Italy lover and he or she will probably say "God bless you." The island is just too peaceful and sleepy to be popular, but for some this is exactly what makes it such a find.

After a short drive from the dock, you reach the hotel, which is set among lush landscaping, and fronts on a beach walkway that runs along the coastline. The public rooms are cool and classically elegant, decorated with custom-made Italian tiles, traditional furniture, white walls, tapestries, and original paintings. Fresh flowers are everywhere, and the understated decor features a mix of antiques and art pieces.

The dining room, with lavender tablecloths and tapestry chairs, has picture windows overlooking the dark blue pool and aqua water beyond. You can eat outside, on the terrace, or on the roof garden to catch the breeze and enjoy the fishing boats going out for the catch.

The cuisine is Italian or international, featuring local seafood, of course, and it is graciously served. A pianist plays for the cocktail hour, through dinner, and on into the night, when couples can dance under a moon shimmering on the bay. Each week guests are invited to a candlelight gala soirée on the "Terrazza Grande."

The cool, stylish guest rooms have ceramic tile floors, beds with antique headboards, minibars, TVs, and balconies with panoramic views of the sea. The dominant color is blue, reflecting the sea and sky. Mirrored bathrooms have showers or baths and amenities such as hair dryers, robes, and plants.

What to do here on this quiet island? You can swim in the stunning pool and relax on the little private beach, where topless bathing is an option, and you can participate in a variety of water sports. If you like to walk, you can go to the nearby woods and follow the footpaths or find a private hideaway in the flower-strewn meadow of the park. You can also take a four-hour boat ride around the island.

The most popular activities center on the hotel's well-equipped spa. Since ancient times the thermal waters here have been enjoyed by travelers seeking soothing treatments and relaxation. Today the hotel's spa still offers thermal baths, mud packs, saunas, hydro-massage, and facials.

After an invigorating massage you can sunbathe and sip a Campari on the little jetty that juts into the lapping water. Watch the local children playing nearby on the rocky public beach, catch the distant sounds of family life coming from the fishermen's houses, or gaze at the beautiful castle just across a bridge. Or do all three. It's all part of soaking up the laid-back life in Ischia.

At twilight walk along the beach as the lights turn on in the small buildings in the distance. The peaceful serenity of this place can really creep up on you.

Grand Hotel Punta Molino Terme

Location: On the northern coast of the island of Ischia, near Ischia Porto

Romantic Highlights: Dancing under the moon, shining on the Bay of Naples; candlelight dinner on the seaside terrace

Address/Phone: Lungomare Cristoforo Colombo 23, Porto, Italy; 39–081–991–544; fax 39–081–991–562

E-Mail: reservations@puntamolino.it

Web Site: www.puntamolino.it

U.S. Reservations: Leading Hotels of the World, (800) 223–6800

Owner/Manager: Eugenio Ossani, owner and general manager; Rosario Mazzella, managing director

Arrival/Departure: By boat from Naples seaport of Mollo Beverello: 40 minutes by hydrofoil, 1½ hours by ferry; transfers via limousine to ferry can be arranged on request

Distance from Naples Airport: 24 miles via ferry

Distance from Naples: 24 miles via ferry

Accommodations: 86 rooms; 10 suites

Most Romantic Room/Suite: Ocean-view suite

Amenities: Air-conditioning, minibar, telephone, radio, TV, bathrobe, toiletries, magnifying mirror, safe, hair dryer

Electricity: 220 volts

Sports and Facilities: 2 outdoor pools, 1 indoor pool, beach, spa, water sports, game room; tennis nearby

Dress Code: Casual

Weddings: Can be arranged

Rates/Packages: From €119 (U.S.$112) per night per person, including breakfast, dinner, service charges, and taxes; spa packages available; Honeymoon Package, 10 percent discount on regular rates, welcome bottles of spumante

Payment/Credit Cards: Most major

Deposit: Guarantee with credit card

Government Taxes: Included

Service Charges: Included

Entry Requirements for U.S. Citizens: Passport

HOTEL DANIELI
Italy

To stay at the superdeluxe Hotel Danieli is to embrace the romantic heart and soul of this unique city of gondolas and canals, flower boxes, and footbridges, cathedrals, and ancient architecture. As with every corner of Venice, every nook and cranny of the Danieli begs to be photographed. The fourteenth-century palace of the Doge Dandolo is the central building of three attached wings that house 233 restored rooms and suites of varying vintage, decor, and views, but all definitely in the deluxe category.

Arriving by private water taxi right to the doorstep of the hotel, you walk into what is now a covered courtyard foyer with a gorgeous, golden stairway leading up to the rooms (elevators, of course, are always there for the travel weary). The lobby is sublime, darkly opulent, and unfor-

gettable, with its marble arches, ornate ceilings, breathtaking Venetian glass chandelier, and huge fireplace. The ghosts of such eminent and historic guests as George Sand, Charles Dickens, and Richard Wagner can easily be conjured up as you sip a drink in the Bar Danieli.

Right outside the front door is Venice itself. If you haven't already prearranged a package of sight-seeing and excursions, the concierge will be happy to help you arrange a gondola ride, a guided city sight-seeing tour, an excursion to the islands of the lagoon—Murano, Burano, and Torcello—to see the famed Venetian glass being made (with plenty of opportunity to shop), to visit the school of lace-making, and to tour the ancient cathedral of Torcello.

When you want to take a break from sight-seeing, you can spend the afternoon at the world-renowned Venice Lido (beach). A free water taxi takes you over to the Excelsior Lido Hotel to swim and sunbathe at the swimming pool or right on the beach, with its rows of cabanas. You can try your hand at the nearby casino or take in a round of golf.

On more than one morning, you may very well forgo a breakfast served in your room to eat at the hotel's open-air (in good weather) rooftop Terrace Restaurant to take in the early morning Venetian light and the breathtaking views of the lagoon.

Hotel Danieli

Location: Prime location on Venice's famed lagoon next to the Doge's Palace and near the entrance to the Grand Canal. Situated right in the heart of the city, it is a 2-minute walk to St. Mark's Square.

Romantic Highlights: Venice's opulence and history are combined in this authentically elegant Grand Hotel of the world, which once hosted visiting royalty and ambassadors (and continues to do so).

Address/Phone: Riva degli Schiavoni, 4196, 30122 Venice, Italy; 39–041–522–6480; fax 39–041–520–0208

E-mail: claudio.staderini@starwoodhotels.com

Web Site: www.starwood.com

U.S. Reservations: (800) 325–3535

Owner/Manager: Giuliano Corsi, general manager

Arrival/Departure: By air to the Marco Polo Airport, just outside of Venice, and then by private water taxi from the airport to the hotel; by train (Santa Lucia Station), then 20 minutes by boat

Distance from Marco Polo Airport: 45 minutes by boat

Distance from Venice Center: In the heart of the city

Accommodations: 233 deluxe rooms of varying vintage, decor, and views, including 11 suites and 190 double rooms

Most Romantic Room/Suite: 6 suites, 3 junior suites, and 51 double rooms are available with wonderful lagoon views

Amenities: Air-conditioning, hair dryer, minibar, shaver outlets, TV with international programs via satellite, direct-dial telephone, toiletries; robes in suites; room service

Electricity: 110/220 volts

Sports and Facilities: In season there are many sporting options on Venice Lido. The concierge can arrange tennis, horseback riding, golf, waterskiing, sailboarding, and yachting. Free boat service to the Lido is available.

Dress Code: Casually smart for daytime; dressier in the evening

Weddings: Can be arranged

Rates/Packages: From €440 (U.S.$415) per couple per night for a luxury romance package including accomodations, breakfast, flowers, and Italian spumante; minimum stay, 2 nights.

Payment/Credit Cards: Most major

Deposit: Guarantee with credit card; cancel up to 24 hours in advance without penalty

Government Taxes: 10 percent

Service Charges: Included (at client's discretion)

Entry Requirements for U.S. Citizens: Passport

VILLA D'ESTE
Italy

The ultimate vacation resort on Lake Como, one of the loveliest lakes in the world, is Villa D'Este. Built by a cardinal as his personal home in the sixteenth century, this impressive, neoclassical pleasure palace sits amid ten acres of gardens, manicured lawns, magnolias, and towering trees. Once you pass through the elegant entrance, you will have everything you need to enjoy a relaxed, yet fun-filled honeymoon. In addition to the heart-stopping lakeside setting framed by the high ridges of the mountains, the resort boasts a full range of sports and fitness facilities, several restaurants, a nightclub, and a cozy piano bar.

As you come into the palatial lobby, with its high, vaulted ceiling, graceful white columns, wide double marble staircase, and fine period furniture, you enter another world, where you will be pampered like royalty, but not so much so that it becomes overbearing. The staff here strikes just the right note between service and respect for your privacy.

Each of the 104 spacious rooms and 60 suites is different, and many, including those rooms located in the Queen's Pavilion, have balconies overlooking the lake. Rooms are elaborately decorated with rich, jewel-like fabrics and colors. Chandeliers, comfortable upholstered chairs and sofas, luxurious full drapes pulled back with golden cords and brocade ties, Renaissance-style artwork, and plush carpets give you accommodations fit for a king and queen.

Clark Gable, Paul McCartney, Ali McGraw, Woody Allen, Arnold Schwarzen-egger, John Cleese, and Carly Simon have all stayed here, along with other notables. It's a good place to unwind and fall in love all over again with the person you care most about.

In 1875 Franz Liszt remarked, "When you write of two happy lovers, let the story be set on the banks of Lake Como." No doubt he had in mind strolls along the shore in the moonlight and serene afternoons lying on the banks when he wrote this. But today this is only part of

what you can do here. For active couples there are plenty of options. One of the resort's useful novelties is its large, freshwater pool, which actually floats in the water on its own island, just off the water's edge. There are also an indoor pool and a children's pool as well.

There are eight tennis courts as well as a squash court, waterskiing, sailing, and even hang gliding, along with various sports lessons and clinics scheduled throughout the week. Take a canoe and spend a peaceful afternoon paddling along the waters. If staying fit is on your agenda, you'll find the gym well equipped with the latest exercise and weight-lifting equipment. Or relax in the Turkish baths or saunas and get a soothing massage. Golf enthusiasts can practice their putting on the special green located on the villa grounds and later get in a game at a course just down the road.

All the dining facilities are oriented toward the lake. In good weather meals are served outdoors either on the open-air Verandah, which is covered by bright yellow awnings, or at the large, open Grill Room, set under a canopy of leafy, ancient plane trees; the walls are dense, green hedges, and the views are of the shimmering lake. At breakfast you can order a specially prepared omelet from the trolley and watch it being cooked or you can ponder your choices from the lavish breakfast buffet. Head to the terrace or sit poolside for lunch and enjoy a selection of fresh fruits, salads, fish, and pastas.

At night the Verandah lowers its glass walls to shelter diners from the night breezes and turns up the romance factor with candles, lots of fresh flowers, and soft lights. The presentation of food is a work of art: Grilled salmon is served with red, green, and yellow peppers in the shape of leaves, and a lemon tartlet arrives in a pool of vanilla custard laced by a delicate pinwheel pattern of chocolate and strawberry sauce. You almost hate to stick your spoon into it and disturb the fragile beauty of that confection. But when you do, you'll scrape every last drop from your plate. It's just too good. After dinner, mellow out at the piano bar or dance the night away at the disco.

If you should wish to venture out, you can visit the nearby quaint medieval villages with red-roofed buildings and narrow, winding streets and explore ruins of centuries-old castles and fortresses. One of the best ways to see the area is to take a boat ride around the lake, where you will see spectacular villas.

Villa D'Este

Location: Set on 10 acres on the western shore of Lake Como

Romantic Highlights: Spectacular lakeside setting; floating pool; dancing under age-old trees in the foothills of the Alps; watching the sun set over the lake and the mist waft down from the mountains

Address/Phone: Via Regina 40, 22012 Cernobbio, Lake Como, Italy; 39–031–3481; fax 39–031–348844

E-mail: info@villadeste.it

Web Site: www.villadeste.it

U.S. Reservations: Leading Hotels of the World, (800) 223–6800 or (212) 838–3110; fax (212) 758–7367

Owner/Manager: Jean-Marc Droulers, chairman and CEO; Claudio Ceccherelli, general manager

Arrival/Departure: You can arrange for pickup by the hotel at the airport, but check rates. The resort is easily accessible by car (car rental at airport); helipad at hotel.

Distance from Malpensa and Linate Airports: 27 miles (45 minutes)

Distance from Como: 3 miles; Cernobbio is less than 1 mile; Milan, 35 miles

Accommodations: 104 rooms; 60 suites. Many have balconies overlooking the water; others face gardens.

Most Romantic Room/Suite: Rooms in the nineteenth-century Queen's Pavilion and suites in the main building overlooking lake

Amenities: Hair dryer, telephone, in-room safe, toiletries, air-conditioning, whirlpool tub, minibar, TV, room service

Electricity: 220 volts

Sports and Facilities: 8 tennis courts (6 clay, 2 manteco), squash court, gym, putting green, jogging route with 15 checkpoints, sauna, Turkish bath, 3 pools (2 outdoor, 1 indoor); waterskiing, sailing, canoeing, sailboarding; golf 20 minutes away; spa with health and beauty treatments

Dress Code: Casual sports clothes during day; evening: jacket and ties required for men in the dining room

Weddings: Can be arranged; outside terrace popular

Rates/Packages: €485–€645 (U.S.$457–$608) per couple per night, including buffet breakfast. "Romantic Stay" from €1,557 (U.S.$1,469) per couple per night, includes 3 nights' accommodations, breakfasts, 3 dinners or lunches per person, flowers, plus use of most of the sports facilities

Payment/Credit Cards: Most major

Deposit: Depending on season

Government Taxes: Included

Service Charges: Included

Entry Requirements for U.S. Citizens: Passport

Closed: December–February

POUSADAS
Portugal

If you ever wondered what it would be like to live like a duke or countess or even a king or queen; to dine in a baronial stone hall, walls hung with priceless tapestries; to gaze from your hilltop terrace over the red-tiled roofs and fields of the world below; or to sleep in a bed topped by a crown of gold and crimson–velvet drapes, then catch the next jet to Portugal and check into a pousada. Dotting the countryside are forty-four pousadas, a network of unique places to stay, created in some of the country's most historic castles, palaces, monasteries, and regional structures. Most occupy the highest sites in their area and boast exceptional views of hills, mountains, lakes, and rivers.

From the Pousada de Sao Teotoio in the north, which is built inside the thirteenth-century fortress town of Valenca, to the cliff-top Pousada do Infanta on the southern coast, the pousadas range from the very opulent, including former castles and convents, to much simpler places chosen for their exceptional location—perhaps on a lake or overlooking a river valley. Government owned and operated by Enatur, most pousadas average fifteen rooms. Many have swimming pools, some are located in the middle of medieval walled villages; others peer out over the sea.

Pousadas (derived from the Portuguese verb "pousar," to lodge or repose) were created not only to save some of these wonderful buildings but to provide places to stay where travelers are treated as honored guests. For example, there is the small riverside regional Pousada de Vale do Gaio, a modest, peaceful place where you wake to the sound of a cock's crowing and have breakfast on an outdoor terrace overlooking a shimmering river. Then there is the grand Pousada de D. Joao IV, with its age-burnished walls, once a royal convent. Original frescos and wall paintings have been beautifully preserved; rooms are arranged around the interior courtyard gardens.

There is nothing shabby or slipshod about any of the places in the furnishings, linens, toiletries, or service. Everywhere I went I was impressed by the consistency of the amenities and the cuisine, all the more remarkable when you consider that converting a thick-walled monastery to a first-rate hotel could not have been easy. It is obvious that a great deal of money has been spent to do the job right.

Cuisine served in the pousada restaurants includes a combination of regional specialties and continental dishes presented with flair and creativity. Fresh fish, cataplana de mariscos (seafood cooked in a special pan), steamed lobster, fish stew, frango na pucara (chicken cooked in a clay pot), and cozido a portuguesa (meat stew) are particularly tasty.

Here are details about a few of Portugal's pousadas:

Castelo Obidos, Obidos (north of Lisbon). Hugging the edge of the thirteenth-century walled town, this is the smallest of the pousadas and perhaps the most romantic. Three rooms are in tower suites with dramatic views of the countryside. Tapestries, dark-wood antique furniture, candles (electrified), and thick stone walls provide the proper medieval ambience. 9 rooms.

Castelo de Alvito (southeast of Lisbon). This fifteenth-century mellow stone castle with towers, turrets, and ramparts has hosted kings and queens. Now mere mortals can enjoy royal quarters with modern conveniences. The castle has a lofty reception room, stunning swimming pool, amphitheater, and resident brace of peacocks that sturt their stuff around the grounds. The dining room serves regional dishes and wines from Alentejo, including oven-roasted fish, and pork with coriander. 20 rooms.

Pousada D. Maria I, Queluz (5 miles from Lisbon). This posh pink-and-white confection was once a residence for the king's court. For a peek at what life was like in the eighteenth century among the rich and titled, just across the street is the Queluz National Palace, with its splendid gardens and museum. The pousada is perfect for those who want to enjoy Lisbon during the day but prefer to escape the hustle-bustle of the city in the evening. The excellent restaurant, Cozinha Velha, is housed in the former royal kitchens. Rooms are spacious and furnished with handsome wood furniture and rich brocades. 24 rooms; 2 suites.

Pousada de Santa Luzia, Elvas (on the border of Spain and Portugal). With its airy and comfortable rooms decorated in light pastel colors and cheery painted furniture, this pousada is a good stopover location for those crossing the Caia border. See the 843-arch Amoreiras aquaduct nearby. Good restaurant and large pool and deck. 25 rooms.

Pousada de Sao Francisco, Beja (southeast of Lisbon). A converted thirteenth-century monastery with a lovely swimming pool, gardens, and tennis court. Restaurant has a deserved reputation for superb fish dishes. 37 rooms.

Pousada de D. Joao IV, Vila Vicosa (east of Lisbon). In the sixteenth-century this richly endowed complex was the Royal Convent of Chagas de Cristo. Many of the original altars, tiling, and artwork have been preserved and incorporated into the public and private rooms. Theme rooms include the Astronomy Room and the Painter's Room. Exceptional fresco of the Last Supper in dining room; after dinner fun in the billiard room. 33 rooms; 3 suites.

Pousada de Rainha Santa Isabel, Estremoz (east of Lisbon close to Spanish border). D. Dinis once lived in this thirteenth-century palace with his wife, Queen Isabel. Today a fine pool with a generous-sized terrace and gardens tempt guests to laze the day away, yet there is a lot to see in this walled town. The dining room with its vaulted ceiling has been the setting for many royal meals. 23 rooms; 3 suites.

Pousada de Palmela, Palmela (south of Lisbon). This converted hilltop fortress with stunning views of Lisbon served as the headquarters of the Portuguese Knights of St. James in the thirteenth century. In modern times it has hosted such dignitaries as the President of France and the Queen of Denmark. Glassed-in cloisters overlook a wisteria-clad courtyard. Thick walls and smallish windows create interesting window seats in many of the guest rooms. Some furnishings date back to fifteenth century. Imaginative cuisine. 27 rooms; 1 suite.

Pousada D. Afonso II, Alcacer do Sal (south of Lisbon). Storks nest on poles just outside the entrance to this restored castle, which sits high above the Sado River. Guests enjoy fine views from their balconies of the countryside and red-roofed houses. Interesting mix of antiques and modern furnishings and artifacts. Beautiful gardens, pool, and archaeological museum on grounds. Very good restaurant. 31 rooms; 4 suites.

Pousadas

Locations: If you want to explore Portugal by car, to travel at your own pace, and experience a special place to stay and dine each evening, try plotting your itinerary through the countryside from pousada to pousada. Some are in or on the edge of town; others are in the middle of nowhere (or so it seems).

Romantic Highlights: Red-tile roofs and clusters of white houses in the green-clad moors glimpsed through rectangular spaces between the crenelated walls; huge silk-draped beds; fireplaces; gardens; history, history, history

Address/Phone: Avenida Santa Joana Princesa, 10A PT 1749–090 Lisbon, Portugal; 351–218442000; fax 351–218442085

E-mail: info@pousadas.pt or guest@pousadas.pt

Web Site: www.pousadas.pt

U.S. Reservations: Marketing Ahead, (800) 223–1356

Owner/Manager: Enatur

Arrival/Departure: Most guests fly into Lisbon and rent a car.

Distance from Airports: Varies

Accommodations: 9 to 51 rooms and suites

Most Romantic Room/Suite: Some favorites: The Terrace Suite at Pousada de Evora, where jasmine winds over the wrought-iron balcony; a Tower Suite at Castelo Obidos; Room 108 at Pousada de Rainha Santa Isabel, a kingly room with a blue-and-gold canopy bed; Painter's Suite at the Pousada de D. Joao IV

Amenities: Hair dryer, telephone, radio, laundry service, toiletries; most have satellite TV; minibar, restaurants; some have air-conditioning, fireplaces, whirlpool tubs

Electricity: 220 volts

Sports and Facilities: Most have swimming pools and gardens

Dress Code: Casually smart

Weddings: Can be arranged

Rates/Packages: From $152–$167 per room (high season); $135–$153 (low season); suites $85–$285, including breakfast. Special interest packages available.

Payment/Credit Cards: Most major

Deposit: Guarantee with credit card

Government Taxes: Included

Service Charges: Included

Entry Requirements for U.S. Citizen: Passport

REID'S PALACE
Madeira, Portugal

Madeira has been called a floating garden. Indeed, this 287-square-mile island plunked about 600 miles off the coast of Lisbon, Portugal, in the middle of the North Atlantic, is exuberantly lush with flowers and tropical vegetation. Its volcanic origins have created an island of contrasts: dramatic green mountains; coastal plantations of sugarcane, bananas, and other crops terraced up the hillsides; deep-water bays and clear mountain streams. It's not really a place you come for beaches: It has few. But because of its charm, its beauty, and its subtropical climate, Madeira has been attracting sun seekers from the damper climes in northern Europe for more than one hundred years.

The oldie but goodie grandee of Madeira's many resorts is Reid's Palace. Sitting high on its own promontory on the southern coast near the center of Funchal, Madeira's principal city, Reid's enjoys a commanding view of the Atlantic and the bay. What it lacks in beaches it makes up for in views and service. After all, Reid's has had more than a century to get it right, and it has.

From the time you arrive, you don't have to sniff it out—you know it at once. Reid's is a place "old money" likes to come to. The British-style hotel's guest list amassed over the years reads like a *Who's Who*: Sir Winston Churchill, Prince Edward, George Bernard Shaw, Gregory Peck, Queen Ingrid of Denmark, and Roger Moore, to name a few.

With its clubby bars, polished antique furniture mellowed with lemon oil, crystal chandeliers, silk brocades, and cushioned wicker terrace furniture as well as contemporary amenities like air-conditioning and modern baths, Reid's continues to be *the* place to stay in Madeira.

There are 164 rooms and suites located in the main Victoria building and in the newer wings. Most have balconies facing the sea. Those on the upper floors of the main building are preferred for their views and their character, aged like fine wine over the years. (Madiera, of course.)

There is no sandy beach, but you'll hardly care! The pools are so close to the water, you'll swim and sunbathe in total bliss enjoying sea-breezes and wonderful water views. In addition to a freshwater pool off the terrace, there is an ocean pool reached by steep stairs (or an elevator) from the top of the cliff to sea level. As the tides rise and fall, the pool fills and lowers. Carved into the cliffs are several level places and even open caves furnished with chaises for private lounging and viewing of the sea. A stairway leads into the sea for hardy ocean swimmers.

Reids has two all-weather tennis courts and lovely gardens that stretch out to the seaside cliff. A variety of massages and spa treatments are offered and the saunas are free to guests.

For elegant, traditional dining, try the Main Dining Room, the only restaurant in the hotel that requires that men wear jacket and tie. Soft pink linens, crystal and table lamps dating from 1891—the original lamps—marble columns, fresh flowers, chandeliers, and high ceilings painted with clouds prompt you to speak in hushed tones and sharpen your table etiquette. A four-course meal costs about $45; a la carte entrees run around $20–$25.

Les Faunes is more casual and notable for its Picasso prints. On Friday singing waiters entertain and special theme dinners are held throughout the year. The Garden Restaurant overlooking the pool and sea is the place for breakfast and light fare; Trattoria Villa Cliff, an informal open-air restaurant, features Italian cuisine; and Reid's famous afternoon tea is served on the open-air terrace or in the lounge.

Do yourself a favour and at some point, order scuburd. The fish is an ugly black and white eel-like thing—you'll see them draped over the tables in the markets. But its taste is pure bliss...sort of a cross between sea bass and halibut. Tender, lightly deep-fried, its delicious.

Most rooms in the hotel have recently been redecorated, lightening up the whole look. Fortunately, the redo has incorporated the best of the characteristics of the original guest room decor, which made these rooms unique and special.

Reid's Palace

Location: Perched atop a cliff overlooking the Bay of Funchal

Romantic Highlights: Wrought-iron balconies overlooking sea; Old World elegance

Address/Phone: P-9000 Funchal, Madeira, Portugal; 351-291-717171; fax 351-291-717177

E-mail: reservations@reidspalace.com

Web Site: www.reidspalace.com

U.S. Reservations: Leading Hotels of the World, (800) 223-6800; fax (212) 758-7367; Orient Express Hotels, (800) 524-2420

Owner/Manager: Anton Küng, general manager

Arrival/Departure: Transfers to and from Funchal Airport included in honeymoon package; otherwise can be arranged for a fee ($50 for private transfer per car); approximately $25 per carload for taxi

Distance from Funchal Airport: 30 minutes; 75 minutes by air from Lisbon

Distance from Funchal Center: 10 minutes

Accommodations: 164 rooms and suites

Most Romantic Room/Suite: #840, decorated in pretty blue and white, is sunny and light with a balcony; #572 has two balconies; Room #872 on the corner of the main house has a huge patio; and room #674 has a crown-draped, king-size bed, large patio, and lots of blue-and-white tile.

Amenities: Air-conditioning, hair dryer, minibar (free soft drinks and beer), TV, radio, telephone, personal safes

Electricity: 220 volts

Sports and Facilities: 2 heated saltwater pools, rock pool, seaside terrace/swimming area, 2 all-weather tennis courts, Ping-Pong, billiards, sauna, gym, and massage; waterskiing, scuba diving; golf at Santo da Serra and Palheiro Golf Club courses; hiking trails nearby; deep-sea fishing

Dress Code: Casual during day; jacket and tie for men in the Dining Room and jacket in cocktail bar after 7:00 P.M. and in Les Faunes

Weddings: Can be arranged

Rates/Packages: €259.40–€399.00 (U.S. $244–$376) regular season; €399.00–€496.30 (U.S. $376–$468) holidays; suites, €616.00–€1,643.50 (U.S. $581–$1,551); €820.50–€1,798.20 (U.S. $774–$1,697) holidays; per room per night, including buffet breakfast, use of tennis courts, windsurf boards, sauna, gym, pools, shuttle, minibar with soft drinks and beer, service charges, local taxes, and VAT; honeyoon and meal plans available.

Payment/Credit Cards: Most major

Deposit: Credit card deposit

Government Taxes: Included

Service Charges: Included

Entry Requirements for U.S. Citizens: Valid passport

Some feature lots of decorative tile and garden patios.

In and around Reid's there is plenty to do. For about $8.00 you can rides in a gondola from Funchal to the top of the hill about three and a half miles. Your "reward" besides incredible views out to sea, is the opportunity to return in a two-person wicker toboggan, which charges down the streets guided by two very fit young men, each holding a short rope attached to the back of a runner.

You'll want to take time to explore the island and perhaps walk along one of the LeVadas, or water channels, built to direct the water down and through the mountains. The LeVadas cut through some of Madiera's most dramatic terrain and at times the walking paths get very narrow, especially along the edges of the cliffs.

Those craving yellow-gold sandy beaches head to Porto Santo, a flattish island about a two-and-a-half hour ferry ride from Madeira. Boat trips around the island, game fishing, golf, and scuba diving can also be arranged.

Of course, one of the joys of visiting Madeira is becoming acquainted with Madeira, the wine. You will learn about the complexity of the wine: how a particular vintage can taste as good as fine cognac. Most of the Madeira wine companies, such as Vinhos Barbeito's, Blandy's, and Henriques & Henriques, have shops and tasting rooms in Funchal that are open to the public.

ASIA AND THE PACIFIC

BEDARRA ISLAND
Australia

When you hear an Australian say, "Going troppo, mate," he or she could be heading to Bedarra Island, a sunny tropical bit of paradise located just off the northern coast of Queensland—Great Barrier Reef territory. For this cheery saying means you're going to a place guaranteed to provide lots of hot sun, sand, and sea. Bedarra offers all this and more—or less, depending on how you look at it. It's secluded; it's quiet. Very quiet. Here there are no schedules to follow and very little in the way of nightlife.

A white, sandy oasis in the middle of a brilliant turquoise sea, Bedarra Island is a small, intimate resort. Staying here is much like staying at the home of a wealthy relative who just happens to be out of town: Members of the staff are in attendance and have been told to do everything in their power to keep you happy. And they do!

At this sybaritic destination, besides being waited on, you're quite welcome to help yourself to anything you desire, at any time. If you want something special, all you have to do is ask. Caviar? They'll bring it. An omelet at three in the afternoon? They'll cook it. Want to go over to nearby Dunk Island for some action? They'll get the boat fired up. You just name it.

Your multilevel villa is yours alone. Crafted from native timbers, it sits on stilts amid lush gardens. Ceilings are high, with exposed beams; floors are made of highly polished wood. The bright, airy decor reflects the colors from outside. Linens are smooth and lovely; pillows are puffy, soft down. (If you want something different, just ask.) Towels are thick and thirsty and are changed often.

Each of the fifteen villas has a balcony, a good place to enjoy your welcome bottle of champagne while gazing out at the sea. Only a few steps from the beach, each villa comes with a king-size bed and a separate lounge area with CD stereo system, TV, video, and fully stocked complimentary minibar.

Since Bedarra is a very private island, you'll have no trouble finding innumerable places to be alone. Discover hidden coves; walk in the lush rain forest that flourishes alongside the beaches; or float side by side on rubber rafts. Swing gently in one of the hammocks slung between palms on the beach, or ask for a picnic hamper filled with delicious food and champagne to take with you to a secluded spot.

Although Bedarra's chefs find new ways to tempt you daily, they also make a point of asking if you have any personal requests. The open bar, which is available to you twenty-four hours a day, is stocked with domestic and imported beers, champagnes, fine vintage red and white wines, spirits, and liqueurs.

The restaurant, which is round and constructed of local woods, overlooks the gardens and turquoise lagoons, a perfect setting for that special romantic dinner. Enjoy the excellent cuisine and be sure to top it all off by indulging in a delectable Pavlova (a meringue dessert). There are only fourteen other couples at most, so if you're looking for a lively nightlife with lots of socializing, this might not be the place for you to come. If, however, a serene, beautiful natural setting and lots of pampering by an extremely competent and caring staff appeal, then Bedarra is worth the trip.

Bedarra Island

Location: On Bedarra Island, 3 miles off the tropical northern Queensland coast

Romantic Highlights: Very, very quiet private island; lovely beaches

Address/Phone: P.O. Box 1033, Bedarra Island via Townsville, Queensland, Australia 4810; 61–7–4068–8233; fax 61–7–4068–8215

E-mail: reservations@poresorts.com

Web Site: www.poresorts.com

U.S. Reservations: P&O Australian Resorts, (800) 225–9849

Owner/Manager: P&O Australian Resorts, owner; Caroline Henry, resort general manager

Arrival/Departure: Private resort launch transfer to and from Dunk Island airstrip

Distance from Dunk Island Airstrip: 15-minute launch ride

Distance from Cairns: About 108 miles from Cairns to Mission Beach, from there by launch or plane to Dunk Island, then by launch transfer to Bedarra Island

Accommodations: 15 private, two-level and split-level villas crafted from native timbers

Most Romantic Room/Suite: Villa Number 1 is the most secluded.

Amenities: Hair dryer, toiletries, air-conditioning, ceiling fans, ISD telephone, radio, ironing facilities, TV, VCR, bathrobes, CD stereo system

Electricity: 240 volts

Sports and Facilities: Tennis, use of motorized dinghies, island hiking, paddleskis, sailing, swimming, snorkeling, fishing, sailboarding. Guests may use sporting facilities at nearby Dunk Island, just 15 minutes away, at no extra charge.

Dress Code: Casual

Weddings: Can be arranged

Rates/Packages: All-inclusive rates, from AU $890 (U.S.$496) per person per night, includes accommodations, 3 meals daily, open bar, snacks, tennis, water sports, and laundry. "Romantic Moments" package from AU $3,750 (U.S.$2,092) includes 5 nights' villa accommodations, meals, open bar, massage, and transfers. Stay 7 nights and receive an 8th night free.

Payment/Credit Most major

Deposit: Credit card guarantee; no charge for cancellation made 30 days prior to arrival date; less than 30 days, a one-night charge

Government Taxes: Included

Service Charges: None

Entry Requirements for U.S. Citizens: Passport

CHATEAU YERING HISTORIC HOUSE HOTEL
Australia

As much as I love Melbourne, I recommend you escape for a few days into the countryside to visit Yarra Valley's more than thirty wineries and its exceptional parks. My choice of where to stay? Chateau Yering, an historic Victorian house hotel (circa 1854), a grand mansion with floor-to-ceiling windows, verandas, and sweeping lawns. It provides a superb base for exploring the rich, rolling wine country of the Valley. In fact, Yering Station winery is just next door.

Paul de Castella, who came to Melbourne from Switzerland, purchased Yering Station in 1850, developing it into a world-class winery. In 1889, Yering wine received the only "Grand Prix" award given to the Southern Hemisphere at the Paris Exhibition. The chateau, constructed by De Castella in 1854, quickly became the social mecca of the region. A newspaper article reported in 1889, "The Chateau is a substantial building, surround by a 15-foot verandah. On entering one is struck by the loftiness of the rooms, and the handsome fittings and decorations which equal those to be found in an old English home. Mr. de Castella is noted for his hospitality and most of the Governors and visitors of note in the early days have been royally entertained here."

Chateau Yering (Yering was the Aboriginal name for the region) sits on 250 acres bordering on the Yarra River. The hotel is furnished with period pieces, fine paintings, and rich fabrics. Many of the pieces have been brought from England, including the antique Georgian four-poster bed in the Archer suite and the pair of red leather wing chairs in the library.

In the drawing room, below the original delicately stencilled barrel ceiling, great vases of fresh flowers sit on highly polished tables, and pastel floral artwork, Oriental carpets, gleaming parquet floors, rosewood tables, and swagged silk brocade drapes create a peaceful place to relax.

Deep yellows and reds predominate in the library and dining room. Outside, there are wonderful gardens and a delightful garden pool open in warmer months.

The gardens which date back to the mid-1800s, contain exotic trees and plants such as the giant Chilean wine

palm and bunya bunya pines along with a pergola covered with wisteria and roses.

There are just twenty rooms and suites, each different. Rich brocades, tapestries, chintz, and silks create an elegant ambience. French doors open onto private balconies or verandas. The River suites have king-size beds, claw-foot baths, separate showers, antique furniture, and views of the hills, and rooms located in the historic stables feature antique four-poster beds, open fireplaces, marble baths with spas, and garden verandas. Suites come with sitting rooms.

The long windows in Eleonore's Restaurant reveal faraway vistas of the countryside. Here you enjoy regional wines, fresh local produce, and creative cuisine like crayfish tortellini served on crushed potato with salmon roe and a champagne and watercress sauce and Yarra Valley quail saltimbocca with sage and prosciutto served with a saffron and vanilla risotto and Madeira jus. For the main course you might have Barramundi served with gingered pear, sweetbreads, stewed cabbage, and port wine foie gras reduction or perhaps rabbit served with buttered spinach or lamb served in a puff pastry with roquette pesto and summer vegetables.

For dessert, there is vanilla, white chocolate, and apricot pudding served with Domaine Chandon Cuvée Riche ice cream, anise-flavored crepes, and a confection made of meringue, mango sorbet, raspberry sorbet, mascarpone cheese, and rose-scented geranium jelly. The crème brûlée is especially hard to resist.

Light meals and breakfast are available at Sweetwater Cafe, a light-filled atrium paved in stone and furnished with cane chairs and tables. Both restaurants feature freshly baked breads and local wines such as Yarra Yarra Sauvignon/Semillon, Yarra Valley Hills Riesling, and Yarrabank Cuvee. A small timber-panelled bar is located next to the library.

In addition to the vineyards, Chateau Yering is close to the Healesville Wildlife Sanctuary where indeed you can see kangaroos hopping in the grasses and koala bears draped over the limbs of eucalyptus trees.

Chateau Yering Historic House Hotel

Location: On 250 acres amidst the vineyards of the Yarra Valley about an hour from Melbourne

Romantic Highlights: Views of vineyards; fireplaces; four-poster beds

Address/Phone: 42 Melba Highway, Yering, Yarra Valley, Victoria, Australia 3770; 613–9237–3333; fax: 613–9237–3300

E-mail: info@chateau-yering.com.au

Web Site: www.chateau-yering.com.au

U.S. Reservations: Contact the hotel directly

Owner/Manager: Len and Elly Milner, owners; Sue O'Brien, manager

Arrival/Departure: Helicopter transfer from the airport can be arranged as well as transfers by car

Distance from Melbourne Airport: 50 minutes

Distance from Melbourne: 35 miles (50 minutes)

Accommodations: 20 rooms and suites

Most Romantic Room/Suite: Stable Suite in winter; Yering suites in summer, with a separate living room, queen "half tester" bed, spa bath, open fireplace, stereo TV with DVD player, and private staircase entry to suite. Yarra suites have separate sitting rooms, king-size beds, spa baths, balconies, stereo TV in both bedroom and sitting room, and DVD players.

Amenities: Spa baths, stereo TV with video player, 24-hour room service, toiletries, some have fireplaces

Electricity: 240 watts

Sports and Facilities: Pool, tennis court, pétanque (French *boules*), croquet, and board games; golf and hot air ballooning available nearby

Dress Code: Resort casual

Weddings: Yes

Rates/Packages: From AU $435–$895 (U.S.$242–$499) per night including breakfast, wine tasting, taxes, and service charges. "A Romantic Affair" package priced from AU $625 (U.S.$348) per couple per night, includes suite accommodations, dinner, breakfast, bottle of wine, bouquet of flowers, and special gift.

Payment/Credit Cards: Most major

Deposit: 50 percent deposit required to confirm

Government Taxes: Included

Service Charges: Included

Entry Requirements for U.S. Citizens: Passport

HAYMAN
Australia

Hayman, a long, low, sprawling property with reflecting pools filled with swans, tropical gardens, waterfalls, and palm-lined beaches, is designed for romance. The Great Barrier Reef is close by, but you may find it hard to tear yourself away from your Hayman Island paradise. Situated at the tip of the Whitsunday Islands, this luxurious 245-room resort is the only place on the 726-acres. And what a place!

It takes a bit of doing to get here, but it's worth it. First you have to get to Australia; then you can fly from Sydney, Brisbane, Cairns, or Townsville to Hamilton Island, where you board a sleek yacht for the fifty–minute cruise to Hayman. While onboard, you enjoy complimentary flutes of champagne and get all the registration formalities out of the way so that you can head right to your room on arrival.

The resort, which stretches along a cove on the southern part of Hayman Island, fronts a beach. Some say the waters around this island offer some of the finest sailing in the world. Hayman, 3 miles in length and 2 miles wide, is shaped like a crescent with mountains running along its spine, punctuated by a tall peak standing 820 feet above sea level. The island is covered with a dense blanket of native eucalyptus trees, and the Australian bushland goes right to the edge of the white beaches. In 2001, Hayman completed a two-year AU $18 million (U.S.$10 million) development program that included refurbishing the rooms and introducing new Palm, Pool, Beach, and Lagoon wings with new room categories.

All rooms, suites, and penthouses have either private balconies or terraces with views of the pools, lagoons, and beaches or gardens. Rooms are low-key but elegant, decorated in soft pastels, natural textures and rich woods that complement the tropical setting. All rooms come with large glass patio doors, white sliding louvers, handwoven rugs and dhurries, original paintings and sculpture, comfortable upholstered chairs and sofas, and lavish marble baths. The one-, two-, and three-bedroom penthouses on the top floor of the Lagoon Wing are each decorated in a different style, accented with a stunning selection of furnishings and objets d'art. You can choose from a variety of themes including Greek, Japanese, Italian palazzo, Moroccan, South Seas, contemporary, North Queensland, California, Art Deco, and French provincial.

You don't have to be water-oriented to be enraptured by the dazzling freshwater pool floating in the midst of a huge saltwater lagoon—it's seven times larger than an Olympic pool. There is also an intimate pool surrounded by palms, tropical gardens, and fish ponds. Here you'll have as much privacy as you want. Wander through exotic gardens and along the beaches and never see another soul.

In addition to a full range of water sports facilities and five tennis courts, Hayman has an excellent health club equipped with computerized workout equipment, such as rowing machines, aerobicycles, and treadmills, along with spas, saunas, and steam rooms. Want to be pampered? Indulge in a Swedish or aromatherapy body massage.

Many things make Hayman an exceptional resort, but its proximity to the Great Barrier Reef really sets it apart. This incredible natural wonder is more than 1,200 miles long and is made up of 2,000 individual reefs and 71 coral-based islands. Snorkelers and scuba divers universally classify the reef as the ultimate underwater experience. The waters around Hayman churn with fish of all shapes and colors, and even for a rank novice it is a thrill to glide above and through their world. If you prefer to stay dry, you can opt for a glass-bottom boat ride or a helicopter or seaplane excursion, which will take you directly over the reef.

Hayman has its own marina and offers chartered fishing excursions aboard the *Sun Aura*, a 40-foot game-fishing boat. Since these waters offer some of the finest fishing in the world, you might get lucky and catch some dinner, which the Hayman chefs will be happy to prepare for you.

In all there are five restaurants, each one featuring its

own unique fare. There is also an extensive wine cellar of more than 35,000 bottles. La Fontaine is the most formal, with Waterford chandeliers and Louis XVI furniture. Its "cuisine moderne" is outstanding and beautifully presented. There is also the Oriental, where you can try Moreton Bay "bugs," a cross between lobster and crab, served in an outstanding black bean sauce. The menu includes food selections from China, Malaysia, Thailand, and Japan. Fresh herbs from the resort's gardens are used in preparation of the meals. Hayman bakes its own breads and makes chocolates and ice creams. La Trattoria is a lively, informal, indoor/outdoor Italian bistro featuring pastas, salads, and antipastos at moderate prices. Azure, a new dining venue built on the site of the former Coffee House and fronting the beach, offers contemporary Australian-style dining specializing in fresh regional seafood prepared in an open kitchen and served inside or outdoors on an enlarged deck extending over the beach. The Beach Pavilion offers daily blackboard specials, barbecues, snacks, and drinks. And there is always room service, available at any hour. After dinner you can enjoy nightly performances by resident and guest artists.

Hayman's guests give the staff high marks for professionalism, friendliness, courtesy, and dedication. These, combined with an idyllic setting and superb facilities, add up to a top-notch honeymoon resort.

Hayman

Location: 20 miles from the Australian mainland, on 726 acres of one of the Whitsunday Islands

Romantic Highlights: Private dinners for two on beach or in tropical gardens; themed penthouses filled with antiques; island picnics and snorkeling on Bali Hai and Langford Reef

Address/Phone: Great Barrier Reef, North Queensland, Australia 4801; 61–7–49–401–234; fax 61–7–49–401–567

E-mail: reserve@hayman.com.au

Web Site: www.hayman.com.au

U.S. Reservations: Leading Hotels of the World, (800) 223–6800, (800) 4–HAYMAN

Owner/Manager: BT Hotels Ltd., owners; Lloyd Donaldson, general manager

Arrival/Departure: Fly Qantas to Hamilton Island, where guests board one of Hayman's 3 luxury yachts for the 50-minute trip to the island. A minibus will pick you up at the wharf for the 5-minute ride to the resort complex.

Distance from Hamilton Island Airport: 50 minutes by boat plus 5 minutes by minibus

Distance from Hamilton Island: 25 miles (approximately 50 minutes)

Accommodations: 234 rooms and 11 penthouse suites

Most Romantic Room/Suite: One of the 11 penthouses or the newly renovated Lagoon suites

Amenities: Air-conditioning, TV, Movielink, telephone, ceiling fan, minibar, in-room safe, refrigerator, tea/coffeemaker, hair dryer, toiletries, robe and slippers

Electricity: 240 volts

Sports and Facilities: Snorkeling, Hobie-Cats, sailboarding, paddle skiing; use of 5 tennis courts, golf target range, putting green; billiards, table tennis, badminton, and hiking. Scuba, fishing, and yacht trips can be arranged.

Dress Code: Casual during the day; jacket required for dinner at La Fontaine; casually elegant at other 4 restaurants

Weddings: Exquisite setting for garden weddings.

Rates/Packages: Rates per couple per night range from AU $560 (U.S.$312) to AU $1,800 (U.S.$1,004) for Lagoon Wing Suite overlooking the Whitsunday Passage. Penthouses are priced from AU $2,000 (U.S.$1,116). Honeymoon package, priced at AU $3,196 (U.S.$1,783) per couple, includes chilled wine and chocolates, private dinner, massage for two, and tax.

Payment/Credit Cards: Most major

Deposit: 1 night; cancellation 1 week prior to arrival for full refund.

Government Taxes: 10 percent

Service Charges: Included

Entry Requirements for U.S. Citizens: Passport

SILKY OAKS LODGE & HEALING WATERS SPA

Australia

This one is definitely for the adventurous couple. Located on the edge of the Daintree Rain Forest National Park, Silky Oaks Lodge gives you the wilderness experience without the bugs and the cold showers. Look up into the treetops from the Mossman River as the night arrives, and you'll see the twinkling lights and windows of cottages glowing through the leafy canopy of the forest. Silky Oaks Tree-houses are built on stilts to sit high in the dense tropical foliage and constructed of wood inside and outside. Large sliding glass doors open onto a veranda with a hammock for two, giving you a marvelous perch from which to view the world below. Tarzan and Jane would have loved it.

The Treehouses are spacious, comfortable, and very private with sitting areas, queen-size beds, and lots of windows. Although it's set in the Mossman River Gorge in a lush ancient rain forest, you'll find that your private tree-house chalet has air-conditioning, an en suite bath, a hair dryer, telephone—even a minibar. From your veranda look carefully and you may be able to catch a glimpse of a platy-pus or tortoise. Or, most certainly, a resident bush turkey.

Winner of several tourism awards, the lodge features a superb open-air restaurant set high in the treetops over-looking the natural rock swimming pool and the river that flows below. The observation and guest lounges, which are ringed with large windows, are furnished with rattan chairs with comfortable cushions and Oriental carpets.

The lodge, Treehouses, and rain forest are connected by a series of paths and boardwalks on stilts. The new Healing Waters Spa is located in an attractive timber treehouse. The treatment rooms are designed to soothe and calm, with a decor of natural colors and textures and the sound of running river waters in the background.

There is plenty to do at Silky Oaks. You can go kayak-ing, hiking, and swimming and even play tennis. And, of course, the diving rearby is fantastic. Silky Oaks is only 75 minutes from Cairns, the jumping-off point for the Great Barrier Reef, which is really a must-see. Guided rain forest walks led by a naturalist are comlimentary and, to help you understand what you see, you can refer to the lodge's impressive selection of books in the library.

Just outside your doorstep is a whole world of inter-esting flora and fauna to discover. After morning tea at the lodge's Tree House Restaurant, you can walk to the World Heritage–listed Daintree National Park, the oldest living rain forest in the world, where you will be surrounded by huge trees, primitive plants, and a myriad of birds, butter-flies, and little creatures such as lizards. Sling bridges take you over bubbling creeks, and marked paths show you the way to some spectacular sights—electric-blue butterflies, bright yellow-and-green birds, and tiny frogs.

Take a refreshing dip in the crystal-clear billabong, a natural pool surrounded by big boulders and lush tropi-

Silky Oaks Lodge & Healing Waters Spa

Location: Adjoins the Daintree Rain Forest National Park, on the northern bank of the Mossman River Gorge, near Port Douglas and Cairns

Romantic Highlights: Very private wilderness chalets; hammocks in the trees

Address/Phone: Finlayvale Road, Mossman; P.O. Box 396, Mossman 4873, Australia; 61–7–4098–1666; fax 61–7–4098–1983

E-mail: resorts.reservations@poresorts.com.au

Web Site: www.poresorts.com.au

U.S. Reservations: P&O Australian Resorts, (800) 225–9849

Owner/Manager: Shane McNally, manager

Arrival/Departure: From Cairns you can rent a car, take a limousine or go by bus (check at desk in airport). Pickup can also be arranged at various Cairns hotels.

Distance from Cairns Airport: 1¼ hours by limousine; AU$270 (U.S.$150) round-trip per car

Distance from Cairns: 16 miles north (20 minutes) from Port Douglas; 51 miles (1¼ hours) from Cairns

Accommodations: 44 private Treehouses on stilts located near the lodge overlooking the lagoon or the treetop canopy or situated deeper in the rain forest itself

Most Romantic Room/Suite: 6 riverhouses where you enjoy seclusion and your own special view of the rain forest

Amenities: Air-conditioning, ceiling fan, minibar, tea/coffee facilities, hair dryer, toiletries, clock radio, telephone; massages available; nightly turndown service, laundry service, ironing board/iron, bathrobes

Electricity: 220 volts

Sports and Facilities: Hiking in the rain forest, tennis, swimming, canoeing, river kayaking, horseback riding, wilderness safaris, bicycling; trips to the Great Barrier Reef; golf at the Mirage Country Club (20 minutes from Silky Oaks); fishing, night animal spotting, Aboriginal tours, river cruises, rain forest, picnics, and the Healing Waters Spa

Dress Code: Casual

Rates/Packages: AU $640 (U.S.$357) per couple per chalet per night; three-night package, AU $960–$1,185 (U.S.$535–$661) per person, double occupancy, includes accommodations, breakfasts, dinners, guided rain forest walks, and a Great Barrier Reef Cruise or wilderness safari

Payment/Credit Cards: Most major

Deposit: Credit card guarantee

Government Taxes: Included

Service Charges: None

Entry Requirements for U.S. Citizens: Passport

cal foliage. Take a picnic lunch (provided by the lodge) for a fun day on your own. Or explore the rain forest on horseback, retracing the steps of the old teamsters. Back at the lodge's bar, you can make new friends from all over the world.

The food is worth writing home about. This may look like a wilderness lodge, but there is nothing primitive about the cuisine served here. You may not be able to remember exactly what you ate, but you will remember that the food was some of the tastiest you've ever had—anywhere. Fresh tropical fruits and lots of great seafood from the nearby Barrier Reef along with Asian and Continental dishes are prepared with great skill. As one recent guest put it, "Every day we really looked forward to returning to the lodge for dinner. It got to be a habit."

There are several companies, such as Tauck Tours and Swain Australia, that take you to Australia and combine a wilderness adventure with a stay at Silky Oaks. A typical program takes in the Daintree Rain Forest, Cape Tribulation, and the Bloomfield Track and includes a Daintree River cruise. Maybe you'll catch a peek at an estuarine crocodile sunning on the riverbanks.

TURTLE ISLAND
Fiji

Some call it the most romantic place on earth. Apparently Columbia Pictures thought so, as they chose this island as the site for their 1980 movie *Blue Lagoon* starring Brooke Shields. The original 1949 version with Jean Simmons was also shot here.

This is a true fantasy island, where you live in your own thatch-roofed beachfront *bure* (cottage), spend lazy barefoot days on the beach, and get to know other couples.

When Turtle was simply a relatively unknown Fijian island located somewhere in the South Pacific, Richard Evanson, an American, came here to find a simpler life apart from the hectic world of television, where he had achieved success working on the West Coast. Evanson liked it so much, he stayed, eventually purchasing the island in 1972 and building a small resort with the help of Joe Naisali, a Fijian.

In constructing Turtle, Evanson was extremely careful not to upset the beauty and balance of the environment. He planted thousands of trees, including many Honduras mahoganies, carved a small road from the underbrush to go around the island, and protected the natural development of Turtle with a 500-year-old trust. Small and intimate, Turtle is a jewel not only because of its unspoiled physical beauty but also because of the interaction of its guests with the warm, loving Fijian people. Sitting under a banyan tree and singing with guests and staff in the late evening can be a spiritual experience.

The minimum stay of six nights gives you time to relax, unwind, and explore Turtle's many pleasures. Turtle's all-inclusive fee frees you to go with the flow. No bills to sign. No need to wonder about additional charges, since everything is included—even deep-sea fishing, scuba diving, and drinks.

A seaplane brings you to Turtle from Nadi, Fiji's main airport. As you approach, you'll see the brilliant colors of the Blue Lagoon and miles of white, powdery sand ringing the island. From the time you step from the boat to the shore, you are warmly attended to by a very hospitable staff who call you by your first name (only first names are used here). If you have any special requests or needs, they'll already know about them from the questionnaire you filled out before you came. Like a white omelet every morning? You'll get it. Don't eat meat? No problem. Be prepared for some great meatless selections.

Fifteen traditional thatched-roof two-room *bures* built of coral stone are roomy, comfortable, and private with separate sitting areas, louvered windows, wet bars, "his and her" baths, four-poster beds, and rattan furniture. Handwoven, twenty-one-foot vaulted ceilings arch over wheat-colored walls and mellow wood or terra-cotta floors. Ten grand *bures* have private Jacuzzis, king-size beds, outdoor lily ponds, and verandas. And perhaps best of all, you have plenty of space around your bure, which is located directly on the beach of the Blue Lagoon.

Lali drums and guitar music announce cocktail time. After cocktails, guests enjoy dinner under the stars and have a choice of dining alone or with other guests. Food is fresh and delicious, with an emphasis on organically grown produce and fruits just picked from the trees. Turtle's three-acre garden provides an abundance of tropical delights and gourmet delicacies. Grilled lobster with lemongrass, all kinds of seafood, fresh fish caught earlier in the day by local fishermen, accompanied by wine from Turtle's extensive wine cellar, are prepared with skill and flair. Try *Kokoda*, a Fijian dish of fish marinated in lime and coconut milk, or mud crabs dipped in tangy vinaigrette.

At Turtle you have so many choices: Go horseback riding or have a champagne picnic on the beach; take a nap in a hammock strung between two coconut palms; hike into the jungle hillsides; or head to one of fourteen private beaches to spend a romantic afternoon in the sun. Here the sea is calm, with gently rolling waves, perfect for swimming and snorkeling. There are weekly *lovo* feasts and Fijian sing-alongs, where you share *kava*, the Fijian ceremonial drink.

You will probably find the most difficult thing about Turtle is leaving. After a week here, among some of the friendliest people you'll find anywhere, life for you will be just like a beautiful song—"*Vovosa malva mai vei au.*"

Turtle Island

Location: 500-acre privately owned island in the South Pacific

Romantic Highlights: Thatched beachfront cottages; 14 private beaches you can reserve just for you; dining by candlelight on the beach or on a mountaintop; intimate gourmet picnics

Address: P.O. Box 9317, Nadi, Fiji Islands 72921; 10906 SE Thirty-ninth Street, Suite A-1, Vancouver, WA 98682-6789

E-mail: usa@turtlefiji.com

Web Site: www.turtlefiji.com

U.S. Reservations: (877) 2–TURTLE; fax (360) 253–3934

Owner/Manager: Richard Evanson

Arrival/Departure: Fly from Los Angeles nonstop to Fiji with 5 flights weekly. Round-trip transfer via seaplane from Nadi, Fiji, to Turtle Island is $380 per person, including tax (make arrangements when booking your Turtle Island stay).

Distance from Nadi International Airport: 30 minutes

Accommodations: 14 suites (*bures*)

Most Romantic Room/Suite: Grand *Bures*

Amenities: Ceiling fans, hair dryer, iron/ironing board, tea and coffeemaking facilities, CD player, toiletries, beach bag, bathrobe, stocked refrigerator, snorkeling gear, next-day laundry service

Electricity: 240/110 volts

Sports and Facilities: Water sports such as boating, scuba diving, windsurfing, snorkeling, sports fishing; hiking on trails, horseback riding

Dress Code: Casual (sandals or barefoot), cotton shorts, T-shirts, and swim suits. Pack light, as you are limited to 33 pounds of luggage for the seaplane flight. Extra luggage can be stored at Turtle's facility in Nadi.

Weddings: Can be arranged.

Rates/Packages: $1,200–$1,934 per couple per night for everything, including accommodations, activities, meals, all beverages (even unlimited champagne), excursions to neighboring islands (Sunday only), use of boats and water sports equipment, all services, and 10 percent tax. Seven-night package starting from $9,160 per couple, includes all nightly rate inclusions plus seaplane fare.

Payment/Credit Cards: Deposit by credit card; final payment by check

Deposit: $2,000 at booking; balance due 45 days prior to your arrival. If you cancel, you can be rescheduled for another date within a five-year period, but no refunds.

Government Taxes: 10 percent included

Service Charges: Not necessary. If you wish, you can contribute to staff Christmas fund when you leave.

Entry Requirements for U.S. Citizens: Passport

BORA BORA LAGOON RESORT
French Polynesia

A full moon rises over Mt. Otemanu, the crenellated peak that inspired the legends of Bali Hai. The moon's rays shimmer on the glassy lagoon like a king's ransom of silver. This is the vision that awaits when you step onto your lanai (terrace) at the Bora Bora Lagoon Resort, an exclusive enclave set on a private isle off Bora Bora. Many consider Bora Bora to be the loveliest island in French Polynesia, with its mountaintops soaring heavenward like the skyline of an emerald city. Here a necklace of barrier reef is clasped around a perfectly blue, perfectly clear lagoon.

The resort is located on Motu Toopua, an islet in the lagoon that's just five minutes by boat from Bora Bora's main town, Vaitape. There are no roads, no electricity (the hotel uses generators), no other businesses—just twelve acres of tropical gardens and views of the mountains, reefs, and fields. After arriving by private launch at the hotel's long pier, you're taken to the main building, constructed of lava stone and bamboo, with local *aito* logs supporting the roof. Here you're welcomed with a lei and refreshing drink of coconut water.

You'll stay in Tahitian-style *farés* (bungalows, pronounced fa-RAY, Tahitian for "home"), with peaked roofs thatched with pandanus palm leaves. One wall is made up of louvered panels that you can slide open to the views and prevailing breezes. Each room offers a king-size bed and separate bath with a deep soaking tub and shower as well as a TV and VCR. The most romantic quarters are the overwater bungalows, built on stilts above the opalescent lagoon. A small stairway leads down to the water, so you can swim right from the deck.

Inside, the rooms reflect Polynesian chic, with tapa cloth hangings, coconut-shell inlays, and lovely floors of lustrous yucca wood streaked with a yellow and brown grain. Decorator fabrics come from French Polynesia and intertwine tones of ocean turquoise and sunset red. The most unusual piece of furniture is the glass coffee table: The top slides back so you can feed morsels of bread to the multicolored fish that gather below . . . an unusual twist on a "floor" show. The underwater spectacle is even illuminated at night!

The so-called beach bungalows are actually located in the gardens. Although they have the exact same decor as the over water accommodations, they lack the magic of the sea-moored *farés*.

The rooms and facilities at the resort continue to be updated. The latest renovation took place in 2001.

The resort has two different restaurants, including the Otemanu Room for formal dining. Once a week the resort schedules a Tahitian feast, with roast suckling pig and a folkloric dance show.

Bora Bora Lagoon offers plenty of activities—and delicious ways of doing nothing at all. A quarter of a mile of white-sand beach stretches alongside the transparent waters, and there's a marvelous pool that flows right to the edge of the tiles—the largest swimming pool in French Polynesia. Practice your strokes on the two lighted tennis courts (racquets and balls are available if you didn't bring your own). At the fitness center you'll find exercise machines and free weights. Learn to paddle an outrigger canoe, or opt for a massage in your own room or at the spa facility.

Feel adventurous? You can also choose from a roster of intriguing excursions (which cost extra) each day. Tops on your list should be a four-wheel-drive expedition around Bora Bora. Dauntless Land Rovers crash through jungle, revving up steep, rocky, muddy, pothole-wracked tracks to some dynamite scenic overlooks. For thrill seekers there are the shark feeds. Wearing snorkel gear, you watch safely from the shallows as dive masters serve up chunks of raw fish to black-tip sharks, which circle just a jaw's breadth away. Other activities include helicopter tours and snorkel excursions.

Exciting as these excursions are, your most vivid memories will be of the spectacular scenery in Bora Bora.

Bora Bora Lagoon Resort

Location: Motu Toopua, a small, roadless coral island within the Bora Bora Lagoon

Romantic Highlights: Tahitian-style *farés* (bungalows) built on stilts right over the lagoon; private island setting; magnificent views of the Bora Bora mountainscape; unusual adventures like shark-feeding expeditions

Address/Phone: Motu Toopua; B.P. 175, Vaitape, Bora Bora, French Polynesia; 689–60–40–00; fax 689–60–40–01

E-mail: bblr@mail.pf

Web Site: www.boraboralagoonresort.orient-express.com

U.S. Reservations: Orient Express Hotels, (800) 860–4095; Leading Hotels of the World, (800) 223–6800

Owner/Manager: Bernard Sarme, general manager

Arrival/Departure: At Bora Bora Airport, you are whisked to the resort across the lagoon on a private motor launch.

Distance from Bora Bora Airport: 15 minutes

Distance from Vaitape: 5 minutes by boat

Accommodations: 50 over-water bungalows (6 over water at end of pontoon); 27 beach bungalows; 21 garden lagoon bungalows; 2 family bungalows

Most Romantic Room/Suite: Over-water bungalows

Amenities: In-room safe, minibar, electric ceiling fan (air-conditioning is not needed), hair dryer, telephone, in-house video system, TV, double sinks

Electricity: 220 volts

Sports and Facilities: 2 tennis courts, swimming pool, outrigger canoes, pedalboat, snorkeling, sailing, windsurfing, fitness center; deep-sea fishing, waterskiing, parasailing, jeep safaris, sunset sails, massages, sharkfeeding, and scuba diving can be arranged.

Dress Code: Tropically casual

Weddings: Can be arranged. (The cermony however, is not legally recognized in the U.S.)

Rates/Packages: $520–$770 per couple per night. Total Experience Package for 4 days/3 nights, $3,200 per couple, includes accommodations in an over-water bungalow, American breakfast and lunch daily, dinner for two, shark-feeding excursion, 4-wheel drive excursion, parasailing, half-day rental in a FunCar, transfers, and use of tennis courts, fitness room, and nonmotorized watersports

Payment/Credit Cards: Most major

Deposit: Guarantee with credit card

Government Taxes: 11 percent

Service Charges: Included

Entry Requirements for U.S. Citizens: Passport and outbound ticket; if you're staying more than 1 month, you may need a visa.

HOTEL BORA BORA

French Polynesia

Remember those pictures of thatched huts perched on stilts over turquoise blue water? This is it. Bora Bora, the Grace Kelly of islands, flawlessly beautiful. Home to Hotel Bora Bora, a member of the prestigious Amanresorts group, this South Seas paradise appeals to sophisticates willing to go the extra mile to experience the exotic.

As your plane zooms in on this small island (only 4 miles long and 2½ miles wide), you'll spot palm-thatched bungalows half hidden in the greenery. Crystalline waters in blues, greens, and turquoise swirl around the white-fringed shoreline. Green volcanic peaks that run like a spine down the middle of the island soar toward the brilliant blue sky.

When you arrive, take off your watch, lie back, and soak in the scenery and seamless service. Many of those on the Polynesian staff have been working at the resort for over twenty years and truly know how to anticipate whatever it is you need.

Constructed of cedar, the individual bungalows and farés are spread over grounds that have had more than thirty years to grow lush and lovely. All have hand-tied, thatched pandanus (palm) roofs, private bars, radio/cassette players, and roomy tiled baths with freestanding, oval, wood-rimmed tubs and separate showers. Deluxe bungalows are located on the beach and have separate lounges and sundecks with steps leading to the water. Superior bungalows are also located on the beachfront and come with a small patio facing the sea and a hammock nearby. Bungalows have patios and are set in the gardens.

For the most fun opt for one of the bungalows over the water. Some are in the shallow lagoon waters; others are situated on a coral reef in a deeper section of the lagoon. Each of the over-water bungalows features an enormous room more than 750 square feet; a king-size, four-poster bed swathed in mosquito netting; sliding glass doors leading out to a deck with a pandanus shade overhang; and steps to a small platform, where you can sit on the edge and dangle your feet in the water. Floor-to-ceiling louvered panels allow the sea breezes to slide in, and you have a generous-size sitting area and dressing area with loads of storage space.

Farés, which are located on the beach and in the gardens, are very roomy and come with a living room; a bedroom with a king-size, four-poster bed; an en suite sitting room; a bathroom; and a large sundeck. Eight farés—very spacious, with 1,200 square feet—have private swimming pools enclosed in courtyards furnished with cedar lounges and comfortable cotton cushions; three have outdoor Jacuzzis set into sundecks.

You can eat at the Matira Terrace restaurant overlooking the lagoon or at the Pofai Beach Bar. Both have lofty thatched roofs and are open on all sides to great views and cooling sea breezes. By the time you realize that your dinner and drink tab is heading skyward like the volcanoes, you really won't care much; but be prepared. Meals are not included in the rates (unless you get the Honeymoon package, which gives you some breaks). Entrees can range from $15 upward; a reasonable bottle of wine, $35 and up.

You are entertained nightly by local musicians; a Tahitian dance show is held twice a week.

Many of the activities center on the water: picnics to deserted islands, outrigger canoe rides, sunset cruises, and sailing. You'll find the snorkeling very good just offshore—the fish will eat bread right out of your hand. If you want to explore the colorful underwater world farther out, you can take one of the reef trips.

There is a scuba diving program for all levels of divers. Beginners can take a resort course or go all the way to certification. There are also catamaran sails, fishing excursions, deep-sea and saltwater fly-fishing, moonlight horseback riding, helicopter tours, island tours, jeep excursions, shark-feeding expeditions, and a library with enough books to fill any extra hours you may have.

A special package combines three nights in a *faré* at Hotel Bora Bora and a private yacht charter for three nights with full crew service aboard *Tara Vana*, a 50-foot catamaran.

If you want to experience something really wild, for about $600 you can take part in the Polynesian Ceremony, a sentimental marriage ceremony performed by a Polynesian group leader at sunset. At the lagoon's edge on the main beach, the site is decorated in the Polynesian style and the ritual accompanied by dancers and musicians. Flower crowns and leis crafted from native gardenias are offered and the couple is presented with a *tapa* cloth certificate at the end of the ceremony.

Hotel Bora Bora is restrained, in harmony with its graceful surroundings and the gentle, graceful people who live and work here. It will take you very little time to shrug off the jet lag, sink your toes in the sand, and get into the rhythm of a world that moves at a pace you can absorb.

Hotel Bora Bora

Location: On the southwestern coast of the island of Bora Bora, 150 miles northwest of Tahiti in the Leeward Society Islands

Romantic Highlights: Over-water thatched bungalows; king-size beds covered with clouds of gauzy net

Address/Phone: Point Raititi, Bora Bora, French Polynesia; 689–60–44–60; fax 689–60–44–66

E-mail: hotelborabora@amanresorts.com

Web Site: www.amanresorts.com

U.S. Reservations: toll free 800–2255–2626; reservations@amanresorts.com

Owner/Manager: Amanresorts International Pte. Ltd; owner; Peter Wynne, manager

Arrival/Departure: Transfers from Bora Bora Airport are complimentary; VIP airport express services available on request

Distance from Bora Bora Airport: 7 minutes; flying time between Tahiti and Bora Bora is 45 minutes.

Distance from Vaitape: 3½ miles

Accommodations: 54 Polynesian-style bungalows and *farés* set amid the gardens, on the beach, or over the lagoon

Most Romantic Room/Suite: Over-water bungalows numbers 118 to 128 or a *faré* with in-deck Jacuzzi or private pool

Amenities: Ceiling fans, hair dryer, minibar, safe, telephone (optional), bathrobes, and slippers

Electricity: 110/220 volts

Sports and Facilities: 2 tennis courts, snorkeling, outrigger paddles and sailing, canoes, billiards, table tennis, basketball, and volleyball; optional activities include jeep excursions, glass-bottom boat tours, sunset cruises, reef trips, deep-sea fishing, scuba diving, shark feeding, and sailing and hiking excursions

Dress Code: Casually chic

Weddings: Can be arranged, but the marriage may not be legally recognized in the United States

Rates/Packages: From $500–$750 per couple per night; Honeymoon package for approximately $2,200 per couple includes 3 nights' accommodations transfers, special in-room bed-of-flowers decoration, fruit and French champagne, 3 á la carte breakfasts, 1 candlelight dinner with wine served on the terrace of your *faré* or bungalow, sunset cruise.

Payment/Credit Cards: Most major

Deposit: Guarantee with credit card;14 days notice (30 days in high season) must be given for any cancellations.

Government Taxes: 11 percent

Service Charges: Not included; not encouraged

Entry Requirements for U.S. Citizens: Passport and outbound ticket; if you're staying more than 1 month, you may need a visa.

AMANDARI
Indonesia

If you believe that the best things come in small packages, Amandari is just further proof. You'll find this little jewel of a hotel perched dramatically on a cliff overlooking the Ayung River Gorge, on the exquisite island of Bali. Below are sweeping views of terraced rice paddies and tiny villages, palms, and orchids, a dreamscape to savor in luxury. Designed as a Balinese village, Amandari, one of the very special Amanresorts properties, has thirty garden suites, some with private pools and garden courtyards.

What better place to go to celebrate your union than in Bali, which is legendary for its beauty. The graceful, sarong-clad people sway as they walk, balancing goods on their heads. The land is green and lush, with sinuous rice paddies, and the island is ringed by soft, white sand beaches and clear water.

Traditional dancers greet you at the open-air lobby, with its thatched-roof, templelike facade; floors of local marble; and carved teak furniture made on the island. The adjacent library/lounge offers comfortable chairs and a chance to learn about the surroundings and the gentle, artful Hindu culture.

The villages in the neighboring area each specialize in a different art form: Ubud is known for painting; Mas, for woodcarving; Celuk, for gold jewelry. The hotel can arrange to drive you around the island, where days can be spent bargaining for art and soaking in the rich culture. Each village also has its own distinctive dance, performed to the percussive music of the gamelan. Visitors can enjoy watching a new presentation each night at the open pavilions.

Dining here takes advantage of the views. The restaurant, overlooking the river, is dreamy with candlelight and soft music and serves fine international and Indonesian cuisine. The lounge offers spectacular views; a poolside bar features light meals.

Activities include tennis, hikes into the gorge, biking in the villages, and rafting on the Ayung River. But the loveliest activity of all has to be swimming in one of the most beautiful pools in the world. Contoured in the shape of a rice terrace, the pool appears to meld into the valley beyond. With the reflection of the clouds spreading out over the water, it seems as if you are swimming right up to the edge of the gorge. At one end is a pavilion, where at sunset the ringing sounds of the gamelan fills the air.

Suites are spectacular, some with private pools. Each is enclosed in its own garden courtyard and has a private entrance. Steep paths and stone steps lead to other bungalows and down to the river and the villages. Duplexes have spiral staircases that go up to the bedroom. All suites have polished marble floors, teak furnishings, four-poster beds with hand-painted canopies, and patios with sunken marble tubs hidden behind Balinese walls. Decorative sliding wall screens, creamy white walls accented by wood trim, and lovely paintings and sculpture further enhance the accommodations.

The high-pitched thatched roofs, oversize daybeds, elegant Asian furnishings accented with native art, flowers, glass walls overlooking the beauty of this island, and sarongs provided to each guest to wear to temple ceremonies—all are wondrously romantic things.

Amandari, which means "place of peaceful spirits," is aptly named.

Amandari

Location: In Ubud, Bali, in the center of the Indonesian archipelago

Romantic Highlights: Sunrise walk to the river; scent of frangipani; gamelan concert at sunset; private garden pools; swimming in a pool that seems suspended in midair

Address/Phone: Ubud, Bali, Indonesia; 62–361–975–333; fax 62–361–975–335

E-mail: amandari@amanresorts.com

Web Site: www.amanresorts.com

U.S. Reservations: Toll free 800–2255–2626; reservations@amanresorts.com

Owner/Manager: Amanresorts International Pte. Ltd.

Arrival/Departure: Complimentary transfers provided from airport

Distance from Bali Airport: 45 minutes

Distance from Ubud: 5 minutes

Accommodations: 30 luxury suites enclosed in private courtyard, 11 with private pools; duplex suites have outdoor garden showers and queen-size beds. The Amandari Suite is available with 1 or 2 terrace-style bedrooms and a separate living room pavilion; the suite's 40-by-18-foot pool overlooks the gorge.

Most Romantic Room/Suite: Asmara Suite and Ayung Suite are duplex accommodations with private pools and views of the rice terraces and valley. The Amandari Suite has a separate living room pavilion, pool, and outdoor-dining *bale* of teak and bamboo.

Amenities: Hair dryer, toiletries, air-conditioning, ceiling fans, mosquito netting, twin vanities, minibar/refrigerator, garden patio, in-room safe, radio, sunken marble tub, 24-hour room service

Electricity: 220 volts

Sports and Facilities: Swimming in main or private pool, rafting, trekking, biking, tennis court, and a fully equipped health and fitness center

Dress: Casual; shorts not allowed in temple areas of villages

Weddings: Can be arranged

Rates/Packages: $600–$1,200, rooms; $1,750–$2,950 suites; per couple per night, excluding tax

Payment/Credit Cards: Most major

Deposit: Guarantee with credit card at time of reservation. For refund, 14 days' notice (30 days in high season) must be given; in the event of a no-show, the first 2 nights' charge along with transfer costs will be charged to the credit card or deducted from the prepayment.

Government Taxes: 11 percent

Service Charges: 10 percent

Entry Requirements for U.S. Citizens: Passport

AMANWANA
Indonesia

Ever thought of spending your honeymoon in a tent on some exotic, almost deserted South Pacific island? If so, then Amanwana, on the island of Moyo in Indonesia, may be your ticket to romance. There are only about 2,000 inhabitants on the entire 120-square-mile bit of land, and it's not exactly easy to reach. You need to get to Bali, take a plane and then a boat, and after about two hours you should finally be pulling up to the jetty of the Amanwana resort. You'll have to look hard to see anything, for this little spot of heaven has been carefully placed in this dense, jungle-like forest—no trees were cut down during its construction, and all the work was done by hand.

Amanwana, which means "peaceful forest," is part of the upscale Amanresorts group, which has created unique, very special small vacation places in harmony with nature. Amanwana, the first in the resort company's hideaway category, is like going camping and having your cake, too. Its clever design combines the sense of camping in the wild with the luxuries of modern-day conveniences such as air-conditioning, king-size beds, and double tile vanities.

Set on an island that is a wildlife reserve, the spacious tented rooms are more luxurious than many resort hotel accommodations. The canvas ceiling swoops to a peak in the center of the room over the bed, which is enveloped in an umbrella of filmy netting falling from a high round crown. The canvas, which extends over an outside veranda, is actually roped and pegged to the ground. Here the similarity between this accommodation and the tent you slept in at summer camp ends. The floor of your room is polished teak; there is a generous sitting area with two corner sofas covered in a natural, off-white fabric, and there are practical, well-designed, but simple tables and chairs as well as a desk.

Three sides of the tent are windows with off-white, cotton accordion shades, and there are beautiful straw mats on the floors. Original native sculpture, tapestries, and paintings decorate the off-white walls. The bathrooms are really an unexpected pleasure, boasting double vanities, beautiful twin mirrors in teakwood frames, teak louvered windows, a shower and toilet, plus baskets containing toiletries on the shelf. And the rooms are air-conditioned as well as cooled by ceiling fans.

The tents are randomly linked by paths that lead to the beach, the reception area, and the dining pavilion. Located in a bungalow, the reception area has a library stocked with lots of books, and the decor is pure Indonesian, with hand-hewn wooden tables and stools and original wall hangings, carvings, and paintings.

The open-air pavilion, where you find the bar, restaurant, and lounge, is located under a soaring ceiling of woven bamboo. Views are of the sea; food is basic, fresh, and good with choices from both Western and Asian cultures; and dinner is by candlelight. In fact, since the lighting tends to be less than bright even in your rooms, you'll find the mood can readily be called seductive anywhere you are in camp after the sun goes down.

There is a teak sundeck perched on the edge of the shoreline with coral steps leading to the water. Lounges,

Amanwana

Location: On island of Moyo, east of Lombok and Bali

Romantic Highlights: A hideaway close to nature; luxury tented "villas"

Address/Phone: Moyo Island, West Sumbawa Regency, Indonesia; 62–371–22233; fax 62–371–22288

E-mail: amanwana@amanresorts.com

Web Site: www.amanresorts.com

U.S. Reservations: Toll free 800–2255–2626; reservations@amanresorts.com

Owner/Manager: Amanresorts International Pte. Ltd.

Arrival/Departure: Most transfers to Amanwana from Bali are in a Cessna Caravan amphibian. The state-of-the-art eight-passenger floatplane lands on the bay directly in front of the resort. Flying time is 65 minutes and guests need to arrive at the airport in Denpasar just 30 minutes before the flight. Round-trip transfers are $550 per person.

Distance from Denpasar Airport: About 3 hours total travel time from door to door

Accommodations: 20 luxury tents with king-size beds and en suite bathrooms

Most Romantic Room/Suite: Open-front tents closest to the shoreline

Amenities: Hair dryer, toiletries, air-conditioning, ceiling fans, mosquito netting, twin vanities, minibar, veranda

Electricity: 220 volts

Sports and Facilities: Trekking excursions, boating, snorkeling, cruise excursions, sports fishing, jungle cove massage; freshwater dipping pool; scuba diving can be arranged

Dress Code: Casually smart

Weddings: Can be arranged

Rates/Packages: $750–$875 per tent per couple; includes all meals, water sports, and nonalcoholic beverages

Payment/Credit Cards: Most major

Deposit: Guarantee with credit card deposit within 7 days of acknowledgment from the Bali Central Reservations Office; should a reservation be canceled within 7 days of arrival date or in the event of a no-show, the first night's charge along with transfer costs will be charged to the credit card or deducted from the prepayment.

Government Taxes: 11 percent room tax

Service Charges: 10 percent

Entry Requirements for U.S. Citizens: Passport or round-trip airline tickets.

Closed: January 15–March 15

Note: It is recommended that you start taking antimalaria medication (e.g., doxycycline) before you arrive.

which are sturdy and constructed of wood and have upholstered cushions, provide a great inducement for those who want to lie back and relax in the sun. You can also have a private dinner on the deck or on the beach.

Activities are centered on the crystal-clear turquoise sea and the land. A guided trek into the tropical forest takes you to a beautiful inland waterfall, where you can swim in the pools created by the cascading waters. Walk under the wide tamarind, banyan, and native teak trees; catch a glimpse of monkeys, deer, and wild boar.

Or head out to sea for a late-afternoon sail and see the sun go down over the Flores Sea. Amanwana also has a fleet of nine vessels, including an outrigger canoe that can take you on a cruise of the area, stopping for a picnic on the beach along the way.

Scuba enthusiasts will love it here. The island is ringed with a wonderful coral reef, and a number of interesting dive sites are accessible right from the front of the camp as well as by boat. Beginner courses are $110 excluding tax; PADI International Certification and other instruction are also available.

Keep in mind that the rainy season is from December to March; the rest of the year is pretty dry.

For a real South Pacific experience, you might try combining a stay at Amanwana with two or three nights at one or more of the other Amanresorts. (Please see descriptions of Amanpuri and Amandari in this chapter.)

KAMANDALU RESORT & SPA
Indonesia

If you have decided to go all the way to exotic Bali for your honeymoon, consider including a stay at the Kamandalu. Granted it's not on the beach, but for those who want to really soak up Balinese culture, this little gem of a place, set on a tropical forested hillside with green paddy fields spreading out below, would be an excellent choice. Enhanced by accommodations that have been designed to replicate a typical Balinese village, Kamandalu is located very near Ubud, home of many gifted artists from Indonesia and other parts of the world, who come to live and work in this serene environment.

Just a short shuttle ride from the resort, you'll find a bustling little town and the artists and craftspeople who live and work here.

At Kamandalu, villa cottages with traditional thatched roofs hover just below the tall palms, which have been profusely planted on the hillside. Since the villas cling to the curved terraces of the hillside, you may have to walk many steps up (or down) a hill to get where you're going.

All villas and pavilions have garden showers, marble floors, modern baths with sunken marble tubs; the villas have a *bale bengong* (sitting area). They come with modern amenities such as air-conditioning, minibar, TV, in-house movies, audio system, in-room safe, and garden showers.

The simplest and smallest of the villas features an outdoor garden shower; the deluxe villas are more spacious, have better views and outdoor Jacuzzis, and come with private sunbathing areas, pools, and valley views. The villas, designed in the typical thatched Lombok-style *sasak* (house), each contain a courtyard garden and two separate rooms.

Many villas have king-size beds that are richly decorated with Balinese canopies and headboards. Furniture is simple yet elegantly styled in wood with traditional Balinese fabric cushions. Ceilings are lofty and show the intricate underside of the thatched roofs.

Meals are served in the Petulu Restaurant and highlight cuisine from Bali along with international specialties. There is also the Cempaka Bar and Lounge as well as a library bar with panoramic views of the rice terraces.

The resort has a large swimming pool, tennis courts, and hiking and jogging trails. If you feel adventurous, you can go whitewater rafting.

The Kamandalu Heritage Herbal Spa, a new addition to the property, offers health and beauty care treatments. Experience the soothing essences of selected *jamus*, herbal mixtures used in various treatments offered at the spa.

In its commitment to the local culture and people, Kamandalu has provided a nearby village with clean water and an easy access to the hotel temple, which is built into the hills. Villagers come here to present their offerings to God. While you're staying at the resort, you'll see the villagers quietly going about their business, tending the rice fields and driving their ducks to the paddy to eat.

Sometimes in the distance you may hear the music of a special festival or celebration. Kamandalu is a tranquil place located in close proximity to authentic villages, not to be mistaken for the hub of Bali's tourist nightlife. The main pool may have a swim-up bar and you may have twenty-four–hour room service, but if you want discos and nightclubs you'll have to go somewhere else. Here when the sun goes down, life slows. You relax; you enjoy.

Kamandalu Resort & Spa

Location: In the highlands of central Bali, just north of Ubud

Romantic Highlights: Showering in a private walled Balinese shower under the stars; your own thatched pavilion overlooking emerald-green paddy fields and the Petanu River

Address/Phone: Jalan Tegallalang, Banjar Nagi, P.O. Box 77, Ubud, Bali, 80571 Indonesia; 62–361–975–825 or 62–361–975–835; fax 62–361–975–851

E-mail: sales@kamandaluresort.com

Web Site: kamandaluresort.com

U.S. Reservations: Contact hotel directly

Owner/Manager: Francisca Widjaja, director sales and marketing

Arrival/Departure: Guests are picked up from the airport; cost is $25 one way.

Distance from Bali Airport: 1-hour drive

Distance from Ubud: 1 mile

Accommodations: 58 thatched-roof pavilions and villas set in private walled enclosures; each is designed as a typical Balinese house, some with *bale bengongs* (sitting areas) overlooking the rice paddies and hillside and outdoor showers; some have private pools and separate living rooms

Most Romantic Room/Suite: Jacuzzi or Pool Villas

Amenities: Air-conditioning, in-room safe, minibar, I.D.D. telephone, audio system, satellite TV, toiletries, coffee and tea maker, hair dryer; garden showers, some with Jacuzzis and private pools, in-house movies

Electricity: 220 volts

Sports and Facilities: Large swimming pool with swim-up pool bar and children's pool, tennis court, jogging track, hiking trails, nature walks; white-water rafting can be arranged

Dress Code: Casually elegant

Weddings: A mock wedding in traditional rich red and gold Balinese costumes available to guests booking Balinese Wedding package

Rates/Packages: $200 per room per night for a pavilion; $300–$525 for a villa. A Romantic Indulgence package, $1,355–$1,973 per couple, includes 4 days/3 nights in Pool or Garden Villa, breakfasts either in your villa or in the Pudak Restaurant, transfers, fruit basket and welcome drink, spa treatment, candlelight dinner, and a barbecue dinner.

Payment/Credit Cards: Most major

Deposit: Credit card

Government Taxes: 11 percent

Service Charges: 10 percent

Entry Requirements for U.S. Citizens: Proof of citizenship; passport best

AMANPURI
Thailand

In Sanskrit *Amanpuri* means "place of peace." It is. No discos, no slot machines, no traffic noise. Amanpuri, the first of twelve intimate Amanresorts, is a haven from the fast-paced world many of us live in. Once here you'll have plenty of time to unwind and soak in the tranquillity and beauty of Amanpuri. In fact, doing nothing in an exotic place is exactly what many come here for.

One thing for sure: You'll know you're in Thailand when you arrive in Amanpuri. Most of what has been built here has been created out of local materials made by local craftspeople.

The main roof of the Grand Sala, the centerpiece of Amanpuri, soars to 40 feet. Its multiple, pitched roofs and columns are reflected in the rectangular pool, which is filled to the brim with the clearest of water. The Grand Sala, simply yet elegantly decorated with live orchids and antique furniture, is where you are greeted when you arrive at Amanpuri. At that time a manager is assigned to look after you for the duration of your stay.

Built on three levels into the trees and tropical foliage of a former coconut plantation, forty pavilions are spread out over twenty acres. They stand on stilts linked by elevated walkways. The design of the resort is refined, with guest pavilions and the Grand Sala integrated into a harmonious whole. Steep-pitched roofs curve to a sharp peak—like Buddhist temples—and buildings are constructed of wood accented by earthy, red-hued trim.

You'll find a well-equipped gym with treatment rooms where you can be pampered with massages, facials, and other soothing delights. The Grand Sala, a huge open-air reception area with a lounge and pool, is on the second level.

A lot of natural materials such as bamboo, stone, and teak are used throughout the resort. You'll find caned chairs, baskets, stone walls, and teak floors.

Pavilions are very spacious, containing 1,200 square feet including the bedroom, dressing area, bath and shower, outdoor sala (sitting area), and sundeck. Each bedroom is quietly elegant. Decor doesn't jump out and hit you with a resounding "wow!" Rather it seduces with

creamy, white walls; floor-to-ceiling decorative wood panels; fiber rugs; carved furniture; soft, handwoven cottons and silks; pottery; plants; and Thai sculpture. Bathrooms are enormous, designed for two; closets have enough drawers to hold an entire winter wardrobe.

Although some rooms have good ocean views, most are located in the dense palm groves overlooking the gardens. When Amanpuri was built, the integrity of the land was respected.

The Terrace Restaurant features fresh seafood and continental and Thai specialties daily; and surprise, there is also an Italian restaurant where you can dine by candlelight on the veranda overlooking the sea. Musicians will serenade you as the moon rises over the water. Service is seamless, gracious. If you prefer a quiet party for two in your pavilion, you can call on room service any hour.

You'll find a wide range of water sports activities on the beach, including sailing, sailboarding, Hobie-Cats, and snorkeling. Amanpuri has an excellent marina and maintains more than twenty yachts, available for charter. Pack a picnic, your snorkeling gear, and flippers, and explore some of the neighboring islands and bays close to the resort. Or climb aboard a restored classic Chinese junk for a sunset cruise.

Want to see some of the wonderful life beneath the sea? Check out the H2O Sportz operation, a full-service PADI facility geared to scuba divers of all abilities. The resort course will give you a basic introduction to diving; for the more advanced and certified divers, there are trips to a number of world-class dive sites for exploring underwater caves and crevices as well as coral reefs and walls.

The resort has a library with a collection of more than 1,000 books and a gift shop where you can purchase a variety of Asian artifacts, including jewelry, textiles, pottery, and small sculptures.

It's a long way to this part of the world, so consider seeing both Thailand and Indonesia. Stay at Amanpuri in Thailand, Amandari in Indonesia, and/or Amanwana, a luxury "tented" island resort on the tiny island of Moyo, near Bali. All are members of the Amanresorts group.

Amanpuri

Location: On the island of Phuket, off the southern coast of Thailand

Romantic Highlights: Private treetop pavilions; serene island retreat

Address/Phone: Pansea Beach, Phuket Island, Thailand; 66–76–324–333; fax 66–76–324–100

E-mail: amanpuri@amanresorts.com

Web Site: www.amanresorts.com

U.S. Reservations: Toll free 800–2255–2626; reservations@amanresorts.com

Owner/Manager: Amanresorts Internatinal Pte. Ltd.

Arrival/Departure: Complimentary transfers provided from Phuket Airport; frequent air service from Bangkok daily (1-hour flight)

Distance from Phuket Airport: 12 miles (20 minutes)

Distance from Phuket Town: 10 miles

Accommodations: 40 pavilions, each with its own outdoor *sala* (sitting area); also 30 guest villa homes, with two-, three-, or four-bedrooms, each with a black-tiled pool and separate dining room and living room. A live-in maid and cook attend to all guest needs.

Most Romantic Room/Suite: Numbers 103 and 105, with ocean views

Amenities: Hair dryer, toiletries, air-conditioning, ceiling fans, mosquito netting, twin vanities, minibar/refrigerator, sundeck, in-room safe, stereo cassette system, 24-hour room service

Electricity: 220 volts

Sports and Facilities: 2 lighted tennis courts, pool, gym, Aman Spa, beach club, sailing, sailboarding, snorkeling, waterskiing, deep-sea fishing, scuba diving; golf nearby; island cruises

Dress Code: Casually smart

Weddings: Can be arranged

Rates/Packages: Pavilions, $525–$1,260 per couple per night; villa homes, $1,470–$6,300 per couple per night, including transfers. (Prices subject to change mid-May to mid-October.)

Payment/Credit Cards: Most major

Deposit: Guarantee with credit card at time of reservation; for refund, 14 days' notice (30 days in high season) must be given; in the event of a no-show, the first 2 nights' charge along with transfer costs will be charged to the credit card or deducted from the prepayment.

Government Taxes: Approximately 18.75 percent

Entry Requirements for U.S. Citizens: Passport that is valid for duration of stay and ongoing or round-trip airline tickets.

Note: It is recommended that you start taking antimalaria medication (e.g., doxycycline) before you arrive.

AFRICA

CAPE GRACE
South Africa

You couldn't ask for a better location. Overlooking the new international yacht basin on Cape Town's recently renovated Victoria and Alfred Waterfront, Cape Grace is within walking distance of the aquarium and all the shops, craft stalls, restaurants, and other attractions.

After only three years, Cape Grace was voted "Best Hotel in the World" by *Condé Nast Traveler* Readers' Choice 2000 and was the hotel of choice when President Clinton came to Cape Town during his presidency. Its rooms may not be the largest I have ever experienced, its appointments the most spectacular, or the facilities over the top, still the overall package is one of perfection.

From the seamless service to the terry slippers placed on a white cloth on the floor in the perfect position for you to slip into them while sitting on your bed, Cape Grace doesn't miss a beat. The reservations people speak several languages including Axhosa, Norwegian, and Swedish; the scones are set out for afternoon tea; and you are even offered complimentary shoeshines. (The only remotely nitpickable thing I could find was that the elevators were a tad slow.)

Rooms are quietly yet elegantly appointed. Traditional furniture, floral prints along with rich tapestry fabrics, Oriental carpets, upholstered stools and benches, Cape art, and fresh flowers create a soothing yet uplifting haven

after a day of sight-seeing. Some rooms have balconies and all have French doors overlooking either the harbor or Table Mountain, which looms in the background. From my room, I got a close-up view of the marina, the yachts, fishing boats, and the complex of attractive waterfront buildings.

The baths are spacious with enclosed toilet areas, double vanities, and walk-in closets. Each room has a sitting area and there is a desk with a strip of converter plugs that accommodates most countries' personal appliances.

Tea is served throughout the afternoon in the library on the waterfront terrace at a cost of about $5. You'll agree it's the bargain of the century when you see the full table of goodies such as salmon sandwiches, fresh fruit, jams, pastries, tarts and other tasty items. Forget your book? The library shelves are well stocked with a variety of interesting reading materials.

Bascule, a cozy, intimate bar with the air of a private yacht with its brass-rimmed round "porthole" wall designs, is carved into the hillside around the pool. Come here often and you can have your own wine bin with an engraved name plaque. Norman Pieters, owner of Karell's African Dream Vacations, maintains a selection of wines in his bin (along with two cans of his favorite beverage, Coca Cola). His clients are invited to select a bottle of wine, compliments of Karell's.

Here you can relax in large comfortable chairs and sip a cocktail. The bar stocks more than 400 whiskies and the wine cellar is filled with top South African selections as well as wines from other parts of the world. Each evening at six guests are invited to come to hear about the history and local viniculture of the Western Cape and to sample South African wines.

Quay West Restaurant, with its high windows opening onto the gardens and pool and natural color palette, is effectively decorated in a clean minimalist style. Canvas "sails" create a visual boundary between the bar area and the dining room, which is furnished with wicker chairs, graceful iron chandeliers, and red-tile floors. A glass conservatory overlooks the pool and gardens. In the evening this unpretentious restaurant turns divinely elegant with candles and soft lights. At breakfast fresh fruits of all kinds, hot dishes, rolls, breads, meats, cheeses, cereals, yogurts, jams, jellies, and fresh-squeezed juices create a feast for the eyes as well as appetite.

Cape Grace offers a variety of in-room spa services including aromatherapy massage, deep-tissue sports massage, reflexology, and Swedish message as well as mani-

Grande Roche

Location: Amidst a vineyard in fertile Paarl Valley just 30 minutes from Cape Town.

Romantic Highlights: Cooing doves; terraces overlooking vineyards and valleys; cottages with thatched roofs

Address/Phone: PO Box 6038, Plantasie Street, 7622 Paarl, South Africa; 27–21–863–2727; fax 27–21–863–2220

E-mail: reserve@granderoche.co.za

Web Site: www.granderoche.com

U.S. Reservations: Contact the hotel directly or Relais & Château (800) 735–2478. For a complete tour of the wine country and Southern Africa, contact Karell's African Dream Vacations (800) 327 0373; Web site: www.karell.com.

Owner/Manager: Horst W. Frehse, general manager

Arrival/Departure: Most arrive by car; transfers available

Distance from Cape Town International Airport: 30 minutes

Distance from Cape Town: 30–40 minutes

Accommodations: 35 rooms and suites: 1 honeymoon suite, 18 terrace suites, 10 duplex suites, 5 executive suites, 1 junior suite

Most Romantic Room/Suite: Honeymoon "Stable" Suite located in a separate building at the end of the rear courtyard. It has a private roof terrace, king-size bed, and Jacuzzi. Also the two-story thatched suites: "Dalphine" at the end of a block of terrace suites, with a view of the vineyards; and "Bamboo," furnished with Oriental accents.

Amenities: Air-conditioning, minibar, radio, TV, telephone, heated towel rails, double vanities, robes, radio in the bathroom, tea and coffee service, fax facility (optional), 24-hour room service, valet service, gift shop

Electricity: 210 volts

Sports and Facilities: 2 pools, 2 tennis courts, hiking trails, fitness center with sauna, steambath and fitness equipment, bicycles, horseback riding, and on-site chapel. Hot air ballooning, fishing, squash, and golf nearby (Paarl Golf Club)

Dress Code: Casually smart

Weddings: Weddings can be held in the historic "Slave Chapel," which seats just 8 people. A Wedding Package priced at Rand 10,730 (U.S.$1,021) includes 2 nights' accommodations in the Honeymoon "Stable" Suite, a champagne breakfast, buffet breakfast, massages, services of a hairdresser, organist, flowers, cake, and dinner.

Rates/Packages: Per room rates from Rand 1,350-2,650 (U.S.$128–$252) low season; Rand 2,050-3,300 (U.S.$195–$314) high season

Payment/Credit Cards: Most major

Deposit: By credit card

Government Taxes: Included

Service Charges: Not included

Entry Requirements for U.S. Citizens: Passport

Closed: June–August

MALAMALA
South Africa

Rattray Reserves, which owns MalaMala, a vast game reserve, operates three camps. Where you stay depends on your budget and what you are looking for in the way of a safari experience. You can't really go wrong whichever place you stay.

On a knoll overlooking the Sand River, MalaMala Main Camp, the most luxurious and the most expensive of the three camps, features spacious thatched-roof cottages overlooking the Sand River. Rooms are beautifully furnished with king-size beds or side-by-side twins, soft carpets, African art, rattan chairs and headboards, and spacious bathrooms. Large French doors open onto terraces and most rooms have two baths, dressing areas, and closets.

Guests at Main Camp enjoy flexibility when it comes to how long the game drives last and when the drives take off. The lodge, a spacious airy room with high-beamed ceilings, extends out to a large deck, a perfect place to watch the wildlife below.

In the midprice range is Victorian-style Kirkman's, and Harry's is the least expensive and newest camp, having been recently rebuilt from the ground up. All three are efficiently run operations with excellent staffs. The difference in price is reflected in the size of the rooms and appointments as well as the range of flexibility and services.

For example, Harry's bedrooms have one very large bath, not two as in Main Camp; and you might have to share your safari drive with other guests instead of a having a private vehicle. But this does not mean that quality is compromised. All three camps have infinity pools, *bomas*, a viewing terrace,

bar, and lounge and share the MalaMala game-viewing ground, and all rangers are superbly trained and highly competent. Perhaps Norman Pieters of Karell's Africa Dream Vacations summed it up best when he said, "The animals don't know what you're paying when they decide to show up."

At MalaMala it's all about game. Your wake-up call comes about 5:30 A.M. After a cup of tea or coffee in the lodge, you climb into an open Land Rover and, with a ranger-driver and armed tracker aboard, head into the bush for a magic morning of game viewing. You may see a mother cheetah sitting under a tree with her four cubs, or you may pick up the trail of a lioness loping along, her tail swaying back and forth. You'll get close to giraffes and elephants, warthogs, kudu, and waterbucks. Later, back at the lodge, you'll feast on a lavish breakfast.

Afternoons at camp are spent as the animals spend them: leisurely. You can take a nap, swim in the pool, or sip a cool drink under the shade of a tree.

Night drives begin in late afternoon after tea while the sun is still hot, but beware: Once the sun goes down, it may cool off rapidly. Bring a jacket.

Often it's a matter of tracking animals wherever they go. Each drive brings new discoveries. On my recent visit, in order to keep abreast of a mother leopard as she led her two cubs to dinner (a baby impala she had killed earlier and hidden under a tree), our amazingly skillful driver/ranger kept the cats always in sight. We plunged through the bushes, crossed a sand-bedded stream, and

ducked under thorn acacias.

As evening turned into night, our ranger kept up with the determined cats who seemed totally oblivious to the sound of our vehicle. We were told that the leopards were so used to the noises of the vehicles, we were for now part of their world and fortunately not a member of their food chain.

Our tracker played a spotlight on the trio as they silently walked through the bush. Finally the mother sat down as her son prowled around looking for the hidden catch. When he found it, he dragged it into a thicket and began his meal.

Back at the lodge the meals are served in an air-conditioned dining room or outside in the *boma*, a traditional South African open-air gathering spot. You sit in a large circle with everyone facing a log fire blazing in the center of the area. Your meal includes beautifully prepared fresh local fruits and vegetables and game meats such as venison and impala. After dinner, dancing and entertainment is provided under the starry South African skies.

Each MalaMala camp has a cozy bar where people gather in the evenings after the game drives to compare their sightings. It's always a challenge to see if you qualify for the prestigious "Big Five Club"—spotting lion, leopard, rhino, elephant, and buffalo.

MalaMala's rangers are highly trained and qualified; all have university degrees in areas like ecology or zoology; and all have an intimate understanding of animals and their relationship to their environment.

During a two-night, three-day safari trip, you'll have time for four game drives and one or two game walks. For a more leisurely pace, stay three nights.

I would suggest you roll your safari experience into a two-week South Africa trip visiting Cape Town, the wine and garden regions, and Bushman's Kloof, an area where you can see 10,000-year-old Bushman rock drawings. You can also combine a safari in South Africa with game viewing in a Botswana tented camp. Karell's African Dream Vacations, specialists in this part of the world, can arrange travel to South Africa as well as Botswana, Zimbabwe, Namibia, and Zambia.

The romance of MalaMala is a heady concoction of exotic safari experiences; warm, knowledgeable people; exceptional accommodations; and brilliant African skies.

MalaMala

Location: MalaMala Game Reserve, a private, 45,000-acre game reserve adjacent to Kruger National Park, in the northeastern part of the country

Romantic Highlights: Moonlight safaris; thatched *rondavels* overlooking Sand River

Address/Phone: MalaMala Game Reserve, Box 2575, Randburg 2125, South Africa; 27–789–2677; fax 27–886–4382; fax to camp 2713–735–5686

E-mail: reservations@malamala.com

Web Site: www.malamala.com

U.S. Reservations: Tim Farrell & Associates, P.O. Box 3029, Westport, CT 06880; (203) 845–0304; fax (203) 845–0448; safaritim@aol.com. For a full southern Africa program including a safari to MalaMala, contact: Karell's African Dream Vacations, (800) 327–0373; Web site: www.karell.com.

Owner/Manager: Michael Rattray, C.E.O./managing director; Nils Kure, camp manager

Arrival/Departure: MalaMala offers daily direct flights from Johannesburg into the MalaMala airstrip. You can also fly from Johannesburg to Skukuza Airport, where you will be met by rangers from the MalaMala camp.

Distance from Skukuza Airport: 14 miles (½ hour)

Distance from Skukuza: 13 miles

Accommodations: 25 *rondavels*

Most Romantic Room/Suite: Suites, #15, #17 and #19

Amenities: Air-conditioning, ceiling fans, and electric shaver plug, *New York Times* fax daily, laundry service, hair dryer

Electricity: 220 volts

Sports and Facilities: Wild game viewing, swimming pool, guided bush walks, walking safaris

Dress Code: Bushveld casual; during winter (May to September) very warm clothes, including a windbreaker, are essential.

Weddings: Can be arranged

Rates/Packages: Main Camp from about $500 per person; Kirkman's Kamp from $300 per person; and Harry's from $275. Includes accommodations, meals, game drives, walking safaris, laundry, transfers and VAT.

Payment/Credit Cards: Most major

Deposit: 50 percent deposit required to secure accommodations; balance due 30 days prior to arrival.

Government Taxes: Room tax, Rand 5.70 (U.S. 54 cents) per person per night

Service Charges: Included

Entry Requirements for U.S. Citizens: Passport and return or onward ticket required. Check whether visa is necessary.

SELOUS SAFARI CAMP
Tanzania

You hear them: the steady chomp, chomp of hippos munching their way to the nearby lake. You've zipped up your tent, turned the gas lantern on the back deck down low, and are lying in bedlistening. Other animal sounds you can't identify mingle with the cacophony of tree frogs. You feel vulnerable, but you have been assured by rangers that the night-roaming creatures won't invade your territory. Finally you sleep.

It is still dark when you hear the gentle clatter of a tea pot and plate being placed on the small wooden table on your deck. "Good morning," says the man softly before moving on to the next tent. You quickly throw on your khaki shorts, shirt, and walking boots; give yourself a good spray of Cutter Back Woods; and go out to the deck to pour a cup of tea and eat a cookie, a delicious chocolate-peanut-butter concoction.

The rising sun is just beginning to tint the sky pink and gold as you meet your guide to begin the walking safari. You are in the southern tier of Tanzania in the Selous Game Reserve, the second largest wildlife park in Africa—three times the size of the better-known Serengeti National Park and the famed Ngorongoro Crater to the north—and home to more than 50,000 elephant. In the next two hours, walking single file behind your guide, you'll see a variety of birds and animals, perhaps even catch a glimpse of the elusive wild dogs or eland.

Safari walks and game drives take place when the animals are most active: the late afternoon, at night, and in the early morning, before the sun is up. At Selous Safari Camp, you'll track game on foot, in rugged open Nissan safari vehicles that run over brush like World War II tanks, and by boat.

There are many kinds of safaris and styles of accommodations, from superluxurious camps where the closest you come to camping is walking to dinner on a gravel path to camps set on wooden platforms with tents that zip up to keep out the critters. The Selous Safari Camp is a tented camp, but it is certainly not one where you have to rough it.

The camp has twelve tents set on raised platforms and divided into two "rooms" with mesh "windows" and a canvas wall that can be dropped or pulled back. One section contains the bedroom that opens onto a deck. It is

furnished with two single beds that can be converted to a king-size bed on request, rush carpets, a bureau, chairs, and solar-powered lights. The other section has a private toilet (which flushes quite nicely) and a wooden vanity table with mirror and ceramic basin; your shower is just outside attached to your tent by a privacy screen. Water is heated by solar power.

Outside is the vast sprawling Selous, much less developed for tourism than other game reserves (you seldom see another vehicle except for those operated by your own camp) your wildlife experience is rich, personal. "It's the real Africa," explained Frank Cary, head guide at the camp.

After a morning game walk, back at camp we enjoyed bacon and eggs along with fresh juice and breads in the *dungo*, a thatched-top, open-air dining room/lounge/bar that sits high on wooden stilts overlooking the river. That afternoon we went on a game drive. When our driver learned from his radio that there was a pride of lions in another part of the park, our SUV, which up to this point had been creeping along, took off in a cloud of dust. Finally we reached the lions, full and lazy from having just finished the prime portion of a downed giraffe. One of the females rolled over on her back and went to sleep. A male with a rather scruffy mane lolled nearby. A peaceful family outing. Vultures sat in trees nearby waiting for their go at what was left of the carcass.

During the drive we saw impala grazing under the acacia trees and perky warthogs trotting along, short, stiff tails straight up as they scurried into the underbrush. Giraffes stared at us before loping away followed by herds of zebra.

A mother elephant silently glided into the bushes followed by her small baby. Kudus hid camouflaged in the trees, and antelopes, waterbucks, and wildebeests darted across the landscape. We passed colonies of sparrow weavers who had woven their nests in the thorny trees and herds of elephant moving as one in the distance.

Late in the day, we took a boat safari on the Rufiji River where we saw flocks of bright blue and emerald birds, white-throated bee eaters, a pied kingfisher, monitor lizards, squadrons of dragonflies, and a goliath heron, the largest heron

species in the world. A hippo chomped on grass by the water's edge until he saw us and plunged underwater. A water buffalo cooled off in the river up to his belly and several crocodiles slithered into the water upon hearing us approach. The sun was setting as we returned to the camp dock silhouetted by tall palms that dotted the reedy wetlands.

Dinner was a surprise: We had not expected gourmet-style cuisine with a hint of Asian seasoning out here in the bush. But manager Sal Economos, originally from the New York area, is really into food and enjoys presenting new flavors and dishes. You can eat alone at a cozy candlelit table or join others and share animal sightings and travel tales. The chef prepares fresh vegetables, fruits, and meats seasoned with a hint of Asian herbs and spices accompanied by perhaps a merlot or champagne. For a special treat, the Selous staff will set up a private table in the bush.

Though the wildlife is the main attraction, there are other things to enjoy. Chill out at the 25-foot garden pool or vent your bragging rights with a drink in the *dungo*.

For a two-week honeymoon, we suggest you combine the remote Selous experience with a few days on safari in the more developed Serengeti National Park and the famed Ngorongoro Crater in northern Tanzania. The vast, open plains of the Serengeti contain the largest concentration of migratory game animals in the world; the Ngorongoro Crater, a huge unflooded, collapsed volcanic crater, has more than 30,000 big animals including the rare black rhino. Complete your holiday at a beach resort on the island of Zanzibar, the ancient trading port of the sultans of Oman.

Selous Safari Camp

Location: In Tanzania's 21,000-square-mile Selous Game Reserve, the second largest of Africa's game reserves, yet one of the most remote

Romantic Highlights: Getting close to nature; starry nights in the bush

Address/Phone: P.O. Box 1193, Dar es Salaam, Tanzania; 255–022–2134802; fax 255–022–2112794

E-mail: info@selous.com; noltingaac@aol.com

Web Site: www.selous.com; www.africa-adventure.com

U.S. Reservations: Africa Adventure Company (800) 882–9453

Owner/Manager: Sal Economos, manager

Arrival/Departure: Fly from Dar es Salaam by scheduled charter, a 45-minute flight. Rangers meet the plane.

Distance from Selous Airstrip: 5 minutes

Distance from Dar es Salaam: About 200 miles

Accommodations: 12 tents on raised platforms

Most Romantic Room/Suite: All the tents are the same; you may request that the twin beds be converted to a king-size bed.

Amenities: Solar-powered bedside light (goes off around 11 P.M. when it runs out of juice), in-tent toilet and vanity with mirror, flashlight, small fan

Electricity: 220–224 volts (but don't even think of bringing a hair dryer)

Sports and Facilities: Game drives; pool

Dress Code: Bushveld casual

Weddings: Can be arranged.

Rates/Packages: About $320 per person per night includes meals, game drives, walking safaris, and park fees; alcohol, laundry, and tips are extra. The Africa Adventure Company offers a fourteen- to eighteen-day program in Tanzania including game drives in the Ngorongoro Crater, the Serengeti, and Selous with overnights in tented camps and lodges as well as 2 to 4 nights at a beach island resort in Zanzibar. Priced from $3,250 per person.

Payment/Credit Cards: Most major; cash preferred for purchases at camp

Deposit: 30 percent; full amount due 75 days before departure

Government Taxes: Included except for airport departure taxes (about $20)

Service Charges: Ask your safari provider for tips recommendations for staff and driver guides.

Entry Requirements for U.S. Citizens: Passport; visa ($50) can be obtained either before you leave or on arrival at the airport.

INDEXES

SEASIDE RESORTS

RESORTS WITH TENNIS

RESORTS WITH GOLF ON PREMISES
(*Note*. Many other resorts offer golf nearby.)

Sandals St. Lucia Golf Resort & Spa, 124
Woodstock Inn & Resort, 54

RESORTS WITH HORSEBACK RIDING

Ahwahnee, The, 4
Boulders, The, 2
Grande Roche, 214
Greenbrier, The, 56
Hotel Hana Maui, 32
Inn at Spanish Bay, 12
La Casa Que Canta, 146
Maroma, 136
Nisbet Plantation Beach Club, 118
Schlosshotel Lerbach, 170
Silky Oaks Lodge & Healing Waters Spa, 194
Turtle Island, 196

IN-CITY/TOWN HOTELS

Cape Grace, 212
Equinox, The, 52
Feathers Hotel, The, 152
Hotel Danieli, 178
Hotel Goldener Hirsch, 150
Inn of the Anasazi, 46
Pousadas of Portugal, 182
Radisson Edwardian Hampshire Hotel, 158
White Barn Inn, The, 40
Woodstock Inn & Resort, 54

RESORTS WITH AREA SKIING

Ahwahnee, The, 4
Amangani, 58
Chateau du Sureau, 8
Equinox, The, 52
Hotel Goldener Hirsch, 150
Inn of the Anasazi, 46
Snake River Lodge & Spa, 60
Sonnenalp Resort, 22
Wawbeek, The, 50
Woodstock Inn & Resort, 54

ADVENTURE/SAFARI LODGES AND RESORTS

Ahwahnee, The, 4
MalaMala, 216
Silky Oaks Lodge & Healing Waters Spa, 194
Selous Safari Camp, 218
Snake River Lodge & Spa, 60
Wawbeek, The, 50

RESORTS WITH PRIVATE POOLS

Ahwahnee, The, 4
Amandari, 202
Cap Juluca, 76
Cobblers Cove Hotel, 88
Hacienda Katanchel, 142
Half Moon Golf, Tennis, and Beach Club, 108
Hotel Bora Bora, 200
Hotel Villa del Sol, 144
Kamandalu Resort & Spa, 206
La Casa Que Canta, 146
La Samanna, 128
Point Grace, 130
Sandals Royal Bahamian Resort & Spa, 84
Sandals St. Lucia Golf Resort & Spa, 124
Spice Island Beach Resort, 104
Windjammer Landing Villa Beach Resort & Spa, 126

RESORTS WITH IN-ROOM FIREPLACES

Ahwahnee, The, 4
Amangani, 58
Auberge du Soleil, 6
Auberge Wild Rose, 70
Boulders, The, 2
Chateau du Sureau, 8
Chateau Yering Historic House Hotel, 190
Chatham Bars Inn, 42
Equinox, The, 52
Feathers Hotel, The, 152
Four Seasons Biltmore, 10
Hartwell House, 154
Inn at Spanish Bay, 12
Inn of the Anasazi, 46
La Pinsonnière, 72
La Valencia, 14
Le Manoir aux Quat' Saisons, 156
Longueville House, 172
Meadowood, Napa Valley, 16
Mirbeau Inn & Spa, 48
Post Ranch Inn, 18
Rancho Valencia, 20
Sonnenalp Resort, 22
Snake River Lodge & Spa, 60
Wawbeek, The, 50
White Barn Inn, The, 40
Woodstock Inn & Resort, 54

PHOTO CREDITS

Many thanks to the following people and resorts for providing photographs: pp. i, 98–99, and 132–33, Rosewood Hotels & Resorts; pp. iii and 100–101, Hyatt Regency Grand Cayman; pp. v and 6–7, Auberge du Soleil; pp. vi, 1, and 26–27, Little Palm Island; pp. vii and 48–49, Mirbeau/© James Scherzi; pp. viii and 156, Le Many thanks to the following people and resorts for providing photographs: pp. I, 98– 99, and 132–33, Rosewood Hotels & Resorts; pp. iii and 100–101, Hyatt Regency Grand Cayman; pp. v and 6–7, Auberge du Soleil; pp. vi, 1, and 26–27, Little Palm Island; pp. vii and 48–49, Mirbeau/© James Scherzi; pp. viii and 156, Le Manoir aux Quat' Saisons; pp. x and 8–9, Chateau Sureau; pp. xii and 64–65, Banff Springs Hotel; pp. xiii and 46–47, Inn of the Anasazi; pp. 2–3, The Boulders; pp. 4–5, Yosemite Concession Services Corporation/Keith S. Walklet; pp. 10–11, Four Seasons Biltmore; pp. 12–13, Pebble Beach Company; p. 16, Meadowood Napa Valley; pp. 18–19, Post Ranch Inn at Big Sur; pp. 20–21, Rancho Valencia; pp. 22–23, Sonnenalp Resort of Vail; pp. 28–29, Four Seasons Maui/© David Franzen; pp. 30, Halekulani Hotel/Steve Murray; pp. 31, Halekulani Hotel/Dyess 1197; p. 32, Hotel Hana-Maui/S. Franz; p. 33, Hotel Hana-Maui; pp. 34–35, Kona Village Resort; pp. 36–37, Manele Bay Hotel/Jeffrey Asher; pp. 38, Mauna Lani Bay Hotel/© Ric Noyle; pp. 39, Mauna Lani Bay Hotel; pp. 40–41, White Barn Inn; p. 45, Wauwinet; pp. 50–51, Nancy Howard; pp. 52–53, The Equinox; pp. 54–55, Woodstock Inn & Resort; pp. 56–57, The Greenbrier; pp. 58–59, Amanresorts International; pp. 60–61, Snake River Lodge & Spa; p. 63 and 66–67, Chateau Lake Louise; pp. 68–69, Jasper Park Lodge; p. 70, Wild Rose Inn; pp. 72–73, La Pinsonnière; p. 75, John Dyson; pp. 76–77, Cap Juluca; pp. 78–79, Curtain Bluff; pp. 80–81, Hyatt Regency Aruba; pp. 84–85, 111–12, and 124–25, Sandals Resorts; pp. 88–89, Cobblers Cove; pp. 90–91, Cambridge Beaches; pp. 92–93, The Reefs, Bermuda; pp. 94–95, Peter Island; pp. 102–3, Casa de Campo; pp. 104–5, Spice Island; pp. 106–7, SuperClubs Resorts/Len Kaufman; pp. 108–9, Half Moon Hotel; pp. 114–15, Couples Resorts; pp. 116–17, Four Seasons Nevis Resort; pp. 118–19, Nisbet Plantation Beach Club; pp. 120–21, Horned Dorset; pp. 122–23, Anse Chastanet Hotel; p. 127, Windjammer Landing; p. 128, La Samana; p. 129, La Samana/© Shirley Sherwood; p. 130, Point Grace/© Fish Frames; p. 131, Point Grace; pp. 135 and 146–47, La Casa Que Canta; pp. 136–37, Maroma; pp. 138–39, Ritz-Carlton Cancun; pp. 142–43, Hacienda Katanchel/Eric Sander; pp. 144–45, Hotel Villa del Sol/Michael Calderwood; pp. 149 and 184–85, Reid's Place; pp. 150–51, Hotel Goldener Hirsch; pp. 152–53, Feathers Hotel; p. 154, Hartwell House and Spa; pp. 158–59, Radisson Edwardian Hotels; pp. 162–63, Chèvre D'Or; pp. 164–65, Château St. Martin; pp. 166–67, Château Eza; pp. 168–69, Hotel de Mougins; pp. 170–71, Schlosshotel Lerbach; p. 172, Longueville House; pp. 174–75, Excelsior Palace Hotel; pp. 176–77, Grand Hotel Punta Molino; p. 179, Hotel Danieli; p. 180, Villa D'Este/© Moreno Maggi; p. 181, Villa D'Este; pp. 187, 200–205, and 208–9, Amenresorts International; pp. 188–89 and 194–95, P&O Australian Resorts; pp. 190–91, Chateau Yering; pp. 192–93, Hayman; pp. 196–97, Turtle Island; pp. 198–99, Bora Bora Lagoon Resort; pp. 206–7, Kamandalu Resort & Spa; pp. 232–33, Cape Grace; and images by PhotoDisk and Peter Sispoidis.

The following photos are by the author: pp. 14–15, 42–44, 83, 96–97, 126, 140–41, 155, 157, 160–61, 182–83, 211, and 214–19.

ABOUT THE AUTHOR

KATHARINE D. DYSON is a freelance writer who specializes in travel. For this book her work has taken her around the world researching and writing about the best romantic spots. Her articles have appeared in many newspapers and magazines, including *Modern Bride, Romantic Escapes, Country Victorian, Bride & Groom, Elegant Bride, Specialty Travel Index, Golf Digest, Fitness Magazine,* and *Jax Fax Travel Marketing.* She writes a bi-weekly travel and food column for several Fairfield County, Connecticut, newspapers. She is a member of the Society of American Travel Writers and Golf Writers Association of America, a recipient of the Quill and Trowel Award from the Garden Writers Association of America, and a consultant for A&E Network for their "Top 10 Most Romantic Resorts" series.

For further information log onto the author's Web site at www.honeymoonsaway.com.